JUSTIFICATION AND LEGITIMACY

A. John Simmons is widely regarded as one of the most innovative and creative of today's political philosophers. His work on political obligation is regarded as definitive, and he is internationally respected as an interpreter of John Locke.

The characteristic features of clear argumentation and careful scholarship that have been hallmarks of Simmons's philosophy are everywhere evident in this collection. The essays focus on the problems of political obligation and state legitimacy as well as on historical theories of property and justice. Cumulatively, the collection presents a distinctive social and political philosophy, exploring the nature of our most fundamental rights and obligations and displaying the power and plausibility of Lockean ideal theory.

The volume will be eagerly sought out by students and professionals in the fields of philosophy, political science, and law.

A. John Simmons is Commonwealth Professor of Philosophy at the University of Virginia. His previous books are *Moral Principles and Political Obligations* (1979), *The Lockean Theory of Rights* (1992), and *On the Edge of Anarchy* (1993).

JUSTIFICATION AND LEGITIMACY

Essays on Rights and Obligations

A. JOHN SIMMONS

University of Virginia

 CAMBRIDGE
UNIVERSITY PRESS

2001

PUBLISHED BY THE PRESS SYNDICATE OF THE UNIVERSITY OF CAMBRIDGE
The Pitt Building, Trumpington Street, Cambridge, United Kingdom

CAMBRIDGE UNIVERSITY PRESS
The Edinburgh Building, Cambridge CB2 2RU, UK
40 West 20th Street, New York, NY 10011-4211, USA
10 Stamford Road, Oakleigh, VIC 3166, Australia
Ruiz de Alarcón 13, 28014 Madrid, Spain
Dock House, The Waterfront, Cape Town, 8001, South Africa

http://www.cambridge.org

First published 2001

Printed in the United States of America

Typeface Baskeville 10/13 pt.   *System* QuarkXPress [BTS]

A catalog record for this book is available from the British Library.

Library of Congress Cataloging in Publication Data

Simmons, A. John (Alan John), 1950–
Justification and legitimacy: Essays on rights and obligations / A. John Simmons.
        p.   cm.
ISBN 0-521-79016-6 (hb) – ISBN 0-521-79365-3 (pbk.)
1. Political obligation.   2. Legitimacy of governments.   3. Human rights.   I. Title.
JC329.5 .S55   2001
323'.01 – dc21   00-023590

ISBN   0 521 79016 6   hardback
ISBN   0 521 79365 3   paperback

CONTENTS

v

INTRODUCTION

Justification and Legitimacy brings together a closely related set of my papers in social, political, and legal philosophy. All of the papers assembled here concern the basic rights and obligations of persons, citizens, and states, and nearly all express my most recent thoughts on these subjects. All of these papers also exemplify or defend one particular approach to the fundamental questions of social, political, and legal philosophy. This approach begins with an examination of the natural moral condition of persons: that is, an examination of the basic rights and duties persons possess and of the special moral relationships into which they can enter (or in which they can find themselves), independent of their roles as members of organized political societies. The basic assumptions on which this approach is founded are: (1) that all persons, whenever and wherever born, begin their moral lives (upon rising to the status of full moral agents) with a substantial body of moral rights and duties, and (2) that the rights in question centrally include, and perhaps add up to no more than, a broad right of self-government or independence (both from other persons and groups and from states).

A person's standing as a legitimate subject of some government must then be understood, on this approach, as the result of a special kind of departure from that person's natural condition. The political realm is to be analyzed in terms of permissible transitions from the natural condition to the condition of political membership. The rights and duties of states and governments, the moral limits on the state's employment of coercive political power, and the demands of social justice are all to be explained by delineating the (actual and morally permissible) processes by which persons make the transition from the natural to the political condition.

This approach to political philosophy, then, constitutes a straightforward rejection of what we might call "political naturalism" – according to which the natural condition of persons born within the territories of political societies is one of political membership and political obligation. The political relationship is by contrast, according to the view espoused here, essentially "artificial" (that is, a product of human artifice), however "natural" it may be for us to create and live in political societies.

The best-known practitioner of this approach to social and political philosophy, of course, was John Locke, though many philosophers since Locke (and a few before him) have explicitly or implicitly practiced it as well. We can see Locke's commitment to this approach just by noticing the most prominent claims in his writings. For instance, it would not be misleading, I think, to identify as the central theses of Locke's *Second Treatise of Government* the following: (1) All persons are naturally free and equal; (2) persons can acquire natural property rights by laboring on unowned nature; and (3) all legitimate political power derives from the consent of those subject to it. In defending the first thesis, Locke lays out his view of persons' basic rights and duties. All persons are by nature equally subject to the requirements of natural law and equally entitled to govern their own lives within the constraints of that law. In defending the second thesis, Locke explains one of the most basic and politically important sources of special rights and obligations. Persons are by nature capable of making for themselves (without the need for conventional, legal, or political sanction) full private property rights in fair shares of the earth and its resources; and it is only by the voluntary subjection of such property to the jurisdiction of a state that states can legitimately achieve their familiar territorial dimensions. The third thesis, of course, gives us Locke's view of the only legitimate ground for the transition from our natural to our political condition. Without their free consent to membership in some legitimate political society, persons remain always in their natural moral condition, however thoroughly political their lives may otherwise seem to be.

Locke's work thus identified as the three central problems the political philosopher must address: the nature and justification of our natural rights to self-government, the nature and justification of natural rights to property, and the nature and justification of political obligation and of governmental or state legitimacy. The papers collected in this book all explore, directly or indirectly, these three central problems of social, political, and legal philosophy. All the papers concern either the substance of the moral relationship between citizen and state or the extent of and grounds for individual natural rights. I do not, of course, always employ Locke's methods or follow his arguments, nor do I always accept anything like the conclusions Locke defended; but I do take my approach to these issues to be throughout Lockean in spirit, following the same basic orientation to these areas of philosophy and taking the same issues to be fundamental.

The first eight of the twelve papers assembled here address, in one way or another, the nature of the citizen–state relationship, dealing principally with the problems of political obligation and state legitimacy. Of these, only one ("'Denisons' and 'Aliens' . . .") attempts a detailed or scholarly treatment of Locke's own consent theory of political obligation and legitimacy, despite the broadly Lockean orientation of all of the papers. In "'Denisons' and 'Aliens'" I offer both a new interpretation of Locke's consent theory and a defense of the theory I attribute to Locke as the soundest position for a consent theorist to take. Some of the other papers on these themes aim instead to refute currently popular rival accounts of political obligation and legitimacy. Two, for instance ("The Principle of Fair Play," "Fair Play and Political Obligation"), have as their target the fair play or fairness account of political obligation, according to which the citizens of reasonably just polities who have accepted the beneficial results of the cooperative sacrifices of their fellows owe an obligation to reciprocate by doing their fair shares in supporting the political scheme. This account, I am distressed to report, seems to enjoy more support today than it did when I first argued against it in 1979, which explains my return to the subject after twenty years. My conclusions about this account remain highly skeptical. Two other papers ("Associative Political Obligations," "External Justifications . . .") argue against the view of political obligation as an "associative" or "role" obligation, a view taken very seriously in Locke's own day (and during several periods since) that is once again quite popular today. It is also a view that is diametrically opposed to the voluntaristic approach to such issues that I favor – and that Locke favored as well, if not, perhaps, in so wholehearted a fashion as do I. "Associativists" hold that our political obligations are binding on us simply by virtue of our occupation of certain social, institutional, or associational positions or roles. If my arguments against this view are sound, they effectively undermine theories of political obligation that are Hegelian or Wittgensteinian (or, more broadly, communitarian), as well as views like Dworkin's "liberal associativism."

In another of the papers dealing with political obligation ("The Obligations of Citizens . . ."), I try to provide some general organizing principles for discussions of political obligation, and I briefly lay out the grounds for my systematic rejection of all attempted defenses of political obligation. This paper, in addition to thus helping to motivate those that follow it, offers a useful illustration of the practical bearing of arguments concerning political obligation on political policy issues – in this case, on the justification of military conscription. "Philosophical Anarchism" has as its objective a clear description and defense of my favored position on this subject, a position toward which all of the best arguments about political obligation seem to me to push us. This position is that all actual states are illegitimate, but that there may nonetheless be good moral grounds for supporting (or, at least, not resisting) the activities of many states. Finally, in "Justification and Legitimacy" I try to place all of the preceding arguments in a broader context, defending a Lockean view of the relationship between these concerns about political obligation and state legitimacy, on the one hand, and additional dimensions of institutional evaluation (such as virtue or justice), on the other. I argue that evaluations of states in terms of their legitimacy should be understood to be distinct from, and to vary independently of, their evaluations in terms of justice or goodness (i.e., that which "justifies" states), in opposition to the dominant schools of contemporary political philosophy.

The remaining four papers collected here address the other central areas of concern in a Lockean approach to social, political, and legal philosophy, though again only one ("Makers' Rights") includes any extended consideration of Locke's own views. "Human Rights and World Citizenship . . ." discusses both Locke's and Kant's (rival) views of the natural moral condition of persons; it also tries to clarify the ways in which our views on that subject should affect our picture of the primary focus of loyalty for citizens, thus providing a perspective on the viability of the "cosmopolitan" stance in moral and political philosophy.

The last three papers ("Original-Acquisition Justifications . . ." "Historical Rights . . . ," "Makers' Rights") all concern the idea of natural property rights and allied historical accounts of distributive justice. Property is, according to the approach practiced here, a particularly important special natural right (with important correlated obligations) for a number of reasons. The private property (or use rights) of individuals in land is the material out of which states' territories must be constructed in order for those territories to be legitimately subject to state jurisdiction. And the rights that politically associated persons must be understood to retain over their land and possessions constitutes one of the important limits on legitimate governmental power. Further, of course, many prominent conceptions of social justice revolve around or centrally feature respect for individual rights to property. A proper appreciation of the nature and grounds of natural property, then, is essential not only to a Lockean, but to any, approach to social, political, and legal philosophy. The papers on property included here are all designed to defend (and to modify in ways that render more plausible) historical theories of property – and, in a more limited way, historical theories of justice – of the sort defended by Locke. I try to argue on behalf of these theories in something like their traditional form, maintaining that they in fact have the resources to respond to the familiar dismissive objections (e.g., of contemporary irrelevance and justificatory impotence) that recent philosophy has tended to casually advance and endlessly repeat. I try as well to orient my discussions so that they will bear in obvious ways on some actual examples of historical injustice and property violations, such as the case of Native American peoples.

I have dealt before with many of the issues addressed in these collected papers, particularly in my three previous books (*Moral Principles and Political Obligations* [1979], *The Lockean Theory of Rights* [1992], and *On the Edge of Anarchy* [1993]). The papers assembled here begin, in effect, where those books left off, though they presuppose no knowledge of my arguments there. These papers for the most part represent my most recent thoughts on these subjects and constitute, I think, substantial improvements upon and additions to the work done in those books. For those curious about my earlier arguments, one of the papers in this collection ("The Obligations of Citizens . . .") does contain a summary of (and a slightly different way of characterizing) the general case that I made against political obligation in *Moral Principles and Political Obligations*. But virtually all of the papers here are otherwise essentially freestanding. Ten of the twelve papers in this book were written since the publication of my last book. Two ("Fair Play and Political Obligation . . .", "Human Rights and World Citizenship . . .") have not been previously published in English, while the others were published in a variety of (not always particularly accessible) places.

Two of the papers in this collection, however, are considerably older than the others, and their inclusion here requires some justificatory comment. "The Principle of Fair Play" (originally published in 1979) is included here principally to accompany and motivate a second (very recently completed) paper on the same topic ("Fair Play and Political Obligation . . ."), in which I both develop my earlier view and respond to some of the criticisms of my position that have been advanced during the past two decades. The other older paper, "The Obligations of Citizens and the Justification of Conscription" (from 1983), is included for different reasons. First, as already noted, it reorganizes and briefly summarizes my principal arguments against political obligation and so should help readers see more clearly the general grounds for my philosophical anarchist conclusions. But it also contains a discussion of (and arguments against) the approach to the problem of political obligation that was Locke's chief target in his *Treatises*; namely, the view of political obligations as identical to (or strongly analogous to) filial obligations. This paper thus not only supports the case made in other papers in this collection against political obligation conceived of as a "role" or "associative" obligation. It also seems a particularly fitting contribution to an effort to sustain and expand a Lockean approach to normative philosophy.

I hope that readers will agree that the twelve papers collected here make genuine advances on some of the central problems of social, political, and legal philosophy. These papers should, at the very least, help to clarify the character, virtues, and limits of a broadly Lockean approach to those fields. Perhaps they will also, as I hope, help to convince readers that such an approach is genuinely fruitful in ways that require that it be taken very seriously by contemporary philosophers. For the conclusions this approach yields, however unfashionable they might be, seem to me to have considerable force in specifying the regulative ideals in light of which social and political philosophy should proceed.

ACKNOWLEDGMENTS

The author gratefully acknowledges the following publishers' permission to reprint previously published material:

"The Principle of Fair Play" originally appeared in *Philosophy and Public Affairs* 8:4 (Summer 1979), 307–337. Copyright 1979 by Princeton University Press.

"The Obligations of Citizens and the Justification of Conscription" originally appeared in R. K. Fullinwider (ed.), *Conscripts and Volunteers* (Totowa, NJ: Rowman & Allanheld, Publishers, 1983), 73–88. Copyright 1983 by Rowman & Allanheld, Publishers.

"Associative Political Obligations" originally appeared in *Ethics* 106:2 (January 1996), 247–273. Copyright 1996 by the University of Chicago Press.

"External Justifications and Institutional Roles" originally appeared in *The Journal of Philosophy* 93:1 (January 1996), 28–36. Copyright 1996 by The Journal of Philosophy, Inc.

"Philosophical Anarchism" originally appeared in J. T. Sanders and J. Narveson (eds.), *For and Against the State* (Lanham, MD: Rowman & Littlefield, Publishers, 1996), 19–39. Copyright 1996 by Rowman & Littlefield, Publishers.

"Justification and Legitimacy" originally appeared in *Ethics* 109:4 (July 1999), 739–771. Copyright 1999 by the University of Chicago Press.

"'Denisons' and 'Aliens': Locke's Problem of Political Consent" originally appeared in *Social Theory and Practice* 24:2 (Summer 1998), 161–182. Copyright 1998 by Social Theory and Practice.

"Human Rights and World Citizenship: The Universality of Human Rights in Kant and Locke" originally appeared in German only (under the title "Menschenrechte und Weltbürgerrecht – die Universalität der Menschenrechte bei Kant und Locke") in K. Dicke and K. Kodalle (eds.), *Republik und Weltbürgerrecht* (Weimar: Böhlau Verlag, 1998).

"Original-Acquisition Justifications of Private Property" originally appeared in *Social Philosophy & Policy* 11:2 (Summer 1994), 63–84. Copyright 1994 by the Social Philosophy and Policy Foundation.

"Historical Rights and Fair Shares" originally appeared in *Law and Philosophy* 14:2 (May 1995), 149–184. Copyright 1995 by Kluwer Academic Publishers.

"Makers' Rights" originally appeared in *The Journal of Ethics* 2:3 (1998), 197–218. Copyright 1998 by Kluwer Academic Publishers.

THE PRINCIPLE OF FAIR PLAY

I

The traditional consent theory account of political obligation can be understood as advancing two basic claims. (1) All or most citizens, at least within reasonably just political communities, have political obligations (that is, moral obligations or duties to obey the law and support the political institutions of their countries of residence). (2) All political obligations are grounded in personal consent (express or tacit). Today most political philosophers (and non-philosophers, I suspect) are still prepared to accept (1). But (2) has been widely rejected largely because it entails, in conjunction with (1), that all or most of us have undertaken political obligations by *deliberate consensual acts*. And this seems not even approximately true. If it is not true, then (1) requires a defense employing a more complex account of special rights and obligations than the one offered by consent theory.

One popular way of defending (1) relies on what has been called "the principle of fair play" (or "the principle of fairness").[1] Advocates of this principle argue that promises and deliberate consent are not the only possible grounds of special rights and obligations; the acceptance of benefits within certain sorts of cooperative schemes, they maintain, is by itself sufficient to generate such rights and obligations. It is these arguments

---

1 These are John Rawls' two names for the principle, from "Legal Obligation and the Duty of Fair Play," *Law and Philosophy*, ed. S. Hook (New York: New York University Press, 1964) and *A Theory of Justice* (Cambridge: Harvard University Press, 1971). The same principle was alluded to by C. D. Broad in "On the Function of False Hypotheses in Ethics," *International Journal of Ethics* 26 (April 1916), and developed by H. L. A. Hart (see below).

I want to examine. I begin with a brief discussion of the principle of fair play as it has appeared in recent philosophical literature. From there I proceed to a more general evaluation of the principle (in Sections II and IV) and of the theory of political obligation with uses it (in Sections III and V).

The first concise formulation of the principle of fair play was provided by H. L. A. Hart:

> A third important source of special rights and obligations which we recognize in many spheres of life is what may be termed mutuality of restrictions, and I think political obligation is intelligible only if we see what precisely this is and how it differs from the other right-creating transactions (consent, promising) to which philosophers have assimilated it.

Hart's explanation of the "special transaction" he has in mind runs as follows:

> When a number of persons conduct any joint enterprise according to rules and thus restrict their liberty, those who have submitted to these restrictions when required have a right to a similar submission from those who have benefited by their submission. The rules may provide that officials should have authority to enforce obedience . . . but the moral obligation to obey the rules in such circumstances is due to the cooperating members of the society, and they have the correlative moral right to obedience.[2]

While Hart does not refer to this source of special rights and obligations in terms of fairness or fair play, he does note later that "in the case of mutual restrictions we are in fact saying that this claim to interfere with another's freedom is justified because it is fair."[3] We can understand him, then, to be claiming that, in the situation described, a beneficiary has an obligation to "do his fair share" by submitting to the rules when they require it; others who have cooperated before have a right to this fair distribution of the burdens of submission.

Hart's brief account of the principle of fair play, of course, leaves many important questions unanswered. What, for instance, are we to count as an "enterprise?" Are only participants in the enterprise obligated to do their part, or do obligations fall on all who benefit from the enterprise? Why is a set of rules necessary? Clearly a fuller treatment of the principle is essential for our purposes, and John Rawls provides one in his 1964 essay, "Legal

2 "Are There Any Natural Rights?" *Philosophical Review* 64 (April 1955): 185.
3 Ibid., pp. 190–191.

Obligation and the Duty of Fair Play."[4] There Rawls builds on Hart's account to give both a more complete account of the principle of fair play and an extensive discussion of its application to constitutional democracies. His central presentation of the principle echoes Hart's:

> The principle of fair play may be defined as follows. Suppose there is a mutually beneficial and just scheme of social cooperation, and that the advantages it yields can only be obtained if everyone, or nearly everyone, cooperates. Suppose further that cooperation requires a certain sacrifice from each person, or at least involves a certain restriction of his liberty. Suppose finally that the benefits produced by cooperation are, up to a certain point, free: that is, the scheme of cooperation is unstable in the sense that if any one person knows that all (or nearly all) of the others will continue to do their part, he will still be able to share a gain from the scheme even if he does not do his part. Under these conditions a person who has accepted the benefits of the scheme is bound by a duty of fair play to do his part and not to take advantage of the free benefits by not cooperating.[5]

The context within which obligations (or duties – Rawls is not very concerned here with the distinction between them) of fair play can arise, as described by Rawls, can be seen to exhibit three important features, parallel to those we can discern in Hart's account.

(1) There must be an active scheme of social cooperation. This does not really advance us much beyond Hart's "enterprise," but I think that both writers clearly intended that the principle cover a broad range of schemes, programs, and enterprises differing in size and in significance. Thus, both a tenant organization's program to improve conditions in an apartment building and an entire political community's cooperative efforts to preserve social order seem to qualify as "enterprises" or "schemes of social cooperation" of the appropriate sort. Rawls does set two explicit conditions, however, which help us limit the class of "schemes" he has in mind. First, they must be "mutually beneficial." This condition is, I think, implicit in Hart's account as well; indeed, the principle would be obviously objectionable in its absence. Second, the schemes must be just. This condition is nowhere alluded to by Hart, and I will consider it carefully in Section II.

---

4 See fn. 1 above. The versions of the principle which Rawls presents elsewhere do not differ substantially from this 1964 version; however, contrary to his claims in this version he does argue in *A Theory of Justice* that this principle cannot be used to account for political obligations.
5 "Legal Obligation and the Duty of Fair Play," pp. 9–10.

(2) Cooperation under the scheme involves at least a restriction of one's liberty. Rawls does not mention here, as Hart does, that this restriction must be in accord with a system of rules which govern the scheme by determining the requirements of cooperation (although his later "institutional" language does follow Hart's requirement). Frankly, I can see no good reason to insist that the enterprise be governed by rules. Mightn't an enterprise be of the right sort which, say, assigned burdens fairly but not in accord with any preestablished rules? Cannot doing one's part be obligatory under considerations of fair play even if "one's part" is not specified by the rules?

(3) The benefits yielded by the scheme may be received in at least some cases by someone who does not cooperate when his turn comes; here Rawls again makes explicit a condition which Hart clearly has in mind (since "free riding" is a problem only when this condition obtains). But Rawls adds to this the condition that the benefits in question can be obtained only if nearly all of the participants cooperate. I confess that I again do not see the necessity of this condition. Would it be any less unfair to take the benefits of the cooperative sacrifices of others if those benefits could still be obtained when one-third or one-half of the participants neglected their responsibilities towards the scheme? Would this make that neglect justifiable? Surely not. A scheme which requires uniform cooperation when only 50 percent cooperation is needed may perhaps be an inefficient scheme; but it is not clear that this would make considerations of fair play inapplicable. Consider a community scheme to preserve water pressure. This scheme prohibits watering lawns in the evening, when in fact if half of the members watered their lawns there would be no lowering of water pressure. Surely this is an inefficient plan, compared to alternatives. But once the plan was instituted, would a member be any more justified in watering his lawn in the evening than if only a few people's so doing would lower the water pressure? I think it is clear that he would not be. Certainly free riding is more dangerous to the scheme's successful provision of benefits when Rawls' requirement obtains; it may then be even more objectionable in those cases. But this additional objectionable element seems to have nothing to do with considerations of *fair play*.[6]

---

6 This argument also seems to me to provide an effective response to a recent attack on the principle of fair play made by M. B. E. Smith, in "Is There a Prima Facie Obligation to Obey the Law?" *Yale Law Journal* 82 (1973). Smith argues that failing to cooperate in a scheme after receiving benefits is only unfair if by this failure we deny someone else benefits within the scheme. But my example is precisely a case in which the failure to cooperate may not

Rawls' account seems to conform to either the letter or the spirit of Hart's account fairly consistently. One significant addition Rawls makes, however, is to move beyond Hart's simple requirement that an individual must benefit from the scheme in order to become bound. Rawls specifies that the obligation depends on "our having accepted and our intention to continue accepting the benefits of a just scheme of cooperation. . . ."[7] We have, then, a move from mere benefaction in Hart's case, to a positive *acceptance* of benefits in Rawls' account. (The "intention to continue accepting benefits" seems quite beside the point here, and Rawls drops that clause in later versions; I shall ignore it.) While the distinction between benefiting and accepting benefits is usually not easy to draw in actual cases, that there is such a distinction, and that it is of great significance to moral questions, is undeniable. Suppose that I am kidnapped by a mad doctor and dragged to his laboratory, where he forces on me an injection of an experimental drug. When I discover that as a result of the injection my intelligence and strength have greatly increased, it is undeniable that I have benefited from the injection; but it would be a simple abuse of language to say that I had "accepted" the benefits which I received. It seems clear, then, that we can distinguish, at least in some cases, between mere receipt and positive acceptance of benefits. And it seems equally clear that this distinction may play a crucial role in determining whether or what obligations arise from my having benefited from another's actions.

To have accepted a benefit in the right sense, I must have wanted that benefit when I received it or must have made some effort to get the benefit or, at least, must not have actively attempted to avoid getting it. I will try to be more precise about this distinction later; here I want only to suggest that Rawls apparently does not see mere benefaction as sufficient to generate an obligation of fair play. He stresses instead the necessity that the benefits be voluntarily accepted by the beneficiary.

II

I want now to return to consider briefly another of Rawls' conditions for the generation of obligations of fair play. The condition states that only

---

deny anyone else benefits within the scheme. And still it seems clear that failure to cooperate is unfair, for the individual's failure to do his part *takes advantage* of the others, who act in good faith. Whether or not my cooperation is necessary for benefiting other members, it is not fair for me, as a participant in the scheme, to decide not to do my part when the others do theirs. For these reasons, Smith's argument is unpersuasive.

7 "Legal Obligation and the Duty of Fair Play," p. 10.

when the scheme or institution in question is just can any obligations of fair play (relative to that scheme) arise. This claim is part of a more general thesis that we can never be bound to support or comply with unjust arrangements. Although Rawls never advances this general thesis in so many words, it follows from his (unacceptable) claim that *all* obligations are accounted for by the principle of fair play, conjoined with the absence of any natural duties which could account for such a bond.[8]

Rawls' requirement that the scheme of cooperation be just is put forward quite casually in the essay we have been considering; and although he calls it an "essential condition," as far as I can see he offers no defense of this claim. Even in the more recent statement of this requirement in *A Theory of Justice*, we are given little in the way of justification. While he suggests that the condition is necessary to guarantee the requisite "background conditions" for obligation, he elaborates on this point only by suggesting a (strained) analogy with the case of promise-making: "extorted promises are void ab initio."[9] I have argued elsewhere that this observation is quite irrelevant.[10] It is a failure in terms of voluntariness that renders extorted promises non-binding, and the injustice of an institution need not affect the voluntariness of either consent to its rules or acceptance of benefits from it. Rawls' only argument for his "justice condition," then, seems to be a non sequitur.

As Rawls supplies us with no real argument for the justice condition, let us try to construct some for him. Two sorts of arguments suggest themselves as defenses of this condition; the first concerns the purpose of the scheme or the ends it promotes, while the second more directly concerns distribution within the scheme. Our first argument would run as follows: we cannot have obligations to do the morally impermissible, or to support schemes whose purposes are immoral or which promote immoral ends. Since unjust schemes fall within this category, we cannot have an obligation to cooperate within unjust schemes. Now there are a number of difficulties with this as a defense of Rawls' justice condition. One obvious problem is this: why does Rawls only disqualify *unjust* schemes, rather than all schemes which promote or aim at *immoral* ends? Why does Rawls not include the more general prohibition?

The reason is, I think, that while these immoral ends of the scheme

---

8 *A Theory of Justice*, p. 112.

9 Ibid., p. 343.

10 A. John Simmons, "Tacit Consent and Political Obligation," *Philosophy & Public Affairs* 5, no. 3 (Spring 1976): 277–278.

provide us with a reason for working against it, the justice condition is meant to be tied to the principle in a more intimate fashion. But what is this fashion? Thus far, nothing we have said about fair play seems to have anything to do with the moral status of the scheme's purposes. The intuitive force of the principle of fair play seems to be preserved even for criminal conspiracies, for example. The special rights and obligations which arise under the principle are thought to do so because of the special relationships which exist between the cooperating participants; a fair share of the burdens is thought to be owed by a benefiting participant simply because others have sacrificed to allow him to benefit within a cooperative scheme. No reference is made here to the morally acceptable status of the scheme. Simple intuitions about fair play, then, do not seem to provide a reason for disqualifying unjust cooperative schemes. Rather, they suggest that obligations of fair play can, at least sometimes, arise within such schemes.

But perhaps another sort of support can be given to Rawls' condition. This second argument concerns distribution within the scheme, and it certainly has the Rawlsian flavor. We suggest first that, in effect, the justice condition amends the principle to read that a person is bound to do his fair share in supporting a cooperative scheme only if he has been allocated a fair share of the benefits of the scheme. Previously, the principle of fair play required only that the individual have accepted benefits from the scheme in order to be bound, where now it requires that he have accepted benefits *and* have been allocated at least a fair share of benefits. The role of the justice condition now appears to be important, to be an intimate feature of our intuitions about fair play. For if a scheme is just, each participant will be allocated a fair share of the benefits of cooperation; thus, anyone who benefits at all from the scheme has the opportunity to benefit to the extent of a fair share (although he may *accept* less than this). We are guaranteed that the principle of fair play will only apply to individuals who have been fairly treated. Our feeling that a person ought not to have to share equally in supporting a scheme that treats him unfairly is given voice in this condition. The justice condition, then, on this argument, serves the purpose of assuring that a man is bound to do his fair share only if he is allocated a fair share of benefits (and accepts some of them).

I think that this is an important feature of our intuitions about fair play, and it also seems a natural way of reading Rawls. In fact, this may be the argument that Rawls is suggesting when, in elaborating on the principle, he notes that if the scheme is just, "each person receives a fair share when all (himself included) do their part."[11] (Rawls' observation is, strictly speaking, false; the justice of a scheme does not guarantee that each person either receives or accepts a fair share.) But if this *is* the argument Rawls intends for his justice condition, there are serious difficulties for it to overcome. The motivation for including the requirement is (on this reading) to guarantee that an individual not become bound to carry a fair share of the burdens of a cooperative scheme if he has been allocated less than a fair share of its benefits; it is unfair to demand full cooperation from one to whom full benefits are denied. But if *this* is our reason for including the justice condition, we have surely included too much. Why should we think that the whole scheme must be just for this sort of intuition to be given play? Rawls' justice condition requires that *everyone* be allocated a fair share of benefits if *anyone* is to be bound by an obligation of fair play. But the reasons we have given for including this condition seem only to require that for a particular individual to be bound, *he* must be allocated a fair share. This says nothing about the allocation of benefits in general, or about what benefits *others* are allocated. If some individuals within an unjust scheme are allocated less than a fair share of benefits, then our reasons would support the view that *they* are not bound to carry a fair share of the burdens. But nothing said yet about feelings of fair play seems to exempt from obligation those individuals to whom a fair share of benefits is in fact allocated within an *unjust* scheme. So again the point of Rawls' justice condition comes into doubt.

There arguments may prompt us to think more about the notion of a "fair share" of the burdens of cooperation. For if we understand by this phrase a share of the total burden proportionate to the share of the total benefits allocated to the individual, then we may have no problem in accepting that anyone who accepts *any* benefits from a cooperative scheme is bound to do his "fair share." Our belief that only an individual who is allocated a fair share of the benefits is bound to cooperate may be false. For it seems eminently fair to hold that each is bound to cooperate to the extent that he is allowed to benefit from a cooperative scheme; thus, those who are allocated the largest shares of benefits owe the largest share of burdens. But even one who is allocated a very small share of the benefits is bound to carry a small share of the burdens (provided he accepts the benefits).

Now it is clear that these intuitions cannot be given full play in the case of schemes whose burdens cannot be unequally distributed. But there may seem to be other difficulties involved in the interpretation of the fair-play

11 *A Theory of Justice*, p. 112.

principle sketched above. First, it seems to entail that the better-off are bound to support unjust schemes which favor them, and the more discriminatory the scheme, the more strongly they must support it. And second, it seems to entail that those who are allocated tiny, unfair shares of the benefits are still bound to cooperate with the unjust scheme which mistreats them. These may again seem to be good reasons to limit the principle's application to just schemes. I think this appearance is misleading. For, first, the principle under discussion does not entail that the better-off must support unjust schemes which favor them. While it does specify that they are obligated to repay by cooperation the sacrifices made in their behalf by the other members, the injustice of the scheme is a strong reason for opposing it, which gains in strength with the degree of injustice. Thus, there are moral considerations which may override the obligations of fair play (depending, of course, on the degree of the injustice of the scheme, among other things). And if we think of the burdens as sacrifices to be made, it seems only fair that the unjustly favored should be heavily burdened. As for the apparent result that the unjustly treated are still bound to support the scheme (even if to a lesser degree) which discriminates against them, this result can also be seen to be mistaken. For if we remember that benefits must be *accepted* in order for an individual to be bound under the principle, the unfairly treated have the option of refusing to accept benefits, hence sparing themselves the obligation to support a scheme which treats them unfairly (and they have, as well, the duty to oppose such unjust schemes, regardless of what obligations they are under). The idea, then, is that only if they willingly accept the benefits of the scheme are participants bound to bear the burdens of cooperation, and only then in proportion to the benefits allocated to them.

I am not sure just how much of the Hart-Rawls conception of the principle of fair play this analysis captures. But the considerations raised above seem to me to be good reasons for rejecting Rawls' "justice condition." While we can, of course, agree with Rawls that intolerably unjust schemes ought not to be furthered (and, in fact, ought to be opposed), there is no logical difficulty, at least, in holding that we may sometimes have obligations of fair play to cooperate within unjust schemes. And the arguments suggest that there may be no nonlogical difficulties either.

III

I want to pause here to comment briefly on the theory of political obligation which uses the principle of fair play, and specifically on the changes which this account introduces into our conception of political obligation. There are, of course, important continuities between this "fair-play account" and the traditional consent theory account mentioned earlier. While one approach locates the ground of obligation in the acceptance of benefits and the other in consensual acts, both are "obligation-centered" accounts and, as such, both stress the essential voluntariness of the generation of the obligation.[12] But defenders of the fair-play account of political obligation wish to stress as well its significant departures from consent theory; the fair-play account requires a cooperative scheme as the context within which obligations arise, and obviates the need for *deliberate undertakings* of obligation. How these changes might be thought to constitute improvements over the consent theory account seems fairly clear.

First, the fair-play account involves viewing political communities in a different way than consent theory; specifically, they are viewed as "communities" in a fairly strict sense. We are to understand political communities as being fundamentally, or at least in part, cooperative enterprises on a very large scale. Citizens thus are thought to stand in a cooperative relationship to their fellows, rather than in an adversary relationship with the government. And this former view may seem to some more realistic than the latter.

But clearly the major advantage which the fair-play account of political obligation is thought by its advocates to have is that of providing a *general* account of our political bonds. No deliberate undertaking is necessary to become obligated under the principle of fair play. One can become bound without trying to and without knowing that one is performing an act which generates an obligation. Since mere acceptance of benefits within the right context generates the obligation, one who accepts benefits within the right context can become bound unknowingly. This is an important difference from consent theory's account, which stressed the necessity of a deliberate undertaking. Thus, while one can neither consent nor accept benefits (in the right sense) unintentionally, one can accept benefits without being aware of the moral consequences of so doing (while being unaware of the moral consequences of consenting defeats the claim that consent was given). The significance of this difference, of course, lies in the possibility of giving a *general* account of political obligation in the two cases. For

---

12 By "obligation-centered" I mean simply that according to the account most or all of the people who are bound by political bonds are bound by *obligations* (that is, moral requirements originating in some voluntary performance). "Obligation-centered" accounts are to be opposed, of course, to "duty-centered" accounts.

consent theory's failure to give a general account stemmed from the lack of citizens in modern states who had voluntarily undertaken political obligations in the sense required. At least initially, however, it seems much more plausible to suggest that most or all of us have accepted benefits, as is required under the principle of fair play. Thus, the possibility of giving a general account using this principle seems to be vastly increased over one which uses a principle of consent. This would *not* be the case, however, if accepting benefits in the right sense required having an understanding of the moral consequences of such acceptance. For certainly most citizens who receive the benefits of government do not have such an understanding.

Exactly what "accepting the benefits of government" amounts to, of course, is not yet entirely clear. Neither is the identity of the "cooperative scheme" embodied in political communities. These points will be discussed as we continue. My aim here has been simply to mention what might seem to be advantages of the fair-play account; whether or not these "advantages" are genuine remains to be seen. But regardless of the advantages this account may have over the consent-theory account, it surely falls short on one score. Consent is a *clear* ground of obligation. If we are agreed on anything concerning moral requirements, it is that promising and consenting generate them. In specifying a different ground of obligation, the account using the principle of fair play draws away from the paradigm of acts that generate obligations. And to those who are strongly wedded to this paradigm of consent, such as Robert Nozick, the principle of fair play may seem a sham.

IV

In Chapter 5 of *Anarchy, State, and Utopia*, Nozick argues against accepting the principle of fair play as a valid moral principle, not just in political settings, but in any settings whatsoever. He begins by describing a cooperative scheme of the sort he thinks Hart and Rawls have in mind, and then suggests that benefaction within that scheme may *not* bind one to do one's part:

> Suppose some of the people in your neighborhood (there are 364 other adults) have found a public address system and decide to institute a system of public entertainment. They post a list of names, one for each day, yours among them. On his assigned day (one can easily switch days) a person is to run the public address system, play records over it, give news bulletins, tell amusing stories he has heard, and so on. After 138 days on which each person

has done his part, your day arrives. Are you obligated to take your turn? You *have* benefited from it, occasionally opening your window to listen, enjoying some music or chuckling at someone's funny story. The other people *have* put themselves out. But must you answer the call when it is your turn to do so? As it stands, surely not. Though you benefit from the arrangement, you may know all along that 364 days of entertainment supplied by others will not be worth your giving up *one* day. You would rather not have any of it and not give up a day than have it all and spend one of your days at it. Given these preferences, how can it be that you are required to participate when your scheduled time comes?[13]

On the basis of this example and others, Nozick concludes that we are never bound to cooperate in such contexts (unless we have given our consent to be constrained by the rules of the cooperative scheme).

Now, to be fair, Nozick does not simply pick the weakest form of the principle of fair play and then reject it for its inadequacy in hard cases; he has, in fact, a suggestion for improving the principle in response to the cases he describes. Having noticed, I suppose, that the case described above favors his conclusions largely because of the negligible value of the benefits received, Nozick suggests that "at the very least one wants to build into the principle of fairness the condition that the benefits to a person from the actions of others are greater than the cost to him of doing his share" (Nozick, p. 94). There is certainly something right about this; something like this must be built into the idea of a useful cooperative scheme. On the other hand, we can imagine a defender of the principle saying "if you weren't prepared to do your part you ought not to have taken *any* benefits from the scheme, no matter how insignificant." Nozick, of course, has more to say on this point, and so do I.

Even if we do modify the principle with this condition, however, Nozick has other arguments against it. "The benefits might only barely be worth the costs to you of doing your share, yet others might benefit from *this* institution much more than you do; they all treasure listening to the public broadcasts. As the person least benefited by the practice, are you obligated to do an equal amount for it?" (Nozick, p. 94). The understood answer is no, but we might agree with this answer without agreeing that it tells against the principle. For if we understand that "doing one's part" or "doing one's fair share" is not necessarily "doing an equal part," but rather "doing a part proportionate to the part of the benefits received," then the one who ben-

---

13 Robert Nozick, *Anarchy, State, and Utopia* (New York: Basic Books, 1974), p. 93. Citations of Nozick in the text refer to this work.

efits least from a cooperative scheme will *not* be bound to share equally in the burdens of cooperation. I argued for this interpretation in Section II, and if we accept it, Nozick's PA system example may no longer seem so troublesome. For we might be willing to admit that the individual in question, because he benefited so little, was bound to cooperate but not to the same extent as others who benefit more from the scheme. Would being obligated to do one's part in the PA scheme seem quite so objectionable if one's part was only, say, an hour's worth of broadcasting, as opposed to that of the PA enthusiasts, whose parts were one and a half days of broadcasting? There are, perhaps, no clear answers to these questions.

But surely the defender of the principle of fair play will have more fundamental objections to Nozick's case than these. In the first place, the individual in Nozick's PA example does not seem to be a *participant* in the scheme in the sense that Hart and Rawls may have in mind. While he does live in the neighborhood within which the scheme operates, and he does benefit from it, he is still very much of an "innocent bystander." The PA system scheme has been built up around him in such a way that he could not escape its influence. And, of course, the whole force of Nozick's example lies in our feeling that others ought not to be able to *force* any scheme they like upon us, with the attendant obligations. The PA case would be precisely such a case of "forced" obligation. So naturally we may find Nozick's criticism of the principle of fair play convincing, if we believe the principle to entail that we *do* have obligations under the PA scheme.

But it seems clear that Hart and Rawls did not mean for the principle to apply to such cases of "innocent bystanders" (though admittedly neither emphasizes the point). Nozick's case seems to rest on a reading of the principle which runs contrary to the spirit of their remarks, a reading according to which the principle binds everyone who benefits from a cooperation scheme, regardless of their relations to it. And Nozick is surely right that a moral principle which had those results *would* be an outrageous one. People who have no significant relationship at all with some cooperative scheme may receive incidental benefits from its operation. Thus, imagine yourself a member of some scheme which benefits you immensely by increasing your income. Your friends and relatives may benefit incidentally from the scheme as well if, say, you now become prone to send them expensive presents. But the suggestion that their benefiting in this way obligates them to do their part in the scheme is absurd.

Hart and Rawls can most fairly be read as holding that only beneficiaries who are also participants (in some significant sense) are bound under the principle of fair play. And on this reading, of course, Nozick's PA system example does not seem to be a case to which the principle applies; the individual in question is not a participant in the scheme, having had nothing to do with its institution, and having done nothing to lead anyone to believe that he wished to become involved in the scheme. The example, then, cannot serve as a counter-example to Hart's principle. In fact, all of Nozick's examples in his criticisms of Hart are examples in which an "outsider" has some benefit thrust on him by some cooperative scheme to which he is in no way tied (see Nozick's "street-sweeping," "lawn-mowing," and "book-thrusting" examples, pp. 94–95). But if I am right, these examples do not tell against the principle of fair play, since the benefits accruing to "outsiders" are not thought by Hart and Rawls to bind under that principle.

The problem of specifying who are "outsiders," and consequently whose benefits will count, is a serious one, especially in the political applications of the principle. And it seems that the problem may provide ammunition for a serious counterattack by someone such as Nozick against the principle of fair play. We have maintained, remember, that only "participants" or "insiders" in the cooperative scheme are candidates for being obligated under the principle to do their share in cooperating. Those "outsiders" who benefit from the scheme's operation are not bound under the principle of fair play. But how exactly do we differentiate between these outsiders and the insiders? What relationship must hold between an individual and a cooperative scheme for him to be said to be a participant in some significant sense?

This is a hard question to answer, but we have already considered some cases where an individual is *not* a participant in the right sense. Thus, merely being a member of some group, other members of which institute a scheme, is not enough to make one a participant or an "insider." Although Nozick's man is a "member" of an identifiable group, namely his neighborhood, this "membership" does not suffice to make him a participant in any scheme his neighbors dream up. Normally, we would want to say that for an individual to be a real participant in a cooperative scheme, he must have either (1) pledged his support or tacitly agreed to be governed by the scheme's rules, or (2) played some active role in the scheme after its institution. It is not enough to be associated with the "schemers" in some vague way to make one an "insider" or a participant; one must go out and do things to become a participant and to potentially be bound under the principle of fair play.

Now we can imagine an opponent of the principle accepting these remarks concerning whose benefiting will count, and accepting our criticism of Nozick's PA system counterexample, and still responding to our discussion by posing the following dilemma. We are agreed, the Nozickian begins, that "outsiders" fall outside the scope of Hart's principle; not just anyone who benefits from a cooperative scheme will be bound to do his share in it. And we are agreed that mere membership in some group, other members of which conduct some cooperative scheme, is insufficient to make one an "insider." And we are agreed that one becomes an "insider" by the means described above, perhaps among others. But the problem is this. In becoming an "insider" one must do something which involves either an express or a tacit undertaking to do one's part in the scheme. So if the principle of fair play can bind only "insiders" in a cooperative scheme, it will bind only those individuals who have *already* become bound to do their part in the scheme in becoming "insiders." The principle is superfluous; it collapses into a principle of consent. All and only those individuals who have actually undertaken to do their part in the scheme are bound by the principle of fair play to do their part in the scheme. Benefiting under the scheme is quite irrelevant, for benefiting only counts under the principle for "insiders." But "insiders" are already bound to the scheme, whether they benefit from it or not.

This argument, if it is acceptable, counts heavily against the principle of fair play. For that principle was supposed to show us how individuals could become bound to some cooperative enterprise *without* actually giving their consent to it. But if the principle can only plausibly be thought to bind those who have already consented to going along with the enterprise, the principle's usefulness becomes highly doubtful. We can explain whatever obligations participants in the enterprise are thought to have simply in terms of a principle of consent, quite independent of considerations of fair play.

But is this sort of argument acceptable? It is true that I cannot become a participant in the right sense without giving at least tacit consent to the scheme. Surely many participants in cooperative schemes have given their consent, either express or tacit, and are bound to their schemes regardless of what else they do to bind themselves. But these are not the individuals with whom Hart and Rawls are primarily concerned. With all our discussion of "participation," we are overlooking a feature of the principle of fair play which Rawls saw as essential to the generation of the obligation. The principle of fair play does not specify that all participants in cooperative schemes are bound to do their part, or even that all participants who benefit from the schemes are so bound. It states rather that those who *accept* the benefits of a cooperative scheme are bound to cooperate. This distinction between accepting benefits and merely receiving benefits has been lost somewhere in the shuffle. It is a distinction which is *completely* overlooked in Nozick's discussion of the principle of fair play. But it seems to me that this distinction is crucial in settling the problem of how to distinguish participants (or "insiders") from "outsiders."

For Rawls and Hart, the principle of fair play accounts for the obligations of those whose active role in the scheme consists of accepting the benefits of its workings. One becomes a participant in the scheme precisely by accepting the benefits it offers; the other ways in which one can become a participant are not important to considerations of fair play. And individuals who have merely *received* benefits from the scheme have the same status relative to it as those who have been unaffected by the scheme; they are not in any way bound to do their part in the scheme unless they have independently undertaken to do so. If, as I've suggested, the acceptance of benefits constitutes the sort of "participation" in a scheme with which Rawls and Hart are concerned, we can understand why neither Rawls nor Hart specifically limits the application of the principle to *participants* in the scheme. This limitation has already been accomplished by making obligation conditional on the acceptance of benefits. This means, of course, that the principle cannot be read as the outrageous one which requires anyone at all who benefits from the scheme to do his part in it.

But understanding the principle in this way also helps us see why the Nozickian line of argument we have considered cannot succeed. The Nozickian tried to persuade us that an individual could not become a participant, or an "insider," without doing something which amounted to giving his consent to do his part in the scheme. But it seems clear that a man *can* accept benefits from a scheme and be a participant in that sense without giving his consent to the scheme. And further, such acceptance of benefits *does* seem to obligate him to do his part. Let me support and clarify this claim with an example.

Imagine that in Nozick's neighborhood the need for public entertainment is not the only matter of concern. There is also a problem with the neighborhood's water supply; the water pumped through their pipes has developed an unpleasant taste and an odd yellow tinge. A neighborhood meeting is called, at which a majority votes to dig a public well near the center of the neighborhood, to be paid for and maintained by the members of the neighborhood. Some of the members clearly give their consent to the proposed scheme. Others, who vote against the proposal, do not. Jones, in particular, announces angrily that he wants to have noting to do with the scheme and that he will certainly not pledge his support. Nothing, he claims, could make him consent to do such a ridiculous enterprise. But in spite of his opposition, the well is dug, paid for, and maintained by the other members of the neighborhood. Jones, as expected, contributes nothing to this effort.

Now the benefits of clear, fresh water are available to the neighborhood, and Jones begins to be envious of his neighbors, who go to the well daily. So he goes to the well every night and, knowing that the water will never be missed, takes some home with him for the next day. It seems clear to me that Jones is a perfect example of a "free-rider." And it also seems clear that, having accepted benefits from the scheme (indeed, he has gone out of his way to obtain them), he has an obligation to do his part within it. But he certainly does not seem to have *consented* to the scheme. We have, then, a case in which an individual has an obligation to do his part within a cooperative scheme which is *not* accounted for by a principle of consent. We would, I think, account for that obligation precisely in terms of fair play. Jones has made himself a participant in the scheme by accepting its benefits, although he has refused to give his consent. So the Nozickian argument does not succeed.

I have tried to show, then, that the principle of fair play does not collapse into a principle of consent. While many participants in cooperative schemes will be bound to do their parts because they have consented to do so, many others will be bound because they have accepted benefits from the scheme. The obligations of the latter will fall under the principle of fair play. We should not think, because of the peculiarity of Jones' position in our example, that only the obligations of free-riders like Jones will be accounted for by the principle. For it is possible to *go along* with a cooperative scheme (as Jones does not) without consenting to it, becoming bound through one's acceptance of benefits. In fact, I think that *most* participants in cooperative schemes do nothing which can be thought to constitute consent. It is not necessary to refuse to give one's consent, as Jones does, in order not to give it. Consent is not given to a scheme by any behavior short of express dissent. Most participants in cooperative schemes simply go along with the schemes, taking their benefits and carrying their burdens. But if they do not expressly undertake to support the schemes, and if their behavior does not constitute a response to a clear choice situation, I do not think that we can ascribe consent to them. Certainly by going along with a scheme, we lead others to *expect* certain future performances from us; but this does not show that we have *undertaken* to perform according to expectations. Thus, the obligations which participants in cooperative schemes have (relative to those schemes) will not normally be grounded in consent.

The reading of the principle which I have given obviously places a very heavy load on the notion of "acceptance," a notion to which we have as yet given no clear meaning (and Rawls and Hart certainly give us no help on this count). It is not, as I suggested in Section I, at all easy to distinguish in practice between benefits that have been accepted and those that have only been received, although some cases seem clearly to fall on the "merely received" side. Thus, benefits we have actively resisted getting, and those which we have gotten unknowingly or in ways over which we have had no control at all, seem clearly *not* to be benefits we have accepted. To have accepted a benefit, I think, we would want to say that an individual must either (1) have tried to get (and succeeded in getting) the benefit, or (2) have taken the benefit willingly and knowingly.

Consider now Nozick's example of the program that involves "thrusting books" into unsuspecting people's houses. Clearly the benefits in question are merely received, not accepted. "One cannot," Nozick writes, "whatever one's purposes, just act so as to give people benefits and then demand (or seize) payment. Nor can a group of persons do this" (p. 95). I am suggesting that, on the contrary, the principle of fair play does *not* involve justifying this sort of behavior; people are only bound under the principle when they have accepted benefits.

Nozick's first-line example, the PA scheme, however, is slightly more difficult. For here the benefits received are not forced upon you, as in the "book-thrusting" case, or gotten in some other way which is outside your control. Rather, the benefits are what I will call "open"; while they can be avoided, they cannot be avoided without considerable inconvenience. Thus, while I can avoid the (questionable) benefits the PA system provides by remaining indoors with the windows closed, this is a considerable inconvenience. The benefits are "open" in the sense that I cannot avoid receiving them, even if I want to, without altering my life style (economists often have such benefits in mind in speaking of "public goods"). Many benefits yielded by cooperative schemes (in fact most benefits, I should think) are "open" in this way. A neighborhood organization's program to improve the neighborhood's appearance yields benefits which are "open." And the benefits of government are mostly of this sort. The benefits of the rule of law, protection by the armed forces, pollution control, and so on can be avoided only by emigration.

We can contrast these cases of "open" benefits with benefits that are only "readily available." If instead of a PA system, Nozick's group had decided to rent a building in the middle of town in which live entertainment was continuously available to neighborhood members, the benefits of the scheme would only be "readily available." A good example of the distinction under consideration would be the distinction between two sorts of police protection, one sort being an "open" benefit, the other being only "readily available." Thus, the benefits which I receive from the continuous efforts of police officers to patrol the streets, capture criminals, and eliminate potential threats to my safety, are benefits which are "open." They can be avoided only by leaving the area which the police force protects. But I may also request *special* protection by the police, if I fear for my life, say, or if I need my house to be watched while I'm away. These benefits are "readily available." Benefits which are "readily available" can be easily avoided without inconvenience.

Now I think that clear cases of the acceptance of benefits, as opposed to receipt, will be easy to find where benefits which are only "readily available" are concerned. Getting these benefits will involve going out of one's way, making some sort of effort to get the benefit, and hence there will generally be no question that the benefit was accepted in the sense we have described. The principle of fair play seems most clearly to apply in cases such as these. These will be cases where our actions may obviously fall short of constituting *consent* to do our part in the scheme in question, but where our acceptance of benefits binds us to do our part because of considerations of fair play. When we accept benefits in such cases, it may be necessary that we be aware that the benefits in question *are* the fruits of a cooperative scheme, in order for us to be willing to ascribe any obligations of fair play; but it will *not* be necessary that some express or tacit act of consent have been performed.

The examples of "open" benefits are, of course, harder to handle. Nozick's comments seem quite reasonable with respect to them. For surely it is very implausible to suggest that if we are unwilling to do our part, we must alter our life styles in order to avoid enjoying these benefits. As Nozick suggests, there is surely no reason why, when the street-sweeping scheme comes to your town, you must "imagine dirt as you traverse the street, so as not to benefit as a free rider" (p. 94). Nozick's comments here do not, however, strike against the principle of fair play in any obvious way. For as I have interpreted it, the principle does not apply to cases of mere receipt of benefits from cooperative schemes; and the cases where the benefits are "open" in this way seem to be cases of mere receipt of benefits. Certainly it would be peculiar if a man, who by simply going about his business in a normal fashion benefited unavoidably from some cooperative scheme, were told that he had voluntarily accepted benefits which generated for him a special obligation to do his part.

This problem of "acceptance" and "open benefits" is a serious one, and there are real difficulties involved in solving it. It may look, for instance, as if I am saying that a genuine acceptance of open benefits is impossible. But I would not want to be pushed so far. It seems to me that it is possible to accept a benefit which is (in one sense) unavoidable; but it is not at all the *normal* case that those who receive open benefits from a scheme have also accepted those benefits. In the case of benefits which are only "readily available," receipt of the benefits is generally *also* acceptance. But this is not so in the case of open benefits. I suggested earlier that accepting a benefit involved either (1) trying to get (and succeeding in getting) the benefit, or (2) taking the benefit willingly and knowingly. Getting benefits which are "readily available" normally involves (1) trying to get the benefit. It is not clear, however, how one would go about *trying* to get an open benefit which is not distributed by request, but is rather received by everyone involved, whether they want it or not. If open benefits can be accepted, it would seem that method (2) of accepting benefits is the way in which this is normally accomplished. We can take the open benefits which we receive willingly and knowingly. But doing so involves a number of restrictions on our attitudes toward and beliefs about the open benefits we receive. We cannot, for instance, regard the benefits as having been forced upon us against our will, or think that the benefits are not worth the price we must pay for them. And taking the benefits "knowingly" seems to involve an understanding of the status of those benefits relative to the party providing them. Thus, in the case of open benefits provided by a cooperative scheme, we must understand that the benefits *are* provided by the cooperative scheme in order to accept them.

The necessity of satisfying such conditions, however, seems to significantly reduce the number of individuals who receive open benefits, who can be taken to have *accepted* those benefits. And it will by no means be a standard case in which all beneficiaries of a cooperative scheme's workings have accepted the benefits they receive.

I recognize, of course, that problems concerning "acceptance" remain. But even if they did not, my reading of the principle of fair play, as binding only those who have accepted benefits, would still face difficulties. The fact remains that we *do* criticize persons as "free riders" (in terms of fair play) for not doing their part, even when they have *not* accepted benefits from a cooperative scheme. We often criticize them merely because they *receive* benefits without doing their part in the cooperative scheme. Let us go back to Nozick's neighborhood and imagine another, more realistic cooperative scheme in operation, this one designed to beautify the neighborhood by assigning to each resident a specific task involving landscaping or yard work. Home owners are required to care for their yards and to do some work on community property on weekends. There are also a number of apartments in the neighborhood, but because the apartment grounds are cared for by the landlords, apartment dwellers are expected only to help on community property (they are expected to help because even tenants are granted full community membership and privileges; and it is reasoned that all residents have an equal interest in the neighborhood's appearance, at least during the time they remain). Two of these apartment dwellers, Oscar and Willie, refuse to do their part in the scheme. Oscar refuses because he hates neatly trimmed yards, preferring crabgrass, long weeds, and scraggly bushes. The residents do not feel so bad about Oscar (although they try to force him out of the neighborhood), since he does not seem to be benefiting from their efforts without putting out. He hates what they are doing to the neighborhood. Willie, however, is another case altogether. He values a neat neighborhood as much as the others; but he values his spare time more than the others. While he enjoys a beautiful neighborhood, the part he is expected to play in the cooperative scheme involves too much of his time. He makes it clear that he would prefer to have an ugly neighborhood to joining such a scheme.

So while the others labor to produce an almost spotless neighborhood, Willie enjoys the benefits resulting from their efforts while doing nothing to help. And it seems to me that Willie is *just* the sort of person who would be accused by the neighborhood council of "free riding," of unfairly benefiting from the cooperative efforts of others; for he receives exactly the same benefits as the others while contributing nothing. Yet Willie has not accepted the benefits in question, for he thinks that the price being demanded is too high. He would prefer doing without the benefits to having the benefits and the burdens.

So it looks as if the way in which we have filled out the principle of fair play is not entirely in accord with some common feelings about matters of fair play; for these common feelings do not seem to require acceptance of benefits within the scheme, as our version of the principle does. It is against these "ordinary feelings about fair play" (and not against the "filled-out" principle we have been describing), I think, that Nozick's arguments, and the "Nozickian" arguments suggested, strike most sharply.

But Willie's position is *not* substantially different from that of the salesman, Sam, whose sole territory is the neighborhood in question. Sam works eight hours every day in the neighborhood, enjoying its beauty, while Willie (away at work all day) may eke out his forty weekly hours of enjoyment if he stays home on weekends. Thus, Sam and Willie receive substantially the same benefits. Neither Sam nor Willie has done anything at all to ally himself with the cooperative scheme, and neither has "accepted" the fruits of that scheme. Willie is a "member" of the community only because the council voted to award "membership" to tenants, and he has made no commitments. To make the parallel complete, we can even suppose that Sam, beloved by all the residents, is named by the council an "honorary member." But if the neighborhood council accused Sam, the salesman, of "free riding" and demanded that *he* work on community property, their position would be laughable. Why, though, should Willie, who is like Sam in all important respects, be any *more* vulnerable to such accusations and demands?

The answer is that he is *not* any more vulnerable; if ordinary feelings about obligations of fair play insist that he *is* more vulnerable, those feelings are mistaken. But in fairness to Nozick, the way that Hart and Rawls phrase their account of the principle of fair play *does* sometimes look as if it expresses those (mistaken) feelings about fair play. As Rawls states it,

> The main idea is that when a number of persons engage in a mutually advan-
> tageous cooperative venture according to rules, and thus restrict their liberty
> in ways necessary to yield advantages for all, those who have submitted to
> these restrictions have a right to a similar acquiescence on the part of those
> who have benefited from their submission. We are not to gain from the coop-
> erative labors of others without doing our fair share.[14]

This certainly looks like a condemnation of Willie's actions. Of course, the way in which Rawls fills out this idea, in terms of accepting benefits and taking advantage of the scheme, points in quite a different direction; for on the "filled-out" principle, Willie is not bound to cooperate, and neither is the salesman.

It looks, then, as if we have a choice to make between a general principle (which binds all beneficiaries of a scheme) which is *very* implausible, and a more limited principle which is more plausible. I say that we have a choice to make simply because it seems clear that the limited principle is much more limited than either Hart or Rawls realized. For if my previous suggestions were correct, participants in cooperative schemes which

---

14 Rawls, *A Theory of Justice*, p. 112.

produce "open" benefits will not always have a right to cooperation on the part of those who benefit from their labors. And this does not look like a result that either Hart or Rawls would be prepared to accept. Perhaps it is, after all, just the result Nozick wished to argue for.

V

When we move to political communities the "schemes of social cooperation" with which we will be concerned will naturally be schemes on a rather grand scale. We may, with Rawls, think that the maintenance of the legal order should be "construed as a system of social cooperation," or perhaps we will want to identify all the workings of that set of political institutions governing "political society" generally as the operation of "the most complex example" of a cooperative scheme (as Hart seems to).[15] The details of the interpretation which we accept are not particularly important here. We must simply imagine a cooperative scheme large enough that "doing our part" will involve all of the things normally thought of as the requirements of political obligation; and regardless of how we characterize this scheme in its particulars, the difficulties involved in an account of political obligation using the principle of fair play will be common to all particular versions.[16]

To begin, we face an immediate problem of "membership," of distinguishing the "insiders" from the "outsiders." Ideally, of course, the account wants all and only the citizens of the state in question to be the "insiders" relative to the cooperative scheme in operation in the state. The "all" in "all and only" can be sacrificed here, since an account which applies only to some members of a political community is not obviously objectionable; but the "only" in "all and only" must not be compromised. For obvious reasons, we cannot accept an account of political obligation which binds non-citizens to do their part in the cooperative political enterprises of a foreign country.

But most "insiders" or citizens, even in constitutional democracies, seem to be very much in the same sort of position as Nozick's man. They are not obviously tied to the grand cooperative scheme of political life any more

---

15 Rawls, "Legal Obligation and the Duty of Fair Play," p. 17; Hart, "Are There Any Natural Rights?" pp. 185–186.

16 One limitation is obvious from the start. Only reasonably democratic political communities will be candidates for a fair-play account of political obligation; for only where we can see the political workings of the society as a voluntary cooperative venture will the principle apply.

than Nozick's man is tied to his PA scheme. We are, after all, born into political communities; and being "dropped into" a cooperative scheme does not seem significantly different from having a scheme "built up around you."

I tried to suggest earlier, of course, that the right way to distinguish the "insiders" relative to some scheme was through the notion of the "acceptance" of benefits from that scheme. While it is clear that at least most citizens in most states *receive* benefits from the workings of their legal and political institutions, how plausible is it to say that they have voluntarily *accepted* those benefits? Not, I think, very plausible. The benefits in question have been mentioned before: the rule of law, protection by armed forces, pollution control, maintenance of highway systems, avenues of political participation, and so on. But these benefits are what we have called "open" benefits. It is precisely in cases of such "open" benefits that it is least plausible to suggest that benefits are being *accepted* by most beneficiaries. It will, of course, be difficult to be certain about the acceptance of benefits in actual cases; but on any natural understanding of the notion of "acceptance," our having accepted open benefits involves our having had certain attitudes toward and beliefs about the benefits we have received (as noted in Section IV). Among other things, we must regard the benefits as flowing from a cooperative scheme rather than seeing them as "free" for the taking. And we must, for instance, think that the benefits we receive are worth the price we must pay for them, so that we would take the benefits if we had a choice between taking them (with the burdens involved) or leaving them. These kinds of beliefs and attitudes are necessary if the benefaction is to be plausibly regarded as constituting voluntary participation in the cooperative scheme.

But surely most of us do not have these requisite attitudes toward or beliefs about the benefits of government. At least many citizens barely notice (and seem disinclined to think about) the benefits they receive. And many more, faced with high taxes, with military service which may involve fighting in foreign "police actions," or with unreasonably restrictive laws governing private pleasures, believe that the benefits received from governments are not worth the price they are forced to pay. While such beliefs may be false, they seem nonetheless incompatible with the "acceptance" of the open benefits of government. Further, it must be admitted that, even in democratic political communities, these benefits are commonly regarded as purchased (with taxes) from a central authority, rather than as accepted from the cooperative efforts of our fellow citizens. We may feel, for instance, that if debts are owed at all, they are owed not to those around us, but to our government. Again, these attitudes seem inconsistent with the suggestion that the open benefits are accepted, in the strict sense of "acceptance." Most citizens will, I think, fall into one of these two classes: those who have not "accepted" because they have not taken the benefits (with accompanying burdens) willingly, and those who have not "accepted" because they do not regard the benefits of government as the products of a cooperative scheme. But if most citizens cannot be thought to have voluntarily accepted the benefits of government from the political cooperative scheme, then the fair-play account of political obligation will not be suitably general in its application, even within democratic states. And if we try to make the account more general by removing the limitations set by our strict notion of "acceptance," we open the floodgates and turn the principle of fair play into the "outrageous" principle discussed earlier. We seem forced by such observations to conclude that citizens generally in no actual states will be bound under the principle of fair play.

These suggestions raise serious doubts about the Hart-Rawls contention that at least some organized political societies can be thought of as ongoing cooperative schemes on a very large scale. While such a claim may be initially attractive, does it really seem reasonable to think of any actual political communities on the model of the kinds of neighborhood cooperative schemes we have discussed in this chapter? This seems to me quite unrealistic. We must remember that where there is no consciousness of cooperation, no common plan or purpose, no cooperative scheme exists. I do not think that many of us can honestly say that we regard our political lives as a process of working together and making necessary sacrifices for the purpose of improving the common lot. The centrality and apparent independence of governments does not make it natural to think of political life in this way.

Perhaps, then, we ought not to think of modern political communities as essentially or in part large scale cooperative ventures. No doubt there is a sense in which society in general (and political society in particular) can be understood as a "cooperative venture," even though no consciousness of cooperation or common purpose is to be found. Social man is thought of as governed by public systems of rules designed to regulate his activities in ways which increase the benefits accruing to all. Perhaps it is this rather loose sense of "cooperative scheme" which Hart and Rawls have in mind when they imagine political communities as cooperative schemes.[17] But we should remember that whatever intuitive plausibility the principle of fair

17 See Rawls, *A Theory of Justice*, for example, pp. 4, 84.

play has, derives from our regarding it as an acceptable moral principle for cooperative schemes in the *strict* sense. Clearly the considerations which lead us to accept the principle of fair play as determining our obligations in the context of a neighborhood organization's cooperative programs may in no way be mirrored in the context of "cooperative schemes" understood in the loose sense mentioned above. So that while talk of cooperative schemes on the level of political communities may not be obviously objectionable, such cooperative schemes will not be among those to which we should be inclined to apply the principle of fair play.

These brief remarks all point toward the conclusion that at very best the principle of fair play can hope to account for the political obligations of only a very few citizens in a very few actual states; it is more likely, however, that it accounts for no such obligations at all. While we have seen that the principle does not "collapse" into a principle of consent, we have also seen that in an account of political obligation, the principle has very little to recommend it, either as a supplement to, or a replacement for, principles of fidelity and consent. In particular, the main advantage which the fair-play account was thought to have over consent theory's account, namely, an advantage in *generality*, turns out to be no advantage at all.[18]

18 This paper is an abbreviated and revised version of material from Chapter V of *Moral Principles and Political Obligations* (Princeton University Press, forthcoming). I would like to thank David Lyons and the editors for helpful suggestions about earlier drafts of the paper.

2

FAIR PLAY AND POLITICAL OBLIGATION: TWENTY YEARS LATER

I

My 1979 essay "The Principle of Fair Play"[1] had two principal objectives. The first was to defend the principle of fair play (against critics like Nozick[2]) as a valid principle of moral obligation, a principle not reducible to or deriveble from some more basic or fundamental principle of obligation. The essay's second objective was to refute accounts of political obligation (like those of Hart[3] and the early Rawls[4]) that centrally employed that principle.

My general strategy in support of the former aim was to delineate a plausible version of the principle of fair play (or "principle of fairness," as it is more commonly called today) that could be collapsed into or ultimately reduced to neither a principle of consent nor some nonvoluntarist principle of morally obligatory reciprocation for benefits received (such as a principle of gratitude). Defending a voluntarist version of the principle allowed me both to remain true to Hart's and Rawls' original goal – that of "introducing" a principle that could capture some of the voluntarist force of traditional contract theory's account of political obligation, without embracing contract theory's "fictions" or anarchistic implications[5] – and to

---

1 *Philosophy and Public Affairs* 8:4 (1979).
2 Robert Nozick, *Anarchy, State, and Utopia* (Basic Books, 1974), 90–95.
3 H. L. A. Hart, "Are there Any Natural Rights?," *The Philosophical Review* 64 (1955), 185–86.
4 John Rawls, "Justice as Fairness," 59–64, and "Legal Obligation and the Duty of Fair Play," 117–29, both in S. Freeman (ed.), *John Rawls: Collected Papers* (Cambridge, MA: Harvard University Press, 1999).
5 Hart, 63; Rawls, "Justice as Fairness," 55–60.

defend a principle that seemed to me far more plausible than any version of it which would allow the mere receipt of benefits from a cooperative scheme to obligate beneficiaries to reciprocate (against which version Nozick's arguments appear to tell so forcefully). But defending a voluntarist version of the principle of fair play also required me to meaningfully distinguish mere (nonvoluntary) receipt of benefits from voluntary acceptance of benefits, and to show that obligation under the principle was tied solely to instances of the latter. That distinction, in turn, required an account of the psychological conditions that must be satisfied – particularly in the case of "open" or "public" goods – for an instance of getting a benefit to count as well as an instance of voluntarily accepting it. I argued that "accepting a benefit involved either (1) trying to get (and succeeding in getting) the benefit, or (2) taking the benefit willingly and knowingly."[6]

My strategy in support of the essay's second objective was much simpler. I argued that contemporary political societies simply do not constitute cooperative schemes of the sort necessary to generate obligations under the principle of fair play. And, relatedly, typical citizens of those societies generally fail to satisfy the psychological conditions that would make their enjoyment of the benefits their governments provide constitute voluntary acceptance of benefits from a cooperative scheme. Here the arguments were both conceptual – i.e., concerning what counts as a genuinely cooperative venture – and based on simple empirical observation. My conclusion, of course, was that the principle of fair play, properly articulated, simply does not apply to, and hence cannot explain the political obligations of, typical citizens of typical (Western) contemporary societies.

I continue to believe that the principal arguments and conclusions of my 1979 essay are correct; but they have been so widely attacked during the two decades since that essay's publication that a further elaboration, reply, and defense of my position now seems appropriate.[7] Few critics of my arguments have challenged the status of the principle of fair play as an independent moral principle – though it does seem to me quite natural to

---

6 "The Principle of Fair Play," 329. That one can freely accept something that one cannot avoid receiving seems as evident to me as that one can freely opt to stay in for the evening, even when one's broken car would prevent one from going out. In both cases, the satisfaction of certain psychological conditions (e.g., one's beliefs, attitudes, preferences) will determine the matter.

7 I have previously addressed some criticisms of my position in "The Anarchist Position: A Reply to Klosko and Senor," *Philosophy and Public Affairs* 16:3 (1987), 270–75, and in *On the Edge of Anarchy: Locke, Consent, and the Limits of Society* (Princeton: Princeton University Press, 1993), 251–60.

wonder whether the principle's force might in fact be captured by more basic principles grounding the rights and duties concerned with (collective) property.[8] Rather, critics have mostly opted for one of two strategies in rejecting my conclusions. First, they have tried to defend different, nonvoluntarist versions of the principle that make it seem more widely applicable to persons in existing political societies (which, they acknowledge, don't look much like genuinely voluntary cooperative schemes). Second, other critics have tried to portray actual political societies as in fact being more voluntary and cooperative than my picture of those societies allows, making even a voluntarist version of the principle seem applicable after all to typical citizens. Occasionally, critics have tried to combine these two approaches, defending a more weakly voluntarist version of the principle than my own, while asserting that real political societies are at least weakly voluntary schemes.[9] Again, as in the first two approaches, the obvious goal here is to show that the political obligations of many real citizens can after all be accounted for (at least in part) by the principle of fair play.

In what follows, I will try to respond to these challenges. Nonvoluntarist and weakly voluntarist versions of the principle of fair play, I will contend, in fact confuse concerns about *fairness* in cooperative ventures with quite different sorts of moral concerns, and so offer us a conception of fairness that is either a muddled, mixed moral notion or no notion of fairness at all. Attempts to portray actual political societies as voluntary cooperative schemes, I will argue, utilize an idea of cooperation that, when employed in discussing the principle of fair play, undermines that principle's own intuitive support.

II

In its most general possible form, the principle of fair play asserts that those who benefit from the good-faith sacrifices of others, made in support of a mutually beneficial cooperative venture, have a moral obligation to do their parts as well (that is, to make reciprocal sacrifices) within the venture. The kind of unfairness condemned by the principle is that involved in *taking advantage of* or *exploiting* the sacrifices of persons who have freely assumed

8 Richard Arneson has argued that Lockean principles of property and "mutual benefit" principles (like the principle of fair play) are justified in the same general way, though not, as far as I can see, that the latter are reducible to the former ("The Principle of Fairness and Free-Rider Problems," *Ethics* 92:4 [July 1982], 624–26).

9 See especially Gregory Kavka, *Hobbesian Moral and Political Theory* (Princeton: Princeton University Press, 1986), 410–13.

the burdens associated with maintaining mutually beneficial schemes. Typical instances of so-called "free riding" involve this sort of unfairness. But as these typical instances clearly show, such unfairness need not do any direct harm to the cooperative scheme at issue or reduce the benefits participants in that scheme can expect to receive. If I ride the bus without franking my ticket or cheat a little on my tax return, the effects of my alleged free-riding – either on others or on the scheme providing the benefits – are likely to be negligible or nonexistent. Unfairly taking advantage of the cooperative sacrifices of others *may* do *direct* harm to them or their scheme, as when my grossly excessive use for lawn-watering of a small local water supply during a drought causes my neighbors to have insufficient drinking water. Or such unfair advantage-taking may do *indirect* harm, as when my influential example of noncooperation causes many others to defect from the scheme as well.

But in many cases of unfair advantage-taking, the moral wrong done involves no harming at all, but only (what we can call) unfair "self-selection" – in which individuals select *themselves* for the privilege of doing the limited amount of free riding that the cooperative scheme can tolerate without harm. If all the drivers in Smallville freely cooperate to leave the breakdown lane on the local highway clear, it is unfair for Edgar to select himself as the one who will avoid the traffic by driving in that lane, even if it is true that the cooperative scheme in question can tolerate a limited amount of free riding before the benefits it provides (e.g., a safe place to deal with disabled vehicles, easy access for emergency vehicles) are threatened. Though Edgar is only, as it were, "taking up the slack" in an inefficient scheme, it seems plain that a real concern for fairness would dictate that any opportunities for nonharmful free riding themselves be fairly distributed to all participants in the scheme (e.g., each driver receives a pass entitling him to drive in the breakdown lane on a particular day of the year). Where (as in this case) no such fair distribution of opportunities is possible or practical, however, no participant is entitled to select himself for those opportunities, since every participant has at least as much claim on the benefits of nonharmful free riding as any other, and since honoring all such claims would undermine the scheme. Self-selection takes advantage of the good-faith sacrifices of others, by forcing them to bear alone the full cost of a mutually beneficial scheme. Notice that this unfairness does not amount *solely* to granting preferential treatment to oneself, since such preferential treatment is routinely morally permissible. The unfairness lies in the way that self-selection exploits or takes advantage of others' good-faith sacrifices – an advantage-taking that occurs, I maintain, only when one freely takes the benefits of cooperation with the requisite beliefs and preference structure, *not* when one merely unavoidably receives those benefits while going about one's normally permissible business.

It is worth noting here that accounts of political obligation centrally employing the principle of fair play are typically chiefly concerned with this sort of unfair self-selection. Citizens are said on such accounts to be morally obligated to do their fair shares in the cooperative schemes of political life. But the political schemes supplying the (usually public) goods at issue can normally tolerate a substantial amount of free riding (e.g., tax cheating, draft dodging, and other covert disobedience to law) without any direct or indirect harm to the schemes or their participants. The obligation that allegedly accounts for our political bonds is principally the obligation to refrain from unfair self-selection.

Direct or indirect harmfulness to a cooperative scheme, then, is not a *necessary* property of those actions from which the principle of fair play directs us to refrain. Neither is such harmfulness a *sufficient* condition for unfair advantage-taking. For unless the participants in a cooperative scheme have a prior right that others refrain from actions that will frustrate their scheme, such actions are not unfair (i.e., contrary to the requirements of the principle of fair play). When a group of my neighbors unilaterally decides to refrain from installing backyard swimming pools, with the goal of greater peace and quiet (no sounds of splashing, children shrieking, evening pool parties, etc.), I surely cannot be accused of taking unfair advantage of their sacrifices when I install a pool in my own yard (which it is otherwise perfectly permissible to do), even if by doing so I undermine their scheme. For my actions gave them no reasonable grounds for expecting my compliance with the rules of their scheme. Only my free participation in their scheme or my voluntary acceptance of the benefits it provides could make it *unfair* for me to act in (otherwise perfectly legitimate) ways that threaten their scheme – though there might well be moral reasons of other sorts (e.g., the importance of their happiness) that make refraining a good, or even the right, act. This, of course, is just the point that Nozick's discussion of the principle of fair play drives home so effectively.

III

It is, however, a point that has not gone unchallenged. Several philosophers and political theorists have argued that the voluntariness of one's participation in (or one's acceptance of the goods supplied by) a cooperative scheme is at least sometimes irrelevant to one's obligations under the principle of fair play. Mere *receipt* of benefits, without any voluntary acceptance, it is argued, may be sufficient for obligation (within just cooperative schemes) where: (1) those who receive the benefits do not accept them (i.e., take them willingly and knowingly) only because of their bizarre, ignorant, or short-sighted beliefs;[10] (2) the benefits in question are "pure public goods" and so *cannot* be accepted or rejected;[11] or (3) the benefits are very large or significant.[12]

Defenders of (1) certainly have a point, though it is not, I think, a point that will much affect their hopes of presenting a defensible fairness account of political obligation. I have argued, remember, that only those who accept benefits from cooperative schemes can be bound (by considerations of fair play) to reciprocate, and that acceptance (in the relevant case of public goods) involves taking benefits willingly and knowingly (so that, e.g., one understands the source and costs of the benefits, prefers their provision in the manner provided to nonprovision, and so on). But suppose that I consume the benefits a scheme produces, yet fail to count as an accepter of those benefits only because I have bizarre or ignorant beliefs about the source of the benefits (say, I think they are manna from heaven or the gift of a mysterious benefactor) or because I grotesquely undervalue the benefits according to my own conception of the good. Am I not still obligated to reciprocate, despite my failure to take the benefits "willingly and knowingly"?

The answer, I think, is more complicated than defenders of (1) seem to acknowledge. It seems clear that culpable or negligent ignorance of the source, nature, or value of the benefits one enjoys will not (by itself) excuse one from obligation under the principle of fair play,[13] any more than my genuine but thoroughly negligent ignorance of the rules of restaurants can excuse me from the obligation to pay for the meal I have freely ordered and eaten. But mere, nonnegligent ignorance is, I believe, another matter. One's consumption of cooperatively produced public goods that one non-

---

10 Arneson, 631–32; Kavka, 411; Kent Greenawalt, *Conflicts of Law and Morality* (New York: Oxford University Press, 1989), 127–28; George Klosko, *The Principle of Fairness and Political Obligation* (Lanham, MD: Rowman and Littlefield, 1992), 48–54.

11 Arneson, 619–21.

12 Kavka, 412; Klosko, 39–48; Steven DeLue, *Political Obligation in a Liberal State* (Albany: State University of New York Press, 1989), 8–11; George Christie, "On the Moral Obligation to Obey the Law," *Duke Law Journal* 1990:6 (1991), 1324–26.

13 As Arneson rightly observes (Arneson, 632). See also Kavka, 411, and Jonathan Wolff, "Political Obligation, Fairness, and Independence," *Ratio* 8:1 (1995), 96.

culpably believes to be already paid for or to be free for the taking will, in standard cases, obligate one not at all. For it is the responsibility of those who cooperate to produce open or public goods to inform or otherwise make clear to consumers their expectations of reciprocation, *not* the responsibility of consumers to pay for what they unavoidably and innocently consume. If my neighbors cooperate to put on a concert, expecting those who listen to reciprocate later but never announcing this fact, I acquire no obligation to take up an instrument and help form a band, just because I innocently listened to the concert during my morning walk.

This conclusion remains true, I believe, even if I *would* have been willing to accept the cost in order to enjoy the benefit.[14] There are many benefits I receive each day from others that I *would* have been willing to pay for had payment been requested as a condition of their enjoyment – e.g., the wonderful joke I overhear you telling others, the lovely music wafting from your open window as you practice your cello, the sight of the adorable toddler staggering down the sidewalk; but in none of these cases, as in so many others of our enjoyment of such positive externalities, is reciprocation in any way obligatory, even if I later learn that payment was expected. What makes considerations of *fairness* an issue is not mere benefaction from the efforts of others, but benefaction where failure to reciprocate would *take advantage of* others. And we do not take advantage of others (in this way) unless we choose to profit from their good faith, cooperatively intended sacrifices (or should know that we are doing so) without reciprocating. That the benefits we receive are real and substantial, even according to our own values and preferences, is, I maintain, quite irrelevant to our obligations of *fair play* (though it might, I will argue, be relevant to *other* sorts of moral judgments). And this turns out, as should be no real surprise, to have dire implications for fairness accounts of political obligation. Most citizens of contemporary political societies could not count as accepting public goods from a cooperative political scheme, even if there were (as there is not) a real cooperative scheme producing those goods. Typical citizens neither suffer from negligent beliefs about the source, costs, and value of the public goods they consume nor take those goods willingly and knowingly.

Defenders of (2) and (3), however, will no doubt contend that my examples above seem persuasive only because they involve goods that are not pure public goods or goods that are relatively trivial and unimportant. Klosko, for instance, maintains that it is the insignificance of the benefits involved in Nozick's examples that makes his conclusions about them seem

---

14 Here I disagree with Kavka (Kavka, 411) and Greenawalt (Greenawalt, 127).

persuasive. Where the goods at issue are, by contrast, "presumptively beneficial" – that is, indispensable to a decent life for (almost) anyone, so that
all can be presumed to want them – mere receipt of goods from the workings of a cooperative scheme is sufficient to obligate one to do one's
part within that scheme.[15] The following example shows, I think, that
defenders of (2) and (3), like Klosko, are mistaken in their claims.

Suppose there is a severe drought in my rural neighborhood, where we
are all dependent for water on our wells, wells that are now drying up. I
am hard at work, successfully digging a new, much deeper well in my backyard to supply my family. But my neighbors, instead of doing the same, opt
to dig a long trench along our neighborhood road and beyond, diverting
water from a river several miles away, so that all will have access to running
fresh water in front of their homes. If I decline to participate in my neighbors' scheme, have I breached an obligation of fair play by benefitting as
a free rider? It seems plain to me that I have not. I may demonstrate a lack
of public spirit, show that I am a bad neighbor, or fail in my duties of charity
or beneficence toward my well-deprived neighbors. But one thing I have
plainly *not* done wrong is to unfairly *take advantage of* my neighbors' good-
faith, cooperative sacrifices. Though they have provided me with a benefit
– the availability of fresh water in front of my home is clearly a benefit for
me, even if I don't use it (just as a hospital's availability is a benefit, even
if I never happen to be seriously ill or injured) – I can hardly count as
riding free on a scheme that I want nothing to do with and whose benefits
I do not even actively utilize.

But notice that the *reason* there is no obligation of fair play in this
example is the *same* reason that there is no obligation of fair play in Nozick's
well known examples, despite the fact that the benefits in Nozick's examples are quite trivial, while the benefit in my example is a *presumptive public
good.* The magnitude of the benefit, or the number of people for whom it
counts as a benefit, seems quite irrelevant to the intuitive force of the arguments. What *is* relevant, on the other hand, is that in neither my example
nor Nozick's do the individuals in question have the correct preference
structure to count as free riders. One does not breach an obligation of fair
play unless one chooses to take advantage of (or should know that one is
taking advantage of) the cooperative sacrifices of others. Free riders take
the benefits others provide without reciprocating, while at the same time
preferring receipt of the benefits at the prescribed price to doing without
the benefits altogether or to trying to supply them independently in an

15 Klosko, 39–44.

alternative fashion. An individual's preferences may, of course, be unusual or eccentric; but provided these preferences are not based in negligent belief or ignorance, this hardly makes it any less wrong to impose on her the burdens associated with others' schemes, of which she wants no part.

If I genuinely cannot do without a public good, supplied as it is and at the price demanded for it, then I will probably freely accept it. But then the basis of my obligations is my free acceptance of the goods, my bringing myself into the cooperative scheme that supplies the goods. The value or importance of the goods is irrelevant. Important goods are, of course, *more likely* to be freely accepted at the demanded price than are trivial goods. But it is free acceptance, not presumptive value, that does the moral work in the argument. And if that is true, then the standard objections (e.g., of the later Rawls and Nozick) to fairness theories of political obligation succeed. And Klosko can avoid their force only by abandoning any real reliance on intuitions concerning *fairness*, relying instead on our intuitions about various natural duties we might have to diminish the needs of others or to contribute to projects that make community life possible, regardless of how little we might stand to *personally* benefit from such activities.

If I ought to help my neighbors with their water project, it is not because otherwise *I* will wrongly benefit as a free rider by having water run through my yard. It is because the success of the project is essential to *them* or to the neighborhood or to maintaining a community, even if *I* don't care about such things at all. Klosko repeatedly emphasizes "the great importance" of presumptive public goods in arguing for our obligations to contribute to their provision. This is, I believe, revealing. Klosko is *not* emphasizing what a *fairness* theory of political obligation should emphasize. Klosko, like many others who defend such theories, makes the easy but fatal slide from genuine concerns about *fair play* (i.e., not taking advantage of cooperators) to quite distinct moral concerns about required charity or beneficence (i.e., helping provide others with what they need), justifiable paternalism (i.e., requiring others to accept what they themselves need), and moral necessity (i.e., contributing to projects in ways that others have a prior right to, *independent* of our having benefitted from their sacrifices within a cooperative scheme).[16] Where Klosko's conclusions

---

16 For instance, it might be argued (with Kant) that all have an obligation to participate in the creation of a just state (and all have a right that others join them in this project), *not* because otherwise they will benefit as free riders, but rather because of the independent moral importance of justice. Such an argument asserts the moral necessity of participation, but not the *unfairness* of nonparticipation.

seem plausible, it is only because they draw on our intuitions about these rather different moral concerns, not on intuitions about fair play.

Return now to my drought-burdened rural neighborhood and imagine a change in the story that makes the example more closely analogous to actual political cases. Suppose that when my neighbors dig their trench to bring in fresh water, they dig it over the only place on my property where I could have dug an adequate well (a well, let's say, that I had planned to begin digging the next day); and when I attempt to divert the trench so that I can dig my well, I am forcibly prevented by my neighbors from doing so. In such a case collective action has *precluded* the possibility of private provision (or non-provision) of the public good in question. When I proceed to use water from the trench, having no viable options permitted to me, does fair play require that I make appropriate trench-related sacrifices (say, maintaining and dredging out the trench)? While I have bene-fitted in significant ways from the cooperative sacrifices of others, there is something deeply unconvincing about the claim that I *owe* my neighbors reciprocation for essential goods that they, in effect, *forced* me to take from them, denying me the option to provide the goods for myself or to do without. Surely, in such a case, only if I *prefer* benefitting from the cooper-ative scheme to benefitting from self-provision (or to doing without) could I be accused of unfairly taking advantage of my neighbors when I refuse to do my part in the scheme. Thus, I maintain that even in the case of pre-sumptive public goods, voluntary acceptance of those goods is required for obligation under the principle of fair play. It will, of course, not surprise readers when I observe that the most important public goods received from the workings of our political societies are normally provided in conjunc-tion with the coercive prohibition of alternative efforts at self-provision (or the acceptance of non-provision).

Let us add one final wrinkle to my example. Suppose that in my rural neighborhood, residents have long been taxed (assessed, required to pay dues) by a neighborhood committee in order to pay for various public pro-jects (road construction and maintenance, a playground, water trenches, etc.), and these tax revenues seem fully adequate to fund the projects in question. Nonetheless, residents are still expected to make various further cooperative sacrifices, contributing to maintenance of the projects, and the like. When I use the water trench or playground or roads – things for whose construction and maintenance I have already paid my fair share in tax dollars – but decline to make any of the further cooperative sacrifices expected of residents, can I then be counted as a free rider, as one who unfairly takes advantage of others?

IV

Many critics of my 1979 essay accepted (at least *arguendo*) my account of the principle of fair play and the conditions under which it generates moral obligations, but still rejected my treatment of fairness accounts of political obligation. My attack on those accounts, it is claimed, was based on unrealistic (or "overly skeptical"[17]) empirical claims about actual political societies – societies which in fact exhibit far more cooperative structure, and are inhabited by far greater numbers of willing accepters of public goods, than my remarks in that essay suggested. Many people in many countries both understand the cooperative origins of the benefits they receive from their political orders and regard those benefits as well worth the price they must pay for them in taxes and in the required sacrifices of obedience to law and support of government.[18] The principle of fair play – even when it is understood in a relatively voluntaristic fashion, rather than as a principle that ties obligation to mere receipt of benefits – does in fact apply to and explain the political obligations of many typical citizens in typical (reasonably just) states.

These critics might, perhaps, concede that *if* an individual genuinely and strongly preferred self-provision (or non-provision) of some benefit supplied by his political society, and if he was coercively prevented from pursuing these options, then that individual, despite having unavoidably enjoyed society's provision of that benefit, would not have an obligation of fair play to contribute to the scheme supplying that good. After all, such an individual could hardly be accused of taking unfair advantage of others. But, it will be claimed, very few typical citizens satisfy this description with respect to very many of the public goods political societies provide.

Some of these critics might even concede that there is a serious "baseline problem" to be resolved here,[19] and that we cannot simply *assume* the answer most favorable to defenders of fair play accounts of political obligation. That is, assuming (as the theorists in question do) that obligations of fair play only arise within schemes supplying benefits that are greater than the costs imposed by the schemes (so that the schemes count as "mutually beneficial"), we must ask against which baseline (i.e., com-

17 Arneson, 633.
18 Arneson, 633; Kavka, 411; Greenawalt, 135–36; Chaim Gans, *Philosophical Anarchism and Political Disobedience* (Cambridge: Cambridge University Press, 1992), 61–62; Richard Dagger, *Civic Virtues: Rights, Citizenship, and Republican Liberalism* (New York: Oxford University Press, 1997), 73–75.
19 Kavka, 410; Greenawalt, 141–42.

pared with which condition *ex ante*) we are assessing the benefits political societies provide. It is far too easy to simply gesture at the horrors of a Hobbesian "war of all against all," concluding that of course all citizens benefit on balance from cooperative political schemes, standing as we do far above the level of well-being we would "enjoy" during a solitary, nasty, short life.[20] The relevant baseline of comparison must include the effects of efforts at self-provision (or small group provision) of goods like security, efforts that would undoubtedly occur (even if they could not be completely successful) in any realistic nonpolitical condition. And the baseline employed must allow us to factor into the calculated costs of political life not only the *obvious* costs (e.g., taxes, military service, frequently unreasonable restrictions, helplessness in the face of massive impersonal power, etc.), but also the less obvious costs – at least considering seriously the charges of the classical anarchists (among others) that modern states magnify (or even create) much of the alienation and violence that we fear when we imagine life *without* states. And with this in mind, we must ask: should our baseline for comparison involve the imagined lives of individuals like ourselves, but devoid of our political organization; or should it employ instead the lives of individuals as (we imagine) they would be had there never been any political associations?

These seem to me interesting and difficult issues, issues that certainly must be persuasively addressed before any fairness account of political obligation could be said to have been convincingly defended. But the difficulty I wish to address here is a different, and I think more basic, problem for those who try to defend such accounts. For I think these defenders have not adequately considered which features of cooperative schemes actually give rise to our intuitions that obligations are owed to their participants, which features give rise to our sense that to take benefits without reciprocating would be to take unfair advantage of others. In 1979 I wrote, perhaps too cryptically, "where there is no consciousness of cooperation, no common plan or purpose, no cooperative scheme exists."[21]

It is this idea that I wish briefly to further explore here, for it is an idea that, surprisingly, has been widely and confidently rejected. Arneson argues, for instance, that no "spirit of developed [or 'full-blooded'] cooperation" is necessary for the existence of an appropriately obligation-generating cooperative scheme; indeed, the core idea of the principle of fair play is nothing more than that of a "fair return for services

20 John Horton, *Political Obligation* (Atlantic Highlands, NJ: Humanities Press, 1992), 93–94.
21 "The Principle of Fair Play," 336.

rendered."[22] And Klosko, while using as his principal examples cases involving people freely "banding together" to produce public goods,[23] in fact appears to allow that nobody has to have done anything voluntarily for an appropriate cooperative scheme to be in force.[24] Dagger, similarly, claims that it is sufficient that the political order provides a salient coordination point for and organization of private action; no consciousness among "participants" that they are cooperating is necessary for the generation of obligations of fair play relative to the political cooperative scheme.[25]

The general spirit of these contentions strikes me as seriously misguided, as seriously misunderstanding the source of our belief that riding free on cooperative schemes is wrong. *Genuine* cooperation between persons requires far more than a (broadly) successful coordination of their actions, with no consideration given to the *motives* of the "participants." There is a vast moral difference between a genuinely collaborative effort for mutual benefit – a case of "working together" – and a competitive practice governed by conflict-limiting rules, observed by most (for their own reasons), even where such limitation is preferable to its absence.[26] Indeed, it is perfectly possible that groups of individuals could completely *unwittingly* act in a coordinated manner that quite accidentally produced benefits for themselves and others. Or they could, with the entirely selfish intention of benefitting themselves at a *serious cost* to others, act on *misinformation* sufficient to accidentally produce a beneficial coordination.[27] Or they could deliberately collaborate to charitably benefit others (along with themselves), with no expectation whatsoever – indeed, with horror at the very idea – that others will feel obligated to make reciprocal sacrifices.[28] In all these cases, it would simply be ludicrous to suggest that a mutually beneficial cooperative scheme exists, or at least that a scheme exists of the right sort to impose on all who benefit from it obligations of fair play to reciprocate. "Services" may have been "rendered," but no "fair return" is due.

As Donald Regan has persuasively argued, genuine cooperation involves a real (and successful) attempt to achieve a jointly valued outcome by coor-

22 Arneson, 631–33.   23 Klosko, 52–53.   24 Klosko, 148.

25 Dagger, 47, 74. Dagger, oddly, seems to believe that consciousness of cooperation *is* necessary to the existence of (and hence to obligations within) *small* cooperative schemes, but not to the existence of large ones. This curious asymmetry is not explained.

26 Horton, 92–93.

27 Donald Regan, *Utilitarianism and Co-operation* (Oxford: Oxford University Press, 1980), 130–31.

28 Rolf Sartorius, "Political Authority and Political Obligation," in W. Edmundson (ed.), *The Duty to Obey the Law* (Lanham, MD: Rowman and Littlefield, 1999), 154.

dinated behavior.[29] No explicit agreement on a plan for the cooperative scheme is necessary,[30] but true cooperation does require a proper motivation on the parts of the cooperating parties and their correct understanding of their basic situation, as well as the correct behavior to achieve coordination.[31] Merely "behaving correctly" (without further reference to one's motivation and understanding) is insufficient to qualify one as a cooperator.

It seems clear that the actual motivations of actual citizens who "behave correctly" in our political societies, thereby rendering to others the service of a (relatively) secure and peaceful environment, could only with considerable idealistic polishing be made to shine with this genuinely cooperative glow. Nor do I intend by this to demean that typical motivation. For a good part of it is undoubtedly the quite laudable desire to refrain from harming others, to actively assist them, and in other ways to do what is regarded as *independently* right or obligatory. Much of the rest of the motivation is blind habit and fear of punishment. But very little of it involves the serious attempt to coordinate behavior with others for mutual gain that true cooperation requires.

This is important, I think, because our intuitions about fair play are drawn from our experiences with small-scale schemes that *are* cooperative in this strong sense. These intuitions are extended only by analogy to large-scale, impersonal, indifferently motivated schemes. And in the case of the *political* analogy, the analogy is plainly strained beyond the breaking point, appearing plausible only in the most memorable moments of voluntary and wide-ranging public sacrifice (e.g., when the boys march off to [defensive] war).

It is such conscious sacrifice for the common good (among other things), not the mere (habitual or coerced) "rendering of services," that gives rise to our sense of the demands of fair play. It is the former phenomenon that is familiar to us from small-scale, strongly cooperative schemes. In typical small-scale cooperative ventures (e.g., those involving cooperative games, or the joint projects of neighborhoods or small voluntary associations), others make deliberate sacrifices in support of mutually beneficial goals, while *relying* on us to do the same – and while having reasonable grounds for such reliance, since we are participants as well, sharing the same goals and understandings. Indeed, others act in such contexts only *because* they think they have reasonable grounds for believing that (at least) most of us will freely make the same sacrifices. Otherwise, they would

29 Regan, 127.   30 Ibid., 131–32.   31 Ibid., 127–30.

endure a cost pointlessly. It is *these* features of the strongly cooperative setting that make us feel that it would be wrong to fail to do our parts, that to refrain from doing so would be to *take advantage* of the good-faith sacrifices of others, and thus to act unfairly (just as the ball player who will only bat and never take the field fails to play fair with his fellows).

To even approach the character of the typical *political* "cooperative scheme," we must add at least the following features to our picture of the strongly cooperative, small-scale venture. First, add massive impersonality and a long tradition of taking the benefits received from the "scheme" without much thought and regarding the burdens associated with the scheme as inevitable (like death). Next, add coercive enforcement of the scheme's rules, so that noncompliance routinely brings punishment, along with a considerable distance between the origins of the enforced rules and the people against whom they are enforced. Add as well the sanction of personal morality, so that much noncompliance is regarded as wrong quite independent of the status of the rules as the rules of a "cooperative scheme," along with a mindless reverence for law and authority. Finally, add the well-supported awareness that (at least) where noncompliance is *not* regarded as independently wrong or harmful, very significant numbers of one's fellow "participants" in the "scheme" would not comply with the rules (or would over-consume the scheme's benefits) were it not for fear of punishment or unthinking habit.

Is this a cynical or "overly skeptical" account of ordinary political societies? Polling ordinary citizens about their true motivations seems pointless in such a context, since the polling procedure itself invariably distorts the data (subjects giving the answers that they think pollsters want, or the answers that will make them feel best about themselves, etc.). Instead, I simply ask you to consider: in cases where no perceived *independent* wrong is at issue, how many of your fellows do you think would comply with law were it not for habit, the threat of punishment, or mindless reverence for law? How many would drive at excessive speeds, cheat on their taxes, consume legally prohibited substances, engage in legally prohibited sexual relations, and so on? Undoubtedly, some of your neighbors would still refrain, though even the least cynical among us must admit that many other neighbors would not (since many of them do not do so now, in the presence of these factors). Very little of the motivation that produces the coordination of action on which rest claims of a political "cooperative scheme," then, can realistically be said to be of the sort necessary to the presence of a strongly cooperative venture.

When we make the additions noted above to our picture of a strongly cooperative scheme, though, it is clear that we leave behind all of the features essential to our sense that fair play requires reciprocation by all beneficiaries. With these additions, we can be confident that others are typically not acting in a good-faith effort to move collaboratively to a mutually preferred state, nor are they typically acting on any reasonable reliance on our voluntary reciprocation, even if their motivations are perfectly honorable or permissible. Thus, neither does our failure to comply with the rules normally constitute *taking advantage* of anyone.

There is undoubtedly a weak sense of "cooperation" in which behavior so indifferently motivated might still be said to add up to a "cooperative scheme," since all (or at least most) are made better off by the "scheme" and none is left perfectly free always to act in egoistically optimal ways without sanction. But there is, of course, also a weak sense of "cooperation" in which the whipped galley slaves can be said to cooperate in their propulsion of the galley. While the former weak sense is undoubtedly of greater moral interest than the latter, just as undoubtedly in neither case does the "cooperative scheme" exhibit any of those features that give rise to our sense of fair play in the first place.

In our most hopeful or idealistic moments – or in those moments when the spirit of self-sacrifice for the common good is most evident in public life – we may imagine that real political societies (in the West, of course) live up to the conditions that would subject us all to political obligations of fair play. After all, it is hard not to be moved by the sight of the young men voluntarily marching off to defend the homeland or to preserve democracy. But it is at precisely that moment that the citizen's understanding of his true situation is most likely to be emotional and unsound. For we should find it at least as hard not to be moved by the indifference and selfishness of our fellow subjects, by the great distances between our governors and ourselves, and by the extraction of funds and the threats of punishment that make up so much of our interaction with our political community. It is hard to understand how anything but an intense desire to view as justified widespread political obligations could lead one to regard these non-cooperative aspects of political life as insignificant to its accurate depiction and to the moral obligations it involves.

3

THE OBLIGATIONS OF CITIZENS AND THE JUSTIFICATION OF CONSCRIPTION

The Obligation to Serve

Most defenses of the military draft offered in contemporary debates must be understood as having conditional form. When conscription is defended in terms of efficiency (on grounds of cost or the resulting quality of personnel, for instance), the conclusion must be read as incorporating a *ceteris paribus* clause: if there are no *other* relevant differences between possible policies, then conscription is preferable (on grounds of efficiency). Similarly, when it is argued that the draft has advantages in terms of fairness (for instance, by distributing burdens more evenly across racial or economic groups), this fact (if indeed it is a fact) has only conditional weight in determining conclusions about the justifiability of the draft. Just as it is possible to pursue efficiently a desirable end by indefensible means, it is possible to distribute burdens fairly that ought not to be distributed at all. An unconditional moral justification or rejection of conscription would deal not only with its efficiency or distributive fairness, but also with more basic moral characteristics of policies of compulsory military service. For example, such policies involve institutionalized forms of coercion, coercion not in response to (or to prevent) transgressions, but in response to birth and continued residence in the territories of the state. And because the efficiency and fairness of coercive interference seem never to legitimate it (a corporate executive may not simply force other persons to work in his plant, no matter how scrupulously he selects them), appeals to efficiency and fairness in defending the draft may seem pointless.

Such appeals seem more weighty, however, and the contest between conscription and alternative policies seems more equal, when two further considerations are kept in mind. First, the practicable alternatives to the coercive policy of conscription may carry heavy moral costs as well. Reliance on unpaid volunteers to man the armed forces would be disastrous. And the employment of paid volunteers, while it involves no actual coercion, does use "compelling offers" to lure the disadvantaged into a dangerous and restrictive occupation.[1] Serious difficulties may then also be involved in the moral justification of noncoercive policies of manpower procurement. But more central to the defense of conscription, and inevitably appealed to by its defenders, is the claim that each (male) citizen has a moral duty or obligation to serve in the military; with this claim courts, legislators, and laymen routinely begin (and often end) their case for the draft.[2] The obligation to serve is viewed as one of the obligations attached to the role of citizen, others being obligations to pay taxes, to obey other kinds of laws (at least within certain limits), and possibly to "bear his fair share . . . in any other joint work necessary to the interest of the society of which he enjoys the protection."[3]

If obligatory military service is a component of each citizen's political obligations, the moral justification of the draft of course seems much more promising. What was condemned as coercive interference can be viewed instead as the enforcement of a moral obligation owed to the state. The moral distance between the compelling offers that create an All-Volunteer Force and the enforced obligations of the draft is diminished, and considerations of fairness and efficiency again begin to look significant. The entire justificatory program for the draft, then, seems to turn on these central claims about political obligations. I will focus my attention on these claims by examining the contention that there is a community-wide obligation or duty to serve in the military and by discussing the moral justification of conscription.

To reduce the discussion to the size of a chapter, I will make several preliminary points and simplifying assumptions. I will assume, first, that if there is an obligation or duty to serve in the military, this obligation is a species of some more inclusive type of obligation – that is, that if we have

---

1 How convincing such arguments seem will turn on our more general evaluation of free markets. See Jules Coleman, "Liberalism, Unfair Advantage, and the Volunteer Armed Forces," in *Conscripts and Volunteers*, edited by R. K. Fullinwider (Totowa, N.J.: Rowman & Allanheld, 1983), Ch. 7.

2 See Hugo Bedau's discussion in Part I of "Military Service and Moral Obligation," in *Philosophy and Political Action*, edited by Virginia Held, Kai Nielson, and Charles Parsons (New York: Oxford University Press, 1972).

3 John Stuart Mill, *On Liberty*, chap. 1.

the obligation, we have it for reasons that are familiar as the grounds of other, nonmilitary obligations as well. Thus, the obligation to serve might be a promissory or consensual obligation, or the result of receiving benefits, or might be entailed by a more general duty to support just institutions or promote the general welfare, for instance.[4] Second, I will suppose that the moral requirement to serve in the military must belong to one of the three classes of moral requirement: (1) a requirement generated by some voluntary performance or forbearance (for example, by entering voluntarily into some special transaction or relationship, as in the making of a promise); (2) a requirement binding on all persons regardless of their special performances (such as the "natural duties" not to lie to or assault others); or (3) a requirement based in some special, but not necessarily voluntary, relationship (for instance, parent-child or benefactor-beneficiary relationships). All moral requirements, I maintain, fall into one of these three groups, including any obligation to military service.[5] Now I will try to present here some brief and very general points which suggest that it is extremely unlikely that any widely shared moral requirement to serve in the military falls in either class (1) or class (2).[6] My intention is to motivate the special attention that I will give to class (3) requirements later in this essay.

Let us examine first the moral requirements grounded in voluntary performances or forbearances (class 1). These are, first, obligations arising from promises, contracts, and the giving of consent (tacit or express). But this class will also include obligations of fairness or fair play, which arise when persons voluntarily enter into mutual undertakings or cooperative projects. Voluntary participation in a cooperative scheme, even if no actual promise or deliberate commitment is involved, may ground obligations to do one's share within that scheme, by way of reciprocation for the sacri-

4 What the obligation to serve will not be is its own type, where the principle of obligation covers military service and no other moral obligations. This rules out of consideration the claim that it is self-evident that we have an obligation to military service, and requires the giving of recognizably moral reasons in defense of obligation claims.

5 The distinction between (1) and (2), of course, corresponds to that drawn by H. L. A. Hart, John Rawls, and others. For Rawls, (1) and (2) are "obligations" and "natural duties" (*A Theory of Justice* [Cambridge, Mass.: Harvard University Press, 1971], section 19). The third class does not fit neatly into the Rawlsian classification, but Hart had earlier distinguished between the special rights that correlate with class (3) and other requirements in "Are There Any Natural Rights?," *Philosophical Review* 64 (1955): 186–87.

6 For a more careful and detailed account of these arguments, I regret that I must refer the reader to other work. See my *Moral Principles and Political Obligations* (Princeton, N.J.: Princeton University Press, 1979). For the arguments concerning class (1) requirements, see especially chaps. 3–5; in connection with class (2) requirements, see chaps. 2 and 6.

fices made by others. However familiar such obligations may be in everyday life, it seems clear that no widespread obligation to serve in the military (or to perform any other "duties of citizenship") could be of this sort. The suggestion that all or most citizens freely consent or promise (even tacitly) to serve in the military cannot be taken seriously. Naturalized citizens are virtually the only nonofficeholders who expressly consent to anything in the political sphere, and genuine choice situations that would provide opportunities for native-born citizens to give binding consent are all but unheard of in modern political communities. As philosophers since Hume have argued, wherever emigration is the only viable option to performing the duties of citizenship, free consent to those duties will be unusual; continued residence in a country need not, and routinely does not, occur in response to any fairly presented choice.[7] Neither does it seem plausible to characterize the average citizen as voluntarily participating in some ongoing political cooperative scheme with his fellow citizens, and as bound by considerations of fairness to serve in the military. While some persons surely can be taken to be voluntary participants in a fairly strong sense, many others clearly cannot – the poor, the alienated, and those who are trapped, oppressed, and denied genuine opportunities for a decent life.[8] But the political participation of the vast majority of citizens is neither fully voluntary (or informed) nor simply coerced. Instead it consists of making the best of a situation to which there are no options worth considering. Participation of this sort will not ground obligations of the kind discussed above;[9] thus, very few citizens will be bound by class (1) moral requirements to serve in the military.

It seems equally unlikely that there will be a community-wide moral duty to serve that would fall in my second class of moral requirements. These requirements (the natural duties) are not based in any special transactions, relationships, or performances, but arise because of the moral character of the required action or forbearance.[10] I am bound not to murder, for instance, not because of anything I have done (such as promising not to),

7 David Hume, "Of the Original Contract." For a dissenting view, see Harry Beran, "In Defense of the Consent Theory of Political Obligation and Authority," *Ethics* 87 (1977).
8 And, of course, these very worst candidates for voluntary participants are called first to military service.
9 All of these arguments are by now familiar. See, for instance, Rawls, *A Theory of Justice*, chap. 6; and M. B. E. Smith, "Is There a Prima Facie Obligation to Obey the Law?," *Yale Law Journal* 82 (1973). For more recent arguments against the voluntarist account of political obligation, see note 6 and Rolf Sartorius, "Political Authority and Political Obligation," *Virginia Law Review* 67 (1981).
10 Hart, "Are There Any Natural Rights?," p. 179.

but because of the moral significance of murder.[11] Similarly, duties not to steal or lie, to give aid to those in need, or to promote justice are shared by all persons, regardless of their voluntary acts. It is hard to accept the claim that there is a duty of this sort to serve in the military, for two reasons. First, because these duties are binding on all persons, the content of any such duty will be general. Our duties will bind us, say, to give aid to anyone who is in need or to refrain from stealing *simpliciter* (or under normal conditions); they will not bind us only with respect to particular persons, institutions, or sets of institutions. By making a promise or entering into some other special relationship I can establish a moral tie between myself and some particular party. But the natural duties, not being grounded in special transactions, lack this kind of "particularity."[12] This creates problems for any attempt to characterize our duty to serve in the military as a natural duty, for such a duty could not bind us to service in any particular state (specifically, our state of citizenship). If, for instance, the duty to serve were conceived as part of a natural duty to support just governments,[13] we would be bound to support not only our own just government, but any other as well. And I assume that a natural duty to serve in the military of all just nations is not one we ought to accept as genuine. What needs to be explained is why a government's being *ours* grounds special moral ties to *it*, such as the requirements to pay taxes to it, obey its laws, and serve in its military. We can understand why our government's being just might establish a moral bond to support it, but not why this would establish a bond to support it *over* other just governments. Of course, a government's being ours routinely has consequences that do seem morally relevant: we receive significant benefits from our government that we do not get from any other, and this may seem sufficient to ground a moral bond. That moral bond, however, would be a requirement falling in my third class. What cannot be shown is that there are any candidates for a natural duty (a requirement in my second class) that would bind us to serve in the military of our own country, without (implausibly) binding us to serve in other countries as well. Since, then, we are seeking an account of a moral duty

---

11 My meeting you for lunch, as I promised, on the other hand, is not obligatory for me because meeting you for lunch is an especially good thing to do. It is obligatory simply because it was promised, and may be of quite neutral character independent of the promise.

12 For a more extensive discussion of the problem of particularity, see my *Moral Principles and Political Obligations*, chap. 2.

13 I choose this example, of course, because of its relevance to the prominent theory of this sort offered by Rawls.

or obligation that binds citizens to the performance of their traditional "duties of citizenship," the natural duties seem unlikely to provide an account of the sort we seek.

The natural duties appear unpromising in the role under consideration for a second reason. Some of the natural duties are negative duties (requiring only forbearances) and as such can be strict or "perfect" duties (that is, allowing virtually no discretion or options, requiring scrupulous forbearance). The duties not to assault, murder, lie, defraud, steal, and so on are of this sort. These negative duties, however, seem to have no direct relevance to our problem of a duty to serve in the military. The positive natural duties (those requiring positive action and not mere forbearance), on the other hand, are less strict ("imperfect"). We are not required, for instance, to give aid to those in need or to promote justice when doing so would cost us our lives or reduce us to beggary; such performances are clearly supererogatory. The positive natural duties allow a certain discretion in performance, requiring that we perform only when the costs of doing so are kept within reasonable limits. (Otherwise, of course, the demands made upon us by these duties would consume the whole of our lives.) But these positive natural duties would be precisely the ones at issue were there a natural duty to serve in the military (and to perform the other functions of citizens). And there is very real doubt whether the price of citizenship, when it includes military service (e.g., to carry out foreign police actions), constitutes a cost within reasonable limits. The risk of death and disability, the cost in years and economic opportunities lost, may well be such that military service could not be part of the content of a positive natural duty. Similarly, and perhaps more important, the absence of any substantial realm of discretion allowed by government in the performance of "duties of citizenship" suggests that in requiring performance the government cannot be enforcing an imperfect natural duty.

I hope these quick and sketchy arguments will persuade the reader that we have no moral duty or obligation to serve in our country's military that is either a class (1) or class (2) requirement. This would leave us free to deal exclusively with class (3) moral requirements and would allow some hope of reaching a conclusion about the existence of an obligation to serve. Whether or not the reader is persuaded, however, the remainder of the essay should serve some useful purpose. I will, in the following section, proceed to examine the possibilities for giving a class (3) account of the obligation to military service. This, I take it, is of some independent interest, regardless of the force of my objections to class (1) and (2) accounts.

Finally, in the last section, I will discuss the relevance of both positive and negative claims about the existence of an obligation to serve to an overall moral justification of conscription, thus returning to the questions raised in the opening pages of this essay.

Obligations and Nonvoluntary Relationships

I have suggested that we reject any class (1) account of the obligation to serve on grounds of realism – the voluntary relationships necessary to ground class (1) moral requirements simply are not in sufficient evidence to support such an account. Class (2) accounts were rejected because of their failure to establish any special tie between the citizen and the country in which he is a citizen. In light of these arguments, a class (3) account must look promising, for class (3) requirements *are* grounded in some special relationship (and so establish a special bond) but do *not* require voluntary performances for the generation of an obligation.

More important, perhaps, a class (3) account seems to capture the spirit of the most familiar answers to questions about political obligation. The reason we are obligated to serve our government (or "country"), many argue, is that it so effectively serves us. It provides numerous and substantial benefits at low cost, and it is the duty of those who benefit from the labors of others to reciprocate. Thus, in the earliest recorded account of political obligation (Plato's *Crito*), Socrates argues for political obligations both as reciprocation for benefits provided and as that which is due a "parent" (to which the state is likened). Here the appeal is to two special relationships (benefactor-beneficiary, parent-child), neither of which need be entered voluntarily, and both of which are ordinarily taken to ground special obligations. Similarly, the well-known consent theory of Locke's *Second Treatise* is in fact only a "front" for Locke's view that those who enjoy the benefits of government are bound to repay them.[14] As A. C. Ewing writes:

> The obligation to one's country or state is more analogous to the obligation to our parents than it is to a business relation. Here also the debt is not incurred deliberately . . . and here also it seems to depend, mainly at least, on uncovenanted benefits conferred on us.[15]

14 Simmons, *Moral Principles and Political Obligations*, chap. 4.
15 A. C. Ewing, *The Individual, the State, and World Government* (New York: Macmillan, 1947), p. 218.

Similar views have been suggested by W. D. Ross and (more recently) by J. P. Plamenatz, Jeffrie Murphy, and Elizabeth Anscombe.[16] I will concentrate here on the parent-child and benefactor-beneficiary relationships, as these seem most likely to be illuminating for our purposes. There are undoubtedly other nonvoluntary relationships that ground obligations (for instance, there are commonly supposed to be other kinds of familial obligations), but I will assume that these are not relevant to possible obligations to serve in the military.

Let me begin by asking why so many have found filial obligations to be analogous to political obligations. First, of course, is the fact that both states and parents provide "uncovenanted benefits." But is there any point in comparing the state to a parent rather than to an unrelated benefactor? Are the obligations we owe our parents different from those we would owe a nonparent who benefited us as extensively as a parent? We might suppose that important differences would arise from the fact that the benefits provided by parents are essential benefits that the child cannot provide for himself and there are (routinely) ties of love and friendship between parents and their children. The analogy between state and parent might seem to be strengthened by noting that the benefits provided by government also are essential (they keep life from being nasty, brutish, and short), and would be difficult for individuals to provide for themselves;[17] and there are (routinely) ties of loyalty and concern between citizens and their states. Perhaps, then, the analogy is a solid one, and it would be worth examining what children do owe their parents, as a possible way of seeing whether citizens do owe military service to their states.

It will be conceded by most that very young children have no moral obligations, to their parents or to anyone else. Where the capacities necessary for minimal levels of moral responsibility are absent, so are moral requirements. As Locke would say, the child is born to, not with, a set of rights and duties. Nor do the child's obligations fall upon him like a moral avalanche at some threshold of maturity. Rather, his obligations grow and extend as his rational powers, self-control, and awareness of the needs of

---

16 W. D. Ross, *The Right and the Good* (London: Oxford University Press, 1967), p. 27; J. P. Plamenatz, *Consent, Freedom, and Political Obligation* (New York: Oxford University Press, 1968), p. 24; Jeffrie Murphy, "In Defense of Obligation," in *Nomos XII: Political and Legal Obligation*, edited by J. R. Pennock and J. W. Chapman (New York: Atherton, 1970), pp. 42–43; Elizabeth Anscombe, "On the Source of the Authority of the State," *Ratio* 20 (1978): 16–18.

17 For comments on this line of argument, see my "Voluntarism and Political Associations," *Virginia Law Review* 67 (1981).

others develop. Thus, the child may have some of the duties of an adult before he has others, since he may grasp the point of some moral prohibitions more readily than others (perhaps property violations, for instance, are more difficult conceptually than more direct kinds of harmful behavior). And the child will owe the obligations and duties to his parents that he owes to others.

He may also have obligations toward his parents that he does not have toward others. Popular candidates are the obligation to obey his parents (at least as long as he is a minor) and the obligation to repay the sacrifices made on his behalf when his parents are in need (after he is self-supporting). It is also commonly supposed that special obligations arise from familial ties of love. Let me deal briefly with each of these.

Children, I contend, never owe obligations of obedience to their parents, given normal family relations – e.g., excluding special contracts to obey, etc. Young children do not, because they owe no obligations to anyone; mature children to not, because they have the same rights and obligations as adults.[18] Children in their middle years, of course, cannot be accounted for as easily, but I think it a mistake to ascribe to them obligations of obedience to their parents. A child, of whatever age, clearly does not always act wrongly (even prima facie wrongly) by disobeying parental commands or by breaking parental rules, which may be pernicious or arbitrary. A child does no wrong in refusing to obey his tough father's command to beat up every child in his class, or in reading an assigned book in school against his parents' wishes. He has not failed to discharge a moral obligation when he does not meet his parents' 8:00 P.M. curfew (which may be perfectly in line with what other parents impose). Children certainly do act wrongly in many instances while disobeying their parents. Excessive drinking, use of dangerous drugs, and lack of respect for the property and rights of others may all be both wrong and prohibited by most parents. But if they are wrong it is for the same reasons that they are wrong for adults; other things will be wrong for children for the same reasons that they would be wrong for a sensitive or confused adult. The wrongness is never, however, a function of the parental command or rule having been disobeyed.

An acceptable position seems to me to be this: to the extent that children have moral obligations at all, their obligations are to do those things that are obligatory for adults of similar capacities, not to do what they are

---

18 See A. D. Woozley, *Law and Obedience: The Arguments of Plato's Crito* (London: Duckworth, 1979), p. 67. The remainder of chap. 4 of Woozley's work is also relevant to the points under discussion.

told to do by their parents. As long as they need their parents' help, of course, they may be "obliged" prudentially to obey all sorts of family rules, good, bad, and indifferent. And children will often want to please their parents by obeying, especially where the parents are loving and reasonable in their demands. Parents, on the other hand, do owe special obligations of care and attention to their children. These may be grounded in the voluntary acceptance of responsibility that sometimes accompanies procreation, but we bear special responsibilities as well for even the accidental or unwanted consequences of our actions.[19] Parents have rights also, rights possessed simply in virtue of their parenthood, and which are part of the "package" that comes with these special responsibilities. The rights in question, however, are not rights to be obeyed, held against their children, but are rather rights not to have the functions of parenthood usurped by others, rights which are held "in rem" (against the world at large).[20] These rights may be easily forfeited by abandonment, neglect, or abuse (in short, by the failure to fulfill the obligations of parenthood). Certain kinds of demands made upon children by their parents are within the parents' rights to make. Some of these demands are made rightly by parents. But children are not morally obligated to fulfill any of these demands simply on the grounds that their parents have made them.

Even if the analogy between the child-parent and citizen-state relationships is sound, then, attempts to model our political obligations (including the obligation to obey the state's command to serve in the military) on the obligations children have to obey their parents will fail. But there may be more (or, rather, less) to filial obligations than an obligation to obey. Certain kinds of special consideration or requital of benefits may be due a parent, even if obedience is not. An obvious way to make a case for these more limited obligations is through the idea of obligatory reciprocation for parental sacrifices. But many who have written on the subject have felt that obligations of reciprocation are either not the whole of filial obligations or are not even a part of them.[21] Filial obligations, they maintain, arise (either "as well" or "solely") from the love, friendship, or personal intimacy

19 We can, I think, easily imagine bizarre science fiction or religious stories in which a child was the result of no one's voluntary actions. In such a case, the biological parents would, I believe, have no duties to their child beyond that of giving aid to anyone who needs it.
20 Sartorius, "Political Authority and Political Obligation."
21 A. I. Melden, for instance, holds the former view (in *Rights and Persons* [Berkeley: University of California Press, 1977], pp. 67–68); while Jane English maintains the latter (in "What Do Grown Children Owe Their Parents?," in *Having Children*, edited by Onora O'Neill and William Ruddick [New York: Oxford University Press, 1979]).

of the parent-child relationship. Jane English writes that "the filial obligations of grown children are a result of friendship, rather than owed for services rendered."[22] Where the "love relationship" between parents and their children ceases to exist, she argues, so do the obligations of children toward their parents. This seems to me wrong, as does the suggestion that special moral obligations arise out of "mutual caring." I will try to present a more plausible position.

The central claim of the position I wish to reject is that moral obligations are generated by mutual caring (love, friendship, etc.). On that account, a necessary condition for my having obligations to you (a loved one, say) is my continued caring; obligations cease when the feelings (on either part) that define the relationship cease. But if obligations arose in this way from mutual caring, part of the point of moral obligations would be defeated, for they would no longer be assurances of future behavior on which we could count and around which we could organize our lives. Love and friendship can grow cold and die in puzzling ways and in ways over which those who have the feelings normally have no firm control. Further, after feelings have died the point of ascribing moral obligations comes most clearly into focus. Where love or friendship flourishes, individuals give of themselves without any feeling of obligation or moral compulsion (one might say that talk of obligations cheapens such relationships). But where love ends for one party, the other may be left with frustrated expectations, lost opportunities, and a life structured in a fashion now rendered pointless. There may have been substantial sacrifices, financial or otherwise. To suggest that, when my child feels love toward me, he has moral obligations to consider my interests specially but that, when his heart hardens, he has none, seems to me extremely implausible. What point can obligations have where they can be ended by hardening one's heart? Surely the answer is that any filial obligations arise not from mutual caring, but from some other ground. The moral component of the parent-child relationship is independent of the child's loving feelings (though not entirely independent of parental love). Indeed, a child who must give to his parents out of a sense of duty has almost certainly failed to love them fully. (Of course, the child may still have duties toward his parents even if he never acts out of a sense of duty. This, I think, is the situation in the ideal parent-child relationship.) If mutual caring is not a ground of moral obligation, as I have argued, this defeats yet another potential line of argument for the existence of an obligation to military service. For it will no longer be per-

22 English, "What Do Grown Children Owe Their Parents?," p. 354.

suasive to argue by analogy that the citizen has an obligation to serve that is grounded in his feelings of loyalty or devotion to country.

I return finally to the idea with which we began – that filial obligations are a kind of obligation of reciprocation, and that our obligation to serve in the military may be analogous on these grounds alone. Even on this point, however, it is not easy to make a case for widespread filial obligations (and analogous widespread political obligations). The obvious point that bears on the moral significance of parental provision of benefits is that it is often the parents' duty or responsibility to provide them. The care, attention, and healthy environment that a good parent gives his children can hardly be compared with a gift from some unrelated individual. But that it is a parent's duty to benefit his child does not show, by itself, that no obligation to reciprocate is owed by the child. Sometimes duty-meeting beneficial action requires reciprocation, sometimes it does not. If you are drowning and I ruin my new suit or incur some injury while saving you, few would maintain that you owe me nothing. Perhaps paying for the suit or tending to the injury would be appropriate as a return; if serious risk were involved, perhaps more of a return would be fitting (if it were possible and agreeable to the benefactor). But what is clearly true is that I did no more than my duty in saving you. Had I ignored your plight (perhaps out of concern for my suit), I would have been open to the most severe moral condemnation. There are, then, familiar cases in which the provision of benefits that it is our duty to provide nonetheless grounds obligations to reciprocate. There are obviously other kinds of cases in which it does not.[23] If I have a duty to pay you $10 (which I borrowed from you), you are not bound to reciprocate when I give you the $10. Which of these kinds of cases resembles that in which parents benefit their children (as they are duty-bound to do)? Any resemblance must surely be to the second case, for what is striking about the benefits parents provide is that the parents have themselves *created* the needs these benefits satisfy (by creating the child who has them). Parents not only have a duty to care for their children but are (normally) morally responsible for the necessity of caring for them. It is as if, instead of just pulling you from the water, I had first pushed you in (accidentally or intentionally), making me responsible for your need. In such a case, it is far less convincing to claim that anything is owed me as benefactor; and by analogy it is unconvincing to insist that filial obligations arise from parental benefaction.

23 See my more detailed discussion of these problems in *Moral Principles and Political Obligations*, pp. 179–83.

More, then, than simply caring for a child and seeing that its needs are met will be necessary for the generation of filial obligations. Perhaps extraordinary sacrifices by parents will make a difference;[24] certainly nonbiological parents (or, say, victims of rape), who have voluntarily taken on a child's care without being morally responsible for its existence, will be owed more by their children than biological parents. Even the "gift" of firm but loving guidance, so seldom and with such great difficulty given by parents but so crucial to the child's psychological well-being and potential for happiness, may (in conjunction with more routine benefits) ground special filial obligations. This seems to me to be the proper explanation of the relevance of love to the moral component of the parent-child relationship. Genuine parental love, understood here as a deep emotional commitment to a painstaking and disciplined pursuit of the child's long-term happiness, is so difficult to give fully and wisely that it may count as the kind of benefit that is not simply a straightforward requirement of parental responsibility. If this is so, then filial obligations may be generated by the parent's loving care (though, as mentioned above, in the ideal parent-child relationship the child will not be motivated by any sense of duty or obligation). These obligations will not be grounded in a relationship of mutual caring, but love will be important to their generation.

My conclusion is that children do not, simply as a matter of course, have special obligations of consideration toward their parents. (These arise only in family situations that exhibit further important characteristics.) It would be unfortunate, then, if defenders of a citizen's alleged obligation to serve in the military attempted to demonstrate the generality of this obligation by analogy with "widespread" filial obligations. The requirements of special loving care or extraordinary sacrifice that might ground filial obligations are surely not in evidence in the relations between state and citizen; the features of the parent-child relationship most important to the creation of special obligations, in other words, are simply not mirrored in normal citizen-state relationship. Perhaps, then, those who would argue for political obligations on the strength of the analogy with familial relations have simply missed the mark, as, for instance, philosophers in the Lockean tradition have long argued.[25]

24 English, implausibly I think, denies this, contending that "the quantity of parental sacrifice is not relevant in determining what duties the grown child has" ("What Do Grown Children Owe Their Parents?," p. 354).

25 I assume that by now it will be clear that the mere biological relation of childhood cannot, by itself, ground obligations, and that, by analogy, mere citizenship cannot ground political obligations. Biological parents are surely owed nothing by children they abandon at

We began with an effort to find some nonvoluntary special relationship in which individuals might find themselves, a relationship which nonetheless grounded special obligations for them; thus we hoped to avoid the problems of realism and particularity discussed earlier. Comparisons with the nonvoluntary position "child" seemed not to advance our case very far. But we have not yet considered situations of simple benefaction, independent of family relations. If, as my arguments seem to suggest, we may owe more to unrelated benefactors than we owe to our parents, perhaps we may owe obligations of simple reciprocation to our state, which we would not seem to owe when we try to characterize the state as a kind of parent. The state, after all, is not (as a parent is) responsible for the creation of the needs it satisfies. Will this alter our position substantially? The answer again seems to me to be no.[26]

Though we may have obligations to repay benefits even when we have not voluntarily accepted the benefits, strict conditions of other sorts must be met for this to come about. Not just any receipt of benefits obligates us to reciprocate (as we can easily see when we consider benefits that are forced upon us against our wills, or benefactors who are hopelessly inept and bothersome in their efforts). Now, the state may be in certain ways inept in its provision of benefits, and those benefits may be forced on some citizens against their wills. But let us suppose that, for the most part at least, citizens do not regard themselves as ill-used in the processes that lead to their receipt of the benefits a government supplies. Can we derive from this a moral obligation to reciprocate by serving in the military when service is demanded?

Of several relevant points, and the most important for our purposes here, we must consider the content of an obligation of reciprocation. What we owe a benefactor is almost never determined with any precision by the context, but varies with our capabilities, the benefactor's needs, and the value of and sacrifice involved in providing the benefit. What we certainly do not owe a benefactor is whatever he demands as repayment. Of course, our reciprocation should be at least as responsive to the benefactor's needs as the benefit he provided was to ours. But this does not mean that he is empowered to specify which of his needs we will consider or to what extent we will satisfy it. The best guide to discharging such an obligation is only a very vague sense of what constitutes a fitting return. Put in another way,

---

birth, and states are owed nothing by citizens who benefit not at all from their policies. This point ties in with my insistence that any obligation to serve in the military must be a species of some more inclusive type of obligation.

26 See my *Moral Principles and Political Obligations*, chap. 7, for a fuller development of this claim.

obligations of reciprocation are not "content-specific" in the way that, for example, a contractual obligation is.

These facts seem sufficient to sink any attempt to defend a "reciprocation account" of the obligation to serve in the military (or, more generally, a "reciprocation account" of political obligation). Even if we are obligated to reciprocate for the benefits we receive from government, we are not obligated to reciprocate in all (or perhaps any) of the ways that governments demand. We are not morally required to serve in the military, to obey every law, or to pay precisely the amount of tax imposed on us simply because we are told to do so. The government, as benefactor, has no special claim to dictate the content of our obligation or to pass final judgment on what constitutes a fitting return (governments have needs, for instance, other than military service). And when we recall that the tax load of most citizens in modern democracies is indeed substantial, it is not at all clear that the price government requires us to pay is not grossly out of proportion with the benefits it supplies. When we add to this the observation that the special efforts and sacrifices involved in extending the benefits of government to one additional citizen are minuscule, it is hard to believe that each of us is bound to give up freedom, years of our lives, economic opportunities, and possibly life or limb in the military, all in reciprocation for benefits that our tax dollars have already purchased.

However far we may be bound to reciprocate, then, it seems clear that this obligation falls far short of morally required military service. Indeed, it seems to me unlikely that we have any obligations to repay the benefits of government at all. If I am right, then the most promising, class (3) accounts of the moral obligation to serve must fail. In conjunction with my earlier claims, the conclusion is clear: citizens generally have no moral obligation or duty to serve in the military. Nor should this conclusion be particularly surprising. The ideal of the citizen-soldier dates from times when states were very different than they are now, when the models of participatory scheme and parent-child relationship had considerably more relevance to political philosophy than they do today.[27]

Enforcing Obligations and Infringing Rights

If there is no moral obligation to serve for most citizens, attempted justifications of conscription will be considerably hampered. The defender of conscription must then find some alternative justification for a basically

27 Michael Walzer, "Political Alienation and Military Service," in *Obligations: Essays on Disobedience, War, and Citizenship* (New York: Simon & Schuster, 1970), p. 99; and Bedau, "Military Service and Moral Obligation," pp. 147–48.

coercive policy. In the absence of a moral obligation to serve, an All-Volunteer Force seems almost certain to emerge as the most defensible military policy. For regardless of the "economic compulsion" at work in many voluntary enlistments, there is little doubt that volunteering does create an obligation to serve which may legitimate the coercive practices of the military. I anticipate, however, that some readers will remain unconvinced by my argument that there is no obligation to serve in the military. And because it will be useful as well in understanding attempted moral justifications of conscription, I will very briefly consider what seem to be the consequences for such a justification of both negative and affirmative answers to our question about the existence of an obligation to serve.

Let us suppose, first, that I am mistaken, and that there are in fact community-wide (or at least widely held) political obligations, one of which is the moral obligation to serve in the military. Many apparently feel that the existence of such an obligation would serve, by itself, to justify conscription, but this is not obvious because the connection between obligation and justified coercion is not a simple one. That Jones owes a moral obligation to you (or to someone else), I maintain, does not entail that you are justified in doing whatever is necessary to force Jones to discharge his obligation (and may not entail that you are justified in using coercion at all). Much of the body of philosophical literature on obligation and coercion grows out of John Stuart Mill's classic analyses. Mill maintains that when we say that a man has a moral obligation (or that it is morally right for him to do something, which is Mill's equivalent), we mean in part that he ought to be compelled to discharge it. Mill thus appears to be prepared to claim that the use of at least some coercion is always justified in the enforcement of obligations.[28] More recently, similar claims have been common. H. L. A. Hart commits himself to the position that if I owe you an obligation, you have a "moral justification for limiting [my] freedom."[29] Kurt Baier holds that one of the distinctive things about moral obligations is that it is justifiable to "ensure" that individuals fulfill their obligations;[30] and David Richards writes that "to say that a rule is obligatory is to say that coercion is thought to be justified, in the last resort, to get people to do what the rule requires."[31]

---

28 John Stuart Mill, *Utilitarianism*, chap. 5, paragraph 14.
29 Hart, "Are There Any Natural Rights?," p. 178. Hart's actual discussion concerns rights rather than obligations, but his views on their correlation entail the position I attribute to him.
30 Kurt Baier, "Moral Obligation," *American Philosophical Quarterly* 3 (1966): 223.
31 David A. J. Richards, *A Theory of Reasons for Action* (London: Oxford University Press, 1971), p. 98.

This view is misleading in its simplicity, in ways that affect our interest in the possible justification of conscription (and in ways that do not).[32] One point that needs to be clarified for our purposes is the nature of the "justification of coercion" that an obligation's existence allegedly entails. It is not true that whenever someone has an obligation someone (or everyone) else is morally justified in forcing performance. Just as it can be morally wrong to discharge an obligation, it can be wrong to force another to discharge his obligation. The kinds of conflicts that motivated W. D. Ross's account of prima facie moral requirements are particularly clear examples of this point: it would be wrong for me to ignore the drowning man in order to discharge my obligation to meet you for lunch, and it would be wrong of you to force me to discharge my obligation to you. The only kind of justification of coercion that could possibly follow from the existence of an obligation is a prima facie justification (or justification ceteris paribus), and this mere presumption of a justification could be defeated by any number of countervailing moral considerations. (I will not pause here to discuss the very real possibility that many obligations do not involve even a prima facie justification of coercion. Coercion is, after all, a serious business.)[33]

Even the very limited points made thus far affect the justifiability of conscription. Even if citizens did have a moral obligation to serve in the military, the state would not be justified in enforcing this obligation (through conscription) under many conceivable circumstances. Some of these circumstances involve obligations that outweigh the obligation to serve and are in fact recognized in current practice: the obligation to support dependent family members and the obligations of religious and moral conscience are (or have been) recognized as having overriding importance (and making state enforcement of the obligation to serve indefensible). Similar cases involve nonobligatory services rendered to society. Those who contribute, and will continue to contribute, to the well-being of others and to

32 One problem I will not discuss here concerns who is justified in enforcing obligations (if anyone is). I will assume that if the obligation to serve in the military is owed to the state, then the state is justified (if anyone is) in enforcing it. What happens when the state enforces obligations not owed directly to it is more confusing and is, of course, at issue in resolving problems concerning the Lockean "executive right" or "right of all to punish." See Locke, *Second Treatise of Government*, chap. 2, paragraphs 7–13; Robert Nozick, *Anarchy, State, and Utopia* (New York: Basic Books, 1974), chap. 6; A. John Simmons, "Inalienable Rights and Locke's *Second Treatise*," forthcoming in a collection on rights, edited by H. Miller and W. Williams.

33 This appears to be Nozick's position, at least in his attack on Hart (*Anarchy, State, and Utopia*, pp. 91–93).

the diminishment of suffering often ought not to be forced to serve in the military; their importance to society, even though it is not required by any moral obligation, will have moral weight far greater than their obligation to serve as soldiers. Members of any group or profession may fill this role, although certain doctors, exceptional religious or political leaders, social workers, and those who contribute centrally to other essential services seem likely to be the best candidates. Many other circumstances in which state enforcement of the obligation to military service is illegitimate are not (and by their nature will never be) recognized in actual practice. These are cases in which the conscript is to be used for morally unacceptable purposes. The state may not legitimately enforce obligations by conscription against those who will be employed in unjust or otherwise indefensible wars, police actions, or domestic control. Here the moral obligations a citizen is under to resist conscription will never be recognized by the state, but will be no less real for that. Where it is wrong to serve it cannot be right to force service.

Lest it seem that in spite of these limits to the state's legitimate enforcement of obligations there will still be numerous and routine cases of justified conscription, I would remind the reader of the kind of obligation the state would be enforcing. If there are any widespread obligations to military service (and I have argued that there are not), they will be obligations of the sort least likely to be legitimately enforceable in routine cases. For they cannot be obligations that flow from deliberate commitments (the facts of political life do not include widespread acts of this sort), nor can the failure to serve in the military be seen as directly and clearly injurious to others (and so be morally wrong in the ways that murder and assault are). But these are the kinds of obligations that most clearly justify enforcement. If there is any obligation to serve, it is almost certainly the kind of obligation that includes a wide realm of discretion in time and manner of performance. The state's requirement of prompt compliance to a specific set of demands cannot be viewed as the enforcement (let alone justifiable enforcement) of an obligation of that sort.

Assume now that there is no general obligation to serve, and that each citizen has a moral right not to be coerced by government to serve. Is defensible conscription out of the question in this case? It is not, for just as obligations sometimes ought not to be discharged, so rights may sometimes be legitimately infringed. I do not act wrongly in taking your car without permission (and so violating your property rights) or failing to deliver the product I sold you (violating your contractual rights), if these acts and omissions are necessary to save someone from great and unmerited harm. Our rights may sometimes be infringed in the performance of important duties or to prevent extremely unhappy occurrences. Similarly, we are often not justified in exercising our rights; sometimes we ought not to press moral claims (in the case of positive rights) and should allow others to interfere where we have (negative) rights that they not interfere.

The relevance of these points to the justification of conscription is again readily apparent. Even if citizens have no obligation to serve, certain kinds of social and military emergencies may still make conscription morally justifiable; even if citizens have a moral right not to be conscripted, they may be justifiably conscripted. But because conscription violates many people's rights, and extensively so (causing prolonged loss of liberty and opportunity, and risk of death), justifying emergencies must be very real and very serious indeed. Emergencies of this sort will, of course, also affect the justifiability of conscription favorably if citizens do have an obligation to serve. In either instance, the seriousness of the emergency will throw a corresponding moral weight on the side of legitimating conscription.[34]

It is hard to specify with any precision what constitutes a serious emergency, but the emergencies I have in mind will involve a high probability of significant loss of life or liberty. Natural disasters, epidemics, and civil disturbances may sometimes qualify, although they are unlikely to justify wholesale military conscription. Threat of invasion by a foreign power may also qualify and will routinely justify more coercive interference in the lives of citizens. The imminent overthrow of a government (from within or without), however, which will almost always be counted as an emergency by those in power, will in fact be an emergency serious enough to justify conscription only if the costs (in terms of life and liberty) of overthrow outweigh those of continuation. The continuation of the government might constitute the actual emergency.

Further, not only domestic emergencies may serve to justify conscription, although they seem to be the justifying circumstances most often men-

---

34 Nonpolitical duties may seem to favor conscription in emergencies as well – e.g., our duty to help those in need. But we should remember that such duties are neither owed to the government (making government enforcement questionable), nor do they bind us to specific performances (making the government's specific demands inappropriate). Yet I am sure that many individuals have been moved to volunteer for military service out of the sense of a duty to help; clear cases might be (many of) those Americans who served in British, Russian, and Chinese units during World War II.

tioned in discussions of these points.[35] Foreign crises and suffering must carry the same moral weight as those at home, if we are not blinded by moral parochialism.[36] Only the existence of a special moral tie to our own state (which I have denied) could justify conscription for special attention to domestic emergencies while ignoring emergencies of similar importance abroad. Of course, conscription (and military involvement generally) may not (and very often will not) affect the course of an emergency sufficiently to justify the extensive violation of rights that conscription involves. In that case, neither the seriousness of the emergency nor the probable suffering should be weighed against the cost of conscription; rather, the probability and extent of beneficial effects of conscription must be balanced against the infringed rights and other costs. For instance, even if we judged the conflicts in Korea and Vietnam to have constituted genuine and serious emergencies,[37] the prospects for their successful resolution through foreign intervention were so limited that the probable benefits of conscripting for such intervention could not have outweighed the costs. And because the prospects for successful resolution of foreign emergencies through intervention will generally be far worse than those for overcoming domestic emergencies, conscription to combat domestic emergencies (such as invasion) will have a much higher likelihood of being justified (even though domestic emergency has no special moral priority over foreign emergency).

Responding to an emergency by conscripting may involve moral costs beyond the massive infringement of rights directly associated with conscription. The rights of innocent persons who have not been conscripted but against whom the conscripts are used may also be infringed, and here the wrongness or injustice of a government's cause again bears on the justifiability of conscription. Where conscription, even if it is to avoid dire consequences, nonetheless is for the purpose of aggressing against innocent persons, the magnitude of the emergency involved must be staggering. Aggressive war to protect vital national interests and to avoid domestic disturbances – for instance, to seize needed oil supplies, occupy needed addi-

---

35 For instance, in Walzer, "Political Alienation and Military Service," pp. 117–18, and Bedau, "Military Service and Moral Obligation," pp. 157–58.
36 This point is recognized by Rawls (*A Theory of Justice*, p. 380).
37 I do not think that a case can be made that either instance was a genuine and serious emergency. The probable loss of life and liberty seemed at least as great in responding to the emergency as in ignoring it (not even counting those who died because of the intervention), and the qualities of the governments preserved were not such as to make them worth preserving on independent grounds.

tional living space, or expropriate food-producing territories for a starving nation – involves serious infringement of foreign rights. If such a war is fought through conscription, it will also involve serious infringement of domestic rights. This combination of moral costs (not to mention the possibility of triggering other, greater evils) is unlikely ever to be outweighed by the probable avoidance of suffering that the war would produce. Conscription in wartime will be justifiable only where the war itself is justifiable (and not always then).

But this makes the case for occasional conscription look better than it really is. For in order to be justified the benefits of conscription must not only outweigh its costs, but the policy of conscription must be the morally best approach to reaping those benefits; and conscription must be far enough better in this way than the next best alternative policy that its higher probability for success outweighs the infringed rights which it, but not the alternative policy, involves. But this means that because an All-Volunteer Force involves no overt infringements of rights (and only minimal moral costs of other sorts), conscription to counter emergencies would have to improve the probability of success (over reliance on volunteers) sufficiently to outweigh the massive violation of rights it produces. The difference between the effectiveness of an All-Volunteer Force and a conscripted force could be that great only if the All-Volunteer Force suffered virtual collapse. So even if conscription might otherwise be defensible, it would almost certainly be unjustifiable in virtue of the moral superiority of alternative policies.

But suppose that enlistment or the quality of recruits was so low that the All-Volunteer Force was in fact unable to perform with even minimal competence. And might we not construe the increasing imbalance of military power in the world as itself constituting a military emergency for the United States? There is, of course, no red alert imminence of invasion or nuclear attack, but by the time there was such a concrete emergency, conscription could not possibly be of any use in countering it. We can no longer call out the Minute Men to save the nation. Might we not, then, conscript a force that would be capable of meeting emergencies when they arose? I believe that such a course would be morally unjustifiable, for the same reason that the state is not justified in conscripting a force of citizens to watch and wait for nonmilitary emergencies before there is any concrete indication that they will occur. The loss of liberty and infringed rights such policies involve cannot be justified by the probability of diminished suffering that the existence of such a force involves. The responsibility of government in a modern democracy is not to conscript against an "inevitable" emergency; it is rather to work to make service attractive, to make clear to citizens the value (if any) of a strong deterrent force, and to leave the results to the voluntary decisions of the people whose nation it is.[38]

38 Many of the views expressed here grew out of the enjoyable discussions of conscription I had with Captain George Higgens, Instructor at the United States Military Academy.

ASSOCIATIVE POLITICAL OBLIGATIONS

I

If we owe to [civil society] any duty, it is not subject to our wills. Duties are not voluntary. . . . The awful Author of our being is the Author of our place in the order of existence. . . . He has in and by that disposition virtually subjected us to act the part which belongs to the place assigned us. . . . Parents may not be consenting to their moral relation; but, consenting or not, they are bound to a long train of burdensome duties towards those with whom they have never made a convention of any sort. Children are not consenting to their relation; but their relation, without their actual consent, binds them to its duties. . . . So, without any stipulation on our own part, are we bound by that relation called our country. . . . The place that determines our duty to our country is a social, civil relation. . . . The place of every man determines his duty.[1]

With the possible exception of his reference to the "Author of our being," Edmund Burke's words would not seem out of place in the writings of any number of contemporary authors writing on the problem of political obligation. Ronald Dworkin, for instance, claims in *Law's Empire* that "political obligation . . . is a form of *associative* obligation," a kind of moral requirement that he also refers to as a "communal obligation" or an "obligation of role."[2] Such obligations, Dworkin tells us, are not a matter of choice but

For their helpful comments on earlier drafts of this article, I would like to thank Nancy Schauber, Rüdiger Bittner, Leslie Green, and the referees for and editors of *Ethics*.

1 Edmund Burke, *Appeal from the New to the Old Whigs*, in *Works of Edmund Burke* (Little, Brown, 1866), vol. 4, pp. 164–67.
2 Ronald Dworkin, *Law's Empire* (Cambridge, Mass.: Harvard University Press, 1986), p. 206; my emphasis.

are the special responsibilities assigned by local social practice "to membership in some biological or social group," such as a family or a group of neighbors or colleagues.[3] And John Horton, in his recent book *Political Obligation*, claims "that familial obligations share several features with political obligations, and that the family provides a good example of a context in which obligations are experienced as genuine and rather open-ended, and are not the result of voluntary undertaking. . . . A polity is, like the family, a relationship into which we are mostly born."[4]

Burke, writing two centuries earlier (in 1791), captured much of the spirit of the contextualist, antivoluntarist strain of thought that has come (especially during the past decade) to occupy a central place in the literature on political obligation (and on many other topics in moral and political philosophy). The inspiration for this contemporary movement, admittedly, has not been primarily Burkean. It has more often been Aristotelian or Hegelian or Wittgensteinian or pragmatist in nature. But the strange alliance springing from these (and other) sources has been bound together by many of the same contentions advanced by Burke in the passage above. The most important of these (interrelated) contentions seem to be the following:

1. *Antivoluntarism.* Voluntarists claim that our political obligations can arise only from our voluntary choices to subject ourselves to the political authority of others or to participate in the ongoing cooperative schemes of political life. Voluntarists also typically assert (on the strength of descriptive claims about actual political life) that many of us do in fact have political obligations, born of precisely these kinds of voluntary acts. But antivoluntarists plausibly contend that actual political societies are not voluntary associations nor are they importantly like the voluntary associations

3 Ibid., pp. 195–96.
4 John Horton, *Political Obligation* (Atlantic Highlands, N.J.: Humanities, 1992), pp. 146, 150.
  For other examples of the old and new versions of this position on political obligation, see, e.g., F. H. Bradley: "What [a man] has to do depends on what his place is. . . . We must say that a man's life with its moral duties is in the main filled up by his station in that system of wholes which the state is . . . , by its laws and institutions and still more by its spirit. . . . We may take it as an obvious fact that in my station my particular duties are prescribed to me, and I have them whether I wish to or not" (F. H. Bradley, "My Station and Its Duties," in his *Ethical Studies* [Indianapolis: Bobbs-Merrill, 1951], pp. 110, 112); and Michael Hardimon: "The idea that we have noncontractual familial obligations is one of the most salient beliefs we have. . . . I may also have an analogous obligation to the state. . . . Our roles as family members and citizens are the source of some of the deepest and most important bonds we have" (Michael Hardimon, "Role Obligations," *Journal of Philosophy* 41 [1994]: 342, 344, 353).

we know best. We are for the most part born into political societies and rise into our places as citizens of them without ever freely choosing to participate or to become members.[5] However attractive the social contract theorist's picture of political life may be in other, prescriptive regards, antivoluntarists are right to believe that this picture is not even remotely accurate as a descriptive account of contemporary societies. But further, they argue, insofar as membership in political societies clearly carries with it certain duties or obligations, the nonvoluntary character of membership entails that our political obligations also fall on us independently of our voluntary choices. Thus, the consent theorist's insistence that free consent to political authority is a necessary condition for political obligation must be rejected. Nor should this be a troubling conclusion, they claim, given that so many of our duties, both general (owed to all other persons) and special (owed to particular persons, such as family members, friends, or lovers), seem not to be voluntarily assumed.

2. *The authority of shared moral experience.* Important support for the first thesis (antivoluntarism) derives from the fact that ordinary people do not experience political life as voluntary and from the fact that they do experience many of their duties (including their political duties) as nonvoluntary. Voluntarism does not reflect our shared moral experience. Our claims about, for example, political obligation must be true to moral phenomenology, must be realistic. This thesis is defended in many different forms; but in whatever form it is defended, it appears to have one crucial consequence for the debate about political obligation: it rules out in advance what is commonly referred to as philosophical anarchism. Philosophical anarchists maintain that we (or that most of us) have no political obligations, that all arguments purporting to establish general political obligations fail (perhaps even necessarily fail, as a result of a necessary clash between state authority and the autonomy required for individual obligation). Especially during the 1970s, one popular response to the rejection of voluntarism (as descriptive of actual political life) was precisely to

---

5 The classic statement of this view, of course, is Hume's, in his essay "Of the Original Contract." It is interesting that Locke, the archvoluntarist, seems to agree that most people think this; they "take no notice" of the consent that grounds political obligations "and thinking it not done at all, or not necessary, conclude they are naturally subjects as they are men" (John Locke, *Second Treatise of Government*, sec. 117 [Cambridge: Cambridge University Press, 1960], p. 346). The best-known contemporary statement of the antivoluntarist line is in Rawls; see, e.g., John Rawls, *A Theory of Justice* (Cambridge, Mass.: Harvard University Press, 1971), pp. 336–37, and *Political Liberalism* (New York: Columbia University Press, 1993), pp. 136, 222, 226–27.

embrace some form of philosophical anarchism.[6] But when we accept the second thesis (the authority of shared moral experience), the anarchist response to the first thesis (antivoluntarism) seems to be precluded. For, the argument goes, ordinary people clearly do believe that they have political obligations. Philosophical anarchism, viewed in this light, looks odd and unrealistic;[7] and its efforts to portray ordinary beliefs about political obligation as a kind of false consciousness can never get off the ground.

3. *Particularity.* Another consequence of accepting the second thesis is that any account of political obligation must satisfy what I have elsewhere called the "particularity requirement."[8] Political obligations are felt to be obligations of obedience and support owed to one particular government or community (our own), above all others. Citizens' obligations are special ties, involving loyalty or commitment to the political community in which they were born or in which they reside. More general moral duties with possible political content, such as duties to promote justice, equality, or utility, cannot explain (or justify, or be) our political obligations, for such duties do not necessarily tie us either to one particular community or to our own community. Promoting such values may require the support of many communities, of no existing communities at all, or of communities other than our own.[9] By accepting the particularity requirement, then, the associative obligation theorist can exclude another popular response to the first thesis (antivoluntarism). Rawls, for instance, was pushed by the failure of voluntarism (as a descriptive account) to seek our political obligations instead in his (hypothetical contractarian) account of the natural duty of

---

6 See esp. R. P. Wolff, *In Defense of Anarchism* (New York: Harper & Row, 1970); M. B. E. Smith, "Is There a Prima Facie Obligation to Obey the Law?" *Yale Law Journal* 82 (1973): 950; A. John Simmons, *Moral Principles and Political Obligations* (Princeton, N.J.: Princeton University Press, 1979). Some philosophical anarchists accept voluntarism as a normative thesis about what is necessary for political obligation while rejecting it as descriptively accurate (i.e., rejecting the claim that many actual citizens in actual states have performed the voluntary acts required to obligate them). Others think that political communities are such that no person ever could be obligated to one.

7 Margaret Gilbert, "Group Membership and Political Obligation," *Monist* 76 (1993): 119–20; Horton, pp. 133–35; George Klosko, *The Principle of Fairness and Political Obligation* (Lanham, Md.: Rowman & Littlefield, 1992), pp. 23–26.

8 Simmons, pp. 31–35. Similar appeals to the need for particularity followed in, e.g., Dworkin, p. 193; Klosko, pp. 4–5; and Gregory Kavka, *Hobbesian Moral and Political Theory* (Princeton, N.J.: Princeton University Press, 1986), pp. 407–15.

9 Simmons, pp. 32–34, 154–55. Our general duties would also require different kinds of support for our own political communities under different circumstances. This general style of argument against natural duty accounts of political obligation is followed in *Law's Empire* (Dworkin, p. 193).

justice.[10] But if general duties cannot specially bind us in the proper way to our own political societies, above all others, then the particularity requirement seems to rule out any natural duty approach of this sort.[11] With voluntarism, anarchism, and natural duty approaches all on the sidelines, understanding political obligations as associative or communal begins to seem very attractive.[12]

4. *The analogy with the family.* This tack may seem even more attractive if we question the orthodox Lockean view that familial obligations and political obligations are dissimilar enough to discredit any attempt to understand the latter in terms of the former. A prominent feature of our shared moral experience consists precisely in the obligations we feel toward those with whom we share the nonvoluntary special relationships around which so many of our social practices revolve – Dworkin mentions as examples of such relationships those with family, friends, neighbors, lovers, fellow union members, and colleagues.[13] But surely, we might say, our experience of our political obligations is reasonably similar after all to our experience of these familiar nonpolitical, associative obligations. Both arise from social relationships in which we usually just find ourselves (or into which we grow gradually), both involve no datable act of commitment, and both involve requirements to show a special loyalty and concern.[14]

Indeed, moved by a slightly different spirit, we might wish to even more closely associate familial with political obligations by specifically contrasting these two to the obligations arising from all the other types of social relationship mentioned by Dworkin. Michael Hardimon, for instance, follows Hegel in drawing a sharp contrast between the sphere of civil society and that of the family and state:

> "Civil society," as I understand the term, refers to the domain of private association distinct from the family and the state. It includes, but is by no means

10 Rawls, *Theory of Justice*, chap. 6.
11 Rawls, of course, attempted to particularize his natural duty account by limiting the scope of the natural duty of justice to the support of those just institutions that apply to us. I have argued (Simmons, chap. 6, pp. 32–34) that this move in fact involves the illicit use of nonduty considerations (i.e., those that make application seem morally significant). For a recent attempt to defend a natural duty account of political obligation, see Jeremy Waldron, "Special Ties and Natural Duties," *Philosophy and Public Affairs* 22 (1993): 3–30.
12 Indeed, the only other strategy that has been at all popular (once voluntarism, anarchism, and natural duty theories are rejected) is trying to devise new, nonvoluntarist versions of moral principles that used to be defended in different forms by voluntarists. The nonvoluntarist contract theories I discuss below are one example of this strategy.
13 Dworkin, pp. 195–96.
14 Horton, pp. 145–51, 157–59, 163; Gilbert, "Group Membership," pp. 122–25, 127–28.

limited to, the marketplace. It also comprises the network of voluntary associations which includes unions, professional associations, private clubs, social movements, and neighborhoods. This sphere is governed by a norm of voluntary association. . . . The idea would be that, whereas actual choice is required for obligation within civil society, it is not required for obligation within the family and the state. Within these spheres, noncontractual role obligations may be morally binding.[15]

But even if we agree with Dworkin that states and families do not impose moral requirements on members in a fundamentally different way than do, say, neighborhoods or friendships, we may still be inclined to allow that familial obligations are importantly like political obligations in both their generation and their content.

5. *The normative power of local practice.* These observations may motivate an even stronger view of the locality of political obligations – that is, the view that local associative obligations, including political obligations, are internally justified or self-justifying, that local practice can independently generate moral obligations. One might maintain, for instance, that (*a*) having political obligations is just part of what it means to be a member of a political community, just as having familial obligations is part of what it means to be a family member; (*b*) criteria of membership are in such cases simply social facts wholly determined by social practice; (*c*) the specific content (requirements) of our associative obligations is also simply a social fact; and therefore (*d*) our social practices and the obligations they define require no justification by reference to external moral principles[16] – that is, our practices, to impose genuine obligations, need not be voluntarily accepted, consented to, recognized, maximally useful, or in conformity with any principles external to those practices themselves.

Somewhat less dramatically, one might maintain instead simply that local social practices at least determine the specific content of many obligations (i.e., the behavior required), including the content of our political obligations, even though some external general moral principle must require it if we are to be bound to accept or comply with the requirements of local practice (e.g., the principle of utility might direct us to conform our conduct to the specific requirements of local practice).[17] In either case,

---

15 Hardimon, pp. 352, 353.
16 Horton, pp. 145–48. For the simpler view of local associative political obligations as essentially self-justifying, see Haskell Fain, "The Idea of the State," *Nous* 6 (1972): 25.
17 See Leslie Green, "Consent and Community," in *Political Obligation*, ed. P. Harris (London: Routledge, 1990), pp. 103–6.

however, one would be maintaining that political obligations are not only local in the sense of being owed particularly to one's own country (or community, or government) but also local in the sense of possibly varying quite significantly in content with variations in social location.

II

The theses of antivoluntarism, the authority of shared moral experience, particularity, the analogy with the family, and the normative power of local practice jointly define a definite argumentative space within which the theses' proponents must locate their arguments for (justifications of) political obligation. The theses define this space, of course, in part by just excluding the options of voluntarism, anarchism, and natural duty theories. But the theses jointly require as well that any argument for political obligations characterize these obligations in a special way – namely, as associative obligations or role obligations. We can take an associative obligation to be a special moral requirement, attached to a social role or position (including that of membership in a group), whose content is determined by what local practice specifies as required for those who fill that role or position.[18]

The argumentative space referred to above is, however, still a large space, and many different accounts of political obligation can fit within it (unsurprisingly, given the varied roots from which defenses of the theses have grown). I will concentrate here on a set of three related (styles of) argument for political obligation that satisfy the theses' requirements and that present political obligations as associative in character. These are the three arguments that I take to have enjoyed the most contemporary support. While these arguments are not always carefully distinguished by their advocates, clarity requires that we distinguish them here. And clear exposition will show us, I think, why all three styles of argument should be rejected.

18 Hardimon defines a "role obligation" as "a moral requirement, which attaches to an institutional role, whose content is fixed by the function of the role, and whose normative force flows from the role" (Hardimon, p. 335). His definition thus shares quite a few features with my definition of associative obligation, differing from it primarily where I emphasize social roles and group membership generally (as opposed to Hardimon's emphasis on purely institutional roles) and where I remain neutral on the source of the relevant normative force (as we will see, only some defenders of associative political obligations regard local social practice as normatively independent). And both definitions are obviously quite similar to Dworkin's characterization of associative obligations, despite Hardimon's claims that "role obligations . . . are not usefully thought of as a species of associative obligation" (ibid., pp. 335–36).

The first of the arguments can, I think, be dismissed reasonably quickly. It is presented most transparently in the work of some Wittgensteinian political theorists writing in the 1950s and 1960s. Carole Pateman has dubbed it the "conceptual argument" and Margaret Gilbert the "analytic membership argument,"[19] and versions of it were defended by Margaret MacDonald, Thomas McPherson, and Hanna Pitkin, among others.[20] The conceptual argument attempts to dissolve the problem of political obligation by pointing to the connections of meaning between concepts such as government, state, authority, or citizen (member) and the concept of political obligation. It makes little sense, the argument goes, to ask the traditional questions of why (or whether) we should obey the government with authority over us or of why (or whether) a member of a political community has political obligations. To ask such questions is to betray one's failure to understand the concepts at issue. Having political obligations is just part of what it means to be a member of a political community; being owed obligations of obedience and support by its subjects is just part of what it means to be a government with authority over those subjects. The traditional problem of political obligation thus succumbs to a volley of analytic statements.

That such conceptual arguments cannot succeed in their purpose I take to be reasonably obvious.[21] Even if political obligations for members are entailed by the very concept of membership, it remains meaningful and important to ask what makes a person a member of a political community and thus to ask what grounds the (analytic) obligations of membership (supposing any such exist). Even if governments with authority are, as a matter of meaning, owed political obligations by their subjects, it remains meaningful and important to ask what gives a government its authority, whether any governments with de jure authority exist, what makes a person subject to a government, and, consequently, what grounds those political obligations. These remaining questions about the grounds of political obligation simply are, of course, the traditional questions about political

---

19 Carole Pateman, *The Problem of Political Obligation* (Berkeley: University of California Press, 1985), p. 27; Gilbert, "Group Membership," p. 121.
20 See Margaret MacDonald, "The Language of Political Theory," in *Logic and Language*, ed. A. Flew, 1st ser. (Oxford: Blackwell, 1963), p. 184; Thomas McPherson, *Political Obligation* (London: Routledge & Kegan Paul, 1967), p. 64; Hanna Pitkin, "Obligation and Consent, II," *American Political Science Review* 60 (1966): 39–52, 48.
21 For other arguments to this conclusion, see Simmons, pp. 38–43; Pateman, pp. 27–30, 104; Richard Flathman, *Political Obligation* (New York: Atheneum, 1972), pp. 100–106, 111–12; Green, "Consent and Community," pp. 93–95; Horton, pp. 137–45.

obligation, and they must inevitably reemerge from the smoke generated by the conceptual argument. Indeed, this should have been obvious all along. For were the conceptual argument sound, we would not be able even to understand the claims of rebels and anarchists who deny their obligations. It would be as if they were claiming that a triangle need not be supposed to have three sides. But that the claims of rebels and anarchists are at least meaningful (i.e., not self-contradictory) seems plain. At the very least, we can understand them to be saying that they deny their membership in the political society that claims them as citizens.

Needless to say, it will not do to respond that being a member (or being a government with authority) is just a socially or politically assigned fact about a person (or a set of institutions)[22] so that no inquiry into the grounds for assertions of membership (or authority) is necessary. For it is precisely the normative import of social and political claims that people are members or that governments have authority that are at issue in the traditional debates about political obligation. As a result, it is incumbent on those who wish to extend or develop the conceptual argument to add to it a substantive account of why the local social and political assignments of membership and authority should themselves be taken to be authoritative and, consequently, why the requirements of local social and political practices and institutions should be taken to be binding upon us. This will involve engagement with, rather than the dissolution of, the familiar questions about political obligation; the most interesting efforts to defend the idea of local, associative political obligations all begin by recognizing this fact.[23]

III

I turn now to the first of the more plausible strategies for arguing for associative political obligations – what I will call nonvoluntarist contract theory. This approach is the one most closely allied with that of Burke, who, while rejecting voluntarist consent and contract theories, nonetheless advanced a social contract justification for the binding force of local (and institutional) obligations: "Now, though civil society might at first be a voluntary act, (and in many cases it undoubtedly was,) its continuance is under a permanent standing covenant, coexisting with the society; and it attaches upon

22 This seems to be the response in, e.g., Parekh, "A Misconceived Discourse on Political Obligation," *Political Studies* 16 (1993): 242–43, 249.
23 See, e.g., Gilbert, "Group Membership," p. 121; Horton, p. 145.

every individual of that society, without any formal act of his own. This is warranted by the general practice, arising out of the general sense of mankind. . . . Without their choice [men] enter into a virtual obligation as binding as any that is actual."[24]

The nature of the social contract or standing covenant that binds each of us to our local duties remains always a bit obscure in Burke. The idea is perhaps explained more helpfully in the work of Michael Walzer, which, despite Walzer's professions of voluntarism, really amounts in the end (in my view) to another sort of nonvoluntarist contract theory of political obligation.[25] But the version of this view that can most usefully be discussed here (because of its greater clarity) is that defended by Margaret Gilbert in her article "Group Membership and Political Obligation." According to Gilbert, some shared activities are based on what she calls a "joint commitment," something that can range from a sort of very informal or tacit agreement to a loose, rather vague, mutual understanding. It is essential to joint commitments that "the relevant parties mutually express their readiness to be so committed, in conditions of common knowledge," and the primary function of such commitments "is to establish a set of obligations and entitlements between individual persons to establish a special 'tie' or 'bond' between them."[26] Perhaps most important, joint commitments needn't involve any datable act of commitment (but can "grow up somehow," "just happen," or result from "a process that is considerably extended in time"), and they needn't be fully voluntary (in the sense that entering into and being obligated by them is not precluded by "coercive circumstances").[27]

24 Burke, p. 165.

25 In both *Obligations* and *Just and Unjust Wars*, Walzer maintains that the rights of states and the obligations of citizens rest on consent (Michael Walzer, *Obligations* [New York: Simon & Schuster, 1970], esp. pp. ix–xi, 7–10, and *Just and Unjust Wars* [New York: Basic, 1977], esp. p. 54). But the consent that is relevant turns out in both cases to be given in a kind of informal "contract" that is "hard to describe." It is given "over time," rather than in a series of discrete transfers of authority (*Obligations*, p. xi, *Just and Unjust*, p. 54). It is given by "willing membership" (where the willingness is of "minimal moral significance") and by our sense of ourselves as sharing a "common life" (*Obligations*, pp. 7, 18, ix, *Just and Unjust*, p. 54). Indeed, "'contract' is a metaphor for a process of association and mutuality" (*Just and Unjust*, p. 54), and "consent" is given by "silence" and in "the daily round of social activities and the expectations of peaceful conduct" (*Obligations*, pp. 100–101). We can, then, give our consent and make our contract, recognize and participate in a common life, according to Walzer, without performing any fully voluntary acts or choices of the sort that we would normally describe as consent, promises, or contracts – hence my characterization of Walzer as a nonvoluntarist contract theorist.

26 Gilbert, "Group Membership," pp. 123–24.

27 Ibid., pp. 124–25, 129–30. See also Margaret Gilbert, "Agreements, Coercion, and Obligation," *Ethics* 103 (1993): 679–706, esp. pp. 701–5.

The relevance of these claims to the problem of political obligation appears to be obvious. In most countries, many of the people subject to law and governmental authority speak (and think) of themselves as members of a "plural subject," referring to the country as "our country" and the government as "our government." There is good reason to think, Gilbert claims, that this language expresses their joint commitment to the political community and explains their shared moral experience of felt obligations of obedience and support owed specially to that country (or community, or government). Since joint commitments determine actual (if not, perhaps, moral) obligations, there is good reason to believe that those who feel themselves so obligated do in fact have political obligations. This amounts to an "actual contract theory" of political obligation[28] that is nonetheless consistent with antivoluntarism, with the authority of shared moral experience (and the antianarchist position this allegedly implies), and (obviously) with the particularity and locality of political obligations.

Whatever we may think of Gilbert's general account of joint commitments, there are serious difficulties involved in trying to apply such an account to our political lives in a way that will yield clear political obligations. The actual extent of these difficulties may be obscured by at least three confusions. The first is the confusion of felt obligations with genuine obligations. The mere fact that individuals refer to "our" government and have a vague feeling of indebtedness to "our" country should not, of course, lead us to believe that those individuals in fact have (or even really believe they have) political obligations. Confused, oppressed, or unthinking feelings of obligation are too common a feature of our moral lives to make reasonable such leaps of faith. I will suggest (in Sec. IV) a better way of understanding these phenomena.

A second, related confusion (that may also prompt the illegitimate extension of Gilbert's reasoning to the political realm) is the confusion of political acquiescence with positive, obligation-generating acts or relationships. To be sure, expressions of a willingness to go along with arrangements often look like commitments or consent or agreement; and they can, in proper circumstances, in fact amount to a kind of consent. But a preparedness to go along, even under conditions of full knowledge, is certainly not the same thing as consent or commitment, nor does it have the same normative consequences. One can choose to go along with an arrangement for a time, perhaps even for quite a long time, without thereby undertaking any obligation to continue to go along in the future. My acquiescing

28 Gilbert, "Group Membership," pp. 127–28, 129, "Agreements," pp. 703–5.

to some pushy participant's efforts to organize our game (by, say, assigning team members and specifying rules) in no way commits me to accepting his further plans or pronouncements about the game or about anything else. Neither does the average political subject's expressed preparedness to continue as a participant in the political game entail any commitment (or any obligation) to future obedience to and support of the political community's government.

It is common to argue against such a conclusion by introducing a third confusion, the confusion of reasonable expectations with entitlements. Once again, it may appear that when individuals express a willingness to go along with arrangements, they thereby induce the reliance of others on their continued acquiescence, creating reasonable expectations of future conformity which those others are entitled to see fulfilled. If four friends meet to play bridge every Friday evening for a year, it may be reasonable for each of them to take the behavior of the others to constitute a very loose, informal agreement, obligating each to continue to show up for the game on Friday evenings. There is, as Gilbert puts it, a "tacit understanding" between the friends.[29] But in a case of this sort, of course, there is a more or less continuous, direct, personal contact between the friends, during which there have presumably been many opportunities to make genuine expressions of their joint commitment to the game (or to make clear just how their continued participation in the game should be understood). In short, the tacit agreement undoubtedly refers to something rather more substantial than a mere reasonable expectation of future performance.

By contrast, simple reasonable expectation in no way implies obligation or entitlement in cases where the parties are less directly and personally involved with one another. When a year of Kant's daily walks through town creates in the Königsberg housewives the reasonable expectation that they will be able to set their clocks by his passing, Kant acquires no obligation to continue his walks, an obligation that would, say, override his preference to remain at home one day to read Rousseau. Indeed, even if Kant had maliciously intended to create these expectations by his actions, his actions still would not create for him new obligations. Only a much more direct, explicit, and personal agreement or understanding between Kant and the housewives could accomplish this – that is, could transform reasonable expectations into legitimate entitlements. Kant may well be personally committed to taking his daily walks (out of his desire for good health), but he

29 Gilbert, "Group Membership," p. 124.

has not committed himself to doing so in any transaction with others. Perhaps it is the play on the word "commitment" that seduces here.

The conclusive point against the nonvoluntarist contract theory of political obligation, however, is this: surely when we think of the relationships that typically hold between fellow subjects in some large-scale political community (as opposed to, say, a town or a neighborhood), we see that these relationships much more closely resemble the indirect, impersonal relationship between Kant and the housewives (whose expectations, however reasonable, they were not entitled to demand that Kant fulfill), than they do the direct and personal relationship (laden with tacit commitments) between the bridge-playing friends.[30] If this is true, as I think it plainly is, then it seems that Gilbert's efforts to extend an analysis appropriate only to (certain kinds of) direct, personal, shared activities into an analysis that would cover the very indirect, impersonal, shared activities of residents in the same political community must fail in a reasonably straightforward fashion. For while residents of typical political communities may, like Kant, be committed to various things – to obeying the law, to staying out of legal trouble, to doing what they think is independently right, and so on – they have not normally committed themselves to one another – they have not tacitly agreed together on anything – in a way that would ground for them political obligations. Gilbert (with other nonvoluntarist contract theorists) needs the latter, stronger notion of citizens' commitments to explain citizens' obligations. But the facts of actual political life permit her, if anything, only the weaker notion of citizens' commitments, which explains obligations not at all. And, in any event, of course, insisting on the stronger notion of commitment she needs would in effect involve reasserting the voluntarist picture of political society whose rejection partly motivated the project in the first place.

Ronald Dworkin, although no contract theorist, has advanced arguments that might seem to blunt the force of my objections here. For Dworkin claims that direct, personal relationships between persons are not necessary for grounding associative or communal obligations. He sees that the primary objection to trying to analyze political obligations in the same terms in which one analyzes the nonvoluntary communal obligations between family members, friends, and associates is that communal obliga-

30 Notice that Gilbert's examples of joint commitments all involve very personal shared activities, such as taking a walk together or regularly going for coffee after the meetings of a scholarly society (Gilbert, "Group Membership," pp. 122–24). Perhaps, then, Locke was right after all to insist that political obligations require a rather different sort of analysis than do the more personal obligations of family members to one another.

tions seem "to depend upon emotional bonds that presuppose that each member of the group has personal acquaintance of all others, which of course cannot be true in large political communities."[31] Dworkin's response to this objection is that the conditions on communal obligations are not psychological, but interpretive conditions. While the obligations between group members do in a sense require that they have personal concern for (and thus a sort of personal interaction with) one another, "the concern they require is an interpretive property of the group's practices of asserting and acknowledging responsibilities . . . , not a psychological property of some fixed number of the actual members." So political obligations can turn out after all to be associative or communal, despite the emotional distance between most members of political groups, if the best interpretation of that political group's practices involves appropriate equal concern for all members.[32]

I confess that I find a bit bizarre the suggestion that the best interpretation of a family's "practices" or a friendship's "practices" might involve reciprocal and equal concern, even if the family members or "friends" lacked any attitudes or feelings of concern toward one another. And Dworkin himself admits that "a group will rarely meet or long sustain [the interpretive conditions] unless its members by and large *actually feel* some emotional bond with one another."[33] This certainly has the ring of truth, but it seems a fatal admission. For while Dworkin may still be able to claim that political obligations (in some hypothetical large political community) could be associative or communal, he has in effect admitted that this is very unlikely ever to be the case in actual political communities, since members of such communities seldom "actually feel some emotional bond" with all (or even most) of their fellow members. It is simply not true, either in our own political community or in any others with which we are familiar, that most citizens feel with respect to all of their fellows a deep and abiding concern. In the interest of realism, we must acknowledge that the divisions

31 Dworkin, p. 196. Instead of saying with Dworkin that these obligations "depend upon emotional bonds," I would say that direct, personal involvement permits the actions of individuals to be imbued with a clear significance, thus permitting degrees of commitment to be clearly expressed in action.

32 Ibid., p. 201. Dworkin's argument is obviously rather more involved than this brief summary suggests. Among other things, Dworkin argues that a "true community," one that involves nonvoluntary communal obligations for its members, must in its practices display not only equal concern for all members but also a sense that the responsibilities of members are reciprocal, personal, and special to that group (ibid., pp. 198–201).

33 Ibid., p. 201; my emphasis.

between religions, ethnic groups, races, political parties, castes, economic classes, and so on run too deep for this claim to be convincingly denied. Where one might find the kind of closeness and concern necessary for Dworkin's account of associative obligations, of course, will only be in groups far smaller than the large-scale political communities with which Dworkin claims to be concerned.

The best interpretation of our political practices, then, will not involve the concern and the reciprocity (etc.) on which the attribution of associative political obligations is alleged by Dworkin to rest. Dworkin, of course, believes that because "our own political culture" is best interpreted as a "community of principle" (i.e., one in which people "accept that they are governed by common principles, not just rules hammered out in political compromise"), it satisfies the interpretive conditions of concern and reciprocity.[34] But even if this interpretation of our own (or of some other) political culture were acceptable, which I deny, Dworkin's strong appeals to independent principles of justice and equal concern would come perilously close to rendering superfluous the very local, associative (communal) obligations that were supposed to lie at the heart of his account of political obligation.[35]

34 Ibid., pp. 216, 211. For a helpful and much more detailed discussion of these (and other) aspects of Dworkin's position, see Leslie Green, "Associative Obligations and the State," in *Law and Community*, ed. A. Hutchinson and L. Green (Toronto: Carswell, 1989), pp. 93–118.

35 Insofar as local associative obligations are only "genuine," in Dworkin's view, when the relevant group is both a true community (i.e., when its practices are best understood as involving reciprocity, special and personal responsibilities, equal concern for all members, etc.) and a just community (i.e., it has a nondefective conception of equal concern and is just to those outside the community [Dworkin, pp. 198–205]), it is not clear just how much moral work is actually being done by the requirements of local practice – as opposed to the principles of justice and equal concern that are used to judge the bindingness of local obligations. Dworkin, of course, hopes that the appeal to local obligations will particularize the application of his general moral principles so that those principles can be understood to bind us specially to our own countries (or associations). But what he actually seems to motivate instead is questions about why our own local associations should be regarded as morally central, why they should be taken to be entitled to our special (or even exclusive) support in the face of other, foreign associations that may be better (more just) or more in need of support – given that our own local associative obligations are so easily overridden by the general, external requirements of justice and equal concern. There are also, I think, serious questions about the extent to which our own community as a matter of fact satisfies the model of principle rather than, say, the rulebook or compromise model – what Rawls calls a "modus vivendi." And it seems important to note that Dworkin's identification of true communities (which involve mutual and equal concern) with communities of principle (which involve only the acceptance of common principles) is both questionable and deeply prejudicial to his case.

IV

There is a third, and much more common, general strategy for arguing that political obligations are local, associative obligations, and I will refer to it here simply (and a bit misleadingly)[36] as the "communitarian theory." Under that very broad heading I intend to capture accounts that stress one or both of the following two theses:

1. Some (or all) of our obligations are justified in virtue of the fact that denying these obligations would amount to denying our identities as (at least partly) socially constituted beings. What makes me who I am, what gives me my values and ends, is (at least in part) my occupation of certain local social roles, but occupying these roles conceptually involves having the local, associative obligations attached to them. More specifically for our purposes here, the fact that my identity is partly constituted by my role as a member of some political community means that my identity includes being under political obligations. I cannot meaningfully ask why (or whether) the I-who-am-in-part-constituted-by-certain-obligations has those obligations. Alasdair MacIntyre, for example, has argued that "to be a man is to fill a set of roles each of which has its own point and purpose: member of a family, citizen, soldier, philosopher, servant of God" and that "the rational justification of my political duties, obligations, and loyalties is that, were I to divest myself of them by ignoring or flouting them, I should be divesting myself of a part of myself, I should be losing a crucial part of my identity."[37] And John Horton claims: "Both the family and the political community figure prominently in our sense of who we are. . . . These kinds of institutional involvement generate obligations."[38]

---

36 "Misleadingly" because, first, the conceptual argument and the nonvoluntarist contract theory I have already discussed might also not unreasonably be called communitarian and, second, because the term "communitarian" has come in contemporary literature to stand for any of the enormous variety of positions that oppose themselves in fundamental spirit to those positions described (equally vaguely) as liberal. I will discuss here only a subgroup, although a large subgroup, of the positions on political obligation that might be called communitarian.

37 Alasdair MacIntyre, *After Virtue* (Notre Dame, Ind.: Notre Dame University Press, 1981), p. 56, "Philosophy and Politics," in *Philosophy and Human Enterprise*, ed. J. L. Capps, United States Military Academy Class of 1951 Lecture Series (1982–83), p. 158.

38 Horton, pp. 150, 157. See also, e.g., John Charvet, "Political Obligation: Individualism and Communitarianism," in *On Political Obligation*, ed. P. Harris (London: Routledge, 1990), pp. 65–88, esp. pp. 79–85. One would expect other prominent communitarians, such as Michael Sandel and Charles Taylor, to endorse this position. For the classic statement of the position, see Bradley: "We have found ourselves when we have found our station and its duties, our function as an organ in the social organism. . . . If we suppose

2. Typically accompanying this first, identity thesis is the further, related claim that local social practices (and our roles or places in them) independently determine (some or all) moral requirements. Where the identity thesis stresses the personal incoherence of denying obligations that are conceptually connected to one's true self, this second, normative independence thesis stresses instead the normative force – that is, the power to independently generate obligations – of the local social and institutional rules and practices under the influence of which those true selves developed. The idea of independent generation of obligations is intended to rule out the need for these local practices to be justified by their utility, by their fairness, by our consent to them, or by appeal to any other "external moral principles."[39] This normative independence of local practice is typically argued for in conjunction either with maintaining that local practice is one of a plurality of spheres or sources of moral requirements – as in Hegel's famous distinction between the local obligations of *Sittlichkeit* and the universal obligations of *Moralität* – or else by maintaining that local practice is the only possible source of moral requirements. Most theorists whose sympathies are broadly Aristotelian, Hegelian, or Wittgensteinian either state or assume the truth of some version of this second, normative independence thesis.

Despite the obvious connections between the two theses, I want to respond first to the identity thesis, considered by itself. It is curious, I think, that defenders of the identity thesis take the personal incoherence or unintelligibility allegedly involved in denying certain obligations to constitute a justification for ascribing those obligations as moral requirements. No one, I assume, would claim that all personal unintelligibility of this sort amounts to a justification of ascription of moral obligation. A person who believed himself to be Napoleon could not intelligibly deny his obligation to, say, lead the French army, but this would not show that this person in fact had a moral obligation to lead the French army. Perhaps, we might say, that is only because the person is not really Napoleon. But the same conclusion seems appropriate in the case of someone who really is an agent in the gestapo, someone who can't intelligibly deny the obligations attached by

the world of relations, in which he was born and bred, never to have been, then we suppose the very essence of him not to be; if we take that away, we have taken him away. . . . The state . . . gives him the life that he does live and ought to live" (Bradley, "My Station," pp. 101, 104, 110).

39 Horton, p. 147. As we have seen, Hardimon's account of role obligations characterizes them as moral requirements "whose normative force flows from the role" (Hardimon, p. 334).

local practice to that position. Surely that personal unintelligibility cannot establish a moral obligation to torture suspects, to send innocents to the death camps, and so on, even if these obligations are (as perhaps they were) conceptually connected to gestapo membership. Perhaps, we might say, that is only because the local practice is in this case morally vile. But if only those local practices that satisfy the demands of external moral principles can realize the argumentative goal here (i.e., generate genuine moral obligations), this strongly suggests that the personal unintelligibility of denying local obligations is not, at least by itself, any basis for ascribing moral obligations. Indeed, it seems plausible to contend that only in con-junction with the second, normative independence thesis does the identity thesis have any real force. Only if our identities are partly constituted by our roles in local practices that do independently generate moral obliga-tions can the unintelligibility of denying our role responsibilities give us any reason to ascribe moral obligations. But if the practices in question independently generate moral obligations for those occupying roles within them, the additional appeal to personal unintelligibility then seems per-fectly superfluous and misleading. The personal unintelligibility involved in denying local obligations is a simple consequence of the fact that local practice has assigned an independently generated moral obligation to the occupiers of some role. The personal unintelligibility of denying the oblig-ations is not the reason why persons in fact have the assigned obligations (i.e., it is not the ground of the obligation). That reason is provided by whatever is taken to justify the normative independence thesis.

Now we might, of course, read the first thesis as less about people's socially constituted identities – about the social roles they in fact occupy according to the role-identifying rules of local practice – and more about identification – about the social roles that people identify with, about what they (in reflective moments) take to be their real identities. While local social practice may assign me the political role of U.S. citizen, I only count as a U.S. citizen for moral purposes, with conceptually related political obligations, if I identify with that role. And this identification is what is indi-cated by our speaking of "our" country or "our" government and by our having certain attitudes characteristic of members or by our participating in the group's political life and steadily following its rules – whatever we may say when the obligations of membership become burdensome.[40]

But why would we think that this kind of identification with a social or political role is either a necessary or a sufficient condition for possessing

40 Gilbert, "Group Membership," p. 127; Horton, pp. 152–54, 159.

a moral obligation to abide by the rules of local practice? In the first place, of course, it again seems to matter crucially what kind of practice we are discussing and how well it fares under critical assessment by external moral principles. Oppressed people are frequently brought by long periods of humiliation and indoctrination to identify with their subservient roles and to acknowledge as their own the degrading, locally assigned obligations of second-class members. But this can surely constitute no justification for ascribing to them moral obligations to abase themselves and to selflessly serve their oppressors. And even where immoral practices are not at issue, people can mistakenly identify with certain social roles (and feel obligated by the locally assigned requirements for those roles). I could, on the basis of confusions, lies, or bad information, falsely believe myself to be of Croatian descent or to be the father of a particular child or falsely believe some particular person to be a neighbor. We should not be likely to conclude from such mistaken identification, however, that I have certain associative moral obligations for as long as I mistakenly identify with a role in this way but cease to have those moral obligations at the moment the truth is revealed, at the moment I am stripped of this part of my identity and of my associated sense of obligation.

In the case of membership in political communities, I think, our argument could be similar. Absent any compelling argument for general political obligations (of the sort to which traditional theorists aspire), and absent any compelling argument for the independent binding power of local rules requiring obedience and support (of the sort to which proponents of the normative independence thesis aspire), it seems plausible to dismiss as a kind of false consciousness our feelings of obligation toward our countries of birth or residence. Of course we identify ourselves with "our" countries, "our" governments, and "our" fellow citizens. We have typically been taught from birth to do so, have typically spent our lives in a particular political culture, have been identified with a particular community by those outside our own (for purposes of praise or blame, say), and have associated with and become used to our own ways. That I might feel shame or pride at the acts of my countrymen (or that I might vote in elections and obey the law) is hardly surprising under these conditions. But none of this identification (along with its accompanying feelings of obligation) – none of these ways of speaking and acting – seems, considered by itself, in any way inconsistent with denying that we are morally bound by political obligations to our countries of residence.

Identification with a political community or with the role of member within it is not sufficient for possessing political obligations. Neither is it necessary for this, as can be seen in the simple case of an individual who freely consents to political obligations (out of simple self-interest, say), while continuing to feel no attachments to or identification with the political community to which he (successfully) binds himself. The fact that he does not feel like a member of a group or think like one no more cancels his voluntarily assumed obligations than does the desire of a promise maker to subsequently renege on his promise.[41] One might in desperation, of course, try to cast identification as a sort of consent or free acceptance of obligation and so try to make identification seem after all at least sufficient for political obligation. But this move from identification as self-definition to identification as personal commitment would appear to amount to reasserting the voluntarism that the identity thesis was originally advanced to replace.

V

If I am right in this, it leaves the defense of associative political obligations resting entirely on what I've called the normative independence thesis. While I cannot here deal decisively with that thesis, understood as a general thesis in moral philosophy, I will try to note some reasons for thinking that it too fails to show that political obligations are best thought of as associative or communal. Some of these reasons are also reasons to be skeptical about the general thesis itself; others are reasons only for believing that the thesis cannot properly support the contention that there are communal or associative political obligations.

We are all familiar with moral arguments in favor of compliance with (some) local practices and institutions that nonetheless deny the normative independence ascribed to such practices by the second thesis. Utilitarians have produced arguments for compliance with useful or expedient

---

41 Hardimon considers a similar case: "Role identification and voluntary acceptance are distinct. . . . Imagine a person with strong anarchist leanings who has successfully completed his medical training. Such a person might voluntarily accept the cluster of duties associated with the role of doctor and yet refuse to identify with this role" (Hardimon, p. 359). So, while this is never clearly stated, identification with a role is apparently not, for Hardimon, necessary for possessing the associated role obligations. And it seems that it cannot be sufficient for this either, since (1) he claims that only those roles that are "reflectively acceptable" generate moral obligations, and (2) we can clearly identify with roles that fail this test of reflective acceptability (ibid., pp. 348–51). But it is then unclear why Hardimon insists that "the idea of *role identification*" is an "absolutely vital factor" allegedly ignored by the (and for that reason, defective) voluntarist theories of institutional obligation (ibid., p. 357).

local practices; contractarians (such as Rawls) have defended compliance with (or support for, or promotion of) just local practices and institutions; and consent theorists have always allowed that through voluntary acceptance or agreement we may take on (sign on for) the roles and obligations defined by local practice, thereby acquiring genuine moral obligations to fulfill these local associative obligations (at least where local practice conforms to certain moral standards). The normative work in these arguments is done by independent principles of utility, justice, and consent. And we have seen that even some accounts of political obligation that stress the associative or communal character of that obligation do not in fact allow for the normative independence of local practice – such as Gilbert's account (where the binding force of role obligations derives from the contract that establishes joint commitment to some activity) or Dworkin's (where there is reliance on a general natural duty to comply with certain sorts of local practices).[42]

The pressure to deny the normative independence of local practice derives primarily from one obvious fact and from one broad theoretical disposition. The fact is this: local practices and institutions can be unjust, oppressive, pointless, woefully inefficient, and in other ways normatively defective. We have all seen more than we care to of all of these defects. It seems natural in the face of such examples to maintain that either certification of a practice by some independently justifying moral principle or acceptance of the practice by those subject to it is required for the associative obligations imposed by the practice to be genuine moral obligations. The theoretical disposition is the belief that universality (or at least a generality far broader than the local) is an essential property of moral judgments, including those moral principles that entail ascriptions of local obligation.

The pressure to defend the normative independence of (at least certain sorts of) local practices and institutions likewise derives primarily from one obvious fact and from one broad theoretical disposition. The fact is this: we often seem to ascribe role obligations to persons "without reference to some further moral principle or theory. . . . It is often sufficient to point out that a man is this boy's father to attribute certain obligations on the part of the man towards the boy. It is both unnecessary and misleading to seek some further moral justification for the obligations."[43] The theoretical disposition is the belief that universalism in moral theory is a failed tra-

42 Dworkin, p. 198.   43 Horton, p. 156.

dition – that morality, to be intelligible, must be understood in a more restricted, culturally relativized, or pragmatic (etc.) fashion.

The controversy over the two broad theoretical dispositions is too substantial and complex to be usefully addressed here. But something helpful can, I think, be said about the "obvious facts" appealed to on the two sides of the debate, for at least one of the obvious facts seems considerably less obvious on reflection. Take the (strongest) case of parental obligations. While it may be true that we think mere parenthood sufficient to ascribe certain rights and obligations to parents without seeking some further justification for this ascription, the rights and obligations we feel comfortable in ascribing are not obviously any or all of the obligations assigned by local practices to parents. We do not automatically accept all aspects of the various institutions or practices of family life. Instead, we reject locally assigned parental rights or obligations where these seem cruel or discriminatory or oppressive. We may, for instance, reject established norms of family life that involve paternal priority, abandonment or sale of children, genital mutilation, arranged marriages, and so on.

Nor are the parental rights and obligations we unqualifiedly accept obviously accepted as self-justifying local rights and obligations. We may confidently ascribe to parents obligations of care, tuition, and support precisely because we believe that all parents everywhere, in all times, have owed this to their children. These natural parental obligations simply (and not coincidentally) have the same content as some of the associative obligations assigned to parents by some local practices. And those who feel no need to argue for or justify such ascriptions of parental obligation, those who find such arguments "unnecessary and misleading," may believe (or vaguely feel) that some statements about parental obligations are simply self-evidently true – not that (some or all) local practices are normatively independent.

The fact that we ascribe certain role obligations without feeling the need for further justification, then, does little to demonstrate, or even to support, the contention that most of us believe local practices and institutions to be normatively independent, (let alone the further contention that they are normatively independent, that shared moral experience is authoritative on this matter). But neither does any of the argument thus far establish that local practices are not normatively independent. That conclusion is supposed to be supported by the other obvious fact that we do not take normatively defective local practices or institutions to be capable of imposing genuine obligations on those occupying roles within them. It might seem, however, that one can acknowledge that the injustice or brutality of a practice limits its power to impose moral obligations on its participants without thereby conceding that the normative independence thesis is false. The following two claims, for instance, may seem crucially relevant here:

1. Even where the injustice of a practice or institution limits its power to impose moral obligations on participants, it may not altogether undermine this power. Unjust institutions, depending on the degree and kind of injustice and on the extent to which the injustice is embodied in particular institutional rules, may succeed in imposing moral obligations in some of the instances where they assign institutional obligations but not in other instances.[44] Even under the Third Reich, one could argue, German citizens still had a moral obligation to comply with some of the legal requirements assigned by local practice to their roles as citizens (such as the requirements not to steal or murder, not to drive recklessly, or even not to park illegally), but they had no moral obligation to comply with other institutional requirements (such as those requiring the reporting of disloyal talk or of the location of Jews in hiding).

2. Even if it is conceded that assessment by external moral principles (e.g., principles of justice) can limit and in some cases completely undermine a local practice's power to impose genuine obligations, this does not show that the associative obligations that pass this external scrutiny are themselves justified by external principles. Just practices or institutions may still be self-justifying or normatively independent. "It is one thing to show that a particular institution does not violate other fundamental moral principles or commitments, but quite another to have to show that the institution is *justified* by these other moral principles."[45]

Now, with respect to (1), it may be true that many people believe that they have a moral obligation to obey all laws where doing so does not directly involve them in the performance of wrongful or unjust acts. This belief only seems consistent with upholding the normative independence thesis, however, if they also believe something like (2) – that is, if they also believe that the ability of external moral principles to limit or condition the obligation-generating power of local practices does not show that local associative obligations that are morally binding are themselves justified by external moral principles. So (2) seems the more important of the two claims.

It does seem clear that, as (2) asserts, the mere fact that an obligation-generating practice is externally limited (in its power to generate obligations) does not show that the obligations it succeeds in generating are

44 Dworkin, pp. 203–5. 45 Horton, p. 156.

justified by those external limiting principles. A promise, for example, cannot obligate me to commit murder. This does not show, however, that the principle forbidding murder is what justifies binding promissory obligations;[46] that principle quite clearly has nothing to do with the justification of everyday promissory obligations.

But it is important to note two points about such examples. First, the fact that local practices are limited by, rather than merely conflicting with, external moral principles shows at least that the normative force of local practice is of a lower order than that of the external principles of justice, respect for persons, nonmaleficence, and the like that limit it. This suggests that local associative obligations, conceived of as independently generated by local practice, are at best a reasonably weak sort of moral obligation – in the face of which it seems appropriate to ask why our moral attention should ever be focused locally rather than on the more weighty general moral concerns that require action far beyond (and sometimes in competition with) what is required by our local role obligations. Second, however, the use of examples such as the practice of promising or laws imposing order on social activities really is not the best test for the normative independence thesis. For these practices or institutions are naturally imagined to have compelling external justifications (in terms of their utility, the requirements of fair play, or our tacit or hypothetical consent to them, etc.). So while we can allow that the obvious fact of normatively defective local practices does not demonstrate the falsity of the normative independence thesis, we should not allow this failure to look as if it counts as evidence in favor of the thesis.

The best commonsense test case for the normative independence thesis would be that of a practice that was perfectly morally neutral under assessment by external moral principles. Hopelessly evil local practices impose no genuine obligations because they are condemned by external principles. Beneficial, just, freely accepted practices do impose genuine obligations but apparently only because external principles in those cases require compliance. The normative independence thesis, however, asserts that local practices and institutions can impose genuine moral obligations simply by virtue of being in force, simply by virtue of the social fact that people occupy (by choice or not) roles or stations, with associated role obligations, within these schemes. So what we need is to imagine a practice whose sole salient moral property is that it is in force, which thereby

---

46 Ibid.

takes external principles out of the picture altogether, and then assess this practice's normative power.

This turns out to be (perhaps surprisingly) quite difficult. For the mere fact that a practice is in force entails the presence of practice-related expectations whose frustration produces disutility, involves sacrifices by those who comply with its rules that seem to call in fairness for sacrifices by others under the rules, and so on. So external moral principles seem automatically to be brought back into the picture. But despite this difficulty, there does seem to be at least one claim about morally neutral practices that can plausibly be made. To the extent that a practice seems morally pointless (from the perspective of external moral principles) – to the extent that it is not beneficial or not freely chosen by its participants to advance their projects, say – to that extent it seems very hard to imagine anyone insisting that the associative obligations it assigns have any genuine moral weight. Even mildly beneficial, harmlessly silly practices seem unable to impose any genuine obligations on nonconsenters assigned roles within them. Nor would the fact that such a practice had a firm hold on or a long standing within a social group look like any better reason for supposing it to independently generate moral obligations.

If my claims here seem wildly hypothetical, it is only because it is so hard to imagine a social practice or institution being established in the first place or long surviving if it were utterly neutral from the external moral viewpoint. The practices with which we are familiar all seem to have either an immoral purpose (e.g., the domination of some by others) or a morally positive aim (e.g., the coordination of otherwise harmful private action, the conferral of widely desired public goods, or the creation of opportunities for advancing less widely shared ends). Even nontyrannical, but nonetheless condemnable, practices (such as dueling) could be thought of as having moral properties of both sorts. But the fact that it is so hard to imagine utterly neutral practices that do not seem at the same time just silly is itself, I think, a strike against the normative independence thesis. Where local practices and institutions are imagined stripped of their external moral justifications, possessing only their social instantiation as a salient property, it is difficult to imagine their normative power as sufficient to overcome even the most trivial and mundane presumptions in favor of allowing instead individual liberty and choice. Mere social instantiation, it seems, is unlikely to confer any normative power on a practice.

My suggestion, then, is that it is not so much the familiar actual phenomenon of morally vile local practices that should make us skeptical about the normative independence thesis as it is the hypothetical case of the morally neutral local practice. I acknowledge that the defender of the thesis will have a hard time answering a criticism such as mine in terms that I would find satisfying. For asking questions about why a morally neutral local practice should be thought capable of generating moral obligations seems to amount to asking for a general external justification of the practice that we know in advance cannot (ex hypothesi) be forthcoming. The response, "This is just what the game involves; local practice simply has social and linguistic, hence moral, authority," will not satisfy anyone who wants to argue that how one gets into the game, or the generalizable virtues of the game, are what confer real moral authority. Being born into an (externally) morally neutral structure of institutional roles and responsibilities, in my view, would no more provide one with a moral reason for compliance than being born handicapped would provide one with a moral reason for conforming one's behavior to the local social expectations about activities appropriate to the handicapped.

There are, then, some good reasons to be skeptical about the normative independence thesis – and, consequently, some good reasons to reject claims about the associative character of political obligation. In fact, however, I think the case against associative political obligations is stronger than the case against the normative independence thesis. So, in closing, I will (very briefly) suggest some reasons for believing that even if we are mistaken in rejecting the normative independence thesis, we should still reject claims that political obligations are associative or communal. Suppose, then, that the normative independence thesis is true, that (at least some) local social practices impose (some or all of our) genuine moral obligations, independent of justification by any moral principles external to the practices themselves. Even if this is true, the following arguments show that political obligations, as least, are not associative:

1. If our theory of political obligation is to be true to our shared moral experience, it will have to account for the fact that most people feel that the content of our communal, associative obligations is vague and indeterminate at best. While we are confident that we must show certain kinds of special concern for our family members, friends, neighbors, or colleagues, we are generally not very clear about the exact requirements of even our most central obligations to these communal associates.[47] By contrast, most people have quite a clear sense of at least the bulk of the content

47 Gilbert, "Group Membership," p. 125; Horton, pp. 150–51, 163.

of their political obligations. They feel they must, in at least virtually all cases (i.e., at least where the law is not morally abhorrent), obey the laws of their country, the most central of which, at least, have quite a specific and widely known content. The contrast between our shared experience of vague, indeterminate associative obligations and our shared experience of reasonably precise, determinate political obligations makes it hard to see how an analysis of the latter in terms of the former is at all likely to succeed – at least if the authority of shared moral experience is not questioned. If it is questioned, of course, then the primary intuitive support for associative obligations (i.e., the felt obligations of family members, friends, etc.) is undercut, and competitor theories allegedly eliminated by this authority – such as philosophical anarchism – can once again enter the debate.[48]

2. If our account of political obligation is to be true to our shared moral experience (as the argument for associative political obligations requires), we will have to acknowledge that our experience of, for example, family life is much more communal in nature than is our experience of political life. Political life may not resemble a club or other voluntary association, as communitarians observe. But we cannot honestly say that it much resembles a tribe or a family or a pair of friends or lovers either – or even a group of neighbors who live close together or a group of employees who work closely together. Our sense of community – of shared interests, values, expectations, life prospects, and the like – is, at least for most of us, so much less involved in our political lives than in these other aspects of our lives that it is only a matter of ancient habit that we refer to modern states as political communities at all.

As a result, some communitarians (such as MacIntyre) plausibly charge that modern individuals live in nothing even vaguely like a unified community but live instead either as social atoms or as members of numerous overlapping, substate groups. To which group or institution, after all, do we feel most bound: to our country, to our society, to our locality, to our neighborhood, to our religion, to our race, or to our company? Even, then, if these communitarians are skeptical about traditional accounts of political obligation, they also provide noncommunitarians with good reasons to

48 If we respond by claiming that the content of political obligation is also vague and indeterminate (Horton, p. 163), we simply threaten the basis of the entire argument. Ordinary people, if they believe they have political obligations at all (an assertion that merits testing, although I have not questioned it here), plainly adhere to the idea of reasonably strict obedience to enacted law, not to some vague idea of obligatory special concern for their state.

believe that political obligations in modern states are not correctly thought of as communal or associative.[49]

My conclusion, then, is that political obligation is not a form of associative obligation. The conceptual argument, the nonvoluntarist contract theory, and the communitarian theory have all failed to establish the associative character of political obligation. Further, even if some account of associative obligation succeeded in defending the normative independence of some local practices and institutions, this account could not show our political obligations to belong to the class of associative obligations. While we might then be able to imagine a political community in which political obligations would be associative, we would also have to admit that our own large-scale political communities bear little resemblance to the close-knit group imagination produced. If we have political obligations at all, then, they are not associative obligations. And if we do not have them but should come to have them through changes in our behavior, our political practices, and our institutions, then unless these changes were genuinely revolutionary, our political obligations would still not be associative obligations. An adequate account of political obligation will have to begin instead, I think, by questioning some or all of the five theses (such as antivoluntarism and the analogy with the family) that associative obligation theorists seem too eagerly to accept.[50]

49 MacIntyre writes that in a society such as ours "the nature of political obligation becomes systematically unclear. Patriotism is or was a virtue founded on attachment primarily to a political and moral community and only secondarily to the government of that community. . . . When however the relationship of government to the moral community is put in question both by the changed nature of government and the lack of moral consensus in society, it becomes difficult any longer to have any clear, simple and teachable conception of patriotism" (*After Virtue*, p. 236). Horton replies that in a pluralistic society lacking moral consensus there can still "be some agreement about the desirability of many laws, or even where there is such disagreement . . . there [can] be some mutual accommodation which . . . is generally acceptable" (Horton, p. 168). But this reply seems to amount only to an argument for the possibility of a political modus vivendi in modern states, not for what Dworkin calls a "community of principle." The former condition, however, is consistent only with political obligations so utterly different in character from the associative or role obligations of families, friends, or neighbors that the point of stressing the analogy seems altogether lost.

50 My preferred account of political obligation maintains that few citizens of modern states have political obligations, that associative, communal, role, or institutional obligations require external justification to be morally binding, and that associative obligation theorists go wrong from the start by accepting unqualified versions of the theses of antivoluntarism and the authority of shared moral experience and by accepting any version of the theses of the analogy with the family and the normative power of local practice. Sustaining these claims, of course, would require a far more systematic account of the subject than it has been my business to attempt here.

5

EXTERNAL JUSTIFICATIONS AND INSTITUTIONAL ROLES

In his "Role Obligations,"[1] Michael Hardimon defends an account of the nature and justification of institutional obligations which he takes to be clearly superior to the "standard view." A "role obligation," as Hardimon defines it, is "a moral requirement, which attaches to an institutional role, whose content is fixed by the function of the role, and whose normative force flows from the role" (334). The relevant institutional roles can be political (for example, the role of "citizen"), familial (for example, "sister"), or occupational (for example, "bus driver") (334–35).[2] On the "standard view" of role obligations, Hardimon explains, "*contractual* role obligations are acquired by signing on for the roles from which they derive," while "*noncontractual* role obligations are extremely problematic, if they exist at all" (337; my emphases). Hardimon argues that this standard view presents a "misleading and distorted" picture of role obligations (and of morality generally); and in its strongest form this view still "leaves out" of its understanding of even contractual role obligations an "absolutely vital factor" (337, 357). I shall contend, by contrast, that a differently characterized

---

1 *The Journal of Philosophy* XCI, 7 (July 1994): 333–63.
2 Hardimon tries to distinguish genuine "role obligations," which bind because of one's occupation of an institutional role, from (a) obligations arising from group membership (for example, belonging to an ethnic group), (b) obligations deriving from practices (for example, promising), and (c) obligations flowing from relationships (for example, friendship) (335–36). My own view is that the relevant concepts here – institution, group, practice, and relationship – are far too vague and overlapping to permit any hard distinctions of the sort Hardimon apparently favors. Is it clear that familial obligations derive from institutional roles, rather than from membership in a group, from a relationship, or from a practice?

"standard view" of institutional obligations is "standard" for a very good reason, namely, that it is true.

Hardimon's version of the "standard view" of role obligations could more precisely be called a (very simple) "voluntarist" view. We have, according to this view, only those institutional obligations which we have freely promised or contracted to perform. Institutional obligations which are simply imposed on us (or to which we are born) have no moral force at all. Hardimon rightly notes that this simple voluntarist view is too simple, for there are many ways in which we can voluntarily accept or agree to fill our institutional roles which do not look very much like promises or contracts. Acceptance can be temporally extended rather than a discrete act, and it can be tacit rather than explicit (356–57). Indeed, I would argue that a voluntarist should allow further that we may have moral obligations to perform the tasks attached to our institutional roles even where we have not strictly "accepted" those *roles* at all, but have only freely accepted the *benefits* provided by the schemes within which those roles are defined. Thus, one might have an obligation of fairness to do one's part within a cooperative scheme from which one has willingly benefited, where "doing one's part" consists precisely in performing the tasks attached to an institutionally defined role.

Suppose, then, that we have before us the most sophisticated voluntarist view of institutional obligations, one that incorporates these (and perhaps other) suggestions. Hardimon will still object to this improved version for two reasons. First, and most obviously, the standard view, even in this more sophisticated form, must reject an idea to which "most of us are committed," namely, that we have genuine (that is, moral) but nonvoluntary role obligations "within the family and the state" (362–63).[3] Second, Hardimon claims, any voluntarist view is defective for failing to recognize "the phenomenon of role identification"; people typically perform their role obligations because they identify with their roles, not simply because they feel obligated to do so by the fact of their morally binding voluntary performances (361).

---

3 Hardimon actually says only that the standard view fails to account for noncontractual role obligations that most of us accept. But since (as we have seen) with only minor modifications the standard view could answer this objection (by simply allowing for voluntarily assumed but not literally contractual role obligations), I assume that Hardimon actually intends the stronger claim – that most of us believe there are nonvoluntary (not just noncontractual) role obligations for which any essentially voluntarist view cannot account.

I shall return momentarily to Hardimon's concerns about the standard view. Here, I want to mention a deeper concern about it. The "standard view" Hardimon discusses, even in its more sophisticated form, is, I think, not really a view to which many thoughtful theorists subscribe (nor does Hardimon ever seem to mention any actual proponents of it). It is, in short, not the "standard view" of institutional obligations at all. I say this because it is clear that even those (like myself) who are broadly sympathetic to voluntarist approaches to, say, political obligation or parental responsibility, almost always still acknowledge that not all our moral duties and obligations are voluntarily assumed. We have general, nonvoluntary duties that bind us simply because we are persons – natural duties "not to murder, lie, or coerce," for instance (340, 343). And all but the strictest libertarians among us allow as well that some of these nonvoluntary moral duties require positive performances of us (and not simply forbearances) – for instance, promoting justice or equality or happiness, making charitable donations or otherwise assisting others, and so on. But positive moral duties of this sort may sometimes require us to perform the obligations attached to various institutional roles. Effectively promoting justice or happiness may require us to operate within and abide by the rules of some institutional arrangement. Fulfilling our duties to assist others may, because of problems of coordination and information, require us to fill roles within institutionalized programs of assistance to the needy. Indeed, the simple fact of the salience of institutional options for discharging some of our moral duties may sometimes render these options the means by which those duties can be most fully discharged. On most moral theories, then, institutional obligations may be morally binding even where there is no voluntary undertaking (like "signing on") that ties one to the relevant institutions. It is general, nonvoluntary natural duty that sometimes provides the link, not special, voluntary obligation.

If that is true, then the "standard view" of role obligations cannot be as simple – or as simple to defeat – as the view presented as "standard" by Hardimon. The standard view should instead be characterized as follows: we are morally required to perform the "obligations" attached to our institutionally assigned roles only if either (a) we have performed morally obligating voluntary acts (or series of acts) that require us so to perform, or (b) the way that we can most fully discharge a natural moral duty is by acting in some institutional capacity. The key to *this* understanding of the "standard view" of institutional obligations is not, as in Hardimon's version, the idea of voluntary acceptance. The key is rather the idea of *external justifi-*

cation.[4] We are morally obligated to perform our institutionally assigned "obligations" only when this is required by a moral rule (or principle) that is not itself a rule of the institution in question. Institutions, in short, are not normatively independent, and the existence of an institutional "obligation" is, considered by itself, a morally neutral fact.[5] Institutional obligations acquire moral force only by being required by external moral rules. This, I believe, is the "standard view" of institutional obligations against which Hardimon's case really ought to be directed. It is also the view that is, in my opinion, correct.

Hardimon is curiously indirect in addressing these questions of external justification and normative independence. He seems initially to deny the need for external justification, both in his definition of a role obligation – where he asserts (as we have seen) that a role obligation is a moral requirement "whose normative force flows from the role" – and in his distinction between normative force "flowing from roles" and its deriving from a principle (335). But later it becomes clear that Hardimon cannot really mean that all role obligations are "internally" justified by the existence of "normatively forceful" institutional roles, since he seems to allow that voluntary acceptance is sometimes what grounds such obligations. Perhaps, then, he means only that noncontractual role obligations require no external justification. But his analysis of noncontractual role obligations eventually arrives at the idea that these are morally binding only when "the roles to which they attach are *reflectively acceptable*" (350, my emphasis). This amounts to a kind of weak, hypothetical contractualist standard for the bindingness of noncontractual role obligations.[6] More important, it seems that it must amount as well to an admission of the need for external justification of even noncontractual institutional obligations. For if their reflective acceptability is not what justifies these roles and obligations, there would seem to be nothing morally interesting about them which could

---

4 For a brief discussion of what I here call "external justification" of institutional obligations, see John Horton, *Political Obligation* (Atlantic Highlands, NJ: Humanities, 1992), pp. 155–58.
5 I defended this position at greater length in *Moral Principles and Political Obligations* (Princeton: Princeton University Press, 1979), pp. 16–23. See also Michael Stocker, "Moral Duties, Institutions, and Natural Facts," *The Monist*, LIV (October 1970): 602–24.
6 It is a "weak" standard because of its apparent "subjectivity" (348). Hardimon seems to have in mind appealing here to what is "reflectively acceptable" to each individual person, rather than to what would be acceptable to, say, a fully rational person, unimpaired by various kinds of prejudices, prejudicing knowledge, or vices. This apparently leaves the content of the "reflectively acceptable" quite open and relative to individuals. Oddly, Hardimon conjoins this "subjective" account of the acceptable with an apparently objective account of the just, ruling out role obligations arising within unjust institutions (344).

serve to distinguish them from those role obligations which require our voluntary choices to bind us to them. While Hardimon does not himself put the point this way, he might fairly be read as asserting a general (external) moral duty (at least within the "spheres" of family and state) to perform reflectively acceptable institutional "obligations."[7]

Perhaps, then, Hardimon does not really oppose the spirit of our newly characterized "standard view." On the other hand, he does argue that the voluntarist portion of this standard view is defective for overlooking the "absolutely vital factor" of "role identification." A voluntarist view is said to imply, for instance, "that the only reason doctors do the things that doctors do is that they have promised or agreed to do those things – that they never do them simply because they are doctors. It also suggests, more generally, that people are indifferent to the norms associated with their roles . . ." (361). When we appreciate the fact that people often identify with their institutional roles and that this identification gives them reason to perform the associated role obligations, Hardimon claims, we shall see that voluntarism "conveys a distorted picture of our relation to our roles" (361).

Now, this criticism of voluntarism (and of the voluntarist portion of our new "standard view") seems to me a non sequitur. Voluntarist analyses of institutional obligations are attempts to explain how a moral requirement to perform institutionally imposed tasks can be *grounded* or *justified*. They are not attempts to explain the motivations of those who occupy institutional roles. Doctors may do their institutional duties for many reasons, ranging from simple concern for the well-being of their patients to the desire for financial reward, and including both a consideration for their voluntary "oaths" and their identification with the role of doctor. Voluntarism is no more "defective" for "leaving out" the idea of role identification than it is defective for "leaving out" the idea of financial incentives. It in fact "leaves out" neither, since it is perfectly neutral on the subject of why people in fact perform their role obligations. It is instead only a theory about why (and when) people are morally bound to perform.[8]

---

7 While Hardimon tries to distance his account of role obligations from Ronald Dworkin's account of "associative obligations," the position to which Hardimon comes on institutional obligations is not unlike the one to which Dworkin comes on group obligations. For Dworkin asserts a general "natural duty" to "honor our responsibilities under social practices that define groups and attach special responsibilities to membership," where these groups are reasonably just and otherwise acceptable – *Law's Empire* (Cambridge: Harvard, 1986), pp. 198–204.

8 Similarly, a voluntarist account of parental duties might ground those in the deliberate creations of needy beings (by some parents) and in the voluntary performance of acts that

It may seem that Hardimon must have in mind that role identification is somehow relevant to the ground of role obligations, so that his criticism of the voluntarist view would not turn out to be a simple non sequitur. But Hardimon cannot consistently maintain that role identification is important to understanding the ground of role obligations. For his various claims entail that identification with one's institutional role is neither necessary nor sufficient for being morally bound to perform the obligations attached to that role. We know that role identification cannot be *sufficient* for role obligation because sometimes "people *should not* identify with their roles," and because "unless the institution from which a putative role obligation derives is just, the obligation does not bind" (361, 344; my emphasis).[9] We know that role identification cannot be *necessary* for role obligation on Hardimon's view because he allows that one "might voluntarily accept the cluster of duties associated with the role of doctor and yet refuse to identify with this role," and because when a "role is reflectively acceptable, its obligations bind me whether I reflect or not" (359, 351).[10] So I cannot escape my institutionally imposed role obligations simply by refusing to identify with my roles or by refusing to reflect on the acceptability of those roles. Role identification, it seems, has nothing much to do with the ground or justification of role obligations even on Hardimon's view, just as on the voluntarist's view.

How then can Hardimon's account substantially depart from the spirit of our newly characterized "standard view"? Hardimon stresses, of course, that "most of us are committed to" the existence of morally binding but nonvoluntarily acquired role obligations (at least within the spheres of

have such creation as a possible consequence (by other parents). Such a voluntarist analysis, while perhaps defective, is surely not defective simply because it fails to mention the actual motives parents have for caring for their children – for example, the fact that most parents act out of *love* for their children, not out of a sense of duty. Indeed, in this case role identification obviously comes no closer to being the central or definitive motive for parental activity than does parents' sense of their voluntarily assumed duties.

9 Hardimon at times writes as if role identification is sufficient for role obligation, as when he asserts that such identification gives one "a *moral* reason" to perform one's role obligations (362; my emphasis). But given that people can identify with their roles in unjust institutions, and given that role obligations are in such cases "void *ab initio*" (350), Hardimon simply cannot mean what his remarks might suggest.

10 Many of us "regard our social roles as 'external' to who we are" (345). Hardimon does say that "the appeal to the fact that a person occupies a particular role can fail . . . if the person does not identify with her role" (361). But he seems there to mean not that such a person as a result lacks the assigned role obligations, but only that role identification will obviously not, in such a case, provide the person with a reason for performing her role obligations. ("In such a case we would be better served by saying 'but you signed on for this job'" (361).)

family and state). But, even leaving aside the frailty of appeals to what "most of us are committed to,"[11] we have seen that the view of institutional obligations that seems genuinely "standard" also allows that we may have such nonvoluntary role obligations – for instance, when an "external" moral duty requires us to assist others by performing institutionalized duties of charity, or requires us to reciprocate for certain uncovenanted benefits by playing an appropriate institutional role. So neither Hardimon's focus on role identification nor his emphasis on nonvoluntary role obligations appears to distance his account interestingly from a genuinely standard view of institutional obligations.

Perhaps the true distance is in other dimensions of Hardimon's view. For example, Hardimon's use of the standard of "reflective acceptability" for validating noncontractual role obligations seems to amount to a much weaker requirement than the (newly characterized) standard view's requirement that some external duty mandate the performance of the role obligations. Judging that a social role is reflectively acceptable – "that it is (in some sense) meaningful, rational, or good" (348) – seems far less demanding than showing that performing that role's obligations is the best way to discharge an externally justified moral duty. Arguing for the former claim seems to amount to showing only that the role is *permissible*, while arguing for the standard view's condition amounts to showing that fulfilling the role is *required*.

We might suppose this is a contrast Hardimon would wish to press, for he clearly wants to defend a position that makes institutional norms more "independent" or "self-justifying" than they would appear to be on the standard view. And the weaker the "external" condition for validating such norms, the more independent those norms would seem to be. But we should certainly want to ask Hardimon why the weaker condition – the mere "acceptability" or permissibility of an institutional role – should be thought morally sufficient for the nonvoluntary imposition of a role's associated obligations on unwilling recipients. There are many things it might

---

11 "Most of us" might, of course, suffer from certain kinds of "false consciousness" in the realm of moral "intuition." Political rulers and parents, for instance, both have very strong self-interested reasons for inculcating in subjects and children (respectively) a commitment to nonvoluntary role obligations (of obedience and support). For that reason, even a pure voluntarist position on the state and the family seems far from crazy. A pure voluntarist would argue that (a) institutional "political obligations" (of obedience and support) are morally binding only if voluntarily assumed; and (b) the moral obligations of parents are all grounded in their voluntary acts (see footnote 7 above), while filial obligations are largely fictitious (given the moral responsibility of parents for creating the filial needs that parental benefactions satisfy).

be (in some sense) good to have, that it would certainly not be good to impose on people without their having any choice in the matter. It would be "(in some sense) meaningful, rational, or good" if people (or some people) occupied assigned roles requiring them to spend their time beautifying neighborhoods, discovering and promoting underappreciated artists, and so on. But few of us would be likely to regard as morally legitimate the nonvoluntary institutional assignment of such role "obligations" to the unwilling. The ends at issue, while good "(in some sense)," are not, as it were, good enough to impose that kind of limit on our moral liberty. The standard view's requirement that there be a moral duty at issue if we are to be unwillingly bound to role obligations (by contrast with Hardimon's weak condition of the mere acceptability or permissibility of the role) can be read as an attempt to ensure that only freely chosen or morally imperative institutional roles will impose on us genuine moral constraints.

It might seem that Hardimon in effect acknowledges this point; for he defends (in Hegelian terms) a distinction between the conditions for role obligations within the various "spheres" of civil society,[12] the family, and the state. "Within civil society the only way in which morally binding role obligations can be acquired is by signing on for the roles from which they derive. . . . Actual choice . . . is not required for obligation within the family and the state. Within these spheres, noncontractual role obligations may be morally binding if they are reflectively acceptable" (353). One might, cynically, read this simply as a conservative effort to applaud the imposition of role obligations in those areas of our lives in which role obligations are most forcefully imposed by the most (physically or emotionally) irresistible superiors. But one might also read Hardimon's distinction as an attempt to ensure that institutions are only morally free to have their way with us in those "spheres" where our "deepest and most important" duties are at issue (353). The performance of the institutional duties of citizens and family members, at least where these duties are derived from acceptable versions of those roles, seem vital to securing a decent existence for both individuals and societies.

If that is true, however, it is not the fact that our political and familial roles are merely "acceptable" – "(in some sense) meaningful, rational, or good" – that justifies the nonvoluntary imposition on us of their associated role obligations. Nor is it the fact that these are concrete roles about which

---

12 "Civil society" includes for Hardimon "the marketplace" and "the network of voluntary associations" like "unions, professional associations, private clubs, social movements, and neighborhoods" (352).

we feel strongly. Institutional roles in civil society (for example, doctor or civil rights activist) may also be acceptable in this way and may also be supported by strong feelings; but Hardimon refuses to accept their non-voluntary imposition. What distinguishes the nonvoluntary imposition of *political and familial* role obligations from the nonvoluntary imposition of *civil society's* role obligations for Hardimon must be the morally imperative character of the former obligations, derivable from the (externally certified) moral importance of the tasks those role obligations require us to discharge. If that is true, however, we can expect that performing the former role obligations will be the way some of our external moral duties can be most fully discharged. And that, remember, is the (new) standard view's condition for the moral force of nonvoluntary role obligations, not Hardimon's weaker condition.

My conclusion is that in this respect, as in the other areas we have explored, where Hardimon's account of role obligations in fact departs from the (newly characterized) standard view, it fares badly. Many of Hardimon's apparent departures, however, turn out to be apparent only. The version of the "standard view" Hardimon attacks is a view held by few and a view too weak to put up a very good fight. The "standard view" that I have here defended, the view that Hardimon ought to be addressing, seems in the end unscathed by any of Hardimon's arguments.

6

PHILOSOPHICAL ANARCHISM

Anarchist political philosophers normally include in their theories (or implicitly rely on) a vision of a social life very different from the life experienced by most persons today. Theirs is a vision of autonomous, noncoercive, productive interaction among equals, liberated from and without need for distinctively political institutions, such as formal legal systems or governments or the state. This positive part of anarchist theories, this vision of the good social life, is discussed only indirectly in this essay. Rather, I focus here on the negative side of anarchism, on its general critique of the state or its more limited critique of the specific kinds of political arrangements within which most residents of modern political societies live. Even more specifically, I center my discussion on one particular version of this anarchist critique – the version that is part of the theory now commonly referred to as philosophical anarchism. Philosophical anarchism has been much discussed by political philosophers in recent years,[1] but it has not, I

I would like to thank Nancy Schauber for her insightful comments on earlier drafts of this paper.

1 See, for example, R. P. Wolff, *In Defense of Anarchism* (New York: Harper & Row, 1970); Chaim Gans, *Philosophical Anarchism and Political Disobedience* (Cambridge: Cambridge University Press, 1992), especially chaps. 1 and 2; and John Horton, *Political Obligation* (Atlantic Highlands, N. J.: Humanities Press, 1992), chap. 5. I discuss the sort of philosophical anarchism that I wish to defend in *Moral Principles and Political Obligations* (Princeton: Princeton University Press, 1979), especially chap. 8; "The Anarchist Position," *Philosophy & Public Affairs* 16 (Spring 1987); and *On the Edge of Anarchy* (Princeton: Princeton University Press, 1993), especially section 8.4. Others, besides Wolff and myself, who are frequently identified as defenders of some form of philosophical anarchism (though almost none of them describe their positions in that language) include M. B. E. Smith, "Is There a Prima Facie Obligation to Obey the Law?" *Yale Law Journal* 82 (1973); Joseph Raz, "The Obligation to

think, been very carefully defined or adequately understood. My object here is to clear the ground for a fair evaluation of philosophical anarchism by offering a more systematic account of the nature of the theory and of possible variants of the theory and by responding to the most frequent objections to the theory. I hope by this effort to present philosophical anarchism as a more attractive, or at least a less obviously flawed, political philosophy.

The Illegitimacy of States

Commitment to one central claim unites all forms of anarchist political philosophy: all existing states are illegitimate. I take this thesis to be an essential, if not the defining, element of anarchism.[2] Anarchist commitments to this thesis are usually motivated by prior commitments to volun-

---

Obey the Law," in *The Authority of Law* (New York: Oxford University Press, 1979); Leslie Green, *The Authority of the State* (Oxford: Oxford University Press, 1988); Donald Regan, "Law's Halo," *Social Philosophy & Policy* (Autumn 1986); A. D. Woozley, *Law and Disobedience* (London: Duckworth, 1979); David Lyons, "Need, Necessity, and Political Obligation," *Virginia Law Review* (February 1981); and Joel Feinberg, "Civil Disobedience in the Modern World," *Humanities in Society* 2 (1979). Other general discussions and/or defenses of philosophical anarchism can be found in Jeffrey Reiman, *In Defense of Political Philosophy* (New York: Harper & Row, 1972); M. B. E. Smith, "The Obligation to Obey the Law: Revision or Explanation?" *Criminal Justice Ethics* (Summer/Fall 1989): 60–70; Vicente Medina, *Social Contract Theories* (Lanham, Md.: Rowman & Littlefield, 1990), 150–52; and Michael Menlowe, "Political Obligation," in R. Bellamy, ed., *Theories and Concepts of Politics* (Manchester, U. K.: Manchester University Press, 1993), 174–96.

2 Four qualifications need to be added here: (1) As we will see shortly, anarchists agree on the truth of this thesis but differ about whether the thesis is necessarily or only contingently true. (2) Some theories that probably should be called anarchist by association hold only that virtually all states are illegitimate. (3) How one defines *state* here is obviously a matter of great controversy, especially within anarchist theory. Some prefer to substitute *governments* or *political societies* in their versions of this thesis. Others think that governments or political authorities of certain sorts may be acceptable where *the state* is not. The vagueness on these scores of the thesis, as I have presented it here, should not affect the force of the discussion that follows, and a certain amount of vagueness is necessary, in any event, to give any very general account of the range of theories usually called *anarchist*. (4) Some prefer to describe anarchism as a view about political obligation. Horton, for instance, characterizes anarchism as "a theory or doctrine which rejects the possibility of any morally persuasive general theory of political obligation" (*Political Obligation*, 109). Gans does the same (*Philosophical Anarchism*, 2). I suspect that Horton, at least, intends this account not so much as a generally adequate account of anarchism, but rather only as one adequate for the limited aims of his discussion. I suggest in the text below that while anarchism's denial of state legitimacy entails the denial of political obligation, this former denial is taken by many anarchists to have more far-reaching moral consequences than the mere denial of political obligation.

tarism (to the great moral importance of autonomy or free choice or self-determination, etc.), with existing states then characterized as fundamentally nonvoluntary or coercive;[3] to egalitarianism (to equal rights or equal opportunities or equal access to basic goods, etc.), with existing states then characterized as fundamentally hierarchical, sexist, classist, or otherwise inegalitarian;[4] to the values of community (to the great moral importance of shared ends or feelings of solidarity or sympathy, etc.), with existing states then characterized as alienating or divisive;[5] or to some combination of these positions. Anarchist theories may also be motivated by the perception of inadequacies in all purported defenses of state legitimacy without the necessity of their making any prior commitment to particular values (which the state is seen as frustrating). That is, some anarchisms are driven by a general skepticism about the possibility of providing any argument that shows some or all existing states to be legitimate – a skepticism perhaps taken to be justified simply by the systematic failure of political philosophy to this point to produce any good argument of this sort.

Philosophical anarchism, as a form of anarchism, is of course committed to the central anarchist thesis of state illegitimacy, and, like other kinds of anarchism, philosophical anarchism generally is motivated either by the kinds of commitments or by the kind of skepticism I have just summarized. What is distinctive about philosophical anarchism, I suggest, is its stance with respect to the moral content (or practical force) of judgments about state illegitimacy. Philosophical anarchists do not take the illegitimacy of states to entail a strong moral imperative to oppose or eliminate states; rather, they typically take state illegitimacy simply to remove any strong moral presumption in favor of obedience to, compliance with, or support for our own or other existing states. To make plain the structure of this position, I propose to provide a reasonably general view of the possible range of anarchist positions by specifying certain distinctions along which anarchist positions divide. I do not pretend that the divisions I describe are exhaustive, but I do think that they are the most salient and important divisions.

Perhaps the most basic division between anarchist theories (and also between philosophical anarchist theories) is that between what I call a

---

3 See, e.g., Wolff, *In Defense of Anarchism*, chap. 1.
4 See, e.g., Kai Nielsen, "State Authority and Legitimation," in P. Harris, ed., *On Political Obligation* (London: Routledge, 1990).
5 See, e.g., Peter Kropotkin, *Mutual Aid* (London: Heinemann, 1910), and *The Conquest of Bread* (New York: Vanguard, 1926).

priori anarchism and a posteriori anarchism. A priori anarchism maintains that all possible states are morally illegitimate. Some essential feature of the state or some necessary condition for statehood – say, the state's coercive character or its hierarchical nature – makes it impossible for there to be something that is both a state and legitimate.[6] A posteriori anarchism, by contrast, maintains that while all existing states are illegitimate, this is not because it is impossible for there to be a legitimate state. Nothing in the definition of the state precludes its legitimacy;[7] rather, existing states are condemned as illegitimate by virtue of their contingent characters. A posteriori anarchists may defend an ideal of legitimacy that existing states simply fail to live up to or approximate – for instance, a voluntarist or egalitarian or communitarian ideal of the state – or they simply may be unconvinced by purported a priori arguments for the impossibility of the legitimate state.[8]

6 Wolff's version of philosophical anarchism is a good example of a priori anarchism. Wolff sometimes maintains that the authority that states must exercise in order to be states is inconsistent with the autonomy of individuals that any legitimate state would have to respect. "Hence, the concept of a *de jure* legitimate state would appear to be vacuous" (*In Defense of Anarchism*, 19). Some authors seem mistakenly to identify philosophical anarchism (or anarchism generally) with a priori versions of it. Stephen Nathanson, for instance, characterizes anarchism as the view that "governmental authority is always illegitimate" (*Should We Consent to be Governed?* [Belmont: Wadsworth, 1992], 57); and David Miller's arguments against what he calls philosophical anarchism are really only arguments against those, like Wolff, who find "the very idea of legitimate authority incoherent" (*Anarchism* [London: J. M. Dent & Sons, 1984], 15–16, 29).

7 With the exception of Wolff, all of the defenders of philosophical anarchism listed in footnote 1 (myself included) seem to defend its central thesis as an a posteriori judgment.

8 Other recent discussions of philosophical anarchism gesture at this distinction between a priori and a posteriori anarchism, sometimes in unfortunate ways. Gans, for instance, distinguishes "autonomy-based" anarchism (according to which "it follows from the very meaning of [the duty to obey the law], that its acknowledgement entails a surrender of moral autonomy") from "critical" anarchism ("the denial of the duty to obey the law which is based on a rejection of its grounds") (*Philosophical Anarchism*, 2), but autonomy-based arguments are, as we have seen, only one kind of a priori anarchist approach, with appeals to equality or community, for instance, as clear and familiar alternatives; so these latter approaches are simply excluded by Gans's classifications. Also, Gans's characterization of critical anarchism is sufficiently general to cover any kind of anarchism (every anarchist denies political obligation by denying its grounds). Horton employs a different and more useful distinction between "positive" philosophical anarchism (which "offers a positive argument of its own as to why there are not, and could not be, any political obligations") and "negative" philosophical anarchism (which "simply concludes from the failure of all positive attempts to justify political obligation that there is no such obligation") (*Political Obligation*, 124). Horton's "positive" anarchism appears to be more or less what I have called a priori anarchism, but his "negative" anarchism plainly needs more careful definition, after which it will approach my a posteriori anarchism. "The failure of all positive attempts" is only a reason (let alone a good reason) to reject political obligation if one also believes

Within the class of a posteriori anarchisms we can distinguish theories most fundamentally according to the ideals of legitimacy, if any, that they profess and also according to the optimism that they display about the possibility of realizing the ideal in the actual political world and the distance of the ideal from the actual state of affairs in some or all political societies. Most a posteriori anarchists, of course, are not very optimistic about soon realizing their ideals (if they defend any), nor are their ideals very close to any existing modern political society; indeed, anarchists who are either very optimistic about soon realizing their ideals or who regard the real political world as a reasonably close approximation of their ideals of political legitimacy should be thought of as anarchists in only the most nominal or technical sense.

Whether anarchists defend their central thesis of state illegitimacy as an a priori or an a posteriori judgment, they must defend as well some analysis of the idea of illegitimacy, that is, some position on the moral content of judgments of state illegitimacy. What, for instance, does a judgment of state illegitimacy imply about our rights and obligations with respect to the state? While there are, of course, many senses of *legitimate* and *illegitimate* that we employ in discussing states and governments,[9] the view that probably deserves to be called the traditional view of state or governmental legitimacy holds that legitimacy consists in a certain, normally limited kind of authority or right to make binding law and state policy. State legitimacy or authority is viewed as the logical correlate of the obligation of citizens to obey the law and to in other ways support the state, that is, to the obligation that is usually referred to as political obligation.[10] Most anarchists have embraced something like this traditional conception of state legitimacy, with the consequence that anarchist judgments of state illegitimacy typically are taken to entail that subjects of those illegitimate states have no

---

that these positive attempts add up to a complete or comprehensive attempt (refuting a handful of miserable, silly, half-hearted, or obviously incomplete positive efforts to show that X clearly gives one no reason to believe not-X). "Negative" anarchist arguments thus need to be based either in an ideal of legitimacy (which existing states can be shown not to exemplify) or in some account of what an acceptably complete positive attempt would look like.

9 See, e.g., my *Moral Principles and Political Obligations*, 40–41, 58, 197.

10 It is, of course, now reasonably common for theorists to attempt to deny this traditional (and, I think, perfectly acceptable) correlativity doctrine, defending judgments of state legitimacy and judgments of citizens' political obligations by means of quite different kinds of arguments. For one particularly clear example of such a strategy, see Jeffrey Reiman, *In Defense of Political Philosophy*, xxv, 18, 23, 42–44 (though even Reiman allows that the traditional correlativity doctrine captures "common usage" of the language of legitimacy [pp. 53–54]).

political obligations. These subjects are, of course, still bound by their nonpolitical moral obligations and duties, and these nonpolitical duties will sometimes have the same substance as the subjects' legal requirements. Subjects have no political obligation, however, to obey the law because it is law or to support the political leaders or institutions that try to compel their allegiance.

This, we may say, is the minimum moral content of anarchist judgments of state illegitimacy: the subjects of illegitimate states have no political obligations. We can then define weak anarchism as the position that asserts no more than this minimum content. Weak anarchism is the view that there are no general political obligations, that all (or, at least, virtually all) subjects of all states are at moral liberty to (i.e., possess a privilege or permission right to) treat laws as nonbinding and governments as nonauthoritative. What we can call strong anarchism also accepts this minimum moral content of judgments of state illegitimacy, but strong anarchists hold in addition that a state's illegitimacy further entails a moral obligation or duty to oppose and, so far as it is within our power, eliminate the state.[11] This obligation can be taken to bind either the subjects of the illegitimate state or persons generally; so where weak anarchism says that we may regard the state as one more powerful bully whose commands and actions we may ignore where we can, strong anarchism argues that all such bullies must be deprived of their power to coerce. Weak anarchists, of course, may also hold that on independent grounds some or all states should be opposed and eliminated, but for the weak anarchist, any such obligation is grounded in factors beyond the mere illegitimacy of the states in question. How strong a strong anarchist position is will depend on how weighty or imperative the obligation to oppose the state is taken to be.[12]

This last point plainly raises a second kind of question about the moral

---

11 Strong anarchists may treat this obligation as a uniform threshold obligation or as an obligation that varies in content with the extent of illegitimacy. In the former case, any state that crossed over the threshold of illegitimacy would thereby impose on us an obligation with uniform content to oppose it, regardless of how extensively illegitimate it was. In the latter case, the extent or nature of our obligation to oppose the state would be taken to vary with the extent of its illegitimacy. Illegitimate states are not necessarily equally illegitimate; some may be worse than others and so may require us to more actively (or in some other way differently) oppose them.

12 Some moral obligations – such as the obligation to keep a relatively insignificant promise to meet a friend for coffee – are obviously quite trivial; others – such as the promissory or contractual obligation of a paid nurse to care for a critically ill patient – are clearly not at all trivial. Strong anarchists who nonetheless regard the obligation to oppose the state as relatively trivial weaken their position to the point where it becomes in practice indistinguishable from weak anarchism.

content of anarchist judgments of state illegitimacy: how are we to understand the weight of the rights and obligations said to be entailed by such
judgments? Here there seems to be nothing distinctive about anarchist
views. Anarchists treat questions of moral weight or finality in the same
range of ways that other moral and political philosophers do. At least two
clearly opposed positions on these questions need to be distinguished. An
anarchist can treat the relevant obligations to oppose the state and rights
to treat law as nonbinding as immediately implying final or absolute moral
judgments, or the anarchist may treat these obligations and rights as possibly defeasible moral reasons, understood as these would be within what
I will call a balance-of-reasons view.

On the first approach, to say that there is an obligation to oppose the
state is to say that there is final, conclusive moral reason so to act. The
obligation's weight is overriding or absolute with respect to competing
considerations (i.e., those supporting nonopposition, if any). To say
also that there is a right to treat the law as nonbinding is to say that no
further justification for so treating the law need ever be given. One's rights
trump competing considerations (i.e., those supporting compliance,
if any).

On the second, balance-of-reasons approach, obligations and rights are
treated as strong but variably weighted and certainly not conclusive reasons
for action. Obligations and rights may on this view conflict with and possibly be outweighed by other obligations or rights, or they may conflict with
and be outweighed by reasons for action of other sorts. Strong enough prudential reasons for action, for instance, may override weak obligations, just
as strong enough reasons grounded in the happiness of others may render
unjustifiable our acting on the weak rights that we possess. In short, the
finality or imperativeness of rights or obligations is, on the balance-of-
reasons approach, very much a function of the context within which the
rights or obligations are exercised.[13]

Defining Philosophical Anarchism

We are now, I think, in a position to see more clearly what is and what is
not distinctive about philosophical anarchism. Like other anarchists, philosophical anarchists can defend their central judgments about state illegiti-

---

13 For further discussion of these two views of the weight or finality of judgments of obligation, or right, see my *Moral Principles and Political Obligations*, 7–11, and *The Lockean Theory
of Rights* (Princeton: Princeton University Press, 1992), 93–95, 111–12.

macy on either a priori or a posteriori grounds and, like others, they take this judgment to entail the nonexistence of general political obligations – that is, the removal of any moral presumption in favor of compliance with and support for the state. What is distinctive about philosophical anarchism is that its judgment of state illegitimacy (even of necessary state illegitimacy) does not translate into any immediate requirement of opposition to illegitimate states. This is what leads many to contrast philosophical anarchism to political anarchism.

Philosophical anarchists hold that there may be good moral reasons not to oppose or disrupt at least some kinds of illegitimate states, reasons that outweigh any right or obligation of opposition. The practical stance with respect to the state, the philosophical anarchist maintains, should be one of careful consideration and thoughtful weighing of all of the reasons that bear on action in a particular set of political circumstances. The illegitimacy of a state (and the absence of binding political obligations that it entails) is just one moral factor among many bearing on how persons in that state should (or are permitted to) act. Even illegitimate states, for instance, may have virtues, unaffected by the defects that undermine their legitimacy, that are relevant considerations in determining how we ought to act with respect to those states, and the refusal to do what the law requires is, at least in most (even illegitimate) states, often wrong on independent moral grounds (i.e., the conduct would be wrong even were it not legally forbidden). So there may be a variety of sound moral reasons not to oppose or not to act contrary to the laws of even some illegitimate states.

What does this mean in terms of the distinctions drawn in the first section of this essay? It means, first, that philosophical anarchists must reject the view of obligations and rights as final moral reasons and accept some version of the balance-of-reasons approach, for if the permission right entailed by the absence of political obligations is seen as providing a final justification for disregarding or opposing law and government, no moral reason for supporting a government or complying with a law could ever outweigh our permission right – and this, I am claiming, is one thing philosophical anarchists wish to deny. Second, philosophical anarchists must embrace either what I call weak anarchism or else a version of strong anarchism that takes the obligation to oppose the state to be a relatively weak obligation. Otherwise, of course, they will be committed to a moral obligation of opposition to illegitimate states that will be likely to outweigh any competing reasons for nonopposition or compliance, even within the best illegitimate states. This, again, is a position that philosophical anarchists wish to avoid. What is distinctive about philosophical anarchism, then, is chiefly its position on the weight or finality of the moral obligations and rights entailed by judgments of state illegitimacy.

Can philosophical anarchism intelligibly deny in this way the connection between, on the one hand, the illegitimacy of the state and the absence of political obligation and, on the other hand, a strong obligation or right to oppose and try to eliminate the state? I think it is clear that it can. A state's being illegitimate means that it lacks the general right to make binding law and policy for its subjects (it lacks political authority), and it means that the state's subjects lack the correlative general political obligation to support and comply with it. This by itself, however, entails neither that the state could have no right to command (and citizens no obligation to obey) on some particular occasion nor that the state could have no moral justification for its actions in particular cases (based on moral reasons unrelated to any strict right to act), nor does it entail that citizens, simply because they lack general political obligations, have strong or conclusive rights to oppose the state or act contrary to its legal requirements. Our general duties to our fellow citizens qua persons, our general duties to promote justice and other values, and our other, nonduty moral reasons to treat others well will all often be good reasons not to disrupt the state's functioning or to act contrary to its laws.[14] Within many decent, but still illegitimate, states, serious (e.g., revolutionary) opposition to the state or regular conduct contrary to its laws simply will not be morally justifiable on balance.

To this point, I have been concerned primarily to clarify what philosophical anarchists must say if their position is to be distinctive in the way its primary defenders have wished it to be and if their position is to be at all plausible. Let me add now a few words about what philosophical anarchists should say if they wish their position to be not just distinctive and initially plausible, but also correct. Philosophical anarchists should, in my view, defend their theory, first, as a form of a posteriori anarchism and, second, as a form of weak anarchism.

While it is not possible to show (without presenting a complete defense of an ideal of state legitimacy) that no form of a priori anarchism could be successful, it is hard on the face of things to see how a convincing a priori case could be made by the anarchist. If the anarchist values autonomy or free choice, for instance, it is hard to see why a possible ideal state that promotes or respects these values could not be described. A fully voluntary,

---

14 For a fuller presentation of these lines of argument, see my "The Anarchist Position," especially pp. 275–79.

genuinely contractual democracy could be rejected as an ideal on such voluntarist grounds, it seems, only if the voluntarist anarchist was also prepared to deny the legitimacy of the ordinary practice of promising – on the ground, say, that promissory obligations objectionably constrain freedom, despite their being freely undertaken. This seems too high a price to pay, as R. P. Wolff's failed attempt to defend a voluntarist a priori anarchism clearly shows.[15] Similarly, if the anarchist values equality or community, say, it is hard to believe that a strict egalitarian state, or the kind of state favored by strict communitarians, could not be defended in those terms as an ideal of political legitimacy. If the anarchist argument is only that actual states have never even approximated (and likely never will approximate) these voluntarist, egalitarian, or communitarian ideals, the argument seems persuasive, but that argument is perfectly consistent with a posteriori anarchism. The a priori anarchist must argue not just that there never has been and never will be a legitimate state, but also for the more dramatic and less plausible claim that such a state is not even possible. In anarchist writings such claims have often (mistakenly, in my view) had to be based on assuming that the forms that all modern states have taken provide us with the proper definitional content of the term *state*.[16]

As for my preference for weak over strong anarchism, I have argued already that even if philosophical anarchism is defended as a strong theory,

---

15 Wolff, it seems, cannot bring himself to deny that promises or contracts are morally binding, with the result that in the end he concedes that "a contractual democracy is legitimate, to be sure, for it is founded upon the citizens' promise to obey its commands. Indeed, any state is legitimate which is founded upon such a promise" (*In Defense of Anarchism*, 69), but this, of course, directly contradicts his earlier a priori claim that "the concept of a *de jure* legitimate state would appear to be vacuous" (p. 19). Contractual democracies, on Wolff's view, are legitimate states, but they gain their legitimacy through their citizens' sacrifice of their autonomy. Perhaps this introduces a second notion of "legitimacy*" in Wolff ("legitimate*" states would be those that reconcile citizen autonomy and state authority), and perhaps it is only the concept of the "legitimate*" state that is vacuous, but it is hard to understand how a theorist committed to the importance of autonomy could intelligibly claim both that all promises are morally binding *and* that some promises (i.e., political ones) objectionably sacrifice autonomy. For further difficulties in Wolff's arguments, see Reiman, *In Defense of Political Philosophy*; Keith Graham, "Democracy and the Autonomous Moral Agent," in K. Graham, ed., *Political Philosophy: Radical Studies* (Cambridge: Cambridge University Press, 1982), 113–37; Gans, *Philosophical Anarchism*, 10–41; and Horton, *Political Obligation*, 124–31.

16 The anarchist argument often then proceeds by maintaining that while no legitimate state is possible, it is possible to have a legitimate large-scale, cooperative, rule-governed association that incorporates positions of rightful authority. To me it seems reasonable to call such an association a state, but nothing of substance turns on the language we choose to use.

it still must accept that the obligation to oppose the state is a relatively weak obligation; but there are good reasons to believe further that the mere illegitimacy of a state entails no such obligations (weak or strong) to oppose it. Only if illegitimacy is taken to be a far more inclusive failing in a state than traditional philosophical analyses of legitimacy imply will it entail a moral obligation to oppose the state, for a state can clearly lack the general right to make binding law and policy without being sufficiently evil that it must be opposed and, if possible, eliminated. This is why the idea of, say, a benevolent dictatorship makes sense; there are at least two conflicting moral characteristics of such a state (benevolence, dictatorship), which makes our assessment of it complex.

I take the legitimacy of a state with respect to me and the other moral qualities of a state to be independent variables, just as I take the right of a business to, say, bill me and the charitableness or efficiency of a business to be independent variables. In both cases, the legitimacy or right is a function of its transactions or relations with me, while its other general qualities need have nothing to do with me at all. The fact that a state or a business has virtues appropriate to it cannot, by itself, argue for its having special rights over me or for my owing it special obligations, nor, of course, do these special rights and obligations, where they exist, necessarily override moral duties to oppose a vicious state. Only if the state also has special relations to me will special rights or obligations of that sort follow. Indeed, even if I had quite general duties to promote states or businesses that exemplified the appropriate virtues, these duties would be owed equally to all such exemplary objects, not specially to any particular one;[17] but insofar as even equally illegitimate states will exemplify the stately virtues in different ways and to different extents, if at all, it cannot be supposed that all illegitimate states should be treated in the same ways by their subjects or by others simply by virtue of their common illegitimacy. Some illegitimate states may be hopelessly evil; others, decent and benevolent (though not, for that, necessarily legitimate with respect to all or any particular citizens).

Three Objections to Philosophical Anarchism

Suppose the philosophical anarchist defends, as I have recommended, a weak, a posteriori anarchism, understanding the weight of the rights this

---

17 They would thus not satisfy what I have elsewhere called the "particularity requirement" for accounts of political obligation (*Moral Principles and Political Obligations*, 31–35, 143–56).

entails from a balance-of-reasons perspective. Are there obvious objections to which the resulting position would be liable? There are none, I think, that are convincing. As a start to showing this, I want to mention here and indicate appropriate responses to the three objections that have been raised in the most prominent recent criticisms of philosophical anarchism.

There are two general lines of attack on philosophical anarchism that may be sensibly pursued by its critics. One, of course, is simply to defend a systematic theory of political obligation and state legitimacy and show that it applies to existing states. In my view, efforts along these lines have uniformly failed, but I will not pursue such questions here. The alternative approach is to try to directly discredit the philosophical anarchist's position – for instance, by showing it to be internally inconsistent or to have unacceptable implications. It is criticisms of this latter sort that I will discuss here.

Objection 1: The Hypocrisy of Philosophical Anarchism

Perhaps the most fully developed of these attacks is that mounted by Chaim Gans in his recent book *Philosophical Anarchism and Political Disobedience*. Gans, like many others, argues, in effect, that philosophical anarchism is not really anarchism at all, that it is a "toothless" theory with an "embarrassing gap" between its "radical look" and its quite "tame" practical implications.[18] Further, Gans maintains that philosophical anarchists draw the intuitive support for their view from focusing "on trivial and esoteric contexts, jaywalking at three o'clock in the morning," while simply conforming to common opinion about the need for obedience in more familiar, everyday contexts.[19] More damning still, Gans's analysis of this move by philosophical anarchists is that while they officially reject the well-known arguments for political obligation (and, on the strength of this rejection, proclaim state illegitimacy), they then implicitly rely on these very same arguments (they "resurrect" them) to maintain that even illegitimate states need not always be disobeyed or disrupted. It would be more honest simply to accept the familiar arguments for obedience to law, Gans suggests, especially once we recognize that accepting political obligation does not mean that obedience to law is always morally required.[20]

---

18 *Philosophical Anarchism*, 90, xi. See also, e.g., Miller, *Anarchism*, 15 (where philosophical anarchism is described as "bloodless"), or Reiman, *In Defense of Political Philosophy*, xvi, xxiii–xxiv (where philosophical anarchism is described as "chasing its tail").

19 *Philosophical Anarchism*, 90.

20 *Philosophical Anarchism*, 90–91. These claims are undoubtedly related to Horton's assertion that "most denials of political obligation . . . are more or less disingenuous" (*Political*

Gans's critique of what he calls "critical anarchism" seems to me to miss almost entirely the point of defending weak, a posteriori philosophical anarchism. It does this in several ways. First, and most obviously, it neglects to mention that only by embracing either a radical moral skepticism, or nihilism, or an unconvincing prioritization of moral concerns could a philosophical anarchist give his theory the "teeth" that Gans thinks a true anarchist theory should have. Second, Gans's critique completely – and mistakenly – collapses the very distinction between political obligations and general moral reasons for acting on which philosophical anarchism relies.

On the first point: it is, of course, a matter of only terminological interest whether we call philosophical anarchism a form of true anarchism or instead argue that it is misnamed. I have located the essence of anarchism in its thesis of state illegitimacy; others might argue that its essence is rather advocacy of active opposition to and elimination of the state[21] – in which case, "philosophical anarchism" would be an unhappy name for a still perfectly defensible political philosophy. What it is important to see, however, is what would be required for anarchism to defend the radical practical stance Gans seem to associate with real anarchism. All anarchists – with the exception only of moral skeptics (nihilists) and those embracing extremely eccentric moral theories – must allow that in virtually all modern states, including even those that are deeply unjust and otherwise illegitimate, a significant body of the law's requirements, both criminal and civil, constitutes a formalization, with the backing of coercive sanctions, of independently binding moral requirements. Even, then, if the law has no moral standing, the conduct required by law is often morally obligatory. Similarly, the fact that our illegal actions would cause widespread suffering, unhappiness, and frustrated reasonable expectations surely makes these actions morally suspect, even if their being merely illegal does not.

We should not, then, be very surprised or troubled – as Gans seems to be – to find that both defenders and opponents of political obligation argue for similar practical stances with respect to many of the law's requirements and with respect to revolutionary political activities. That both the anarchist and the defender of state legitimacy find murder, assault, and acts

---

Obligation, 160). R. George Wright also seems to accept this line of argument in *Legal and Political Obligation* (Lanham, Md.: University Press of America, 1992), 280. One recent denial of a general obligation to obey the law that probably is vulnerable to Gans's analysis is in Kent Greenawalt, *Conflicts of Law and Morality* (New York: Oxford University Press, 1989), part 2.

21 See, e.g., Miller, *Anarchism*, 6–7; Reiman, *In Defense of Political Philosophy*, xxii, 48; and Nathanson, *Should We Consent to Be Governed?* 54, 57, 86.

aimed at producing massive and violent social upheaval to be morally indefensible in no way suggests that their theories are really indistinguishable,
for the theories clearly differ importantly both on the source of these moral
worries – independent moral concerns versus violation of general political
obligations – and on the issue of to whom the relevant moral duties and
moral consideration are owed – our fellow citizens qua persons versus our
government or our fellow citizens qua citizens.

Radicalness of practical implications is hardly the only measure of substantive difference in political philosophies. Indeed, to acquire the radical
"teeth" that Gans wants anarchist theories to brandish, these theories have
to either deny the existence of independent moral concerns about murder,
assault, and causing widespread misery or else argue that the evil represented by the existence of the (i.e., every) state is sufficiently great to justify
or require violence and rending the social fabric in an effort to remove
that evil. I, along with many anarchist philosophers, find neither of these
moves compelling. Philosophical anarchism's less radical "teeth" will be
found rather in its assertions that many distinctively political legal requirements – such as payment of certain taxes or military service – along with
many paternalistic and moralistic laws and laws creating victimless crimes
may be disobeyed without moral impropriety.[22] This is no revolutionary
stance, but neither is it addressed to or motivated by only trivial and esoteric contexts.

To turn now to my second concern about Gans's critique, does this anarchist reasoning not just amount to reintroducing, after the official denial
of political obligation, the very same moral considerations that are usually
and properly employed in defending accounts of political obligation? No,
it does not. Anarchists allow for justifiable disobedience in many cases
(such as those noted above) where Gans does not; and, as we will see, anarchists typically reject most of the lines of argument on which Gans relies
heavily, rather than implicitly reintroducing them, as Gans suggests they
do. Indeed, it is not the philosophical anarchist who has implicitly given
up the game to the defender of political obligation, as Gans suggests, but
Gans himself who has unwittingly given up the game to the philosophical
anarchist.

Gans's own defense of political obligation (or, as he usually prefers, of
"the duty to obey the law") is in fact cobbled together from four different
familiar, purported justifications of political obligation – justifications

22 I discuss these claims more fully in "The Anarchist Position," 276–79, and *On the Edge of
Anarchy*, 262–69.

appealing to consequences, fairness, the duty to support just institutions, and communal obligations.[23] Not only, however, does Gans never bother to argue that these varied justifications can all be motivated by one consistent moral theory (let alone give us any hint of what such a theory would look like), but he also accepts many of the well-known shortcomings of these styles of justification, moving on to new arguments in the face of the acknowledged weaknesses of the ones under consideration.[24] The cumulative force of the many arguments is supposed somehow to make up for their individual defects, and then the resulting political obligation is weakened to make its affirmation consistent with substantial levels of disobedience.[25] What Gans then succeeds in presenting (insofar as the argument is successful at all) is less a case for a general political obligation than a list of often, though by no means always, operative reasons – of distinctly variable weight – for refraining from actively disrupting political life in just societies. As we have seen, however, anarchists can of course embrace a similar list without committing themselves to the legitimacy of the state.

Gans's project in effect just ignores the distinction between moral reasons for acting (of variable weight and application) and grounds for a general political obligation. Anarchists can happily allow, for instance, that acting contrary to law will often have profoundly negative consequences for others. It will also often have no such consequences. Where these consequences are at issue, they may constitute moral reasons for doing as the law requires, but this would in most cases be true independent of the law's formalized requirements. It is also true that negative consequences for others often give us some reason to refrain from causing them, even where there is nothing like a strict duty, moral or legal, to refrain. (It is not my duty, moral or legal, to tell a stranger the time of day when she politely requests it.) The moral weight of negative consequences can, for philosophical anarchists, both range far beyond the realm of duty and be regarded as largely independent of the institutional facts of legal requirement. It is very hard to see how anyone could take such a stance to amount to an implicit acceptance of a general political duty to obey the law.

Anarchists also often just reject, rather than deceptively "resurrecting," the other lines of justification for political obligation that Gans defends.[26]

23 *Philosophical Anarchism*, 89.
24 See, e.g., *Philosophical Anarchism*, 71–78, 82–83, 87.
25 Ibid., chaps. 1 and 4.
26 They may reject arguments from a duty of justice because (a) this would bind us to no particular state (but only to all just states) and (b) the justice or injustice of a state varies independently of its legitimacy with respect to particular persons. They may reject

Gans's attempt to piece together a general political obligation from a wide variety of variable moral considerations both fails in its own right, I think, and in effect amounts to admitting that the proper political stance is the one that philosophical anarchism prescribes – namely, the careful weighing of a range of moral considerations that are at issue in some, but not even nearly all, cases of legal disobedience, even within just political societies. No general moral presumption in favor of obedience can ever be defended in this way, nor do Gans's effects succeed in showing how this might be done.

Objection 2: The Radicalism of Philosophical Anarchism

The other two recent criticisms of anarchism that are intended to apply to the kind of weak, a posteriori philosophical anarchism I am defending can, I think, be answered more quickly now that we have a better sense of the extent of philosophical anarchism's commitments. The first of these remaining criticisms, for instance, claims (directly contrary to Gans) that philosophical anarchism's implications are too radical to be intuitively acceptable. Embracing philosophical anarchism, it has been said, will "encourage general disobedience to critical laws" and prove "a tragedy for liberal regimes"[27]; it will have "extreme" and "startling" consequences.[28] We can see now, however, that these claims are far too strong. Philosophical anarchism will not argue for mindless obedience to law, but neither, of course, will most defenders of general political obligations, nor will philosophical anarchists argue for mindless disobedience to law. It argues rather that the simple fact that conduct is required or forbidden by law is irrele-

---

arguments from fairness because (a) it is not unfair to benefit incidentally from schemes in which one has not willingly included oneself and (b) modern states do not sufficiently resemble the voluntary cooperative schemes (in civil society) from application to which the principle of fairness derives its intuitive force. They also may reject arguments from communal obligations because (a) there are no political communities in any strict sense of *community* in the modern political world and (b) communal obligations are not self-justifying, but themselves require some external justification of a sort similar to that required by the very political obligations these communal obligations are invoked to justify.

27 Steven DeLue, *Political Obligation in a Liberal State* (Albany: State University of New York Press, 1989), x, 1.

28 Thomas Senor, "What If There Are No Political Obligations? A Reply to A. J. Simmons," *Philosophy & Public Affairs* 16 (Summer 1987), 260. For similar criticisms, see Tony Honore, "Must We Obey? Necessity as a Ground of Obligation," *Virginia Law Review* (February 1981), 42–44, and George Klosko, "Political Obligation and the Natural Duties of Justice," *Philosophy & Public Affairs* (Summer 1994), 269–70.

vant to that conduct's moral status, even within decent states; we should decide how best to act on independent moral grounds.[29]

The practical recommendations of philosophical anarchism will converge with those of defenders of political obligation wherever legally required conduct is independently required or recommended by moral considerations. The two views will diverge principally where the law prohibits harmless conduct, where it imposes specifically political duties, and where disobedience has no dramatic negative consequences for individuals or for those aspects of their social structure on which they may reasonably rely. The claim that selective, thoughtful disobedience in these latter areas would be "a tragedy for liberal regimes" seems to me, however, most implausible. If the recommendations of philosophical anarchists were generally followed, subjects would regard themselves (within this range of cases) as free to either obey or disobey as their tastes and interests dictated – though, of course, social pressure to conform and the threat of legal sanctions would typically push in the direction of obedience. Even if the choice was uniformly one of disobedience, such actions might very well push states to be more open, cooperative, and voluntary, less coercive in the name of contested moral and religious doctrines, less free with the money and with the lives of their subjects, and so on – in short, to become less statelike. It would presumably be the most liberal states that would have the least trouble with disobedient anarchists, since the most liberal states would have the smallest body of laws whose content could not be independently (i.e., independently of any appeal to general obligations to obey) defended on uncontested moral grounds.

Objection 3: Denying Political Obligation

The last criticism of philosophical anarchism that I will consider here might be said to bridge the two I have discussed already. The argument here con-

---

29 Obedience to law thus stands as much in need of justification as does disobedience. Mark Murphy has argued that philosophical anarchism (by which he means the view that "there is no reason to obey the law as such") does not in fact imply, as I have claimed, that obedience is as much in need of justification as disobedience ("Philosophical Anarchism and Legal Indifference," *American Philosophical Quarterly* [April 1995], 195–98). His argument, however, without his appearing to see it, actually attacks not the implication in question, but the truth of philosophical anarchism – that is, Murphy in effect asserts that there is a reason to obey the law as such, by appealing to MacIntyre's (in my view unjustified) privileging of the status quo. Since the actual, not the believed, reason-giving force of existing law or conventions is precisely what is at issue in the debate over philosophical anarchism, an argument that simply appeals to our ordinary acceptance of actions con-

cerns not the practical implications of philosophical anarchism (on which the two previous criticisms take opposed positions), but the higher order denial of political obligation itself. Philosophical anarchism, the argument goes, is "out of keeping with our general considered judgments," for "the idea that we have obligations to particular countries is a basic feature of our political consciousness."[30] Insofar as we think, as many moral and political philosophers do, that coherence with our considered judgments is an important part of the justification of moral principles (or general moral judgments), and insofar as we agree that general political obligations are a firmly fixed point in our set of basic judgments about political morality, then it may well seem that the anarchist's denial of political obligation must be unjustifiable – unless he can show that these particular judgments (i.e., that we are politically obligated) are suspect in a way that our other basic moral judgments are not.[31]

The philosophical anarchist can avoid the force of this criticism in a variety of reasonably obvious fashions. Most generally, he can of course simply deny that coherence with considered judgments has any (or, at least, such a privileged) place in the justification of moral principles or general judgments. Let us leave that possible response aside, though, and assume for the sake of argument that some version of this coherence method (the Rawlsian version, say) is correct.

There are still at least three convincing avenues of response available to the philosophical anarchist.[32] First, the philosophical anarchist can argue that the alleged considered judgments of general political obligation against which our theoretical judgments are supposed to be measured are not in fact the kind of particular moral judgments that coherence theories can appeal to in their accounts of justification. A judgment of general political obligation is itself a general theoretical judgment, not a provisional fixed point in our pretheoretical moral sensibility (such as, to use Rawls's examples, the particular judgments that slavery and religious intolerance are unjust). As a theoretical judgment, the judgment of general political obligation is either affirmed with the appropriate supporting body of theory or it is not. In the latter case it can be discounted

forming to existing rules (and our questioning of those that fail to conform) is hardly likely to have much force in deciding the debate.

30 George Klosko, *The Principle of Fairness and Political Obligation* (Lanham, Md.: Rowman & Littlefield, 1992), 26, 24.

31 Ibid., 25.

32 Variants of all of these kinds of arguments are advanced in Leslie Green, "Who Believes in Political Obligation?" in this volume, pp. 1–17.

as clearly irrational; and, if the reasons for the theoretical belief offered within the theory do not support the belief, it can again be discounted as irrational. The philosophical anarchist, of course, affirms precisely that the reasons offered do not support the belief; and he may affirm as well that if ordinary persons are in fact committed to this theoretical judgment of general political obligation, they are probably for the most part irrationally committed to a theoretical judgment that requires support that they are unable to provide or even understand.

Second, philosophical anarchists can simply deny that political obligation is for all or even most of us "a basic feature of our political consciousness." While most of us clearly believe that it is wrong, at least most of the time, to do what law forbids, many of us do not believe that it is, for example, wrong to break the law where it harms no one, wrong to use marijuana, engage in oral sex, or refuse military induction on moral grounds, even where such actions are proscribed by law and even within a basically just society. The principles of anarchist political philosophy may square with this set of considered judgments at least as well as do the principles of political obligation.

Finally, philosophical anarchists can offer reasons why judgments of political obligation are more suspect than our basic moral judgments are generally. Where beliefs in political obligation (and the habits of obedience, subjection, or loyalty such beliefs engender) clearly serve the interests of particular powerful classes of persons – those possessing (or actively aspiring to possess) political power, those endeavoring to coercively impose their favored moral or religious vision, and so on – our more basic moral beliefs (e.g., in the wrongness of murder or the injustice of slavery) quite plainly do not (marxist claims to the contrary notwithstanding). Suggestions of manipulation and inculcation as the source of our beliefs are thus far more convincing in the former case (of beliefs about political obligation) than in the latter. Beliefs about political obligation – insofar as we actually have any – are, I think, "suspect" as a kind of "false consciousness" that it serves the interests of powerful others to induce in us.[33] Compared to our more basic moral beliefs, beliefs in political obligation have less compelling justifications and more insidious implications, and they more obviously and constantly advance the interests of some over others.

If I am right in this, then there are ample grounds for rejecting as well this last recent criticism of philosophical anarchism. And if, as I have

33 *Moral Principles and Political Obligations*, 195.

argued, these recent criticisms all fail to establish any substantial defects in the weak, a posteriori anarchism we have been considering, then we have good reason to be confident about the plausibility of such a political philosophy. Only a quite new and unanticipated theory of political obligation and state legitimacy should shake this confidence.

7

JUSTIFICATION AND LEGITIMACY

In this chapter I will discuss the relationship between two of the most basic ideas in political and legal philosophy: the justification of the state and state legitimacy. I plainly cannot aspire here to a complete account of these matters, but I hope to be able to say enough to motivate a way of thinking about the relation between these notions that is, I believe, superior to the approach which seems to be dominant in contemporary political philosophy. Today, showing that a state is justified and showing that it is legitimate are typically taken to require the very same arguments. I will argue that this contemporary stance obscures the difference between two central ways in which we should (and do) morally evaluate states, and it generates confusions about other serious practical issues, such as those surrounding our moral obligations to comply with law.

I begin (in Secs. I and II) with brief discussions of the ideas of justification and legitimacy and with an attempt to capture what ought to be most central in our concerns about these ideas. I turn then (in Sec. III) to two basic ways of thinking about the relation between justification and legitimacy that I want to distinguish: what I will call the Lockean and the Kantian approaches.[1] Next (in Sec. IV), I argue that the minority Lockean approach to this issue captures essential features of institutional evaluation that the

For their helpful comments on earlier drafts of this chapter, I would like to thank Rüdiger Bittner, David Copp, Ronald Dworkin, David Gauthier, Frances Kamm, Thomas Nagel, Nancy Schauber, Samuel Scheffler, David Schmidtz, David Tabachnick, Jeremy Waldron, and audiences at the University of Arizona, the University of California at Berkeley Law School, New York University Law School, Boston University, and the University of Pittsburgh.

1 Though it will become obvious later, I should issue here a preliminary warning that the accounts identified as Lockean and Kantian will depart from the actual positions of Locke

majority Kantian approach does not, and I add (in Sec. V) brief mention of one further complication facing any adequate account of political evaluation.

I

The project of "justifying the state" is one that we tend to associate with the great political treatises of the seventeenth and eighteenth centuries, and especially with those of the philosophers in the social contract tradition, such as Hobbes, Locke, or Kant. We study these historical texts in large measure because of their perceived contributions to a justificatory project that many feel confident in claiming as "the central task of social and political philosophy."[2] But for all this, we are not always as careful as we might be in specifying exactly what this justificatory project amounts to or how the justifications offered differ from other kinds of institutional evaluation defended within the same works. In order to clearly distinguish what I take to be two importantly different dimensions of these philosophical enterprises, I want to begin with some very general thoughts about practical justification.

Justifying an act, a strategy, a practice, an arrangement, or an institution typically involves showing it to be prudentially rational, morally acceptable, or both (depending on the kind of justification at issue). And showing this, in standard cases, centrally involves rebutting certain kinds of possible

---

and Kant in many ways. I seek only to identify the broad "spirit" of these accounts with those of the historical philosophies in question. There are, of course, many other prominent accounts of these matters that are not centrally discussed, or discussed at all, in this article. I take the Kantian account to be the most influential in contemporary political philosophy (though not in contemporary political science) and the Lockean account to be its clearest and most persuasive rival. For that reason I concentrate here on those two accounts. But it is not at all difficult to find in contemporary philosophical literature rival views of the ground of legitimacy claims (though it is harder to find rival accounts of the meaning of such claims). Ronald Dworkin has suggested to me that the natural competitor for the Lockean view is not the Kantian one but, rather, the (older) view that explains justification, legitimacy, and political obligation simply in terms of our having been born and raised in a particular (acceptably just) political community. I have tried to express my skepticism about that approach in "Associative Political Obligations," *Ethics* 106 (1996): 247–73. Another familiar rival view grounds legitimacy in a Hobbesian (rather than a Kantian) version of a hypothetical contract. And Harry Brighouse has identified a "widely shared . . . liberal" conception of legitimacy that requires *both* the satisfaction of hypothetical consent standards and the actual (free, authentic) consent of at least a majority of subjects ("Civil Education and Liberal Legitimacy," *Ethics* 108 [1998]: 719–45, pp. 720–21).

2 James Sterba, *Contemporary Social and Political Philosophy* (Belmont, Calif.: Wadsworth, 1995), p. 1.

objections to it: either *comparative* objections – that other acts or institutions (etc.) are preferable to the one in question – or *noncomparative* objections – that the act in question is unacceptable or wrong or that the institution practices or sanctions wrongdoing or vice. Justification, we might say, is in large measure a "defensive" concept, in that we ask for justifications against a background presumption of possible objection:[3] so we try to justify moral principles by showing them to be true or valid, to defeat the objections of the skeptic or nihilist; we justify coercion against a background general presumption in favor of liberty; we justify our actions in legal settings against concerns about apparent or prima facie illegality; and so on.

A moral theory that is maximizing, that requires that acts or institutions (etc.) be the best possible (in the circumstances) in order to be justified – such as maximizing forms of utilitarianism – will require for justification showing that all comparative moral objections can be met (i.e., it produces what I have called "optimality justifications"[4]). Non-maximizing moral theories, by contrast, may allow that all acts or institutions which avoid breaching applicable moral rules are justified, even if some are in different respects preferable to others (i.e., they produce what we can call "permissibility justifications"). Kantian and traditional natural law theories are often understood in this way, so that justification requires only a showing that all noncomparative objections can be met. If an act or institution is consistent with God's commands, passes the "consistent willing" test of the Categorical Imperative, or avoids infringing anyone's rights, this by itself may move it across the threshold of justifiability.[5]

---

3 I am discussing here only practical (including political) justification, but I believe this point about the "defensive" nature of justification holds as well for, e.g., epistemic justification. Many other claims made here about justification, however, plainly do not apply (or apply in the same ways) to epistemic justification.

4 This terminology, along with some of the ideas in this section, are drawn from my "Original-Acquisition Justifications of Private Property," *Social Philosophy & Policy* 11 (1994): 63–84.

5 Both optimality and permissibility justifications, of course, may involve acknowledging that an act or arrangement can be morally justified even if it is suboptimal or impermissible *in certain respects*. Moral justifications are typically "all things considered" justifications: to show that an act or arrangement is justified (optimal or permissible) is to show that it is best or good enough on balance. Thus, I may maximize utility, performing the only act that classical maximizing utilitarianism regards as justified, even if in doing so I must cause some disutility (e.g., I may push the drowning swimmer away from the overloaded lifeboat). Or my act may be on balance permissible (on a satisficing version of utilitarianism, a rule utilitarianism, or on some deontological moral theory), even if it involves some elements that might otherwise be impermissible, provided that its other elements are sufficiently morally positive to overbalance these negative elements (e.g., I may be justified in breaking my promise to meet you for lunch in order to help a sick friend).

But what is it to justify *the state?* "Justifying *the* state," with its all-inclusive tone, might at first be thought to have to involve showing that *every* possible state is immune to any systematic noncomparative moral objections. Or it might be taken to involve showing that *any* possible state is preferable to (or as good as) any possible condition of statelessness. If we understand "justifying the state" in either of these senses, then justifying the state is, I think, impossible. Many states are and have been hopelessly immoral and extraordinarily dangerous places to live. Even those who find Hobbes's arguments otherwise persuasive seldom agree with his (apparent) contention that life in any kind of state, no matter how violent or oppressive, is to be preferred to any kind of life outside the state.[6] On this point some variant of Locke's (opposed) position seems correct: life in a pure state of nature or in some nonstate cooperative arrangement, subject though it might be to all of the incommodities of insecurity, lawlessness, and vulnerability such a state could be expected to involve, is still a life to be preferred to life in a state ruled by a cruel and unchallengeable tyrant, where injustice is systematic or wildly random and irresistible.[7]

If "justifying the state" is to identify any plausible enterprise in political philosophy, then it should at least be taken also to be accomplished if we can show that one or more specific kinds of state are morally defensible (comparatively or noncomparatively).[8] So, I suggest, we can justify the state by

6 I do not pretend to any serious Hobbes scholarship with this remark, and it may reasonably be contended that for Hobbesians "only a certain *kind* of state is justified" (Thomas Christiano, "The Incoherence of Hobbesian Justifications of the State," *American Philosophical Quarterly* 31 [1994]: 23–38, p. 26). But Hobbes at least appears to believe that (*a*) the presence of true sovereignty defines the state, (*b*) all true sovereignty is necessarily absolute, and (*c*) absolute sovereignty is always justified (i.e., preferable to all nonstate alternatives). It would seem to follow that all real states (of whatever form) are justified. If Hobbes means only that peace is preferable to (active) war, then he is surely correct. But it is obviously true neither that life in a bad state precludes active war between the sovereign and at least some of his subjects nor that life in the state of nature necessarily involves a constant or active war of all against all. If Hobbes means only that any state must be better than the (real or imagined) anarchy of the English Civil War, his claim both seems possibly false and to constitute no justification of *the* state (i.e., all states) at all. We cannot justify an institution by showing it to be at least preferable to the current situation or to the worst of the other imaginable possibilities. The best discussion of these questions, I think, remains Gregory Kavka, *Hobbesian Moral and Political Theory* (Princeton, N.J.: Princeton University Press, 1986), pt. 1.

7 John Locke, *Second Treatise of Government*, sec. 137.

8 Thus, Locke, say, would "justify the state" if he succeeded in his efforts to show that states ruled by limited governments (of the specified sort) are noncomparatively unobjectionable and preferable to even the best state of nature in which we could reasonably hope to live. Hobbes, presumably, would agree with Locke that states which in fact satisfied these standards were "justified" (though neither, of course, prominently uses this language of "justification").

showing that some realizable type of state is on balance morally permissible (or ideal) and that it is rationally preferable to all feasible nonstate alternatives.[9] In the course of such a justification we will typically argue that certain virtues that states may possess or goods they may supply – such as justice or the rule of law – make it a good thing to have such states in the world.

Such a justification, of course, will provide some comfort to those who have chosen to live in a justified state: their choice wasn't a dumb choice – the state is a good bargain – nor was it a choice to participate in an immoral arrangement. But most of us don't choose the states in which we live, and almost none of us chose to live in a *state* (as opposed to something else). It seems plain that standard justifications of the state are offered not to happy participants in states but to those moved by certain kinds of objections to states. The background objection against which such attempts to justify the state are intended to be mounted must be understood to come from the anarchist, who denies that any state can be morally and prudentially justified.[10] A common anarchist view, of course, is that anything that is sufficiently coercive (hierarchial, inegalitarian, etc.) to count as a state is also necessarily, and for that reason, morally indefensible and prudentially irrational. States necessarily do and sanction wrong, or are necessarily in other ways practically inferior to life without the state.[11] Justifying the state would involve showing that these anarchist views are false. And the justification of the state will be stronger as the kinds of states that are justified are more numerous or more like past or existing states – with the strongest possible justification of the state then being of the (unsuccessful) Hobbesian sort.

One can see a contemporary version of this conception of "justifying the state," for instance, in Robert Nozick's well-known political philosophy. For

9 "To justify an institution is, in general, to show that it is what it should be or does what it should do" (David Schmidtz, "Justifying the State," in *For and Against the State*, ed. John T. Sanders and Jan Narveson [Lanham, Md.: Rowman & Littlefield, 1996], p. 82).

10 Locke would probably not have identified his opponents as "anarchists," though the language of "anarchy" dates from the mid-sixteenth century and had become relatively common by the mid- to late seventeenth century when Locke was writing. Many radical tracts and familiar positions of Locke's own day – from the pre-Civil War period to the Glorious Revolution – were recognizably anarchist in tone or substance.

11 We should distinguish between versions of anarchism that in this way deny the state's moral standing on a priori grounds – no possible state can be justified – and those that only reject the state a posteriori, on account of the contingent character of actual states – no existing state is justified. Though most anarchists in one of these ways deny the justification of the state, I have argued elsewhere that the central unifying thesis of all forms of anarchism is in fact rather an overarching denial of state legitimacy ("Philosophical Anarchism," in Sanders and Narveson, eds., pp. 19–39).

Nozick, "the fundamental question of political philosophy . . . is whether there should be any state at all. Why not have anarchy? . . . If one could show that the state would be superior even to [the] most favored situation of anarchy . . . , this would . . . justify the state."[12] Of course, Nozick does not (attempt to) justify the state in an especially strong fashion, for he goes on to argue (in pt. 1 of his book) that only the minimal state is justified; any more extensive state than that, Nozick claims (in pt. 2), cannot be justified. Nozick argues only for the justification of the minimal state; but he does so precisely by trying to show that such a state could arise and function without violating anyone's rights in the process – thus rebutting the anarchist's objection that even the minimal state would necessarily do or sanction wrong (i.e., would violate rights) and so could not be morally justified – and by trying to show that such a state would arise naturally (guided by an "invisible hand") from any state of nature – thus establishing, against the anarchist, that the minimal state is prudentially superior to nonstate alternatives (i.e., that it is desirable to have states).

II

While Nozick is not as clear about any of this as we might wish, it is important to see that this justification of the state is not for him the only dimension of the evaluation of states.[13] Indeed, given Nozick's orientation toward historical (or "pedigree") evaluations of institutional arrangements, his justification of the state in terms of a purely hypothetical account of a minimal state's genesis might seem a complete non sequitur.[14] Showing that it is possible for a (certain kind of) state to arise and function without immorality and that having such a state would be a good thing – that the state is justified, on Nozick's model – is obviously not the same thing as showing that

---

12 Robert Nozick, *Anarchy, State, and Utopia* (New York: Basic Books, 1974), pp. 4–5.

13 See Bernard Williams, "The Minimal State," in *Reading Nozick*, ed. Jeffrey Paul (Totowa, N.J.: Rowman & Littlefield, 1981), p. 33.

14 Nozick does not ever clearly explain his position on this question. So Schmidtz, e.g., understandably maintains that Nozick's attempted hypothetical, invisible-hand, "emergent" justification of the minimal state couldn't really justify the state in any meaningful sense at all (Schmidtz, pp. 93–94). But I believe that Nozick's argument, if successful, would show at least that, according to his Kantian/Lockean right-centered conception of morality, the minimal state is morally justified. If it is logically and physically possible that a state arise and operate without violating anyone's rights, and if such a state would be rationally preferable to nonstate alternatives, then the anarchist objection is rebutted and (in that sense) the state (i.e., that particular kind of state) is justified. See Alan Nelson, "Explanation and Justification in Political Philosophy," *Ethics* 97 (1986): 154–76, 171.

a particular actual state (even of that kind) did in fact arise and does in fact function in morally acceptable ways. Rather than having located a deep confusion in Nozick's thought, however, I think this observation points the way to a quite basic distinction between justification and legitimacy. For notice that Nozick also defends an independent account of state legitimacy. Showing that a particular state is legitimate appears to be for Nozick a function of showing that the actual history of the state's relationship to its individual subjects is morally acceptable.[15]

It is Locke's political philosophy, of course, that provides the model for this sort of distinction between political justification and legitimacy (though Locke himself never uses these terms to describe the distinction).

---

15 Legitimate states have a special, unique right to be the state that operates in the territory (Nozick, p. 134). A state can acquire such legitimacy, according to Nozick, by having its operations consented to by enough residents of its (claimed) territory that it possesses the "greatest entitlement" (in that territory) to exact punishment for wrongdoing (ibid., pp. 108–14, 132, 139–40). So showing a state to be legitimate involves showing that it actually has (or has had) certain kinds of morally unobjectionable relations with those it controls; justifying the state only involves showing, against the anarchist, that it is possible for a state to have such relations and that having states at all is advantageous (so that we would expect them to arise naturally from within a state of nature). Notice that on this model a particular state could apparently be the sort of state that might be justified – it could (in Nozick's case) be a minimal state that provides protection to all within its territories and that performs no redistributive functions – but still not itself be a legitimate state. If, for instance, a minimal state were imposed on a people entirely by force, without any (or many) consenting "clients," it would have no greater right to enforce justice than would some group of its subjects; it could not then be legitimate, even if it did offer protection to all and operate without redistributing holdings. The state's special legitimacy arises from the fact that its consenting clients give it a greater share of the collectively held "right to punish" than is held by any of its competitors (e.g., individual nonclients, cooperative associations of allied nonclients, rival protective agencies [ibid., pp. 139–40]). A minimal state imposed from without would presumably lack such legitimacy and so have only a de facto monopoly on the use of force. Particular states are legitimate in virtue of the actual history of their relations with their subjects, relations that establish the state's right to rule and the subjects' obligation to comply. So we might use a different language and say that such accounts distinguish between the general justification for having political authority and the specific justification for a particular authority's being the authority. For related distinctions, see Joel Feinberg, *Harm to Others* (New York: Oxford University Press, 1984), pp. 6–7; David A. J. Richards, "Conscience, Human Rights, and the Anarchist Challenge to the Obligation to Obey the Law," *Georgia Law Review* 18 (1984): 771–89, 781; and Harry Beran, "What Is the Basis of Political Authority?" *Monist* 66 (1983): 487–99, 489–90, and *The Consent Theory of Political Obligation* (London: Croom Helm, 1987), pp. 12–13. Richard Taylor also distinguishes between general justifications of certain kinds of states, by reference to their good purposes or ends, and demonstrations of the legitimacy of a particular state. But he, unlike the others considered here, proposes a purely positivist criterion for legitimacy. See *Freedom, Anarchy, and the Law* (Englewood Cliffs, N.J.: Prentice-Hall, 1973), pp. 86–105.

But Locke, in my view, is in certain ways clearer about the distinction than is Nozick. For Locke, remember, "no one can be put out of [the state of nature] and subjected to the political power of another without his own consent."[16] Political power is morally legitimate, and those subject to it are morally obligated to obey, only where the subjects have freely consented to the exercise of such power and only where that power continues to be exercised within the terms of the consent given. The legitimacy of particular states thus turns on consent, on the actual history of that state's relations with its subjects. But Locke also offers us (especially in chap. 9 of the *Second Treatise of Government*) a different and quite general argument for the moral and prudential preferability of states ruled by limited governments to life in the state of nature. This other argument is plainly addressed to those who maintain that the state in any form is morally or prudentially inferior to life without the state. Notice that in justifying the (limited) state – by rebutting the anarchist objection – Locke says nothing about the actual consent that is required to legitimate a particular state with respect to its subjects.[17] That the limited state is justified – that having limited states (governments) is on balance a good thing and that we have good reason to create them – does not appear for Locke to show that any particular limited state is legitimate, that any state (government) has the right to rule over any or all persons within its (claimed) domain (i.e., the right to occupy the position of authority).[18]

16 Locke, sec. 95.

17 It is important to see that, on this Lockean model, showing that *the* limited state is justifiable may give us reasons to consent to a particular limited state's rule. But this implies neither that such consent can simply be assumed nor that actual consent is not necessary for a state's legitimacy and for its subjects' obligations. In Hanna Pitkin's well-known reading of Locke ("Obligation and Consent – I," *American Political Science Review* 59 [1965]: 990–99, pp. 995–97, 999), she (mistakenly, in my view) takes (what I here call) his general justification of the state to amount to a move by Locke to replace actual consent with hypothetical consent as the relevant standard of legitimacy.

18 Though Locke is far from clear on this point, it seems likely that the limited state's justification is intended by him to be a necessary condition for the legitimation (by actual consent) of any particular limited state's rule. Consent is necessary – but not sufficient – for legitimacy and political obligation, (in part) because the justification of a type of state is necessary for consent to a token of that type to be binding. We cannot bind ourselves by consent to immoral arrangements. And to this Locke adds that "no rational creature can be supposed to change his condition with an intention to be worse" (Locke, sec. 131). Locke appears to take this latter claim to imply that binding (rational) consent can only be given to states that are demonstrably superior on prudential grounds to (or at least as good as) the state of nature (i.e., that consent given to states whose kinds are not justified in this broad sense cannot bind us). A state must be on balance morally acceptable and a "good bargain" for our consent to succeed in legitimating it. For a defense of this

This Lockean account utilizes one standard moral conception of state legitimacy,[19] and it is this conception of "legitimacy" that I will hereafter have in mind when I use that term. A state's (or government's) legitimacy is the complex moral right it possesses to be the exclusive imposer of binding duties on its subjects, to have its subjects comply with these duties, and to use coercion to enforce the duties. Accordingly, state legitimacy is the logical correlate of various obligations, including subjects' political obligations.[20] A state's "legitimacy right" is in part a right held specifically against the subjects bound by any state-imposed duties, arising from morally significant relations – in Locke's case, consensual relations – between state and subject. It follows that "on balance" state legitimacy may be complete or partial, depending on whether such relations hold with all or only with some of those against whom the state enforces the duties it imposes (though the state is, of course, either fully legitimate or fully illegitimate with respect to each individual under its rule).

I do not here take up at any length questions about how *state* legitimacy is related to *governmental* legitimacy; I focus principally on questions about state legitimacy. Governments can presumably be illegitimate even where the states they govern are not. But state and governmental legitimacy seem not to be independent of one another, since an illegitimate state could not, I think, have a legitimate government. On the Lockean model this is easily explained. According to this model, states ("civil societies" or "commonwealths," in Locke's parlance) earn their legitimacy by virtue of the (unanimous) consent of their members, a consent that transfers to the collectivity those rights whose exercise by a central authority is necessary for a viable political society. Governments are legitimate only if they have been entrusted by the state (society) with the exercise of those same rights.[21] So while a legitimate state might have an illegitimate government (one that,

reading of Locke, see my *On the Edge of Anarchy: Locke, Consent, and the Limits of Society* (Princeton, N.J.: Princeton University Press, 1993), chap. 5.

19 See, e.g., R. P. Wolff, *In Defense of Anarchism* (New York: Harper & Row, 1970), pp. 3–4.

20 State legitimacy, according to this conception of it, includes an exclusive power over subjects to impose duties and enforce them coercively, which correlates with obligations on others to refrain from these tasks. It also includes a right, held against subjects, to be obeyed (i.e., to have any imposed duties discharged). This latter right is the logical correlate of subjects' political obligations. The correlativity of political legitimacy and political obligation has been denied in a number of recent works, most notably in Kent Greenawalt, *Conflicts of Law and Morality* (New York: Oxford University Press, 1989), chap. 4. But while Greenawalt offers convincing arguments for a noncorrelativity thesis, I think his arguments in fact support only the noncorrelativity of (what I am here calling) the state's justification with political obligation.

21 For a defense of this reading of Locke, see my *On the Edge of Anarchy*, chap. 3.

say, acquired its power by force rather than by trust), an illegitimate state could never have a legitimate government since illegitimate states do not possess the rights, transferred to them by their subjects' consents, that must be entrusted by a state to a government in order to legitimate that government.

There are, of course, many other conceptions of state legitimacy, quite different from the strong Lockean conception just described. Some theorists have advocated weaker moral notions of legitimacy, according to which legitimacy is a mere liberty right or "justification right"[22] – a right which correlates with no other parties' obligations (e.g., with obligations to obey the law or to refrain from rival attempts to impose duties). Such notions of legitimacy, as we shall see, sharply diminish the argumentative distance between accounts of state justification and accounts of state legitimacy.

There is also a host of conceptions of state legitimacy – those used in ordinary political discourse and those advocated by various social scientists and political theorists – whose connections to either of the aforementioned moral conceptions of legitimacy are not immediately clear. For instance, we sometimes count states as legitimate if they achieve certain kinds of international recognition – if they are "accepted into the community of nations" – or if they remain stable over long periods of time, exercising effective or unchallenged control over a fixed territory. Or we might call a regime legitimate that was simply "lawful," in the sense that it came to power and continues to govern according to the generally accepted rules of its state, or if it refrained from the persecution or deliberate impoverishment of its subjects (or of particular groups of subjects).[23] Or we might, with the majority of contemporary social scientists (and following Weber), call "legitimate" those regimes that are accepted or approved of by their subjects in certain distinctive ways.

The satisfaction of any of these criteria might, of course, be said to confer on a regime the kind of moral legitimacy we have been discussing.

22 See, e.g., Robert Ladenson, "In Defense of a Hobbesian Conception of Law," in *Authority*, ed. J. Raz (New York: New York University Press, 1990), pp. 36–37: "The right to rule is . . . a justification right . . . [which] by itself implies nothing about either the subject's duty of allegiance to the state or of compliance with the law"; and Christopher Wellman, "Liberalism, Samaritanism, and Political Legitimacy," *Philosophy & Public Affairs* 25 (1996): 211-37, pp. 211–12): "An account of political legitimacy explains why this coercion [i.e., punishment of those within the state's borders] is permissible . . . It is crucial to notice that political legitimacy is distinct from political obligation."

23 Recent international law has tended to treat the persecution of racial, ethnic, or religious groups within their territories as *de*legitimating states. See, e.g., Allen Buchanan, "Theories of Secession," *Philosophy & Public Affairs* 26 (1997): 31–61, pp. 50–51.

But while concerns about a state's stability or lawfulness or about institutional racism and persecution are clearly moral concerns, they are concerns bearing more obviously on what I have been calling the state's justification than on its legitimacy. That a state is stable and lawful and refrains from persecution shows that it is good (or, at least, not bad) in certain ways, but it does not obviously show that the state has the kind of special moral relationship with any particular subjects that gives it a right to rule them. And international recognition, considered alone, plainly tracks the moral legitimacy of states at best irregularly. What, though, of the last, Weberian conception of legitimacy? Its popularity and its apparent similarity to the Lockean, consent-based conception of legitimacy warrants a slightly more extended consideration of this proposal.

One proponent of the Weberian view, Charles Taylor, distinguishes between two senses of "legitimacy" as follows. On his preferred use, legitimacy "is meant to designate the beliefs and attitudes that members have toward the society they make up. The society has legitimacy when members so understand and value it that they are willing to assume the disciplines and burdens which membership entails. Legitimacy declines when this willingness flags or fails."[24] Worries about the possibility of a contemporary "legitimation crisis" are often understood in this way – that is, in terms of the special difficulties faced by today's industrial democracies in maintaining or generating the attitudes of allegiance, loyalty, or identification on which their "legitimacy" (in this first sense of the word) depends.[25] Taylor contrasts legitimacy in this first, "attitudinal" sense with what he calls "the seventeenth century use of the term not to describe people's *attitudes*, but as a term of objective evaluation of regimes."[26]

The majority of the social scientists writing about legitimacy during the second half of this century have, like Taylor, identified legitimacy with members' positive beliefs, attitudes, perceptions, or other "favorable ori-

24 Charles Taylor, "Alternative Futures: Legitimacy, Identity, and Alienation in Late Twentieth Century Canada," in *Communitarianism: A New Public Ethics*, ed. M. Daly (Belmont, Calif.: Wadsworth, 1994), p. 58.

25 See C. Taylor, "Legitimation Crisis?" in *Philosophy and the Human Sciences: Philosophical Papers* 2 (Cambridge: Cambridge University Press, 1985), pp. 248–88. Although Habermas is perhaps the best known of those who have discussed the possibility of a contemporary "legitimation crisis" (in terms of the "contradictions" that weaken advanced capitalism) (e.g., in his *Legitimation Crisis* [Boston: Beacon Press, 1975]), he does not seem to accept the "attitudinal" sense of legitimacy that is being discussed here. If I understand him correctly, Habermas's notion of legitimacy corresponds to neither of Taylor's senses.

26 C. Taylor, "Alternative Futures: Legitimacy, Identity, and Alienation in Late Twentieth Century Canada," p. 58.

entations" toward their society or its regime. In this, as I have noted, they mostly take themselves to be following Weber, who famously attempted to analyze the legitimacy of power solely in terms of people's belief in its legitimacy.[27]

The most familiar criticism of this analysis of legitimacy points to its quite obvious circularity. But this is not a particularly difficult problem to repair, for Weber can be easily corrected to say more carefully (as he himself sometimes does) that the extent of a regime's legitimacy is equivalent to the extent to which its subjects regard its directives as obligatory or authoritative, or regard the regime as lawful, exemplary, morally acceptable, or appropriate for the society. Legitimacy is then just understood as the "reservoir of loyalty on which leaders can draw,"[28] the subjects' beliefs in the regime's authority (or their feelings of allegiance, trust, or other attachment) that will typically produce compliance and support (or at least guilt feelings on occasions of noncompliance and nonsupport).[29]

There are, however, more serious problems facing attitudinal accounts of legitimacy. One is that such accounts make judgments of legitimacy turn out to be about the wrong thing. Just as subjectivist accounts of moral judgment implausibly understand my judgment that an act is wrong, say, as a statement that I have negative feelings about that act – so that the "moral judgment" oddly turns out to be about *me* instead of about the *act* – so attitudinal accounts of political legitimacy make judgments of legitimacy too much about subjects and too little about their states. To call a state legitimate is surely to say something about *it*, about the rights it possesses or the scope of its authority. The attitudes of a state's subjects can at best be part of what argues for its legitimacy, not that in which its legitimacy consists.

It will not do, however, in response to this problem, to simply shift our focus onto the properties of the state that produce feelings of allegiance or

---

27 M. Weber, *The Theory of Social and Economic Organization* (London: William Hodge, 1947), p. 114, and *Wirtschaft und Gesellschaft*, 4th ed. (Tübingen: J. C. B. Mohr, 1956), pp. 23, 157.

28 Tom R. Tyler, *Why People Obey the Law* (New Haven, Conn.: Yale University Press, 1990), p. 26.

29 A second familiar criticism of such attitudinal accounts of legitimacy is that they preclude the possibility of evaluating regimes according to objective standards – that is, they preclude judging regimes in terms of Taylor's second sense of legitimacy. As Hanna F. Pitkin has argued, "Weber in effect made it incomprehensible that anyone might judge legitimacy and illegitimacy according to rational, objective standards" (Pitkin, *Wittgenstein and Justice* [Berkeley: University of California Press, 1972], p. 283). But this objection is hardly likely to impress theorists (like those who typically advance Weberian accounts of legitimacy) who believe that there are no "objective" standards according to which states or societies or regimes can be evaluated.

support, so that legitimacy can be redefined as "the capacity of the system to engender and maintain the belief that the existing political institutions are the most appropriate ones for the society."[30] For there is a second and much deeper problem with all accounts of legitimacy that thus centrally refer to subjects' beliefs or attitudes: no plausible theory of state legitimacy could maintain that a state has the rights in which its legitimacy consists – rights to exclusively impose and coercively enforce binding duties on its subjects – simply in virtue of its subjects' feelings of loyalty or its own capacities to generate such feelings. Surely by now the history of human oppression has taught us how often people come to feel obligated toward and believe in the rights of those who simply wield over them irresistible power, with no more moral authority over them than such power yields. Attitudinal accounts of state legitimacy appear to disregard such lessons. On such accounts states could create or enhance their own legitimacy by indoctrination or mind control; or states might be legitimated solely by virtue of the extraordinary stupidity, immorality, imprudence, or misperceptions of their subjects. Surely none of this is what any of us has in mind when we call a state or a government "legitimate." Of course, even on the more plausible Lockean account of legitimacy we have discussed, a subject's morally legitimating consent may still be given unwisely; but binding consent cannot be given under conditions that make it unfree or uninformed. And it is hard to deny that free, informed consent at least looks like an act that might give one party a right or some authority to direct and coerce another.

That a state is legitimate with respect to a subject will typically, we hope, result in that subject's actually having feelings, beliefs, or attitudes that generate allegiance, support, etc. But this will, of course, not necessarily be the case. States may actually be legitimate with respect to us without their in fact receiving from us much or any support, provided only that we are sufficiently immoral, deceived, stupid, overwhelmed (by war or disaster, say), weak-willed, or manipulated. In such cases it is correct and perfectly natural to say that a state is legitimate, but unstable or unpopular or unsupported. When people fail to uphold a state due to their own shortcomings, rather than to its lack of moral authority, this cannot plausibly be described as a diminution of its legitimacy.

It is a mistake, then, to focus in an account of state legitimacy on the attitudes of subjects or on the capacity of a state to produce or sustain these attitudes. Of course, insofar as it is the positive attitudes and beliefs of subjects that reliably produce their compliance with and support for states or

---

30 Seymour M. Lipset, "Social Conflict, Legitimacy, and Democracy," in *Legitimacy and the State*, ed. W. Connolly (New York: New York University Press, 1984), p. 88.

regimes, instead of the nature of those actual relations with the state that obligate them to support it and give it the right to rule them (relations that may be overlooked or misunderstood or unappreciated), it is understandable that social scientists have tended to focus on these attitudes and beliefs. For, as social scientists, we are rightly interested in what produces compliance and in distinguishing the various causes of compliance (e.g., habit, indoctrination, fear of sanctions, belief in legitimacy, etc.). But we should not confuse these perfectly reasonable concerns with the quite distinct concerns we have about the moral legitimacy of states or governments. For that reason, I will focus here instead on two rival accounts of the relation between justification and legitimacy, both of which are initially plausible and both of which appeal to unquestionably morally relevant features of the citizen-state relationship.[31]

III

Why does the Lockean separate the two stages of his argument, carefully distinguishing two dimensions of the moral evaluation of the state – its justification and its legitimacy? Why doesn't the Lockean simply say: because limited states are morally acceptable (or ideal) and a good bargain, they ought to be accepted by those subject to them; so particular limited states are legitimate and enjoy the right to rule and their subjects have obligations to comply with them?[32] This kind of argument, of course, would tend

31 To be perfectly clear, I should emphasize at this point that nothing turns on whether we use the language of "justification" and "legitimacy" to identify the distinction with which I am concerned (or instead, say, reserve the term "legitimacy" to identify one of the social scientific properties mentioned above). My interest is only in claiming that there is a distinction of some philosophical importance at issue here that can, I think, be happily captured by these terms and that traditional usage encourages us to express in this language.

32 Some readers of Locke (e.g., Pitkin) mistakenly conclude from his remarks on justification and legitimacy that Locke in fact embraced a hypothetical consent standard of justification and legitimacy. If we focus our attention on Locke's justification of the limited state, arguing that in his view this is a state we ought to give our consent to, we may think Locke's account can do without any reliance on actual consent. Legitimate states are just those that are good (i.e., justified – morally acceptable and a good bargain). But such a reading is forced to ignore all of Locke's explicit references to actual consent. This could only be a good interpretive move if there were no philosophical point to distinguishing one's arguments for state justification from those for state legitimacy. I try to show here that this distinction is important. So we hardly do Locke a favor by reading him (with Pitkin) as really wanting to collapse an important distinction that the text indicates he was in fact unwilling to collapse. See my *On the Edge of Anarchy*, sec. 7.2. Another very recent misreading of Locke, similar to Pitkin's, can be found in Jonathan Waskan, "De Facto Legitimacy and Popular Will," *Social Theory and Practice* 24 (1998): 25–56, p. 29, where it is claimed of Locke (as well as Hobbes and Rousseau) that for him "'legitimacy' is roughly synonymous with 'justified' or 'acceptable'."

to make far less significant any distinction between justification and legitimacy – in the sense that those arguments that demonstrated a state's justification would also demonstrate its legitimacy – and would make the universal legitimacy of all tokens follow directly from the justification of a state-type.

In opposition to such a suggestion, the Lockean, I take it, wants to say the following: the general quality or virtues of a state (i.e., those features of it appealed to in its justification) are one thing; the nature of its rights over any particular subject (i.e., that in which its legitimacy with respect to that subject consists) are quite another thing. The legitimacy of a state with respect to you and the state's other moral qualities are simply independent variables, in the same way that the right of some business to provide services to you and to bill you for them is independent of that business's efficiency or generosity or usefulness. It can be on balance a good thing that such a business was created and continues to exist, and its relationship with willing clients can be morally exemplary, without the business thereby coming to have a right to have *you* as a client. The fact that a state or a business has virtues that can be appealed to in order to justify its existence cannot by itself argue for its having special rights over particular individuals. Only interacting with you – and in a way that we normally suppose gives one party a moral right to expect something of another – will seem to "legitimate" its imposition and/or enforcement of duties on you.

The Lockean recognizes, of course, that states have many functions and virtues that businesses typically lack and that there are thus vast differences between them: states have the salience and the power to solve various coordination and assurance problems, to resolve social "Prisoners' Dilemmas," to institutionalize and enforce rights and justice, to empower the suppression of violence, and so on. But the Lockean also argues that in one crucial respect states and businesses are the same: neither one, no matter how virtuous or how useful to its willing clients, can acquire, simply by its virtue or usefulness, the right to insist on participation in its enterprises by unwilling free persons. To deny this is simply to deny the natural freedom of persons, a basic and plausible Lockean premise. Both states and businesses may be entitled (albeit in different ways), simply by virtue of their goodness or the needs or wants of their clients, to resist active efforts to undermine them or to protect their willing clients' consumption of their services. But mere nonparticipation by the unwilling does not constitute an effort to undermine or an attack on clients. And where mere nonparticipation by the unwilling is sufficient to render a state or a business nonviable, that by itself, for the Lockean, amounts to an argument that the state or business has no right to use coercion on the unwilling to insure its continued existence.

A state's legitimacy on this account, then, is its exclusive right to impose new duties on subjects by initiating legally binding directives, to have those directives obeyed, and to coerce noncompliers. This right and its correlative obligations constitute a special moral relationship between that particular state and each particular (consenting) subject. As for the significance of the state's justification, there seem to me to be two possible Lockean positions, depending on how "positive" a conception of morality one thinks consistent with the Lockean approach. According to the first (and my preferred) Lockean position, a state's being of a kind that is justified gives us moral reasons to refrain from undermining it and will typically give us moral reason to positively support that state (or perhaps even to promote the existence of similar states). After all, justice and the happiness of others, for example, look like ends that may require positive promotion by all moral agents. But a particular state's being justified in this way cannot ground any special moral relationship between it and you. For even if you had perfectly general duties to promote justice and happiness, say, and consequently duties to support just or happiness-producing states, these duties would require of you that you support all such states, providing you with no necessary reason to show any special favoritism or unique allegiance to your own just state, and providing none of those states with any special right to impose on you additional duties.[33]

The mere fact that you reside (or are otherwise located) within the claimed territories of a particular just state seems inadequate to "particularize" any general duties of support and compliance to that one just state. For mere residence of that sort guarantees receipt of none of the benefits and participation in none of the cooperative schemes that make loyalty – or even simple obedience to law – appear morally compulsory. Those within the territories of a just state who have no meaningful interaction with it surely owe it nothing more (including even obedience to just law) than do nonresidents. Imagine, to take extreme cases, citizens in dangerous inner-city "war zones" or in isolated or largely ignored parts of the state's territories – both possibilities that are consistent with a state's being tolerably just on balance. In such cases, one's only duties or obligations are those of natural morality (as Locke surely ought to have stressed, rather than retreating to an inadequate account of the "tacit consent" allegedly

33 See my *Moral Principles and Political Obligations* (Princeton, N.J.: Princeton University Press, 1979), pp. 32–34, 143–56.

given by all within the state's territories).[34] But where citizens (or visitors) do significantly benefit from (or in other ways meaningfully interact with) a just state, which is of course more typical, it is if anything this interaction, not any general duty to support or obey just states, that grounds for them a special obligation of compliance (or more) to that particular state. General duties to promote justice or happiness can bind me no more to, say, pay taxes to my own just state than they can to make contributions to some needier just state elsewhere.

A stricter Lockean line on justification would maintain that while we ought not undermine the institutional arrangements of others if they do us (and others) no harm, the mere justifiability of an arrangement need not give us any moral reason at all to support that arrangement. The mere fact that a business is on balance morally acceptable and a good thing to have around seems to give me no moral reason to do anything for it, unless my failure to act will in some way affect the performance of my duties to others. (Must I even support, let alone buy a policy from, some insurance company that is efficient and charitable and offers good bargains on its policies, say?)

According to this stricter Lockean line, my principal (natural) moral duties are to refrain from directly harming others and to do my share in supporting the helpless needy. These duties I am bound to discharge whether I am a member of a legitimate state, a resident of an illegitimate state, or associated with no state at all. Since these are duties that I can discharge independent of institutional arrangements, I am permitted to do so while refraining from supporting or joining myself to even morally exemplary institutional arrangements. I can pass up morally acceptable good bargains if I wish. Indeed, on either Lockean line, I am permitted to decline to join myself to even those morally acceptable arrangements that are essential to the well-being of others, provided only that my participation in those arrangements is not necessary to their success. As long as I mind my moral business, good insurance companies and just states can be created at will by those who want them; but the virtues of these arrangements give them no moral claim on my allegiance. This is what Locke has in mind when he begins his discussion of the consensual creation of legitimate civil societies by saying: "This any number of men may do, because it injures not the freedom of the rest; they are left as they were in the liberty

---

34 For an account of the ways in which I think Locke should have dealt with the issue of tacit consent, see my "'Denisons' and 'Aliens': Locke's Problem of Political Consent," *Social Theory and Practice* 24 (1998): 161–82.

of the state of nature" (*Second Treatise of Government*, sec. 95). If the virtues/justifiability of institutions made by others gave those institutions authority over me, they would "injure" my natural freedom and so be impermissible.

I may, of course, never be able to effectively disentangle myself from de facto states, for they use irresistible force to back their claims of authority over virtually all persons and all habitable land in the world. But the Lockean asks: what could be the source of states' legitimate claims over their specific territories, other than their prior claims of authority over the persons who occupy or use the land? If that authority over persons cannot first be established, states cannot reasonably use claims over the land to compel acceptance of their authority over the persons on the land. And states' claims of authority over nonconsenting persons, the Lockean insists, are insupportable. States are not entitled to demand from unwilling inhabitants anything that one person may not demand from another independent of states.

There is a natural objection to this Lockean account that might be raised here: this talk of a hard distinction between the virtues or the moral quality of a state and the state's relations with individual subjects, we might say, is highly artificial. For surely the state's "moral quality" simply consists in or is largely constituted by the sum of its morally significant relations with individual subjects. Beneficial states are beneficial precisely by creating or distributing benefits to their subjects; just states are just by virtue of treating their subjects justly; and so on. But this objection proceeds too quickly. From the fact that good states provide benefits for subjects (and treat subjects well in other ways) it does not follow that those states have with any particular subject the kind of morally significant relationship that could ground a state's right to impose duties. Just states invariably treat some subjects badly; beneficial states invariably fail to benefit all. Justified states are those that are on balance good things. And even if some state perfectly exemplified all the stately virtues and actually succeeded in benefiting all (and treating all well), it is not obvious that the mere unsolicited provision of benefits (and good treatment) would ground a right to direct and coerce. After all, when some individual treats others well or provides them with unsolicited benefits, we don't generally suppose that this gives her a right to direct or coerce them. There is, then, considerable plausibility in the Lockean insistence that the considerations that justify the state cannot by themselves also serve to legitimate it.

It is not difficult, of course, to imagine still more basic objections to the Lockean account. Indeed, we need not even imagine, since we have in

Kant's *Rechtslehre* a fundamentally different – but still obviously liberal – approach to these matters, an approach that seems to argue against the Lockean distinction between justification and legitimacy. Summarized very roughly and quickly, Kant's argument appears to be this: all persons possess an innate right to freedom, and many persons, even in a state of nature, possess "provisional" property rights ("Division," secs. 15, 44).[35] These rights, however, cannot possibly be respected or enjoyed except in a civil society. Since rights correlate with the obligations of others to respect them, each person has an obligation to leave the state of nature and to accept membership in a civil society under coercive law (sec. 42), "under which alone everyone is able to enjoy his rights" (sec. 41) and reciprocal freedom under law is possible. Any other person living with me in the state of nature "robs me of . . . security and injures me by virtue of this very state in which he coexists with me."[36]

So for Kant the justification of the state – its necessity for the realization of freedom and rights and justice – entails an obligation to enter civil society and accept the duties society imposes. This justification is apparently intended by Kant to at the same time legitimate particular states by binding each of us to obedience to the laws of our own states. No specific actual history of morally significant relations between a particular state and each of its subjects is thought by Kant to be necessary to support the transition from justifying the state to legitimating a particular state with respect to all of its subjects.

Kant's argument, as presented thus far, however, appears objectionably gappy. Kant never explains very clearly, for instance, why I have an obligation to leave the state of nature and live in civil society with others, rather than just a general obligation to respect humanity and the rights persons possess (whether in or out of civil society). Nor does he explain why, if others are already willing members of some secure civil society, my mere refusal of reciprocal membership (without any further wrongdoing) constitutes any kind of injury to those who already have the security they desire. While I may represent some kind of potential threat to members of a secure society (if, say, I do not acknowledge various of their institutional rights as morally binding), I am still nothing like the threat I would be to others in

---

35 Immanuel Kant, *The Metaphysics of Morals*, trans. Mary Gregor (Cambridge: Cambridge University Press, 1991), pp. 63, 85–87, 123—24. "Division" is the title of an unnumbered section of the work.

36 Kant, *Perpetual Peace*, in *Kant: Political Writings*, ed H. Reiss (Cambridge: Cambridge University Press, 1991), p. 98n.

a state of nature, and surely less of a threat to them than are evil fellow members or other sovereign states. If my refusal of membership is public and if I respect the rights those members possess *qua* persons, any threat I represent will be relatively minor and easy to counter. Indeed, it is not even obvious why Kant thinks a general obligation to enter some civil society entails a special obligation to obey the specific laws of a particular state – namely, that in which I find myself.[37] In short, Kant never really seems to explain the crucial inference from justification to legitimacy – from the assertion that the state is necessary for securing rights and freedom to his conclusion that each state has the right to direct and coerce those within the territories over which it claims authority. We shall return to Kant's argument later to see if it can be filled out in a more satisfactory fashion.

Even those contemporary political philosophers who consider themselves Kantians do not embrace this Kantian line of argument in many of its details. But they do seem to share both with Kant, and with many who would not describe themselves as Kantians, Kant's desire to employ the very same arguments in both justifying the state and demonstrating the legitimacy of particular states. Thomas Nagel, for instance, writes that "the task of discovering the conditions of *legitimacy* is traditionally conceived as that of finding a way to *justify* a political system to everyone who is required to live under it."[38] John Rawls similarly says: "The basic structure and its public policies are to be *justifiable* to all citizens, as the principle of political *legitimacy* requires."[39] And Ronald Dworkin begins his discussion of the "general *justification* for the exercise of coercive power of the state" by saying: "This is the classical problem of the *legitimacy* of coercive power. It rides on the back of another classical problem: that of political obligation."[40] Similar claims can be found without

---

37 An obligation to enter (by consenting to) some civil society is presumably identical to neither an obligation to do what such obligatory consent would be consent to nor an obligation to do whatever one's particular society requires of its citizens. Thus, the "gaps" in Kant's argument may be sufficiently large to lead one to conclude that he was in fact simply uninterested in questions about legitimacy (in the Lockean sense), focusing entirely on questions of justification.

38 Thomas Nagel, *Equality and Partiality* (New York: Oxford University Press, 1991), p. 330. My emphasis throughout.

39 John Rawls, *Political Liberalism* (New York: Columbia University Press, 1993), p. 224; my emphasis.

40 Ronald Dworkin, *Law's Empire* (Cambridge, Mass.: Harvard University Press, 1986), pp. 190–91; my emphasis.

difficulty in the writings of many other prominent contemporary political philosophers.[41]

It is not easy, of course, to assess the significance of these claims, in light of the fact that their authors may be using terms like "justification" and "legitimacy" differently than I have been using them here. One possibility is that questions about the justification of the state and questions about state legitimacy are simply being conflated, so that the distinction between justification and legitimacy is being collapsed entirely. This, I have argued, would be to rob political philosophy of a natural and important dimension of institutional evaluation. Another possibility is that the philosophers in question are simply working with a weaker notion of legitimacy than the strong Lockean right of the state to direct, be obeyed by, and coerce subjects. Perhaps legitimacy is being understood as a mere liberty (uncorrelated with any obligations of subjects or others), so that the state's justification is being taken to imply (or to be part of the argument for) state legitimacy as only a kind of moral permission. Finally, these political philosophers might simply be asserting that there is a direct and obvious argument from the justification of a type of state to the legitimacy of all tokens of that type, where legitimacy is being understood in the stronger Lockean sense. The Lockean reply is that both of the first two moves encourage us to ignore an essential respect in which states and political (and other) institutions are and ought to be morally evaluated. The third move – Kant's own claims are an example – is rejected by the Lockean for the reasons now under consideration.

It has been Rawls's work, of course, that has influenced so many of the contemporary political philosophers, Kantian and non-, to whom I have been referring. And in Rawls's work one can plainly see, if not a simple conflation of questions about justification and legitimacy, at least a very distinct narrowing of the differences between the argumentative grounds for

41 For instance: "The *justification* of authority . . . depends on one main argument. . . . The main argument for the *legitimacy* of any authority is that . . . a person is more likely to act successfully for the reasons which apply to him" (Joseph Raz, *The Morality of Freedom* [Oxford: Oxford University Press, 1986], pp. 70–71). "A state is *legitimate* only if, all things considered, its rule is morally *justified*" (Leslie Green, *The Authority of the State* [Oxford: Oxford University Press, 1990], p. 5). "A system of political authority or law can be *legitimate*, can be morally *justified*" (Jeffrey Reiman, *In Defense of Political Philosophy* [New York: Harper & Row, 1972], pp. 41–42). "To *justify* . . . coercive institutions, we need to show that the authorities within these institutions have a right to be obeyed and that their members have a corresponding duty to obey them. In other words, we need to show that these institutions have *legitimate* authority" (Sterba, p. 1). My emphases throughout.

claims of justification and legitimacy. First, Rawls seems relatively uncon-cerned with justifying the state (or a kind of state) in a way designed to rebut the (real or imagined) objections of anarchists or others who favor nonstate forms of cooperation. Rawlsian justification is principally a justi-fication of coercion offered to those who already accept the necessity of living in some kind of state. The only real justificatory question is: what kind of state? Rawlsian principles of justice are to govern "a structure of basic institutions we enter only at birth and exit only by death"; they are principles for the "political" realm, not for the "associational" ("which is voluntary in ways that the political is not").[42] These principles "regulate the choice of a political constitution and the main elements of the economic and social system."[43] What Rawlsian contractors select between is the kinds of constitutionally centered legal systems and large-scale distributive insti-tutions that define the state. They select, in short, the best form for a state to take, not the state itself. The moral necessity of a large-scale politi-cal/economic institutional structure seems to be a background assumption of, not a demonstrated step in, the project of political justification in Rawl-sian political philosophy.

This is one way in which the project of "justifying the state" seems quite different in Rawls's hands (and in the hands of those influenced by him) than in Locke's. There is also another: where for the Lockean, justi-fication involves showing that the limited state is morally acceptable and a good bargain (simpliciter) – that it is objectively permissible and answers to basic human needs and interests – Rawlsian justification is accom-plished instead by showing that the state is acceptable to the particular persons forced to live under its authority (i.e., it is consistent with their (possibly quite diverse) moral beliefs). What Rawls now calls "public justi-fication" – the "best justification" of a conception of justice (and the insti-tutional structure it dictates) "that we can have at any given time"[44] – is accomplished when the reasonable members of a political society can accept it as the best conception even in light of their own various com-prehensive conceptions of the good[45] (i.e., when there is an "overlapping consensus" of reasonable comprehensive views). Importantly, however,

42 Rawls, *Political Liberalism*, pp. 135–36, 137.

43 John Rawls, *A Theory of Justice* (Cambridge, Mass.: Harvard University Press, 1971), p. 7. Rawls repeatedly claims that the basic structure of society, for the regulation of which the principles chosen by the original position contractors are designed, has two parts, the first of which is a political constitution (ibid., pp. 7, 61).

44 John Rawls, "Reply to Habermas," *Journal of Philosophy* 92 (1995): 132–80, pp. 144–45.

45 Ibid., p. 143.

they accept it as best given their recognition of the need for some collective political/economic solution by which all will subsequently be bound.

The state's justification for Rawls is, we might say, doubly relativized by comparison with Lockean justification. It is justification offered to those who already agree that some kind of state must be justified, and it is justification relative to the moral positions of those who will make up the society in question. Even if those moral positions should be illiberal and the state that is justified in light of them should be what Rawls calls "hierarchical," still, "hierarchical societies are well-ordered in terms of their own conceptions of justice."[46]

Notice the ways in which the arguments for a justified state and for the state's legitimacy are drawn together in the Rawlsian account, and the more distinct Lockean versions of these notions are left behind. Justification is now justification to a particular set of persons, not justification "simpliciter," so that "justifying" is now more like "legitimating" the state with respect to those persons (i.e., more like explaining how a state could have rights over some individual). And legitimacy is now grounded not in what those persons actually accept or do (by consenting or by taking benefits, say), but in what it is reasonable to expect them to accept – that is, in their hypothetical endorsement. So "legitimating" is now more like "justifying." As Rawls puts it: "The exercise of political power is legitimate only when it is exercised in fundamental cases in accordance with a constitution, the essentials of which all reasonable citizens as free and equal might reasonably be expected to endorse."[47] Political power is legitimate with respect to a set of persons if it would be reasonable for them to endorse it. So the Lockean notions of justification and legitimacy are both "pushed" toward a Kantian middle ground where the distinction between them virtually disappears: the Rawlsian argument that shows a type of state to be justified also shows all tokens of that type to be

46 John Rawls, "The Law of Peoples," in *On Human Rights*, ed. S. Shute and S. Hurley (New York: Basic Books, 1993), p. 64.

47 Rawls, "Reply to Habermas," p. 148. Nagel, similarly, suggests that the unanimous acceptance of a political arrangement that its legitimacy (and justification) requires "is neither actual unanimity among persons with the motives they happen to have, nor the kind of ideal unanimity that simply follows from there being a single right answer which everyone ought to accept because it is independently right, but rather something in between: a unanimity which could be achieved among persons in many respects as they are, provided they were also reasonable and committed within reason to modifying their claims, requirements, and motives in a direction which makes a common framework of justification possible" (Nagel, pp. 33–34).

legitimate.[48] Both forms of evaluation are now grounded simply in showing that it would be reasonable for a particular set of persons to accept a particular form of political/economic organization.

IV

I want now to explain why I think (what I am calling) the Kantian account leaves behind, unanswered, certain important questions and without warrant diminishes the force of certain forms of institutional evaluation. While it may sometimes appear that the Kantian's privileging of political solutions to the problem of social interaction is just a conservative view of the state, or a resigned acceptance of the inevitable, this cannot really be what's going on. Standing armies, for instance, seem about as inevitable as states, but Kantians certainly are not committed to accepting them. The Kantian argument at work here, albeit behind the scenes, must follow Kant in maintaining that the state is for each of us morally necessary. Promoting justice, respecting others' rights, or doing other duties requires that we cooperate by accepting the duties of membership in acceptable states.

But why doesn't the Kantian say, with the Lockean, that our duties are just to treat others rightly, whether as members of some civil society or not, and that it is up to each of us to choose membership or nonmembership?

48 Rawls's only explicit discussion of the idea of legitimacy (in his "Reply to Habermas") focuses principally on the legitimacy of governments (regimes) and laws, not on state legitimacy, and on the grounds of legitimacy, not the meaning of legitimacy. Accordingly, he there associates legitimacy with "lawfulness," claiming that the legitimacy of specific rulers and laws is a function of "their pedigree," of how they came to power or came to be in force ("Reply to Habermas," p. 175). But the legitimacy (lawfulness) of the pedigree depends in turn on whether or not the constitution that specifies the relevant procedures for determining adequate pedigree is just. The constitution must "be sufficiently just, even though not perfectly just, as no human institution can be that" (ibid.). It seems reasonable to conclude that *state* legitimacy turns, for Rawls, on the justice of the basic structure, as the passage cited in the text above suggests. Legitimate states are those that use their power according to the provisions of a just constitution. It thus seems to me that Rawls's accounts of justice (justification) and legitimacy are much more closely tied together than is suggested by Brighouse (p. 721). What exactly Rawls means by legitimacy – that is, what a state's legitimacy consists in – is less clear. But given his skepticism about citizens' political obligations (*A Theory of Justice*, pp. 113–14), obligations that correlate with (part of) the strong Lockean conception of legitimacy rights, it seems likely that Rawlsian legitimacy is only a liberty (or justification) right. This, of course, might explain why Rawls never makes explicit the form of his argument from justification to legitimacy. It may simply seem obvious to him that a justified state has a "justification right" to rule and use political coercion (though even this limited claim seems to me not at all obviously true, as my arguments in the text suggest).

Being born in a state and living in a state cannot, of course, be made optional (barring unexpected concessions by existing states); but being a member of a state with a member's obligations can be. Contemporary Kantians sometimes do seem to take seriously this ideal of Lockean political voluntarism. Rawls writes that "no society can, of course, be a scheme of cooperation which men enter voluntarily in a literal sense; each person finds himself placed at birth in some particular society. . . . Yet a society satisfying the principles of justice as fairness comes as close as a society can to being a voluntary scheme."[49] Nagel also suggests that "subjection to a political system cannot be made voluntary," but that we should still think of "the search for legitimacy" as "an attempt to realize some of the values of voluntary participation."[50]

The suggestion here seems to be that the ideal of a fully voluntary society should of course guide us, but the (regrettable) facts of political life force us to accept instead nonvoluntarist standards of legitimacy which appeal only to (what Nagel calls) "quasi-voluntariness." There is, however, something disingenuous about this suggestion.[51] For if the ideal of the fully voluntary political society were in any way regulative for them, Rawls (et al.) would be interested in restructuring political societies so as to make the choice of membership (or nonmembership) as voluntary at least as circumstances would permit. And there are many nonutopian possibilities available for doing this, such as offering various classes of citizenship (and "resident noncitizen") options, training and support to make emigration and resettlement a more realistic option, programs to disseminate relevant information, a more formalized choice process, and so on.[52] Advocating and pursuing such changes only makes sense, of course, if one has a

---

49 Ibid., p. 13. See Rawls's similar remarks in *Political Liberalism*, pp. 135–37, 222.
50 Nagel, p. 36.
51 Indeed, Rawls's gestures toward voluntarism just seem inconsistent with the spirit of his project. For societies whose structures have been legitimated (in the Lockean sense) by the free, unanimous consent of their members may have quite illiberal shapes without thereby losing their legitimacy. Highly restrictive religious orders or extremely conservative agricultural communes, empowered by the free, informed consent of all members, could count as perfectly legitimate "societies" on the Lockean model.
52 Paradoxically, perhaps, such "individualist" changes might well also bring an increase in feelings of communal solidarity. Where we feel that we have genuinely chosen our place, we may be less likely to feel oppressed and alienated by aspects of the social world that are "given" and that seem immune to change. Choice is not the enemy of community (contrary to the suggestions of many communitarian thinkers). Indeed, such choice may be essential to both a community's vitality and its virtue (since if virtues must be voluntary, communitarian and republican emphases on artificial means of character formation may be self-defeating).

genuine commitment to political voluntarism. Few of the most prominent contemporary political philosophers, however, have shown any interest in such matters, suggesting that any allegiance they might feel to the voluntarist ideal is at best half-hearted.

In fact it seems clear that contemporary Kantian and hypothetical contractarian political philosophies have illicitly appropriated the justificatory force of voluntarism while being (like Kant) in no real way motivated by it. Kantians think of institutional evaluation in terms of what ought to be chosen by people – that is, in terms of the moral quality of institutions, what makes those institutions good (virtuous, just etc.) – not in terms of people's actual choices. Appeals to hypothetical choice, acceptability, or reasonable nonrejectability have a very different moral basis and force than do appeals to actual choice (or to any other ground of special relationship between individual and institution). Even appeals to what ought to be chosen in light of the individual's own interests and values are quite different in force from appeals to that individual's actual choices.

Appeals to what ought to be chosen (simpliciter) are perfectly impersonal sorts of moral evaluations. Appeals to what ought to be chosen by me, in light of my peculiar interests and values, are more personal but still may be experienced as (possibly paternalistic) groundings for external practical constraints. Appeals to what I have actually chosen, or to other morally obligating features of my political history, by contrast, seem direct and personal. I am constrained only by how I have in fact lived and chosen. This not only makes the moral constraint seem less external and more obvious (explaining why promissory obligations have seemed to so many the least controversial sort of moral obligation, with breach of promise even seeming to some to involve a contradiction). It also makes the constraint more likely to be motivationally efficacious. And it seems appropriate to suggest that a state's authority over an individual ought to depend on some such personal transactions, given the coercive, very extensive, and often quite arbitrary sorts of direction and control that state authority involves.

In a way, of course, contemporary Kantians have demonstrated considerable sensitivity to some of these points. When Rawls rejects purely impersonal "metaphysical" justifications of the liberal state in favor of "political" justification to the state's citizens,[53] he intends a more personal and uncontroversial justification for the use of political power. Similarly, Nagel's insistence that political justification be understood in terms of what is necessary to satisfy the demands of the personal standpoint, as well as the impersonal,

53 Rawls, *Political Liberalism*, pp. 137, 217.

amounts to a clear demand that more personal justifications of power be taken seriously.[54] These accounts of justification seem to aim at a "middle ground" in three related senses. First, they aim for the middle ground between justification understood as the impersonal presentation of objectively good reasons or good arguments to a conclusion and justification understood pragmatically, where my justification fails if my audience is unconvinced by it.[55] The more personal form of Kantian justification – justification in terms of individuals' hypothetical endorsements – recognizes the need to take account of differing viewpoints, so that justifications can hope to convince and motivate those to whom they are addressed, but without surrendering completely to the eccentricities of individual uptake. Second, such justifications aim for the middle ground between impersonal appeals to what is objectively right and personal legitimation by actual individual consent. Justification to others is seen as a matter of meeting those who disagree with us on common ground,[56] and individual consent offers no such ground. Third, more personal Kantian justifications aim for the middle ground between justifying to highly idealized persons and justifying to persons as we actually find them around us,[57] with all of their confusions, alienations, and irrationalities. By utilizing instead justification by appeal to reflective hypothetical endorsement, we try to take seriously the requirement that justifications be offered to persons in their own terms, while still refusing to allow justification to be held hostage by the worst features of actual persons.

Understood in these terms, we should have considerable sympathy for the approach of the new Kantians. My complaint about the Kantian approach, however, is that in striking this middle ground, its dimensions of institutional evaluation become watered-down and one-sided. Rather than in this way searching for a single compromise dimension of evaluation, located somewhere between impersonal justifications and personal legitimations, the Lockean acknowledges instead the moral importance of both of these kinds of evaluation. How we have actually freely lived and chosen, confused and unwise and unreflective though we may have been, has undeniable moral significance; and our actual political histories and

---

54 Nagel, pp. 4, 17–18.
55 See, e.g., Christopher Bertram, "Political Justification, Theoretical Complexity, and Democratic Community," *Ethics* 107 (1997): 563–83, p. 568.
56 "Justification is argument addressed to those who disagree with us. . . . Being designed to reconcile by reason, justification proceeds from what all parties to the discussion hold in common" (Rawls, *A Theory of Justice*, p. 580).
57 Bertram, p. 574.

choices thus seem deeply relevant to the evaluation of those political institutions under which we live. I do not, of course, mean to deny that facts about the justice or goodness or moral quality of an institution – understood both in ("objective") Lockean terms and in (the "political") terms of the hypothetical endorsement of those subject to that institution – are centrally important to its evaluation. But I do wish to claim that we should and do also take facts about the nature of an institution's actual relationship with particular individuals to be crucially relevant to our evaluation of its operation with respect to those individuals. If the former ground of evaluation seems undeniably relevant to questions about which states ought to be permitted to exist and which ought to be opposed, the latter ground seems just as undeniably relevant to questions about the kinds of rights over particular individuals that states can reasonably claim. The Lockean tries to emphasize the importance of both grounds of institutional evaluation. The Kantian, I think, in effect tries to make it seem that the former kind of evaluation – what I have been calling the state's "justification" – can without further argument give us the latter – what I have been calling the state's "legitimacy" with respect to particular persons.[58]

To put this point in a slightly different way, we can say that *generic* evaluations in political philosophy are grounded in the general moral virtues or other positive qualities of political arrangements (such as their justice or reasonable acceptability) or their moral accomplishments for their subjects conceived as a whole (such as increases in social happiness). What we can call *transactional* evaluations[59] are grounded in morally significant features of the specific histories of interaction between individual persons and their polities (features such as the giving of consent or the receipt of benefits, along with the subsequent absence of rights-violations).[60] While states

---

58 For Rawls, the "principle of legitimacy" has "the same basis as the substantive principles of justice" (*Political Liberalism*, p. 225).

59 I use the term "transactional" here with the intention of ignoring one of its senses: that which conveys "negotiation" or "multilateral participation." In the sense I intend here, a "transaction" has occurred even where only one of the parties involved is active (e.g., where one party benefits another without the other's knowledge or participation).

60 It may be initially unclear how my distinction between generic and transactional evaluations in political philosophy relates to others, such as the distinction drawn by Schmidtz between (what he calls) "teleological" and "emergent" justifications. According to Schmidtz, these latter are the "two kinds of justification in political theory" (p. 81). A teleological approach "seeks to justify institutions in terms of what they accomplish," while "the emergent approach takes justification to be an emergent property of the process by which institutions arise" (ibid., p. 82). I believe Schmidtz's account of the two types of justification, as stated at least, is not an exhaustive classification. His conception of a teleological justification is insufficiently broad, since, unlike what I here call generic

are generically evaluated with respect to either humankind as a whole (as in Locke) or the body of subjects of that state as a whole (as in Rawls), the transactional evaluation of states is with respect to individuals and may differ from one to the next. Put in this language, my claim is that the Kantian tries to make generic evaluation the sole real category of institutional evaluation (perhaps because of worries that transactional evaluations of even quite decent existing states will turn out to be negative in many respects).

Much of the Kantian's work here is done for him or her by a specific conception of the "reasonable." If the Kantian can portray a (type of) state as acceptable to reasonable persons, then we will simply seem unreasonable if we insist that transactional evaluations of the state are also morally crucial and possibly in conflict with this favorable generic evaluation of it. If the state's authority is acceptable to the reasonable, then how could we reasonably deny that it has the right to direct and coerce within its territory and that we are obligated to comply? Directing and coercing is, after all, what states are supposed to have authority for.

We must remember, however, what portraying a state as acceptable to the reasonable means for the Kantian. Rawls says that "persons are reasonable in one basic aspect when, among equals say, they are ready to propose principles and standards as fair terms of cooperation and to abide by them willingly, given the assurance that others will likewise do so."[61] But since, as we have seen, the kind of cooperation with which Rawls seems concerned is political cooperation in establishing a just constitution for the state, the "reasonableness" of persons seems to presuppose a certain ori-

justification, it fails to include justifications that appeal to the moral virtues of states in consequence of which those states deserve support. The state (or some kind of state) may be justified by appeal to its virtues, or by appeal to what it might reasonably be expected to accomplish, even if, through bad luck (e.g., natural disaster or war) or lack of public support, say, it actually fails to accomplish much of value. There can be good reasons to support a state that may not be translatable into "accomplishments" by the state (as when people simply fail to act on those good reasons). Similarly, Schmidtz's notion of an "emergent" justification seems to me too narrow, since it includes only justifications that concern the state's origin. Appeals to actual consent, for instance – Schmidtz's paradigm of an emergent justification – may in fact be appeals to consent given over time, not just once (and for all) in "the process by which institutions arise"; and concerns about rights-violations later in the game, rather than at the state's origin, seem to be left out of Schmidtz's classification. My alternative suggestion is that we distinguish institutional evaluations in political philosophy according to whether they appeal to the state's general moral relations with its subjects conceived as a body, or instead to its particular relations with individual subjects.

61 Rawls, *Political Liberalism*, p. 49.

entation toward political organization. If Rawls and his followers allow willingness to reach political agreement with others to function as a central feature of the concept of reasonableness, then what it is reasonable to reject (or to accept) will be in part determined by what it is necessary to accept in order to arrive at a collective political solution to social problems. Rawls argues that all are bound to accept reasonable terms of cooperation and hopes that it is possible to find a consensus on such terms, so that we can achieve more than a mere political modus vivendi. But the consensus in question is a consensus of reasonable comprehensive views, and reasonable views seem to be the views of those who are committed to finding some acceptable terms of political cooperation. But this seems to mean that views that are highly individualistic or pacifistic, say, are condemned by such an account to unreasonableness – and their proponents condemned to obligation to a coercive authority that cannot legitimate itself in their terms – by virtue of their failure to be precommitted to finding political solutions to social problems.[62]

But surely this conception of the "reasonable" should trouble us. It is not obviously unreasonable (though it may be un- or anti- many other things) to prefer solitude and independence to cooperation. More importantly, it is surely not unreasonable to prefer more limited or less coercive, small-scale forms of cooperation to states (and all that states involve). Too much moral content, then, seems to be built (without argument) into the contemporary Kantian conception of the reasonable. So the Kantian political philosopher must, to support this understanding of the reasonable, show us why the refusal to seek and/or abide by "reasonable" or "acceptable" political terms of cooperation is objectionable.

The obvious route to take, of course, is to argue, with Kant, that each person has obligations or duties that can only be fully or effectively dis-

---

62 While I agree with little else in Michael Sandel's critique of liberal political philosophy, I think he is correct to raise the question (against Rawlsian – or what Sandel calls "minimalist" – liberalism) of "why the practical interest in securing social cooperation . . . is always so compelling as to defeat any competing moral interest." Sandel (rightly, in my view) argues that "it is not always reasonable to set aside competing values that may arise from substantive moral and religious doctrines" (*Democracy's Discontent* [Cambridge, Mass.: Harvard University Press, 1996], p. 19). Rawls at one point briefly considers the position of a Quaker pacifist ("Reply to Habermas," pp. 148–49) and argues that because Quakers support a constitutional regime and majority rule (as the best form of political association for those concerned with the rights and interests of all), their view is reasonable, and the decisions of their less pacifistic compatriots can be justified to them. But one who is an *antistate* pacifist, believing (not implausibly, I think) that modern states are by their very natures fundamentally opposed to pacifism, holds what Rawls seems to count as "unreasonable" views, so that no justification of state policy is owed to him.

charged in a state. But a traditional "justification" of the state will not do enough work here. We all know why the contractarians believed it necessary to have states. We know the "Hobbesian" reasons: the state of nature produces frequent "Prisoners' Dilemmas" in which "anticipation" (hence conflict) is the dominant strategy, and it produces "coordination problems" (which require the salient solutions of the state). And we know the "Lockean" reasons: people are biased in their own favor, they get carried away by their passions, they don't always know what's right, and they lack the power and impartiality to enforce the right even where they do know it. And we know the "Kantian/Rousseauian" reasons: in the state of nature persons lack a certain kind of freedom (or autonomy), and true justice cannot be established.

The problem facing the Kantian is that none of these reasons, quite plausibly offered in support of having states, translates naturally into a reason why any particular contemporary person must become or remain a member of some state. Even if the problems Hobbes, Locke, and Kant identified can't be solved without states (a point on which I am not fully convinced), all of these problems of life without states can be solved without unanimous participation, either at the state's formation or later in its history.[63] States can be made without the participation of all in a particular territory, and they can be maintained without the participation of all in their jurisdictions. While it may be more convenient for states to simply impose political duties on all within the territories they claim, it would certainly be possible (and perhaps even optimific) for states to enforce fair rules that severely limit the political duties of unwilling subjects (as well as the political benefits they receive), while still protecting and doing justice for their willing citizens. The establishment of political justice and the enforcement of political rights for willing participants in states neither logically, morally, nor empirically requires mandatory membership (with a member's rights and duties) for the unwilling.

Since we are not often in the business of making states, it is natural at this point in the argument to turn to reasons why remaining in a state's

---

63 Jean Hampton, e.g., justifying the state in a Hobbesian fashion, argues that "there are moral grounds for generating such a remedy [i.e., the state] because these problems [in the state of nature] have a severe negative impact on the well-being of other people. Moreover, in order to work, such a remedy must be *collective* in the sense that *all or most* people in a territory must . . . participate in it so that the warfare will end" (*Political Philosophy* [Boulder, Colo.: Westview, 1997], p. 73; second emphasis mine). But if most participating in the collective solution can solve the moral problem, then some opting out (on, say, individualist, or pacifist grounds) is not necessarily wrong or "unreasonable."

territories without being a member (or accepting a member's obligation) is wrong – that is, why so-called internal emigration is impermissible or unreasonable. But these reasons will mostly correspond to those offered in familiar accounts of political obligation: that residence without discharging political obligations involves breaching one's tacit consent, demonstrates ingratitude, constitutes an unfair acceptance of benefits, etc. I have argued elsewhere[64] that these purported reasons are in fact quite unpersuasive, and the prominent contemporary political philosophers to whom I have been referring seem mostly to have agreed in turning away from them.[65]

Rawls and others argue that certain natural duties bind us to (some kinds of) states within whose boundaries we may find ourselves. We must promote or advance certain goods (e.g., justice) and comply with institutions that apply to us and that advance these goods. But insisting on an obligation of compliance with our own just institutions – as opposed to a duty only to support or not to undermine them – simply begs the question now at issue.[66] And it is hard to see why membership in a state (with its accompanying obligations) is necessary for advancing goods like justice. One can, for instance, support just arrangements in other ways than by specially binding ourselves to one of them. We can speak out against injustice, or we can put our money where our mouths are, or we can put our bodies where our mouths are (like the American pilots who went to China and England to help resist the Japanese and German aggression). If we can act morally without accepting membership in a political community, the Kantian cannot successfully argue that the state is for each of us "morally necessary" or that unwillingness to cooperate to produce shared political solutions is "unreasonable" or morally objectionable. It is, at worst, eccentric, or perhaps "unneighborly."

Kant and Kantians would reply, I suspect, that I have overlooked the obvious moral duties that can only be discharged by accepting membership in a state. Each of us has a duty to contribute to the most efficient provision of that security and welfare to which every person has a right. Since states are necessary for such provision, duty requires that each of us join and participate in a satisfactory political society. It is unreasonable and immoral to decline to do so. This, we might say, is the real intended force

---

64 Simmons, *Moral Principles and Political Obligations*.
65 See, e.g., Rawls, *A Theory of Justice*, secs. 18, 52; and Dworkin, pp. 192–94. Nagel does not deal with these arguments in *Equality and Partiality*.
66 See my *Moral Principles and Political Obligations*, chap. 6; and Dworkin, p. 193.

of Kant's argument (which we considered earlier). The rights of others cannot be respected by us individually but require of us collective efforts.

The Lockean response must be that the Kantian here simply assumes what most needs showing. First, it is hard to accept the idea that the best way to understand the rights of others is as claims on whatever action by us will best promote their security and well-being. On the Lockean view, others have rights against us only that we do our fair shares in contributing to acceptable levels of security and well-being for all. Thus understood, the rights of others can be respected by us individually. Second, even if this Lockean view of rights is mistaken, it is simply not at all obvious that the best way open to me for attempting to provide security and welfare for others is by consenting to membership in and obeying the laws of the state that claims authority over me. If I live in a stable political society, I might well do better to scrupulously avoid undermining the security of others (and the viability of my state) while privately aiding the needy than I would do to simply obey the law and pay my taxes. If I live in an unstable society, dutiful compliance with law may be vastly inferior to private action as a way of respecting others' rights. In any event, it is plainly an empirical question, and not one for which a positive answer can just be assumed, whether political membership best discharges our duties and respects others' rights, even when we understand these duties and rights in the Kantian's preferred fashion. And the question is a question about our duties and rights here and now, not Kant's question about whether persons in a world without states would do best to create them.

If the Lockean is right that opting out of any statist terms of cooperation is morally permissible (because I can do my duty without assuming a member's obligations), then Lockeans are correct in thinking that questions about the state's justification – about how good or just a state it is – require answers quite different from questions about the state's legitimacy with respect to any particular person – that is, about the state's right to direct, coerce, and be obeyed, correlating with the subject's special obligations to the state. These are distinct dimensions of the moral evaluation of states with distinct grounds, both important and possibly in conflict (as in the case of a so-called benevolent dictatorship). The distinctness of these two dimensions of institutional evaluation is lost in contemporary political philosophy's "Kantian" orientation.

For the Lockean, although the justice or goodness – the justifiability – of our state gives us a moral reason not to undermine it, and perhaps to positively support it, we only have an obligation to obey the state's directives, and the state only has an exclusive moral right to direct, be obeyed by, and coerce us if either (*a*) we have directly interacted with the state in some way that grounds a special moral relationship of that sort, or if (*b*) accepting membership in a state is the only way we can fulfill one of our other moral obligations or duties. This is the rule we accept to govern our relations with every other nonpolitical institution or arrangement, where we sharply separate issues of the virtues of those arrangements from issues of our obligations to participate in them.[67] The Lockean position that I favor, then, is that political institutions, while vastly more important and complicated than others, and despite their alleged unique capacity to solve certain assurance and coordination problems, are still in the end only artificial human creations with no natural claims on our allegiance or compliance. And this position, I have maintained, is well motivated in a way that is not true of the Kantian view that has effectively replaced it in contemporary political philosophy.

V

I will conclude by very briefly noting how the two dimensions of institutional evaluation that I have called "justification" and "legitimacy" naturally call for our commitment to a third dimension of evaluation, about which I've as yet said nothing. Legitimacy, I have suggested, is the exclusive moral right of an institution to impose on some group of persons binding duties, to be obeyed by those persons, and to enforce those duties coercively. Legitimacy is thus the logical correlate of the (defeasible) individual obligation to comply with the lawfully imposed duties that flow from the legitimate institution's processes. The proper grounds for claims of legitimacy concern the transactional components of the specific relationship between individual and institution. Because I subscribe to political voluntarism as the correct account of these transactional grounds for legitimacy, and because I believe no actual states satisfy the requirements of this volun-

---

67 Hegel and contemporary Hegelians, e.g., argue, of course, for a sharp distinction between the rules governing "civil society" and those governing the state and so will be unimpressed by the fact that the rule I mention governs our relations with all nonpolitical institutions and arrangements. The state (with the family) is said to be "special" and governed by different rules, rather than being (as the Lockean claims) on one end of a uniformly governed continuum, along with other useful social arrangements. But Hegelian explanations of what is "special" about political arrangements seem to me either to rely on very obscure and dubious metaphysics or to simply beg the questions at issue (e.g., by without argument taking the well-conditioned beliefs of many in the state's natural authority as true and unsuspicious).

tarism, I also believe that no existing states are legitimate (simpliciter).[68]
States become more legitimate as they more closely approach the ideal of
voluntary association, but no existing states are legitimate with respect to
even a majority of their subjects.

That all states are illegitimate in this sense, however, does not imply that
all states are equally bad. States can be more or less fully illegitimate and,
hence, violate rights more or less widely and severely. And while all illegitimate states do wrong in seizing a monopoly on force to which they have
no right, some illegitimate states are in addition hopelessly evil, while
others are decent and benevolent. Some illegitimate states may thus be justified by reference to the good that they do, which is just to say that they
merit our support, and we thus have moral reason to provide it. But saying
that some states merit support is not at all the same as saying that they have
a right to direct and coerce us, which we are bound to honor. Thus far we
have only the distinction between justification and legitimacy, as this distinction works in a philosophical anarchist's political philosophy.

But to these two dimensions of evaluation we really must add a third.
For states may be justified in acting in certain ways on particular occasions,
I think, even if they are neither justified nor legitimate – simply because
anyone would be justified in so acting. States may be justified on balance
in enforcing certain laws, say, even if they are not justified on balance in
existing or are not legitimate with respect to those against whom the laws
are enforced. In my view even the government of the Third Reich was justified in prohibiting rape and punishing rapists, however illegitimate that
government may have been with respect to its subjects and however unjustified was its existence (i.e., however much of an improvement over its rule
even the state of nature would have been). It is important to see that justifications for particular actions or policies are not in any simple way related
to or derivable from justifications for existing or from possession of the
right to be the one who acts or enacts policies.

Anyone may, I think, justifiably restrain would-be rapists. Anyone may, I
think, justifiably push away the drowning swimmer who threatens to swamp

---

68 If all states are illegitimate, how important can questions about legitimacy be? The proper
answer, I think, is that state legitimacy remains an important dimension of institutional
evaluation because where states are legitimate with respect to persons, those states can
justify acting (in the sense detailed below) in more restrictive fashions, and those persons
can justify less in the way of noncompliance and resistance than where states are illegitimate with respect to persons. A state's justification functions similarly to increase state
options and decrease subject options, so that questions of justification would also remain
important even if the anarchist were right that no existing states were justified.

our overloaded lifeboat, even if that actor has no special warrant or right or authority to decide such matters. Some things anyone may justifiably do; some things anyone may justifiably do in crisis situations. From this it follows that a state or government may also sometimes act with justification, even if that kind of state is not justified and even if that particular state is not legitimate. And even if the state is both justified and legitimate, that particular state plainly may act in ways or enact policies that are not morally justified.

Similarly, individuals may sometimes justifiably disobey the law or refuse otherwise to support their governments or states, even if they owe their governments general political obligations; and they may sometimes have no justification for acting contrary to their states' demands or for undermining their states, even if they owe their states no such obligations and have the right to disobey – for we are not always morally justified in exercising our rights.[69] The dimensions in which states may be morally evaluated, then, are more numerous and their interactions more complex and messy than my discussion above suggested.

Locke, I think, was right to stress the important difference between the grounds for the justification of the state and those for state legitimacy. My objective in this article has been to try to preserve the clarity of that distinction from the blurring of it that contemporary political philosophy seems to be bringing about – and to simply mention a third dimension of political evaluation which any complete account of the subject must accommodate.

---

69 Schmidtz has argued that my "claim that legitimizing the state requires a deliberate act but justifying it does not" in fact amounts to a retreat on my part from my proclaimed voluntarist ("emergent") justifications for political obligation and legitimacy to an unacknowledged "teleological" justification (p. 95). But what I discuss in the passages to which Schmidtz refers is not justifying the state, or even legitimating it, but only "a justification of government *action*": even if "a certain government does not have the right to command, its actions may nonetheless be morally justifiable" (*Moral Principles and Political Obligations*, p. 199; my emphasis). One can, I think, coherently support (as I do) voluntarist standards for legitimacy (and political obligation) – for demonstrating a general right to rule – while at the same time denying that the justification for particular actions or policies, of either states or individuals, is uniquely determined by the presence or absence of general state legitimacy (or political obligation).

8

"DENISONS" AND "ALIENS": LOCKE'S PROBLEM OF POLITICAL CONSENT

1

John Locke claims at the beginning of Chapter 8 of his *Second Treatise of Government* that "the only way" one can lose one's natural liberty and be "subjected to the political power of another" is by giving one's "own consent" to enter a body politic (*Second Treatise*, section 95; subsequent references by section number only). As every student of Locke's political philosophy knows, however, by the close of Chapter 8 this apparently simple consent theory of political obligation and authority has been considerably complicated. In particular, Locke's use of the concept of tacit consent (at the end of Chapter 8) raises a host of difficulties for his – and for *any* – consent theory. It is with some of these difficulties that I will be concerned in this paper.

Locke's motivation in drawing his well-known distinction between express consent and tacit consent initially seems plain. If only our own consent can subject us to and obligate us to obey a political authority, and if (as seems to be the case) very few people in actual political societies have done anything that looks much like a declaration of political consent, then we seem to face the disturbing conclusion that few residents of real political societies are bound to obey their political authorities and the laws that issue from them. Locke's avowed purpose in the *Treatises*, however, is precisely to "*make good*" the new King William's "title, in the consent of the people" (Preface; my emphasis). Locke needs, then, a way of characterizing the behavior of ordinary subjects that shows them to in fact have given consent to their political authorities in some subtle, inexplicit fashion – in short, in a fashion that might well have escaped our notice.

So Locke appears to suggest that where *express* political consent requires something like a public oath of allegiance, *tacit* political consent is given merely by having "any possession or enjoyment of any part of the dominions of any government . . . , whether this his possession be of land to him and his heirs forever, or a lodging only for a week." Indeed, Locke continues, tacit political consent is given by simply "travelling freely on the highway" or by just "being . . . within the territories of that government" (119).

Now here Locke obviously confronts, but never really acknowledges, serious problems in trying to explain how such minimal and apparently insignificant performances by people could amount to a morally weighty political consent, given the apparent requirements on binding consent that it be given intentionally and voluntarily. But these problems for Locke are familiar and will not be my primary concern here. Rather, I want to discuss certain further puzzles generated by Locke's use of the idea of tacit political consent. In resolving these puzzles I think we can learn something not only about Locke's political philosophy, but also about how the idea of tacit consent ought to function in a properly framed consent theory of political obligation.

2

Let me begin, then, by identifying the puzzles I have in mind. A casual reading of Chapter 8 of the *Second Treatise* might seem to show us the following things about Locke's conception of tacit political consent.

First, tacit consent generates obligations that have the same *content* as those flowing from express consent, but these obligations have (at least potentially) different *durations*.[1] Those who give tacit consent are "as far forth obliged to the laws of that government . . . as anyone under it" (119). But where tacit consenters are free at any time to "quit" their enjoyment of the commonwealth and leave its territories, unencumbered by any further obligations, express consenters are said by Locke to be "perpetu-

---

1 I intend to distinguish here between the specific obligations undertaken and/or rights alienated by a consensual act – what I am calling the *content* of the consent (or of the consensual obligation) – and the period of time for which the obligations continue to bind (and/or the rights remain out of the possession of) the consenter – what I am calling the *duration* of the consent (or of the consensual obligation). I am aware, of course, that one can also plausibly regard the "duration" of an obligation as simply part of its "content"; but for our purposes here it will be useful to sharply separate these two features of consents and consensual obligations.

ally and indispensably obliged to be and remain unalterably . . . subject[s] to it" (121).

Second, Locke appears to claim that only an "*express* promise and compact" can make a person a "subject or member" of the commonwealth (122; my emphasis). Tacit consent – which Locke now suggests is given by "submitting to the laws of any country, living quietly, and enjoying privileges and protection under them" – generates an obligation to obey the law, but does not make one a *member* of the political society (122).

Third, resident foreigners or visiting aliens count as tacit consenters, just as do most denizens ("denisons") – where by "denizen" Locke appears to have in mind *non-alien*, probably native-born residents.[2] Since most denizens, like most aliens, give their political consent (if at all) by residing in the state, owning land in the state, and "living quietly" while enjoying the law's protection, most denizens would appear to have the same political status as aliens in the state's territories. They are all bound to obedience as long as they enjoy the state's dominions – just as one who lives for a time in another's family must during that time conform to that family's rules (122) – but they are all free to leave and terminate these obligations whenever they please.

These three sets of claims about tacit political consent jointly produce a set of obvious puzzles concerning Locke's position. If only express consent can make one a member of a political society, then no actual societies will turn out to have (or have had) very many members. While there were undoubtedly larger numbers of explicit oath-takers in Locke's day than there are in our own, in neither time have these express consenters constituted more than a small minority of the permanent residents, and in neither time have these express oaths really even been taken to be what confers *membership* in the society[3] (except, perhaps, in the case of the nat-

2 That is, a "denizen" is a resident who does not enjoy membership in some other commonwealth. I suspect Locke is thinking principally of lifelong residents born to non-alien parents. Elsewhere, when Locke refers to "denisons" he pretty clearly has in mind those subjects or members with full political rights (i.e., *not* aliens). See, e.g., *A Letter Concerning Toleration*, para. 27: "All the rights and franchises that belong to him as a man, or as a denison, are inviolably to be preserved to him" (J. Horton and S. Mendus (eds.), *John Locke: A Letter Concerning Toleration in Focus* [London: Routledge, 1991], p. 23). While Locke argues, of course, that "a child is born a subject of no country or government" (118), actual political practice typically involves granting membership rights at majority to (at least) the class of native-born "denizens," but normally *not* to resident aliens or their children (especially, though by no means only, when the children were not *born* in the state's territories).

3 See G. A. Den Hartogh, "Express Consent and Full Membership in Locke," *Political Studies* 38 (1990): 105–15, pp. 108–9, 111; and Julian H. Franklin, "Allegiance and Jurisdiction in Locke's Doctrine of Tacit Consent," *Political Theory* 24 (1996): 407–22, p. 410.

uralization oaths taken by aliens). So most denizens appear to be thrown by Locke into the same group of non-members that includes foreigners on vacation in the state.

Why is this a problem for Locke? Obviously, *members* of the society must, if anyone does, have the full package of rights and duties that we – with Locke – associate with the politics of popular sovereignty: rights like the right to vote, duties like the duty to assist in defending the state from foreign aggression. But if *only* members have these rights and duties and if there are very few expressly consenting members in nonetheless legitimate Lockean civil societies, then the right to vote and determine public policy will be possessed only by a tiny minority of those subject to law, and the defense of the state will fall to a group too small to be adequate to the task. Locke can hardly have desired such consequences, one would think. But if Locke tries to avoid these consequences by extending membership – or at least extending these rights and duties – to *tacit* consenters, following his apparent claim that tacit and express consents create obligations with the same contents, then aliens in the state would appear to earn this kind of membership along with native-born denizens – and Locke can hardly have wanted that result either. Whichever way he goes, we might say against Locke, nobody believes that native-born, lifelong denizens of a state have precisely the same rights and obligations as vacationing aliens. The aforementioned right to vote and the duty to serve in the military, among many others, are often (and without much objection) granted to and imposed on denizens; but only a very odd theory would ascribe such rights and obligations to visiting aliens.

C. B. Macpherson, in his influential discussion of Locke, tries to resolve this puzzle by arguing that for Locke holding *property* in the state is the way one gives *express* consent. The society's members will then turn out to be all and only the propertied – a group that is (at least arguably) not only large enough to perform the tasks of governing and defending the state, but that has an obvious and serious stake in the state's preservation. The propertied will then have the right to make law for and govern over the tacit consenting masses.[4]

However nicely this reading may square with Macpherson's desire to find

---

4 See C. B. Macpherson, *The Political Theory of Possessive Individualism* (Oxford: Oxford University Press, 1962), pp. 248–49. For fuller criticism of Macpherson's position (than that offered below in the text), see (e.g.) my *On the Edge of Anarchy* (Princeton: Princeton University Press, 1993), pp. 88–90; M. Seliger, *The Liberal Politics of John Locke* (London: Allen & Unwin, 1968), pp. 290–92; Richard Ashcraft, *Locke's Two Treatises of Government* (London: Allen & Unwin, 1987), pp. 166–82.

in Locke a close connection between property and political power, however, it is plainly inconsistent both with Locke's text and with common sense. For Locke explicitly asserts that the owner of land "has given nothing but a tacit consent to the government" (121). And surely Macpherson is obliged to explain why the propertyless cannot *also* make themselves members of the society by simply taking an oath of allegiance, making the kind of "*express* promise and compact" to which Locke plainly refers.[5] Even the poor, after all, are capable of speech. So Macpherson's solution is no way out for Locke, even had Locke had the ambitions that Macpherson supposes he did. Our problem of the lumping together of denizens and aliens remains.

Once this puzzle is acknowledged, however, others come naturally to the fore. Why, for instance, should the manner in which political consent is given have any effect at all on the obligations that are created by it? Why should we follow Locke in supposing that an express consent to political authority generates a *permanent* obligation of obedience, while a *tacit* consent generates an obligation with the very same *content*, but with a different *duration*? Why don't all who consent to their political authorities, in whatever manner, have precisely the same moral standings?[6]

Further, though less obviously, if tacit political consent is given by enjoying the dominions of and living quietly under an established government (as Locke seems to be saying at the end of Chapter 8), then it would seem that tacit consenting is only an option for those living in or visiting already established states. Only *express* consent could make one party to the creation of a *new* commonwealth, since at such a time there would be as yet no dominions quietly to enjoy.

But this conclusion, while apparently innocuous enough on its own, would seem to present a problem of consistency for Locke for at least two reasons. First, it would be odd for Locke to insist that only unanimous express consent could legitimate a newly formed government. For if willingly enjoying the state and living quietly in it can count as consenting to its authority in established states, it is unclear why willingly being included

---

5 For further discussion of these (and other related) issues, see Iain Hampsher-Monk, "Tacit Concept of Consent in Locke's Two Treatises of Government," *Journal of the History of Ideas* 40 (1979): 135–39; Paul Russell, "Locke on Express and Tacit Consent," *Political Theory* 14 (1986): 291–306; Den Hartogh, op. cit.; and Franklin, op. cit.

6 Franklin points out that requiring permanent allegiance of tacit consenters would be hard "on ordinary persons who might wish to emigrate to some other country to improve their condition" (op. cit., p. 410). But this, of course, does not yet *explain* why "tacitness" of consent should be taken to affect the duration of consensual obligation.

in and going along with the formation of a new state, even without making any *express* promise to incorporate, should not *also* count as consenting to a *new* state's authority over one.

Second, in a seldom discussed[7] passage in Chapter 6 of the *Second Treatise*, Locke writes about the first monarchies, discussing the process by which grown children naturally came to authorize their fathers to wield *political* power over them – after the father's *paternal* authority over them, exercised during their minorities, had ended. The children, Locke says, would by this authorization have created a new political society, based in their consent, with their father as monarch. But Locke also says that the consent that created this new society was an "express *or tacit* consent" (74; my emphasis), what he in the next section calls "a *tacit* and scarce avoidable consent" (75; my emphasis). In another, equally unnoticed, passage concerning monarchies, this time in Chapter 7, Locke refers to the process whereby some "good and excellent man" can be elevated to a position of political authority, again creating a new civil society. And Locke again says that this man would be so elevated "by a *tacit* consent" of his associates (94). Tacit consent, it seems, can create *new* political societies, in Locke's view, just as easily as it can bind us to those societies that have previously been established by the consent of their founding members. But if that is so, then it must be possible for tacit political consent to be given in ways *other than* by living quietly under and enjoying the protection of established governments – contrary to Locke's apparent suggestions in Chapter 8.

Finally, we may be left wondering by all this just what standing tacit consenting denizens *do* have in Locke's account. Locke seems to tell us that these tacit consenters are not *members* of the society within whose territories they live. Only express consenters have that status. So what is the status of *tacit* consenting denizens? It appears from Locke's previous claims that these tacit consenters can only be characterized as still being in the *state of nature* with respect to the commonwealth, for Locke tells us that "all men are naturally in that state [i.e., the state of nature], and remain so, 'til by their own consents they make themselves *members* of some politic society" (15; my emphasis).

This conclusion about tacit consenting denizens, however troubling, seems actually to be further supported by Locke's well-known arguments (in Chapter 2) for the right of the state to punish aliens who commit crimes within its territories. Locke, remember, uses the "intuitive clarity" of this

---

7 One exception is Jeremy Waldron, "John Locke: Social Contract Versus Political Anthropology," *The Review of Politics* 51 (1989): 20–25. See also Den Hartogh, op. cit., p. 108.

right of states to punish aliens as a step in his argument for a prepolitical, *natural* right (held by each person in the state of nature) to punish moral wrongdoers. Since the visiting alien is still in the state of nature with respect to the commonwealth he is visiting, Locke argues, those who rule the commonwealth are just "men without authority" to the alien (9). Foreign rulers have been granted no "monopoly" on the use of force *by the alien*. But if the foreign ruler is still in the state of nature with respect to the visiting alien, the ruler's right to punish the alien must be a *natural* right, not an acquired political right (and so a right possessed equally by any other person in the state of nature).[8]

And if visiting aliens are still in the state of nature, despite their having tacitly consented, then it seems that most native-born denizens must also still be in the state of nature, having tacitly consented in just the same way as did the aliens. If the tacit consent given by visiting aliens leaves the government in question "without authority" over the aliens, then presumably governments have no authority either over their tacit consenting denizens, despite Locke's apparent attempt to assert the contrary at the end of Chapter 8.

We begin to see a disturbing picture emerging from all of this – one in which many real and for Locke legitimate political societies (plainly including Locke's own) turn out to consist of only tiny groups of express consenting members living in (and having the right to exercise jurisdiction over) vast territories, territories largely peopled with an overwhelming majority of non-member denizens (and a sprinkling of aliens), with respect to all of whom these few members are still in the state of nature. These societies do not look much like the legitimate societies of which Locke elsewhere speaks, societies in which a "multitude" of members give their consents "separately in their turns" (117). Nor do such societies square well with Locke's claims that "it is easy to discern who are, and who are not, in political society together. Those who are united into one body and have a common established law and judicature to appeal to, with authority to decide controversies between them and punish offenders, are in civil society one with another: but those who have no such common appeal . . . are still in the state of nature" (87). It now seems, however, that most native-born denizens, after spending their entire lives in the state, subject to their civil authorities, living their lives under the state's laws, resolving their disputes in its courts, and so on, are in fact still in the state of nature, never

8 On this argument, and more generally on Locke's defense of a "natural executive right," see my *The Lockean Theory of Rights* (Princeton: Princeton University Press, 1992), chap. 4.

having given the express consent that would make them members. It is again hard to believe that this is the account Locke really wants to defend,[9] for on this account his initially sharp and intuitive contrast between civil society and the state of nature would be badly blurred.

These, then, are the "puzzles" generated by Locke's remarks on tacit consent. What I want to propose in response to them is a more plausible, more unified reading of Locke's position than the one a casual examination of the text suggests. Mine will be a reading, I think, that not only has the virtue of resolving these puzzles in a fashion broadly faithful to the text, but that also has the advantage of ascribing to Locke what is an independently plausible position for a consent theorist. While I believe that Locke is ultimately wrong in supposing that many (or, perhaps, any) actual political societies have ever been legitimate by such a plausible consent theory's standards, the position my reading ascribes to Locke is in other respects the one a consent theorist such as Locke *should* embrace.

3

The key to resolving the puzzles I've discussed is obviously going to involve finding a plausible way for the consent theorist to drive a wedge between the moral positions of denizens and aliens, a way that I hope to show is at least implicit in Locke's own account of these matters. And the point that will serve as such a key is the simple observation that Locke, like any reasonable person, plainly does not take *all* consent given in political contexts to be consent *to* the same thing (despite his occasional remarks that might suggest the contrary). There is, of course, for us, as well as for Locke, an immediate and obvious question to be asked about any case of *tacit* consent: since tacit consent is given without any explicit statement or speech act, how do we know what tacit consent is consent *to*? That question remains interesting even if we believe that Locke was wrong in counting mere residence as a way of giving tacit political consent. To explain Locke's answer – and the best answer – to this question, let me begin by trying to be a bit more precise about the concepts of consent, express consent, and tacit consent.

For Locke, "consent" seems to be a "blanket" term covering all kinds of deliberate, voluntary alienations of rights and/or undertakings of obliga-

9 See John Dunn, *The Political Thought of John Locke* (Cambridge: Cambridge University Press, 1969), pp. 139–40.

tion.[10] For Smith to consent is for Smith to deliberately and suitably communicate to another Smith's intention to thereby undertake new obligations toward and/or to transfer new rights to this other. That is, I think, both Locke's conception of consent and a quite reasonable conception in its own right.

Express consent, on the Lockean account, is consent given by positive action of some direct and explicit sort whose sole conventional point is to give consent – such as an oral or written promise or oath, or a positive but nonverbal act that explicitly signifies acceptance or agreement (such as a signal or wave).[11] Tacit consent, by contrast, is consent given without "expressions" of it, as Locke puts it – that is, consent given without verbal or otherwise direct and explicit positive acts. Tacit consent is consent given by *other* kinds of action – kinds of action whose point is not solely to give consent – that nonetheless also count in the circumstances as making a choice to undertake obligations and/or alienate rights. Acts of tacit consent "count" as choices in this way by virtue of being choice-indicating responses to clear, free choice situations – where a "clear choice situation" is a situation in which a morally significant decision is conventionally expected or appropriate.[12]

Thus, Locke seems to believe, it is conventionally appropriate (or otherwise reasonably to be expected) that a visiting alien's decision to enter a foreign country includes a choice to undertake an obligation to obey the host country's laws while there, on the strength of the clear, free choice situation the alien confronts in deciding whether or not to cross the border. For denizens living quietly and enjoying the rule of law, Locke thinks (far less plausibly), there is a clear, free choice situation that they have faced and acted upon – such that continuing to enjoy the state's dominions counts as continuing to choose to be obligated to obey. And when, in the days of the first monarchies, certain children living under their fathers' rule reached their majorities and faced a decision about how to proceed – or when others living with a good and excellent man in their midst faced the need to organize themselves – they faced a clear, free choice situation, in which allowing the naturally predominant person to have his way counted as a tacit granting of authority to that person, even though there was never any direct or explicit expression of consent.

---

10 By "alienation," I here mean either transfer (to another party or parties) or renouncement (whereby the right simply ceases to be possessed by the renouncing party, without transferring to another).

11 See *On the Edge of Anarchy*, pp. 84–85.

12 Ibid., pp. 83–84.

How does all this help us understand what tacit political consent is consent *to?* We can begin to see the answer by noticing that for Locke, even *express* political consent need not involve anything like an explicit statement of the full range of the obligations undertaken in consenting. Taking an express oath of allegiance can obviously be as simple as stating (in appropriate circumstances) "I swear allegiance to government G (or ruler R)." The oath need not explicitly incorporate a list of all the particular obligations under which swearing allegiance to another places one; it is enough that these obligations are *necessary* to allegiance for one's oath to subject one to them. Indeed, even the express consent that creates a new commonwealth need not, in Locke's view, be at all explicit about the particular obligations undertaken. Locke writes:

> Whosoever therefore out of a state of nature unite into a community must be understood to give up all the power necessary to the ends for which they unite into society . . . And this is done by barely agreeing to unite into one political society, which is all the compact that is, or needs be, between the individuals that enter into or make up a commonwealth. (99)

The principle at work here seems to be roughly this: *all* consent, including *express* consent, should be understood to be consent *to* all and only that which is necessary to the *purpose* for which the consent is given, unless other terms are *explicitly* stated. In the case Locke is discussing – that of the express consent that creates a new political society – we should understand the express (but not fully explicit) consent as consent *to* all and only those arrangements necessary to having a peaceful and viable civil society. And, of course, much of the body of the *Second Treatise* is designed precisely to tell us what those minimal necessary arrangements are: a peaceful, viable society requires, in Locke's view, that its members abide by the laws chosen by the majority of the members or their representatives, always provided that these laws are consistent with natural law and thus with the retained rights of individual members (and within the limits famously listed by Locke in Chapter 11, "Of the Extent of the Legislative Power"). It requires as well that members incorporate their landholdings into the territory over which the society has jurisdiction (117, 120); and it requires that members help to uphold the society by doing their part in supporting the society's other necessary functions (140) – for example, by contributing where necessary their "natural [i.e., physical] force" to assist in law enforcement and national defense (130).

Express consent to incorporate (i.e., to become a member) should be understood to be consent to this – to no more and no less – unless alternative arrangements are explicitly specified. Locke allows, for instance, that the express consent of members should be understood to be consent to majority rule "*unless* they expressly agreed in any number greater than the majority" (99; my emphasis). There is, then, a kind of "default content" that political consent should be assumed to have, in the absence of an explicit denial of that content. But if that is true, then it must also be obvious what *tacit* political consent is consent *to*. Since tacit consent is by definition lacking in explicit content, tacit political consent must be understood to be consent to the "default content," to the arrangements necessary for a peaceful, viable society.

It follows from that, of course, that new commonwealths can be created by either express *or* tacit consent, just as Locke's remarks in Chapters 6 and 7 suggest. For all *political* consent normally has identical content, whether it is express or tacit. And it follows as well that the specific manner in which *tacit* political consent is given is irrelevant to its content. If the context and the choice situation are such that our acts count as *political* consent at all, then our acts count as consent to the default content. The context, in Locke's view, may be one of being born in and continuing to reside in a long established political society; or it may be one of reaching majority within a paternally ruled family in the state of nature. In either case, Locke thinks, it is obvious that the choice situation at issue is one that presents only the options of political membership or non-membership. If we give our tacit consent to membership – which in both cases we do by acting *as if* there is a political authority over us – then we undertake the default obligations of membership and transfer to our political society the rights it requires for a stable, long-term existence.

This point, though, should also show us how to "drive the wedge" between tacit consenting aliens and tacit consenting denizens. The choice situations faced by these two classes of persons seem quite different in kind; so we should expect the obligations undertaken (and rights transferred) by the two classes to be interestingly different as well. In neither case is there any explicit content to their consent. So we must apply Locke's interpretive principle for vague or not-fully-explicit consent: such consent is consent to all and only that which is necessary to the purposes for which the consent is given.

What, then, is the purpose of the tacit consents given by, respectively, visiting aliens and native-born denizens? The visiting alien's purpose is (typically) just to secure the protection of the rule of law provided by the host country during the duration of her visit. Since host countries will (typically) only be able to provide such protections on the condition that visiting aliens act lawfully and accept liability for unlawful conduct, what is necessary to the alien's purpose in consenting is just obedience to law and liability to punishment. This, for Locke, is what the alien's tacit consent is consent *to*, in return for which the alien receives the "local protection and homage due to" those with whom the state is at peace (122).

I think Locke is probably right that this is how we should understand the status of typical visiting aliens, at least where there are no more elaborate clear conventional expectations at issue. While some host countries may require aliens to make express promises to be law-abiding (and perhaps to do more than this), even where such express consent is *not* required, the mere act of deliberately and freely entering the host country's territories should normally be understood as a tacit agreement to abide by the host country's laws and to regard oneself as legally liable for noncompliance.[13] The alien's actions count as tacit consent of this sort simply on the strength of shared conventions and political necessities, just as Locke believed.

But with native-born denizens, the relevant choice situation seems quite different. The purpose of denizens in consenting to political authority – when they do in fact consent – is (normally) to secure considerably more than temporary "local protection and homage." Denizens, anticipating long-term (or, at least, not easily terminated) residence in the state, typically wish to enjoy a state that will be stable over the long term, to have their interests adequately represented in state policy decisions (and to be treated with concern by the powers that be), to have the opportunity to influence those decisions (or perhaps even to be eligible to be a decision maker), to enjoy certain kinds of social solidarity, to have access to an array of collectively produced benefits (such as public education, state support of the needy, etc.), to secure similar benefits for their offspring, and so on.

---

13 Locke, of course (and as we have seen), regards the host state's right to punish the alien as the *natural* right to punish wrongdoers with respect to whom one is in the state of nature. So one might try to argue that the visiting alien does not need to *consent* to anything in order to be liable to punishment by the host country, since the alien is *already* liable to this "natural executive right." But this argument fails for two related reasons. First, those in the state of nature (with respect to one another) have the natural right to punish only violations of *natural* law. Many of the laws that host countries will wish to enforce against aliens (such as traffic or parking laws) do *not* duplicate the requirements of natural law and so could not legitimately be enforced by one who wielded only a natural, nonconsensual right to punish. Second, Locke wishes to claim that visiting aliens are *obligated* to obey all of the host country's laws. Since these laws are not all *naturally* obligatory, only the alien's consent could produce such a *general* obligation to obey. See my *The Lockean Theory of Rights*, chap. 4.

But these more extensive goods can only be provided by the common-wealth if its denizens make more extensive commitments to it than do visiting aliens. So the tacit consent of the denizen must, by Locke's interpretive principle, be understood to be consent to more than just obe-dience to law and liability to legal sanctions. As persons with an enduring stake in the commonwealth, when native-born denizens give an inexplicit consent, this must be interpreted differently from that of aliens, though both "enjoy" the same territories. Denizens and aliens may appear to do the very same things in enjoying the state's territories. But they in fact perform quite different acts by virtue of the quite different contexts in which their behavior occurs – just as raising your hand may be in one context an act of voting and in another context an act of bidding at an auction or asking a question.

There is a clear sense, then, in which the tacit consent of the alien is not really best understood as *political* consent at all. It is simply a tacit agree-ment to play by the rules while passing through. As we have seen Locke say, the alien remains in the state of nature with respect to the common-wealth. As Locke also says, "'tis not every compact that puts an end to the state of nature between men, but only this one of agreeing together to enter into one community and make one body politic; other promises and compacts men may make one with another, and yet still be in the state of nature" (14). The visiting alien makes a promise to the host society, to be sure; but it is a promise that leaves the alien still in the state of nature with respect to that society.

The tacit consent of the denizen, however, appears to be a genuinely *political* consent, for the denizen intends an enduring and complex associ-ation with the commonwealth. Notice that Locke never *says* that the tacit consenting landowner or denizen remains in the state of nature with respect to the commonwealth, as he says this of aliens. We earlier merely inferred this standing for denizens from Locke's apparent denial that tacit consenting denizens are members of the society. But denizens seem, by Locke's own interpretive principle, to consent to considerably more than do aliens. Indeed, it seems that they should, by that principle, be under-stood to consent to just what express consenting members of the society should be understood to consent to.

If that is so, however, then it seems clear that tacit consenting denizens *are* members of the commonwealth. Both the alien and the denizen consent to be "subject to" and "obliged to obedience to the laws of that government" whose territories they enjoy (119). All tacit consenters, including aliens, are "as far forth obliged to the laws" as any member (119).

But this is *all* the alien consents to. The denizen agrees to more extensive obligations (payment of taxes, defending the commonwealth, aiding law enforcement, etc.) and receives more extensive rights (franchise eligibility, poor relief, etc.). This amounts to a consent to a kind of *membership*, implied by the very different purposes the denizen has for consenting and the different choice situation he consequently faces. The tacit consenting denizen, like the express consenter, owes the state not just obedience, but allegiance (which includes supporting the state in ways beyond mere obedience). And denizens, like express consenters, must be understood to be owed reciprocal support by the society which can be claimed by them as *entitlements*, not merely as "local homage."

4

Now this is, I believe, the most plausible position for a committed consent theorist to hold;[14] and it is, I suspect, the position with which Locke's whole text indicates that he would have been most content.[15] We have now seen a line of argument, using Locke's interpretive principle (along with additional claims in the text), that certainly points to this position. But we have seen as well, of course, that Locke seems to explicitly *deny* this position at the end of Chapter 8. How can we square Locke's remarks in that place with the interpretation of the *Two Treatises* for which I am here arguing, thus resolving the interpretive puzzles with which we began? If we reexamine Locke's statements about political consent in Chapter 8 with my proposed interpretation in mind, I think, those statements look rather different than they did on our first reading. What Locke actually *says* is this:

First, express consent makes one "a *perfect* member" of that society, a subject of that government" (119; my emphasis). The *tacit* consent given by possessing or enjoying the territories over which a government has juris-

14 By which I mean: this is the most plausible position for a consent theorist who, like Locke, wishes to *affirm* the legitimacy of actual governments in the world and *affirm* the political obligations of typical subjects of those governments. One can, of course, be a "committed consent theorist" – that is, one can believe that only personal consent legitimates governmental control and grounds political obligations – while *denying* that actual governments (and subjects) can be accurately described as consented to (and consenting).

15 I take the evidence presented in this paper thus far on behalf of this reading to constitute a "preponderance" of evidence in favor of it. We can add to this evidence the guess that Locke was unlikely to have wished to deny, for instance, that his fellow tacit consenting landowners were members of the body politic.

diction counts as "submitting" to the government and obliges one to obedience to that government's laws (119). Thus far at least, these claims are plainly consistent with my reading of Locke, a reading on which *all* tacit consenters agree to obey the law, but *some* agree to more than this. And for all this tells us, denizens, landowning and not, might still turn out to be members of the commonwealth, as my reading suggests. For Locke both refers here only to the *perfect* membership of express consenters – leaving room, perhaps, for *other* kinds of membership for tacit consenting denizens – and clearly makes express consent only *sufficient* for membership, not *necessary* (indeed, not necessary even for *perfect* membership).

The passages immediately preceding section 119 should surely also encourage us to hold to the reading for which I'm pressing. Locke there plainly says that sons who inherit land from their fathers ordinarily thereby become *members* of the commonwealth (117), despite his claim only four paragraphs later (as we have seen) that such owners of land have "given nothing but . . . a tacit consent to the government" (121). This certainly seems to entail that native-born tacit consenting landowners, at least, *are* to be viewed as members of the political society in whose territories their land lies. And the obvious lines of argument that might *support* such claims (such as the line I am pushing) will naturally *extend* arguments for membership status to cover *non-landowning* denizens, while *rejecting* membership status for *aliens* (whether they be landowners or not).

Lest we mistakenly take Locke's claims here (about the membership of land-inheriting sons) as showing that Locke's *true* intention was to claim that landowning is a (or the) way of giving *express* consent (thus ignoring Locke's claims in section 121, as does Macpherson), two obvious points need making. First, such a position would commit Locke to the claim that *alien* landowners were members, despite their owing their primary allegiance to a *different* government. And second, Locke also claims of the consent given by inheriting landholders that "people take no notice of it, thinking it not done at all" (117). A consent of which no notice is taken cannot by very *express*; on the contrary, such a consent seems almost certainly to have been thought by Locke to be tacit only, just as he clearly claims in section 121.

After explaining (in section 120) why incorporation into the commonwealth must include the submission of one's lands to the government's jurisdiction, Locke goes on (in section 121) to claim (as we have seen) that those who have given "nothing but a tacit consent" remain at liberty to leave the state and join a new one, while express consenters remain "unalterably" subjects (barring dissolution of the government or lawful expulsion from the commonwealth). Here Locke addresses neither the *member-ship* status of the two kinds of consenters nor what I've been calling the *contents* of their consents (i.e., the specific obligations undertaken and rights transferred). Rather, he addresses only the question of the *duration* of their consensual obligations – a problem to which I will return momentarily.

Finally we arrive at the last and most troublesome passage in Chapter 8, section 122; but even there, Locke seems to lead us in two inconsistent directions, only one of which is apparently inconsistent with my reading of his position. On the one hand, Locke here plainly identifies "members" with "perpetual subjects of [the] commonwealth" and states that "nothing can make" one a subject or member of the commonwealth "but his actually entering into it by positive engagement and express consent and compact." This seems to identify the class of members with the class of express consenters – and by implication to oppose this class to both denizens and visiting aliens – thus producing my original puzzles.

On the other hand, Locke also says here that those who merely "live quietly" in the state – those to whom he is here *contrasting* the members of the society – receive the state's protection only as "homage due to and from those" in its territories with whom the government is not "in a state of war." This would be a *very* odd way to refer to lifelong, native-born denizens and landholders, raising the possibility that the people who Locke here describes as "living quietly" in the state are only the *aliens, not* the native-born denizens. Indeed, Locke goes on to say: "and thus we see that *foreigners*" are bound to submit to the law "as far forth as any denison" (my emphasis). This remark seems to suggest both (a) that it is in fact aliens to whom Locke is trying to deny membership in section 122 and (b) that the class of visiting or resident foreigners is in some fashion usefully to be viewed as *distinct* from that of denizens – suggesting, perhaps, that aliens, while like denizens in being bound to obedience, are *unlike* them in some further important respect(s). And that, of course, is just the reading for which I have been arguing. On my reading of Locke, then, we must take his claim (in section 122) that only express consent makes one a member to either (a) involve an incomplete reference to the "perfect membership" (of section 119), which Locke might believe can *only* be created by *express* consent, leaving a *less* "perfect" (because less "inescapable") membership to tacit consenting denizens; or (b) be an unhappily worded attempt by Locke simply to draw the sharpest possible contrast between the most *committed* and the most *transient* of those who exist within the state's territories, omitting for these purposes any comment on the vast "middle" class of tacit consenting denizens.

5

My best guess as to Locke's reasoning is as follows: Locke wants to argue that *denizen* landholders – principally those who have inherited land from parents who were members of the commonwealth – themselves count as members, incorporated into the society. His problem is that he does *not* wish thereby to find himself committed to granting membership, with its full package of obligations and rights, to *alien* landholders. So Locke argues that *mere* landholding, like *mere* residence, is insufficient for membership in the commonwealth, unless accompanied by some *further* act of "incorporation" (which binds one to primary allegiance to the commonwealth). *Mere* landholding (and residence) give only a *tacit* consent to submit to and obey the laws of the government with jurisdiction. But Locke *also* wants to argue, in part to square his philosophical position with the conventional political practice, that *denizen* landholders *are* members.

How, though, can we distinguish between denizen inheritors of land and alien inheritors, so that only the former class enjoys membership in the commonwealth? Not by arguing that the act of *inheritance* itself conventionally includes incorporation into (hence membership in) the commonwealth, since aliens too can perform this act. Thus, Locke refers in section 117 only to *denizen* inheritors of land becoming members. Not by arguing that landholding implies the desire and need for protection under the commonwealth's jurisdiction, hence an implied consent to membership in the society, for alien landholders have this same desire and need.

The obvious answer is that the native born have a different kind of stake in the commonwealth from resident or visiting aliens, landholders or not. The native born have no *other* state that can claim to be due their primary allegiance, no other state to which they can retreat and in which they will be recognized as members entitled to more than mere protection under the law. With this different kind of stake, we should understand differently the content of the tacit consent at issue. When denizens (allegedly) give tacit consent by holding land (or by residing) in the state, they consent to something different from aliens who consent by holding land (or by residing) in the state. The denizen is not a "perpetual subject," as he would be had he given an express oath of allegiance. But neither is he a *non*-member, still in the state of nature with respect to the commonwealth, as is the visiting or resident or landholding alien. Locke, of course, never quite manages to *say* any of this. But what he does say, I think, is best read as pointing to this position, rather than to the puzzling positions that a casual reading seems to reveal.

These remarks leave one last question: What are we to make of the final "puzzle" I mentioned – namely, Locke's odd claim that express consenters owe *permanent* allegiance to the state, while *tacit* consenters owe allegiance only so long as they continue to be within the state's territories, remaining free to leave unencumbered whenever they choose?[16] There is, I think, more to be said for Locke's view here than my earlier puzzlement over it indicated. Consider the following points, for instance. Express consenters on Locke's account will almost always *also* be tacit consenters. That is, those who give express oaths of allegiance (and the like) – at least once the commonwealth has been established (which is, of course, the period Locke is discussing in section 121) – will *already* count as *tacit* consenters, for Locke, simply by virtue of being within the territories of the state. So express consenters will be doing what tacit consenters do, *plus* something more. And one might, not completely unreasonably, suppose that this additional express act must add *something* to the consequences of tacit consent. But if the *content* of the tacit consenting denizen's consent *already* includes the obligations of membership (as I've argued), then it is hard to imagine what express consent could *add* to the moral consequences of tacit consent except something in the *duration* of those obligations of membership.[17]

To put this point more explicitly in the terms of the interpretation of Locke's position for which I have here argued, Locke might be reasoning as follows. The principle for interpreting the content of vague or inexplicit consent is essentially a *charitable* principle: we should understand the consent to be given to *no more than* that which is necessary to the purpose for which it was given. The tacit consent of the alien is given only to obedience to law and liability to punishment. The tacit *political* consent of the denizen is given to this obedience and liability *plus* a kind of membership in the state and more general obligations of support for it. *Express* political consent is given to this membership as well, as Locke explicitly asserts. But what could be the *purpose* of making an express oath of allegiance, if merely living as a denizen already establishes membership? Surely the purpose

16 Locke has been frequently criticized for his position on this question. For just a few of the many such criticisms, see (e.g.) Seliger, op. cit., pp. 279–80; John Dunn, "Consent in the Political Thought of John Locke," in Dunn's *Political Obligation in Its Historical Context* (Cambridge: Cambridge University Press, 1980), p. 42; and my own complaints (which I here retract) in *On the Edge of Anarchy*, pp. 87–88.

17 Or one might claim (somewhat less plausibly, I think) that giving express consent, *on top* of one's previous tacit consent, is analogous to making the same promise to two different parties. The resulting obligation might be viewed as *stronger* or less easily overridden than if the promise had only been made to one party.

must be to create an even *firmer* bond to the state, reinforcing one's tacit commitment with a public declaration.

But if this is the purpose of express consent, then we must understand the content of any (not fully explicit) express oath of allegiance in terms of what is necessary to that purpose. And what is necessary to that purpose is a more permanent relationship with the commonwealth than that already established by the tacit consent of the denizen. Compare (what I am supposing might be) Locke's reasoning here with how we might reason about the best way to understand the moral significance of other sorts of relationships – say, relationships of "romantic cohabitation." What obligations flow from marriage vows (or other public declarations), as opposed to those that flow merely from living together (monogamously) – leaving aside for now the obvious *legal* consequences of *legal* marriages. Undertaking the relationship of "living together," all by itself and independent of any express promises, might reasonably be taken to involve certain kinds of tacit commitments by the parties involved, commitments that go beyond those presupposed by simple romantic "involvement" of other sorts – such as deeper commitments to a special regard and care for one's mate, mutual support and affection, and so on (think here of the moral bases for legal "palimony" suits). But for those already living together to take *vows* of care and support, in a deliberately public ceremony, might also reasonably be taken to go still further, to involve one in a different and still more serious order of commitment – such as a commitment to making the relationship long-lived, insofar as it is within one's power. What *other* moral point could such a public declaration have, if not to make firmer and more enduring (by making explicit and public) the commitment already made in choosing to live together? And we might then, with Locke, reason similarly about the express consenting denizen. Employing Locke's principle for interpreting inexplicit consent, we might expect him to say of the difference between tacit and express political consent exactly what he does say.

It could be argued, of course, that if tacit and express political consent are both to be understood to be consent to whatever is necessary for having a peaceful, viable political society, then both express *and* tacit consent should be taken to generate obligations of *permanent* allegiance. For viable states can hardly have their members fleeing the state every time soldiers are needed or the taxes come due. But experience has shown us (and had showed Locke, I think) that denizens are not very likely to abandon their homelands in the face of such burdens, at least not in numbers great enough to threaten the viability of the state. After all, even in the face of extremely unpopular wars waged with conscripts, such as the American "police action" in Vietnam, only a tiny percentage of even the war's most dedicated critics seemed to flee their homeland in order to escape the burdens of continued membership. So Locke's point about the differing durations of obligations differently undertaken may well prove defensible after all.

Where, then, are we left by my proposed resolution of the "puzzles" in Locke's discussion of tacit consent? The position I've ascribed to Locke involves, I think, plausible accounts of the concepts of express and tacit consent and a plausible principle for the interpretation of the content of not-fully-explicit consent (of either sort). Contrary to initial appearances, I've argued, Locke has the argumentative resources required to distinguish, in an intuitively appealing way, between the moral positions of express consenters, tacit consenting denizens, and tacit consenting aliens. The members of each civil society will include not only express consenters, but also all tacit consenters whose lives are centrally tied to the society. This is, I believe, what we should *want* Locke to be saying, since this would be the best position for a defender of a consent theory of political obligation and authority.

In the end, however, we are still left only with the best version of a theory that cannot in fact achieve its (and Locke's) ambition of demonstrating widespread political obligation, in any actual political societies, contemporary or historical (including Locke's own). As I've argued elsewhere,[18] even if Locke's consent theory correctly identifies the necessary and sufficient conditions for political obligation and for legitimate political authority, it does not succeed in showing that the actions of typical subjects of typical states in fact do count as binding acts of tacit consent. On this point Locke still faces the by-now-familiar problems I noted at the beginning of this paper: all morally binding consensual acts, tacit as well as express, must be appropriately voluntary and intentional. And this means that *tacit* acts of political consent, in order to satisfy the requirements of voluntariness and intentionality, must be intentional responses to clear, free choice situations. But typical subjects of typical states face neither *clear* choice situations – given the absence of clear conventions governing the choice of membership for denizens – nor adequately *free* choice situations – given the typically very limited range of even minimally acceptable alternatives to choosing full membership in the state. So, in the end, resolving the puzzles of Locke's theory of tacit political consent will not, in my view, resolve the thornier problem of producing a widely applicable theory of

---

18 *On the Edge of Anarchy*, chap. 8.

political obligation. What it *may* do, however, is help show us the way to a *defensible*, even if *not* widely applicable, theory of political obligation – a voluntaristic political philosophy that entails (in conjunction with the facts of actual political life) not widespread political obligation, but rather its virtually complete absence.[19,20]

19 I have defended this position in both *Moral Principles and Political Obligations* (Princeton: Princeton University Press, 1979) and *On the Edge of Anarchy*, chap. 8. For more on the meaning and significance of this "philosophical anarchism" (and for responses to familiar objections to it) see my "Philosophical Anarchism," in J. T. Sanders and J. Narveson (eds.), *For and Against the State* (Lanham: Rowman & Littlefield, 1996).
20 I would like to thank Nancy Schauber and an audience at Bowling Green State University for their helpful comments on earlier drafts of this paper.

9

HUMAN RIGHTS AND WORLD CITIZENSHIP: THE UNIVERSALITY OF HUMAN RIGHTS IN KANT AND LOCKE

I

Kant's cosmopolitanism is nowhere more evident than in his essay *Perpetual Peace*. Cosmopolitan right is there described as "a universal right of humanity,"[1] derived from the idea that "individuals . . . may be regarded as citizens of a universal state of mankind (*ius cosmopoliticum*)."[2] Kant's apparent appeal to the idea of "world citizenship" as the basis for human rights claims, of course, calls to mind both older, Stoic employments of that idea (with no corresponding theory of *rights*) and contemporary uses of the idea to defend robust accounts of universal human rights. Readers of Kant may be disappointed, then, to find him asserting that "cosmopolitan right shall be limited to conditions of universal hospitality," where this "right of hospitality" amounts only to "the right of a stranger not to be treated with hostility when he arrives on someone else's territory."[3] Indeed, cosmopolitan right permits even that this stranger "may be turned away, if this can be done without causing his death."[4] Kantian "citizens of the world," it seems, benefit only quite minimally from their membership in the world community.

Similarly, while Kant in *Perpetual Peace* has much to say about the *civil* rights of citizens (as well as the rights of rulers) within established states, and about the *international* rights of states with respect to one another, his

---

1 Immanuel Kant, *Perpetual Peace: A Philosophical Sketch*, in H. Reiss (ed.), *Kant: Political Writings*, 2nd ed. (Cambridge: Cambridge University Press, 1991), 108.
2 *Perpetual Peace*, 98–99n.
3 Ibid., 105. Kant says the stranger "may only claim a *right of resort*" (ibid., 106).
4 Ibid., 105–106.

few passing references to the *natural* rights of persons or the sacred "rights of man" are quick and vague[5] (and often confined to footnotes[6]). This may create the impression that Kant is not very serious in his support of human rights. Indeed, it may seem that Kant cannot be taking very seriously *either* the rights of man *or* the rights of citizens, if he can argue that rebellion against an "oppressive tyrant" is always "in the highest degree wrong," even when "the rights of the people have been violated."[7]

Kant's cosmopolitanism, then, may seem weak and half-hearted to the contemporary advocate of human rights. My object in this essay will be to explore more carefully Kant's position on world citizenship and human rights, to see whether such skepticism about it is warranted. This will involve talking more seriously about both Kant's theory of rights and the ideas of world citizenship and human rights. I will also in this essay briefly compare the Kantian approach to these issues to another, equally well known approach: the approach employed by Locke (and by contemporary Lockeans). This comparison should help us to see more clearly the range of options available to contemporary defenders of human rights.

II

What does it mean to claim that human beings are all "citizens of the world"? Such claims are typically advanced as part of the defense of two corresponding ideas. The first is the denial of the priority of "the local" – that is, denial of the authoritativeness of local community- or polity-based rules or conventions limiting our responsibilities to those owed exclusively to fellow members of our community or polity. The second idea is the corresponding affirmation of universal rights of respect and consideration, correlated with universal duties to assure or provide these goods to all humankind.

Viewed from this perspective, there is nothing even remotely odd about Kant's use of the language of world citizenship. Like Diogenes the Cynic – who declared "I am a citizen of the world" – and like the great Stoic thinkers who put flesh on the bare bones of that declaration, Kant is plainly committed to the idea that it is the *humanity* of others (or their "rational nature"), not their local communities, cultures, or nations, that chiefly

5 E.g., ibid., 95, 104, 106, 112, 125, 129.
6 E.g., ibid., 99n, 101n.
7 Ibid., 126.

determines our obligations toward them. The categorical imperative requires that we treat others always as ends-in-themselves and thus as possible members of a "kingdom of ends." In this sense, each of us must think of ourselves as part of one moral "community," regulating our actions as if we were all citizens of that world-state (in a condition of perpetual peace) that stands for us as a regulative Idea of Reason.[8] The relation of Kant's moral theory to his doctrine of perpetual peace thus appears to be that "peace will bring with it the entire achievement of the Kingdom of Ends on earth."[9]

As citizens of the world we must take seriously those outside our political (and other local) communities in the same ways that we (aspire to) take seriously those within them. We should, with Plutarch, regard all humans as fellow citizens, even if there is in fact no world-state that grants us all equal world citizenship. The connection between classical Stoicism and Kant's moral philosophy is described by Martha Nussbaum as follows:

> This clearly did not mean that the Stoics were proposing the abolition of local and national forms of political organization and the creation of a world state. Their point was even more radical: that we should give our first allegiance to no mere form of government, no temporal power, but to the moral community made up by the humanity of all human beings. The idea of the world citizen is in this way the ancestor and the source of Kant's idea of the "kingdom of ends," and has a similar function in inspiring and regulating moral and political conduct.[10]

Nussbaum's comparison between Kant and the Stoics certainly seems at least initially apt, especially when we notice that Kant continues in his later (and more systematic) works to refer to persons as citizens of the world.[11] Indeed, Kant even utilizes the Stoics' favorite metaphor of each person standing at the center of a series of concentric circles of association and responsibility, circles expanding from the self to family and friends to city and nation to humanity – with the guiding idea being the desirability of bringing those in the outermost circle closer to the innermost circle. Kant

---

8 Ibid., 109. See also Kant's *The Metaphysics of Morals*, 160–161 (Doctrine of Right, Conclusion [354–355]) (Cambridge: Cambridge University Press, 1991; tr. M. Gregor).

9 Christine M. Korsgaard, *Creating the Kingdom of Ends* (Cambridge: Cambridge University Press, 1996), 33.

10 Nussbaum, "Patriotism and Cosmopolitanism," in J. Cohen (ed.), *For Love of Country* (Boston: Beacon Press, 1996), 7–8.

11 See *Metaphysics of Morals*, 99, 158 (Doctrine of Right, sections 28, 62 [281, 353]).

writes: "while making oneself a fixed center of one's principles, one ought to regard this circle drawn around one as also forming part of an all-inclusive circle of those who . . . are citizens of the world."[12]

At this level, the central purpose of claims of world citizenship is simply "the inclusion of everyone in the domain of ethical concern,"[13] a purpose Kant certainly shares. Here we can distinguish three modern traditions that follow the Stoic idea of world citizenship as equal moral standing. The first, natural law tradition argues for our moral equality in terms of our equality as the creatures (and thus the property) of God, with our consequent equal standing under God's natural moral law for humankind. The second, the Kantian tradition, locates our equal moral standing (or "world citizenship") in the "rational nature" or autonomy shared by all of humanity. The third, utilitarian tradition argues that "everybody [is] to count for one, nobody for more than one" because of our equal susceptibility to pain and equal potential for happiness, hence our equal standings in the "felicific calculus" of morality.

It is perhaps worth noting that none of these "impartialist" defenses of world (moral) "citizenship" has had a completely unequivocal relationship with the defense of universal human rights. While Locke, for instance, defends both a largely traditional Thomistic conception of natural law and one of the most influential modern theories of natural rights, many other (especially earlier) representatives of the natural law tradition either lacked altogether any related theory of natural or human *rights* or gestured only vaguely in that direction.[14] And while contemporary Kantians are often staunch defenders of human rights,[15] Kant himself (as we have seen) appears to have only a very thin conception of human rights. Finally, while both classical and contemporary utilitarians have attempted to defend general theories of human (i.e., universally applicable moral) rights,[16] it has also been a commonplace in contemporary moral philosophy to charge utilitarianism with a systematic inability to "take rights seriously."[17]

---

12 Ibid., 265 (Doctrine of Virtue, section 48 [473]).
13 Amartya Sen, "Humanity and Citizenship," in Cohen (ed.), *For Love of Country*, 115–116.
14 For a good discussion of early theories of (and the rudiments of theories of) natural right, see Richard Tuck, *Natural Rights Theories* (Cambridge: Cambridge University Press, 1979).
15 See, as perhaps the clearest example, the work of Alan Gewirth (e.g., his *Human Rights* [Chicago: University of Chicago Press, 1982]).
16 See, for instance, J. S. Mill's classic utilitarian defense of moral rights in chapter 5 of *Utilitarianism*, and L. W. Sumner, *The Moral Foundations of Rights* (Oxford: Oxford University Press, 1987).
17 See, e.g., Ronald Dworkin, "Taking Rights Seriously," in *Taking Rights Seriously* (Cambridge: Harvard University Press, 1975).

Each of these three modern traditions, then, unequivocally affirms humankind's moral equality (and "world citizenship"), but each has a far less consistent record of convincingly affirming universal human rights. We would thus do well to explore further the connection between claims of moral equality and defenses of human rights. This I will briefly do, principally in connection with the positions of Kant and Locke (as representatives of the first two traditions mentioned above).

To be perfectly clear before proceeding, however, we should recall first that there are *other* positions (beyond those thus far discussed) often associated with claims of universal world citizenship that *none* of these three impartialist traditions obviously (or at least consistently) defends. I refer here to the views (briefly mentioned above) that (a) our "first allegiance" should always be to the community of human beings, even where such allegiance conflicts with (as we might suppose it often would) our duties to our lawful sovereigns, and (b) individual sovereign states ought to be eliminated in favor of a world-state.

Neither Kant nor Locke, for instance, seems to accept either of these views. With respect to (a), Locke in fact appears to want to deny the *possibility* of conflict between our legitimate political obligations (owed to our local political communities) and any larger responsibilities (under natural law) to persons generally. For our political obligations, according to Locke, rest on our actual (express or tacit) consent to the authority of our political communities and their governments; and our consent can only succeed in binding us when it is given to arrangements that are morally permissible (under natural law).[18] Our special allegiance, then, is always owed to that community (if any) to which we have consensually bound ourselves, but this allegiance is necessarily fully consistent with acting on our natural moral duties (owed to all persons).[19] With respect to (b), Locke never even considers, nor seems in any way committed to considering, the abolition of individual sovereign states. Since a group of persons joining together into a sovereign state "injures not the freedom of the rest" of mankind (who

---

18 Locke, *Second Treatise of Government* (Cambridge: Cambridge University Press, 1960; ed. P. Laslett), 330, 347–349, 284 (sections 95, 119–122, 23). For the defense of this interpretation of the cited passages in Locke, see my *On the Edge of Anarchy: Locke, Consent, and the Limits of Society* (Princeton: Princeton University Press, 1993), esp. parts 2 and 4.

19 Locke, of course, allows that citizens may empower their governments to act *for* them in their relations with those outside the political community (creating what Locke calls the "federative power" of the state [*Second Treatise*, 365 (sections 145–146)]). But citizens cannot thereby give up their responsibilities to see to it that they (or their governments, acting for them) discharge their duties to all persons under natural law.

are at liberty to do the same or to remain in the state of nature),[20] there can for Locke be no compelling argument from the moral equality of persons ("world citizenship" in our impartialist sense) to the mandatory dismantling of the system of sovereign states.

Kant's similar rejection of these views is, if anything, even clearer than Locke's. With respect to (a), Kant argues that we must be first citizens of lawful polities, for we can neither secure our rights nor respect the rights of others without subjecting ourselves to the lawful public coercion of the civil condition. Our first allegiance must be always to our lawful sovereign, not to the "moral community," even where that sovereign commands us unjustly.[21] Further (with respect to [b]), while the idea of a world-republic is for Kant in some sense one by which we ought to be guided, he is plainly concerned not only that a world-republic would never be accepted by sovereign states, jealous of their independence,[22] but also that a world-republic would not be desirable even if it could be achieved. A world-state of any sort would either degenerate into tyranny or would have laws whose protective force would be lost when applied over so wide a domain.[23] It is not the world-republic (or "world citizenship" in the fuller sense that implies) toward which we should aspire, according to Kant, but the more reasonable goal of a universal "pacific federation" of sovereign republics.[24] Only in the abstract, in a world humans cannot realize, is the world-state a goal.

Given these apparent limits on the modern aspiration to the ideal of "world citizenship," I shall here treat the measure of the seriousness of one's commitment to that ideal in terms of the robustness of the body of rights and duties acknowledged within the theory. To what extent does the theorist's acknowledgment of the moral equality of persons lead to the recognition of universal human rights and universal duties to respect these rights? It is to that question, specifically in connection with the views of Kant and Locke, that I now turn.

III

To fix the terms of the discussion from the start, let us begin with a definition of "human right" (though any such definition is bound to be con-

20 *Second Treatise of Government*, 331 (section 95).
21 *Perpetual Peace*, 126–127.
22 *Perpetual Peace*, 103, 105.
23 See "On the Common Saying: 'This May be True in Theory, but it does not Apply in Practice'," in Reiss (ed.), *Kant: Political Writings*, 90; and *Metaphysics of Morals*, 156 (Doctrine of Right, section 61 [350]).
24 *Perpetual Peace*, 102; *Metaphysics of Morals*, 156 (Doctrine of Right, section 61 [350–351]).

troversial). I have spoken before of both natural and human rights, and it is common to use these terms interchangeably. I prefer to distinguish them as follows: *human* rights are rights possessed by all human beings (at all times and in all places), simply in virtue of their humanity. *Natural* rights (to give a more Lockean than Kantian account) are those rights that can be possessed by persons in a "state of nature" (i.e., independent of any legal or political institution, recognition, or enforcement). Natural rights thus include both (what Kant calls) "innate" and "acquired" rights. Human rights are those natural rights that are innate and that cannot be lost (i.e., that cannot be given away, forfeited, or taken away).[25] Human rights, then, will have the properties of universality, independence (from social or legal recognition),[26] naturalness, inalienability, non-forfeitability, and imprescriptibility.[27] Only so understood will an account of human rights capture the central idea of rights that can always be claimed by any human being.

If one had only a passing acquaintance with Kant's moral and political works, it might be difficult to guess where he stands on the question of natural or human rights (understood as described above). On the one hand, of course, Kant's defense of the categorical imperative of morality includes a defense of "perfect" moral duties owed to others (Kant's example of a perfect duty to others in the *Grundlegung* is the duty not to make "lying promises"). Such perfect duties, it seems, correlate with others' *rights* to our performances; and the categorical character of the duties suggests that these duties, along with their correlative rights, are in force at all times, in all places, with respect to all other persons. Reasoning of this sort naturally suggests Kant's commitment to a comprehensive set of *human rights* – that is, human rights to the performance by all other persons of all of their perfect duties (owed to others). This set of rights might naturally be expected to include rights not to be murdered, be assaulted, be tortured, be lied to, to have promises broken to one, and so on.

On the other hand, however, Kant's political writings frequently express

---

25 I discuss the various kinds of rights and rights-loss in both *On the Edge of Anarchy*, especially chapters 2 and 5, and *The Lockean Theory of Rights* (Princeton: Princeton University Press, 1992), especially chapter 2.

26 As Alan Gewirth puts it, "the existence of human rights is independent of whether they are guaranteed or enforced by legal codes or are socially recognized" ("The Epistemology of Human Rights," in E. F. Paul, J. Paul, F. D. Miller, Jr. (eds.), *Human Rights* [Oxford: Basil Blackwell, 1986]), 3).

27 Whether or not some or all human rights must be *absolute* – that is, incapable of being overridden by competing considerations – I will not address here. Article 15 of the European Convention of Human Rights specifically makes some human rights (freedom from torture, slavery, and retroactive legal prosecution) absolute.

sympathy for what appears to be a Hobbesian picture of the state of nature. Hobbes, remember, holds that a state of nature will inevitably be a state of active war, and that in a state of war "the notions of right and wrong, justice and injustice have . . . no place"; there can "be no propriety, no dominion, no mine and thine distinct."[28] There are in a Hobbesian state of nature no *rights* (beyond the competitive "right to every thing"); consequently, a Hobbesian can defend no theory of *human* rights. And Kant says some very Hobbesian things about the state of nature. The state of nature, Kant insists, is "a state of war" in which I may treat my neighbor "as an enemy";[29] it is "a state devoid of justice."[30] We might well conclude from such claims that Kant cannot be a defender of *any* human rights, especially given Kant's obvious familiarity with the significance of Hobbes' similar claims and Kant's apparent defense of other Hobbesian positions (e.g., his denial of all rights of political resistance and his insistence that the sovereign is above the law).

So several of Kant's arguments might be taken to suggest either (1) a Hobbesian/positivist account, on which there are no natural or human rights (all rights depending for their existence on social or legal recognition and enforcement), or (2) a Lockean/natural law account, on which all persons are "born to" an extensive set of rights not to be harmed or coerced by others, rights they possess and can fully realize even in a state of nature.[31] There is, however, a third (intermediate) possible position on human rights, one that is suggested, for example, by the wording of the 1948 United Nations Declaration of Human Rights. That document claims (in a way that might seem to echo Kant) that human rights are based in "the dignity and worth of the human person." But many of the human rights subsequently enumerated in the Declaration are rights that could not possibly be possessed in a state of nature, that depend on the existence of quite contingent social arrangements, or that could only be secured in a civil (i.e., political) condition. For instance, the human rights to due process of law (Articles 7, 8, 10, 11), to a nationality (Article 15), to political participation (Article 21), to social security (Article 22), to employ-

---

28 Thomas Hobbes, *Leviathan* (London: Penguin, 1985), 188 (chapter 13).
29 *Perpetual Peace*, 98.
30 *Metaphysics of Morals*, 124 (Doctrine of Right, section 44 [312]). See also ibid., 122, 145 (Doctrine of Right, sections 42, 49 [307–308, 336–336]).
31 For Locke, however, these rights can be *forfeited* by wrongdoing (and so are not exactly *human* rights, in the precise sense delineated above); and added to the (negative) rights not to be harmed is for Locke a positive right to needed *charity*. See my defense of this reading of Locke in *The Lockean Theory of Rights*, chapters 3 and 6.

ment (Article 23), and to paid holidays (Article 24) are all rights that make sense only within (or with an eye to future) economic, social, and political structures that are in no way necessary features of the human condition.[32]

Some human rights, then, are on this view rights to enjoy certain benefits *within* nonnatural institutional structures – that is, they are rights to have such structures created and sustained. *Other* human rights, such as the rights to liberty and security (Article 3), not to be enslaved (Article 4) or tortured (Article 5), or to freedom of movement (Article 13) or expression (Article 19) seem to be rights whose noninfringement in no way depends on the existence of contingent institutional arrangements and which can therefore be demanded and secured within any variation on the human condition, including the state of nature.

A careful reading of Kant might well suggest that something like this third, intermediate position on human rights is closer to Kant's own view than either the (Hobbesian) positivist or the (Lockean) natural law account. Kant appears to reject both the "moral minimalism" of the former account (where neither individuals nor states at war with one another possess any rights correlating with the duties of others)[33] and the "moral self-sufficiency" of the latter account (where rights can all in principle be secured without any institutional creation or cooperation).

To see this, it will be necessary to briefly summarize Kant's taxonomy of rights. Kant defines rights as "(moral) capacities for putting others under obligations."[34] Rights are derived from (are known "in reference to") those of our duties that Kant calls "duties of right" or "juridical duties."[35] These are the duties imposed by juridical moral laws (to be contrasted with "ethical laws") – that is, by those moral laws that require for compliance only external action, rather than also requiring that we act from a specific motive or incentive.[36] Kant's "theory (or doctrine) of Right" (or justice) is

---

32 Indeed, the right to social security is specifically identified as a right possessed by "everyone, as a member of *society*" (my emphasis).
33 The distance between Kant's view and that of Hobbes becomes evident when one attends to the following: (1) à la Locke (and contra Hobbes), there can be *society* in Kant's state of nature; the state of nature excludes only *civil* society (*Metaphysics of Morals*, 67, 121 [Doctrine of Right, Introduction, section 41] [242, 306]); (2) there is for Kant (as we will see below) at least one *innate* right; and (3) against Hobbes, Kant does seem to acknowledge *some* rights and wrongs even in war (*Metaphysics of Morals*, 153–154 [Doctrine of Right, section 57] [347–348]).
34 *Metaphysics of Morals*, 63 (Division of the Doctrine of Right [237]).
35 Ibid., 47, 64 (Introduction to the Metaphysics of Morals, Division of the Doctrine of Right [220, 239]).
36 Ibid., 46 (Introduction to the Metaphysics of Morals [218–219]).

the theory of juridical law (and its possibility of external – i.e., political – lawgiving).[37] This theory of Right is divisible into the theories of civil or Public Right and natural or Private Right. "Right in a state of nature is called private Right."[38]

Rights, Kant tells us, are either natural (when they rest "only on a priori principles") or positive (when they are established by "the will of a legislator"). Rights are also either innate (belonging "to everyone by nature") or acquired (requiring an act, such as a promise or a "taking" of property, to establish them).[39] The rights in these classes can be of three kinds: rights to *do* things, to *possess* things (including, through contract, to "possess" an action performed by another), and to *be* in some state or condition. In each case, to say that "I have a right to X" is to say that X may be justly realized or protected by *coercion*.[40]

Our first interest here is in Kant's conception of private natural right. What kinds of natural innate or acquired rights can persons possess in a state of nature? Kant's answer is that "there is only one innate right: *freedom* (independence from being constrained by another's choice), insofar as it can coexist with the freedom of every other in accordance with a universal law, is the only original right belonging to every man by virtue of his humanity."[41] Further, it seems that *acquired* private rights – rights to property or rights arising from contract – are at best *provisional* in character; we can only *conclusively* acquire rights (to add to our innate right to freedom) in civil society.[42] Indeed, it seems to be precisely because only civil society can make these rights "real" or conclusive that Kant insists that all persons have a duty to *leave* the state of nature (and a right against others that they do so as well).[43] So again we seem to be faced by a theory of rights that acknowledges only the most minimal *human* rights. How then can Kant blithely refer to the "rights of man" as "God's most sacred institution on earth", which must be respected "however great a sacrifice this requires"?[44]

When we consider what Kant must *mean* in affirming his "single" innate right to freedom the answer to this question becomes clearer. Though Kant

---

37 Ibid., 55 (Doctrine of Right, Introduction [229]).
38 Ibid., 67 (Division of the Doctrine of Right [242]).
39 Ibid., 63 (Division of the Doctrine of Right [237]).
40 Ibid., 57 (Doctrine of Right, Introduction [231–232]).
41 Ibid., 63 (Division of the Doctrine of Right [237]). See also *Perpetual Peace*, 99n; "Theory and Practice," 74.
42 *Metaphysics of Morals*, 78 (Doctrine of Right, section 9 [256–257]).
43 See Mary Gregor, "Kant on 'Natural Rights'," in R. Beiner and W. J. Booth (eds.), *Kant & Political Philosophy* (New Haven: Yale University Press, 1993), 65–69.
44 *Perpetual Peace*, 101n, 125.

never explicitly analyzes this right, it must, I think, be understood to be divisible into two quite substantial parts. First, the right of freedom must be seen as including a (private) right to control one's own body and thus to be free from physical harm (coercion, torture, and so on). Kant is willing to allow, for instance, that even in the state of nature, when someone "e.g., snatches an apple from my hand," he "affects and diminishes what is internally mine (my freedom)"; so acts of others which harm or control my body or what is physically continuous with my body *wrong* me by violating my innate right to freedom.[45] Even in the state of nature, then, there are human rights against physical aggression by others.[46] Second, the innate right to freedom includes the right to those further conditions that are necessary to the realization of human freedom. These include the right to be in civil society – so that conclusive acquired rights are possible[47] and the effective enforcement of *all* rights is possible – and the right to be in a civil society of a particular *sort* – that is, one that provides constitutionally for the equality and independence that are implied or encompassed within our innate right to freedom. They include as well the right to be in an *international* community that is at peace.

From Kant's single innate right to freedom, then, flows a quite extensive body of innate human rights, including both rights to decent treatment even within the state of nature and innate rights to the civil and international conditions for full human freedom. When Kant describes the state of nature as a state "devoid of justice," he means only that it is a condition "in which, when rights are *in dispute* . . . , there would be no judge competent to render a verdict having rightful force."[48] In the state of nature, there is no effective enforcement of rights and there is nobody with the authority to settle disputed rights. What Kant does *not* mean by saying that the state of nature is "devoid of justice" is what Hobbes or a rights-positivist would mean by this: that the state of nature is a "moral vacuum"

---

45 *Metaphysics of Morals*, 72 (Doctrine of Right, section 6 [250]). What is "internally mine" is for Kant equivalent to what is "innately" mine by right (ibid., 63 [Division of the Doctrine of Right] [237]).

46 *Provided*, Kant adds, that one intends to try, so far as one can, to *leave* the state of nature and its lawless condition. Those who intend to *remain* in their lawless condition in effect *consent* to the violence of the state of nature and so cannot claim to be wronged by such violence (*Metaphysics of Morals*, 78, 122 [Doctrine of Right, sections 9, 42] [256–257, 307–308]).

47 Kant appears to believe that acquired rights in the state of nature would be too *indeterminate* to permit the settling of disputes. For this, external positive law is required. See Gregor, "Kant on 'Natural Rights'," 68–69.

48 *Metaphysics of Morals* 124 (Doctrine of Right, section 44 [312]).

in which there are no rights and in which no acts count as morally wrong (since *unenforced* rights are no rights at all). Kant's position is thus consistent with his embracing a *serious* theory of the "sacred rights of man." This is, I think, what we should expect of Kant once we have examined his chart of the "Division of the Doctrine of Right." For there Kant plainly equates "the Right of men" with the correlates of our perfect duties (of right) to others.[49] And these perfect duties are, as we have already seen, quite extensive.[50]

So Kant's theory of human rights may after all be similar in certain ways to the third, intermediate position on human rights identified earlier. He can recognize both substantial rights against coercion and aggression, binding even in a state of nature or a condition of war, and rights to certain social, political, and international conditions. All this seems to follow even *without* any consideration of what Kant calls *cosmopolitan* right. Before turning (in section V) to the question of what cosmopolitan right *adds* to Kant's theory of human rights (as we have described it thus far), however, I want to pause briefly to consider (in section IV) the relationship between Kant's theory and that theory which I have identified as its chief competitor: Locke's natural law theory of "human rights."

IV

Despite the fact that both are acknowledged champions of the rights of man, there is clearly one sense in which two moral theories could hardly differ more fundamentally than do Locke's and Kant's. Locke's appeal to divine will as the foundation of morality amounts for Kant to Locke's embracing a heteronomous, hence irremediably flawed, grounding for morality. At another level, however, the similarities between the two theories are quite extensive. Locke, in my view, appeals not only to theological grounding for natural law, but simultaneously to quite independent rationalist bases; and some of Locke's rationalist arguments appear to be quite Kantian in character, including his prominent argument to the conclusion that persons are not "made for one another's uses."[51] Perhaps more strik-

49 Ibid., 65 (Division of the Doctrine of Right [240]).

50 "When Kant speaks of the 'rights of man' in his political writings he is usually referring to the notion that persons are ends who ought to be respected and not simply using a catch-phrase without philosophical foundations" (Patrick Riley, *Kant's Political Philosophy* [Totowa: Rowman and Allanheld, 1983], 38).

51 *Second Treatise*, 271 (section 6). I discuss the Kantian aspects of Locke's moral theory in *The Lockean Theory of Rights*, 39–46.

ingly: (1) both Kant and Locke identify our humanity with our "rational nature;"[52] (2) Locke summarizes all of our natural rights as our "natural freedom," just as Kant includes all human rights in our innate right to freedom; and (3) Locke and Kant acknowledge (or are committed to) a very similar body of basic moral rights against violence and coercion.[53] Like Kant, Locke allows that using violence *yourself* makes it permissible for others to use violence against you in the state of nature.[54] Like Kant, Locke believes that in the state of nature there is inadequate enforcement of our rights and that our disputed acquired (property) rights may need to be "settled" by civil authorities.[55] In the face of all of these similarities in their (apparently quite dissimilar) theories of rights, we may reasonably ask where lie the chief differences between their theories.

One obvious difference, of course, is in Locke's defense of and Kant's spirited rejection of the possibility of conclusive natural (acquired) property rights. Kant refuses (sometimes quite plainly in response to Locke) to extend the scope of our rights over our *bodies* to encompass conclusive rights over external possessions. Locke, famously, derived our rights to external property *directly* from our prior rights over our bodies and to the labor that flows from our bodies. In this dispute, I think Locke in fact has the better argument. For if (as we have seen Kant allows) snatching the apple from my hand violates my innate right to freedom (my *internal* property), then surely so does stealing some possession on which I rely but which is *not* in my hand. The mere fact of physical contact with or control over an external object seems (contrary to Kant's apparent view) quite irrelevant to the effect of theft on my *freedom*. My freedom is plainly as much diminished by your taking the apple from my home (where it waits to be my lunch) as it is by your snatching the apple from my hand (as I carry it home to eat for lunch).

Kant also, of course, objects to Lockean theories of natural property rights on the grounds that they permit one person (by his labor and consequent appropriation) to *unilaterally* impose obligations (to respect the property appropriated) on others.[56] Right must respect the *equal* freedom of all, flowing from "a will that is *omnilateral*."[57] If this is Kant's concern, however, the well-known "Lockean proviso" on takings – that we may by

52 *The Lockean Theory of Rights*, 24–25.
53 Ibid., 59–67, 87–89.
54 Ibid., 149–154.
55 *Second Treatise*, 350–351 (sections 123–126); ibid., 295, 299, 302 (sections 38, 45, 51).
56 *Metaphysics of Morals*, 82 (Doctrine of right, section 11 [261]).
57 Ibid., 84 (Doctrine of Right, section 14 [263]).

our labor appropriate only so much property as leaves "enough and as good" in common for others to take[58] – seems to adequately address that concern, for it limits natural property rights to precisely those that *could* be acknowledged by Kant's "omnilateral [general] will." Property claims that respect the Lockean proviso both acknowledge the equal right to freedom of others (by leaving them a "fair share" in common for their own appropriations) and seem well motivated by the very innate right to freedom that Kant himself defends (since our control over external property is often essential to the successful completion of our projects). Similar things, I believe, can be said (with Locke and against Kant) in favor of conclusive (acquired) *contractual* rights in the state of nature.

This disagreement between Kant and Locke in their theories of "private right" is only the most salient disagreement in Kant's texts, not the most basic or fundamental. Far more basic is the difference between Kant and Locke over what is *necessary* for the realization of our innate right to freedom (or our "natural freedom"). While Kant tries to deny that it is the "fact" of "men's maxim of violence and of their malevolent tendency to attack one another" that necessitates civil society and public coercive law – this necessity, he says, "lies a priori in the rational Idea" of the state of nature[59] – it is awfully hard to believe that the mere *idea* of a state of nature, completely independent of any conception of *human nature*, contains the *necessity* of the civil state for the realization of human freedom. Provided only that people were so good that they generally acted as they would act if they *were* subject to public law with the same substance as the *moral* law, there would plainly be no need for civil society. It is the *fact* that man is *not* good in this way, or not perceptive enough to see where right lies, that necessitates the state. Kant cannot, as he seems to believe he can, defeat the anarchist (who believes civil society to be unnecessary) by appeal to entirely a priori judgments. It seems clear that Kant *must* rely on the fact of men's general lawlessness in the absence of coercive law – a fact to which Kant refers again and again – to justify his belief that our innate right to freedom cannot be satisfied except in civil society.

It is on this point, of course, that Kant and Locke part company: Kant's claim that humanity has a *right* to live in civil society is bound not to be persuasive to one, like Locke, who finds in human nature the potential for

---

58 *Second Treatise*, 288 (section 27). See my discussion of this proviso in *The Lockean Theory of Rights*, 278–298.
59 *Metaphysics of Morals*, 123–124 (Doctrine of Right, section 44 [312]).

uncoerced peaceful coexistence. For Locke the state of nature is an inse-cure and uncertain condition, but it is not (as it is for Kant and Hobbes) a state of war. Man's natural sociability, aversion to violence, and sensitiv-ity to the demands of reason's (God's) law, while not always sufficient to overcome his greed, bias in his own favor, and desire for power, are still sufficiently strong to produce a state of nature full of commerce, cooper-ative enforcement of natural law, and social organization – in short, full of all those things that neither Hobbes nor Kant can imagine existing without coercive public law.[60] And because the state of nature is not for Locke an absolutely miserable and perilous condition, nobody has a *right* that others assist him in escaping the state of nature. The civil condition is desirable, and we are free to create it with others at will; but it is not morally manda-tory that we do so. This difference with Kant turns, I think, almost entirely on Locke's different (and more benign) conception of human nature – however much Kant may protest that his position depends on no such "facts" as a conception of human nature.

Further, of course, for Locke the (comparatively) peaceful character of the state of nature entails that life in only *some* civil societies – those that are *limited* in their powers in the ways that Locke famously proposes – is preferable to life in the state of nature. This belief in turn produces in Locke a liberal theory of political resistance, according to which govern-ments acting *ultra vires* may be resisted and removed by their subjects; for it is better to have *no* government than to suffer under one that abuses and exceeds its legitimate powers. Kant, of course, prominently and repeatedly opposes all theories of justified political resistance, again specifically picking Locke's theory for criticism.[61]

It is hard, once again, not to see this disagreement as springing princi-pally from different conceptions of human nature and consequently from different views about what revolution is likely to accomplish. Kant, appar-ently disturbed by the illiberality of his position or concerned to distance himself from Hobbes, does at one point allow that "the people . . . have inalienable rights against the head of state." But these rights, it turns out, "cannot be rights of coercion."[62] And on Kant's own terms that means that they are not *real* rights at all, but only what Kant elsewhere calls "equivocal

---

60 For a defense of this reading of Locke on the state of nature, see my *On the Edge of Anarchy*, chapters 1 and 2.

61 *Metaphysics of Morals*, 133–139, 161, 176–177 (Doctrine of Right, section 49, Conclusion, Appendix [319–323, 355, 371–372]); *Perpetual Peace*, 118, 126–127; "Theory and Prac-tice," 80–85.

62 "Theory and Practice," 84.

rights."[63] Kant here sides again with Hobbes, however unwillingly. Thus, it seems, the deepest disagreements between Locke and Kant in their theories of rights have much the same basis as the well-known differences between Locke and Hobbes. I leave the reader to judge whether such differences favor the Lockean or the Kantian theory of human rights.

V

I return, finally, to the Kantian idea with which we began: the cosmopolitan right of "universal hospitality." Cosmopolitan right is for Kant one of the three divisions (along with civil [or "political"] right and international right [or the "right of nations"]) of his theory of *Public* Right.[64] Public Right, like Private Right, is *based* in natural law for Kant. For while the binding positive law made by civil legislators will not always simply follow or duplicate the a priori requirements of natural law, the *authority* of legislators to impose on others binding positive law itself derives from natural law. Hence positive law and the whole of Public Right rests on the natural law (that is, on those external or juridical laws "that can be recognized as obligatory a priori by reason even without external lawgiving").[65] Public Right is the sum of those conditions under which the freedom of one can coexist with the freedom of everyone else;[66] it thus expresses the full realization in practice of each person's innate right to freedom. *Civil* right, then, concerns the conditions *within* states, just as *international* right concerns those *between* states, that must be brought about if all humans are to be free, as is their right. That there must *be* states, and that sovereign states must themselves establish a "pacific federation," are the most basic requirements on which the other conditions for civil and international freedom are based.

What, though, are we to make of *cosmopolitan* right? Kant is plainly hesitant even to acknowledge this division of Public Right: witness his quite defensive insistence that "the idea of a cosmopolitan right is therefore not fantastic or overstrained."[67] The reason for Kant's hesitancy seems plain. The argument that supports the existence of cosmopolitan right simply cannot be of the same sort as those that support civil and international

---

63 *Metaphysics of Morals*, 59 (Appendix to the Introduction to the Doctrine of Right [233–234]).

64 *Perpetual Peace*, 98–99n; *Metaphysics of Morals*, 123 (Doctrine of Right, section 43 [311]).

65 *Metaphysics of Morals*, 50–51 (Introduction to the Metaphysics of Morals [224]).

66 Ibid., 56–58 (Doctrine of Right, Introduction [230–233]).

67 *Perpetual Peace*, 108.

right – that is, from the necessity, in order to realize human freedom, of bringing about those conditions that minimize the possibility of individual or international *war*. Kant tells us that "establishing universal and lasting peace constitutes not merely part of the doctrine of Right but rather the entire final end of the doctrine of Right."[68] But what does the cosmopolitan right of hospitality have to do with the essential conditions for peace among humans?

The answer, I think, is that cosmopolitan right has *nothing* to do with the necessary conditions for peace and so is a quite questionable part of the doctrine of Right. Cosmopolitan right thus needs a different sort of rationale. Kant offers two different kinds of argument in support of the existence of cosmopolitan right. The argument on which he settles in the *Metaphysics of Morals* appears to be that the cosmopolitan right of hospitality is based on the permanent possibility of interaction and commerce between nations, which requires hospitality for its completion.[69] But the force of this argument is unclear. Under the heading of *international* right Kant has already described the necessary, hence obligatory, conditions for *peace* among nations. Why should the possibility of further *optional* interaction between nations, interaction that is not necessary for peace and human freedom, impose *duties* and rights on us?

Kant also suggests, however, a second, and I think slightly more promising, argument for cosmopolitan right. The organization of the world into states is necessary if peace and freedom are to be achieved. But this organization has certain costs in human freedom, even beyond the obvious cost involved in limiting our liberty to that which is consistent with a universal law of freedom. For the transition from the state of nature to a world of states means that the world is now covered with the rightful *territories* of the various sovereign civil societies and the private properties of their citizens. But, Kant tells us, we must think of the world as originally the possession *in common* of humankind, and think of every person as having "a right to be wherever nature or chance . . . has placed them."[70] It is on the strength of this right and of the "communal possession of the earth's surface" that Kant (in *Perpetual Peace*) bases the cosmopolitan "right of resort."[71] The world of civil territories potentially limits our freedom to be where nature or chance places us and thus interferes with our innate right to freedom.

68 *Metaphysics of Morals*, 161 (Doctrine of Right, Conclusion [355]).
69 Ibid., 158 (Doctrine of Right, section 62 [352]).
70 Ibid., 72–73, 83 (Doctrine of Right, sections 6, 13 [250–251, 262]).
71 *Perpetual Peace*, 106.

The world of civil territories, then, must be understood to be bound by laws of cosmopolitan right to permit the stranger to be where he finds himself – at least to be there temporarily and without fear of violence.

This minimal cosmopolitan right is one of Kant's concessions to the fact that civil society, so essential to enhancing human freedom, can also limit freedom when the whole earth becomes thus "civilized." The cosmopolitan right of hospitality is "a universal right of humanity" precisely because it is in this way derivable from humanity's innate right to freedom. But the mere right of hospitality is not for Kant the only *human* right that must be acknowledged and respected by all nations and people. As we have seen, the innate right to freedom, and the moral equality and "world citizenship" for all this right entails, has quite extensive consequences for a Kantian theory of universal human rights. The cosmopolitanism of Kant's *Perpetual Peace* is only the final piece of, not the entire edifice of, Kant's account of the "sacred rights of man."

10

ORIGINAL-ACQUISITION
JUSTIFICATIONS OF PRIVATE PROPERTY

I Original Acquisition

My aim in this essay is to explore the nature and force of "original-acquisition" justifications of private property. By "original-acquisition" justifications, I mean those arguments which purport to establish or importantly contribute to the moral defense of private property by: (a) offering a moral/historical account of how legitimate private property rights for persons first arose (i.e., at a time prior to which no such rights existed); (b) offering a hypothetical or conjectural account of how justified private property could arise (or have arisen) from a propertyless condition; or (c) simply defending an account of how an individual can (or did) make private property in some previously unowned thing (where "things" might include not only land, natural resources, and artifacts, but also, e.g., ideas or other individuals). The "original acquisition" to which such justifications centrally refer, then, may be either the first instance(s) of legitimate private property in human history (typically assumed to have been many centuries ago on earth), or only the first legitimate acquisition of some *particular* thing (which might, for instance, have occurred yesterday or occur in the future on Mars). But in either case, the justification will involve or entail the defense of one or more moral principles specifying how unowned (or collectively owned) things can become privately owned[1] – that is, the

---

For their helpful comments on an earlier draft of this essay, I am grateful to the other contributors to this volume, to its editors, and to Nancy Schauber.
1 In other words, arguments of type (a) or (b) will *entail* some argument(s) of type (c).

defense of the kind of principles Robert Nozick has called "principles of justice in acquisition."[2]

Most of the first (i.e., seventeenth-century) generation of sophisticated property theories, of course, were "original-acquisition" (henceforth "OA") justifications of private property. Hugo Grotius, Samuel Pufendorf, Richard Cumberland, and John Locke, for example, all tried to defend at least some forms or aspects of private property precisely by presenting historical accounts (or, on some interpretations, conjectural or hypothetical accounts) of the process which created justified private property from a state in which the earth and its resources were all unowned (or only collectively owned). In large part these accounts were just very creative interpretations of the biblical Genesis story; but they relied in part as well on anthropological and economic data and speculation (about, e.g., primitive economies, the origins of money, etc.). Most important, these accounts were taken by their authors to have *moral* weight, to constitute *justifications* of private property by virtue of portraying the historical process in question as morally untarnished, or even obligatory. They were certainly not intended as morally neutral (or condemnatory) histories of a process, such as we might now offer in discussing the origins of practices like sun worship or human slavery.[3]

These and later OA justifications of private property attempted to secure this "moral weight" for their histories by direct or implicit appeal to a wide range of principles, all of which were supposed to evaluate positively the actions and events involved in the historical genesis of private property. Thus, Pufendorf and Grotius appealed to a principle of fidelity, to emphasize the sanctity of the compact or agreement which allowed division of the earth; Thomas Hobbes appealed to the authority (also "contractual" in origin) of the sovereign who makes the laws creating private property;

---

2 Robert Nozick, *Anarchy, State, and Utopia* (New York: Basic Books, 1974), pp. 150–53. Jeremy Waldron has recently argued for restricting the notion of principles of justice in acquisition (what he calls "PJAs") to those which specify "that the transition to the private ownership of a resource can be effected by the *unilateral action* of the individual who is to be the owner" (Waldron, *The Right to Private Property* [Oxford: Oxford University Press, 1988], p. 263; my emphasis). I use the notion more broadly here. I see no reason to deny that a principle concerns the process of "just acquisition" simply because it specifies that taking possession requires the permission or cooperation (e.g., in making contracts or establishing conventions) of other persons. I discuss below (in Section IV) Waldron's main argument against "*unilateral* PJAs."

3 Original-acquisition *condemnations* of private property, or at least of certain kinds of private property systems, are, of course, also familiar. Take, as obvious examples, the arguments offered by many of the Levellers and by Jean-Jacques Rousseau in his *Second Discourse*.

David Hume appealed to the utility of naturally arising conventions; and Locke appealed to the principle that mixing what is yours with what is not yours may add to the quantity of what is yours. Of these seriously historical OA accounts, my discussion will reveal that I take Locke's to be the one most worth discussing. This is true not only because of the more obvious problems with the competing accounts[4] and because of the obvious connections between Locke's and some contemporary OA justifications, but also because of the apparent "naturalness" and "timelessness" of the principles to which Locke appeals (and hence their apparent lack of reliance on widely varying conventions and laws concerning property).

Interest in questions about the justificatory force of such OA arguments for private property has been rekindled in the past two decades by Nozick's gestures toward a similar OA approach. Nozick tells no story about the genesis of private property (his is an OA justification falling in my class [c]). Indeed, he notoriously refuses to state or defend any theory of just acquisition at all, leaving us to simply assume that he must have in mind some principle which is at least broadly Lockean.[5] But despite the vagueness of his account, Nozick clearly intends to take full advantage of the same set of compelling intuitions as did his OA predecessors: that private property in some form or under some conditions must be morally acceptable, that such ownership must have a point of origin,[6] but that such own-

4 Historical compact theories seem both to involve simple fiction (i.e., concerning the occurrence of a genuine and binding historical agreement) and to appeal to an event with could have no binding force for later persons (i.e., the descendants of the historical contractors). Hobbesian positivism seems too "thin" to count as *justifying* much of anything, deriving authority (and the "consent" of subjects) from mere asymmetry of physical power. Humean conventionalism faces obvious problems in the nonmaximizing character of its associated conception of moral virtue, and particularly in its "conventional rule utilitarian" account of the artificial virtues. Indeed, given the possibility that Hume may be trying to justify many stages in the *evolution* of property conventions (and, consequently, shifts in property systems and relations), it may be misleading to describe his account as an attempted OA justification at all. The Lockean account, by contrast, can at least be restated in a theoretically plausible fashion, or so I argue in my book *The Lockean Theory of Rights* (Princeton: Princeton University Press, 1992), ch. 5.

5 Nozick, *Anarchy, State, and Utopia*, p. 153. Nozick contents himself with arguing that whatever principle of justice in acquisition is defended, it must incorporate a proper version of the Lockean Proviso (ibid., pp. 175–82) – that is, a proviso specifying that appropriators must leave "enough and as good" to be appropriated by others.

6 Judith Jarvis Thomson claims that "the following thesis is accepted by most philosophers nowadays: The Ownership-Has-Origins Thesis: X owns a thing if and only if something happened that made X own it" (Thomson, *The Realm of Rights* [Cambridge: Harvard University Press, 1990], p. 323). Thomson argues that the thesis is in fact true (ibid., p. 336).

ership cannot arise from nothing, requiring instead a morally interesting human act (or set of acts) as cause.[7]

The current state of play, however, seems to be this. There is a solid consensus among philosophers and legal and political theorists that attempted OA justifications of private property, when presented in any even remotely plausible form, in fact have little or no interesting justificatory force. However compelling their intuitive underpinnings might be, they can justify nothing which helps much in our deliberations about the possible moral defense of private property in contemporary society. Indeed, the standard view now seems to be that OA justifications face insuperable difficulties in even presenting their basic components in a theoretically coherent or morally nonrepugnant fashion.

I will argue in this essay that the familiar recent critique of OA justifications of private property is in fact quite unreasonably overstated. I will contend that OA justifications can (properly presented and defended) be forceful for and of interest in contemporary property theory – that is, that we (and not just the libertarians among us) must take OA justifications very seriously in considering viable styles of possible justifications for private property. Showing this will require me to be more careful than is usual in talking about the idea of justification. We must be clear about just what an OA argument can justify and in what way or what respect it justifies (the subject of Section II below). I must also try to defuse a set of powerful and well-known objections to OA justifications (in Sections III and IV). My object will not be to actually defend (or fully state) some particular OA argument, but only to dampen contemporary skepticism about the possible justificatory force of such arguments, considered as a class.

II   Justification

Talk of "justifying private property" is, of course, deplorably vague and ambiguous, however happily such language may be used (without further

---

7 In Locke, of course, the act is the unilateral extension of prior property in one's person and one's labor into things in the external world. In Grotius and Pufendorf, the act is the multilateral historical compact or agreement. Concern that no human acts could *create* property from nothing has led some contemporary philosophers to reject the "Ownership-Has-Origins Thesis" (see note 6 above), and to claim that property must in some sense have existed all along. See, e.g., Hillel Steiner, "The Natural Right to the Means of Production," *Philosophical Quarterly*, vol. 27, no. 106 (January 1977), esp. pp. 48–49; and Eric Mack's reply to Steiner in "Distributive Justice and the Tensions of Lockeanism," *Social Philosophy & Policy*, vol. 1, no. 1 (Autumn 1983), pp. 140–43. Classically, of course, Robert Filmer's *Patriarcha* supplied the best example of the view that the world was owned from the beginning of the human race (by virtue of God's gift to Adam).

explanation) in much of the philosophical literature on property. The "justifications" we actually offer in everyday life for our actions or practices cover a very wide range, from those as weak as merely asserting some favorable property of a thing (e.g., "it gives people pleasure") to those as strong as all-things-considered demonstrations of moral flawlessness or optimality. I will suggest here that the project of "justifying private property" should be understood as that of meeting or rebutting certain kinds of fundamental moral objections to that institution: either "comparative" objections that alternative arrangements are morally preferable, or "noncomparative" objections that the institution of private property involves or sanctions wrongdoing or vice. The full ambiguity of the expression "justifying private property," however, springs from at least two distinct sources. One part of the problem concerns the imprecision of the expression with regard to the "level" of justification that is at issue. A second part concerns the fact that justifications can be either (what I will call) "*optimality* justifications" or "*permissibility* justifications."

Let me begin with optimality justifications and try to distinguish the various "levels" at which they might proceed. Philosophical attempts to "justify private property" are most often attempts to defend the comparative judgment that private property systems, considered as a *general type* of institutional (or possibly preinstitutional) arrangement, are morally superior to alternative types of property systems (as well as to possible arrangements in which there is no form of property at all).[8] Private property (in this general sense) might thus be portrayed as morally optimal because it is more conducive than any alternative type of system to the advancement of the most important moral goals, or because it uniquely (or most fully) satisfies the most important moral rules (where these goals or rules might concern, e.g., human preservation, human happiness, moral character or its development, individual desert, or self-government or nondependence). Less commonly, but still perfectly intelligibly, "justifying private property" is taken to mean presenting the much more specific demonstration that some *particular kind* of private property system is the best possible property arrangement, where the kind in question is distinguished not only from all kinds of non-private property (or nonproperty) arrangements, but also from alternative kinds of private property systems. These alternative kinds might include, say, systems specifying that different packages of rights constitute

---

8 See Waldron, *The Right to Private Property*, p. 60. I here use the notion of a "private property system" in, I think, roughly the way detailed by Waldron (ibid., pp. 31–33, 37–46).

private property or that a different range of things are possible objects of private property rights.[9]

But this most basic ambiguity in "level" (between "general-type" justifications and "particular-kind" justifications) is far from being the only problem we face in trying to understand what is meant by claims to "justify private property." For there are both further "levels" at which justifications, still properly so-called, can be aimed, and different kinds of conclusions that count as "justifying." On the first point, we should remember that it is perfectly common in efforts to "justify private property" to be arguing neither for a general type of property system nor for a specific kind of private property system, but rather for a certain actually instantiated system (or range of systems) – namely, our own private property system or the range of such systems currently instantiated in modern (primarily Western) "market economies." Many theorists both understand our proper task in the justificatory enterprise, and interpret classical OA justifications, in terms of justifying our own (or their own) existing private property system(s). The relevant justifications do not concern some general or particular *ideal*; rather, they are conservative "local-kind" justifications, concerned to show that our own private property system is morally optimal (or optimal for us).

Alternatively, it is also easy to find self-described justifications of private property whose actual goal is only to defend as morally optimal a particular class of claim rights *within* existing property systems. Typically, such justifications will try to uphold the claims or holdings of a particular group or economic class within the society in question (e.g., the society's farmers, factory owners, artisans). And it still seems fair to use the label "justifications of private property" even for arguments of such limited scope (which we can call "local-class" justifications), insofar as they, like the others we have mentioned, are also moral defenses of private property rights, even if they do not involve justifying entire (ideal or local) property systems.

Optimality justifications of private property, then, need not be understood as being all of one sort. But further, "justifications" of private property need not take the form of showing private property to be *the optimal*

9 Waldron contends that "a philosophical argument can determine only, as it were, the general shape of a blueprint for the good society. Even if we find that there are good moral grounds for preferring private property to collective property, we still face the question of what conception of private property to adopt" (ibid., p. 61). But I assume Waldron would happily allow that the more specific demonstration, if successfully completed (contrary to his expectations), would count as a different, and even more powerful, justification of private property.

arrangement at all with respect to some moral goal(s) or principle(s). When I try in my everyday life to morally justify my actions, I do not always do so by arguing that what I did was the very best thing I could have done in the circumstances, by making the comparative claim that it was morally superior to all possible alternatives. Often it is sufficient (i.e., sufficient to constitute a *justification*) to show that what I did was morally *permissible,* or that it was otherwise morally legitimate.[10] All too frequently this is the best that I could even hope to show. My action constituted no wrong to others and exemplified no vice, even if there were other equally justifiable (or even preferable) actions I could have performed instead. There were, in short, no telling moral objections of a noncomparative sort to my conduct.

Similarly, I believe, we should think it sufficient to "justify private property" (in one familiar sense of "justification") if we show that private property (at whatever the relevant "level") is morally permissible or legitimate, even if it is not morally optimal or clearly superior to all alternatives. To show this is to offer a "permissibility justification," an argument that private property does not violate basic moral rules and is not subject to other kinds of basic (noncomparative) moral objections. And permissibility justifications can be aimed at all of the same "levels" as optimality justifications can – at the levels of general types of systems, particular kinds of systems, existing or local systems (or ranges of systems), or classes within existing systems. The familiar attempts to show that private property is the *best possible* (i.e., optimal) property arrangement should be viewed as (attempted) "justifications" of a *stronger* sort, not as justifications of the *only* sort. To justify an ideal private property system or to justify an actual distribution of private property rights, it is enough to show that they fall within the range of the morally acceptable. To suppose otherwise is to accept (mistakenly, in my opinion) the view that at least significant parts of morality must be *maximizing,* that for all possible institutional arrangements there must be top-to-bottom moral rankings within which only the top scores pass. Such a denial of moral *thresholds* requires (to say the least) extensive argument.

One final complication should be mentioned. Moral justifications (and, consequently, moral justifications of private property) need not be even as strong as my characterization of "permissibility justifications" has suggested. In evaluating actions, we may take them to be morally justified (i.e., optimal or permissible) even if we acknowledge that they were wrong or

10 Most moral theories that admit the distinction, of course, hold that moral optimality entails moral permissibility. I assume such a view in these remarks.

impermissible *in some respects*. Morally justified actions – actions which are acceptable, right, or best "all things considered" – may harm or even violate the rights of some person(s), provided the actions have some compensating moral properties that make them on balance best or acceptable (i.e., provided their "right-making" characteristics outweigh their "wrong-making" characteristics). So-called "moral dilemmas" can typically be "solved" only by performing actions which are justified in only this minimal sense. I suggest that we remember this sense of "justification" in thinking about the justification of private property. Private property (at whatever level) might be justified "on balance," even if, say, a private property system involved harm to, disadvantage for, or even violation of the rights of some persons living under that system. Showing that some are harmed or disadvantaged by private property, say, does not suffice to show that the institution of private property is impermissible or even suboptimal (i.e., inferior to possible alternatives). On my reading of Locke's arguments, for instance, his belief that governments are justified in "settling" property within their territories[11] is precisely a belief that they may justifiably decide genuinely controversial claims (i.e., those to which there are legitimate moral objections), in whatever fashion is seen by them to be best on balance.[12]

III   Original-Acquisition Justifications

Having noted the diversity of possible aims involved in "justifying private property," we can return now to OA justifications. What kinds of justifications *are* OA justifications? What exactly have OA justifications been trying to be justifications of? And, more important, what *could* such arguments justify? Why, if at all, should we today have any interest in OA justifications?

We can begin by thinking about the goals of the classical OA justifications of private property. It is obvious, first, that most of these arguments displayed a strong conservative, local bias – that is, that the "level" of private property justifications their authors attempted was at least in part that of defending the private property systems enforced in their own societies.[13]

---

11 John Locke, *Two Treatises of Government*, ed. Peter Laslett (New York: Mentor, 1960), *Second Treatise*, sections 38, 45. Subsequent references to the *Two Treatises of Government* will be by I or II, followed by section number.

12 See my *Lockean Theory of Rights*, pp. 307–18.

13 Thomas Horne argues at some length that Grotius, John Selden, Hobbes, Cumberland Pufendorf, James Tyrrell, and Locke all "accepted the legitimacy of private property in general and, more specifically, the distribution of property that existed in their society" (Horne, *Property Rights and Poverty* [Chapel Hill: University of North Carolina Press, 1990], pp. 10, 17, 31, 48). I state below my disagreement with this position in the case of Locke.

And it is probably fair to say not only that in that respect the classical justifications clearly failed, but that all such attempts have clearly been doomed to failure. None of the classical "justifications" was sufficiently fine-grained, imaginative, or forceful to justify all aspects of any imaginable property system, let alone all aspects of the private property systems in legal force at the time their authors conceived them. More generally, however, it seems true that if "justifying private property" is taken to involve justifying in its entirety some actual property system that has been enforced in a prominent modern political society, then no justification of private property is possible. All actual modern property systems have been in many ways manifestly and systematically unjust – both in the acquisitions and transfers they have permitted and in the limits and redistributions they have and have not imposed. But to admit this is only to admit that one sort of justification of private property (a "local-kind" justification) is not and has not in the past been possible; it is not, in my view, to admit that private property cannot be justified, that a defensible system of private property is not achievable.

In the OA justifications of Locke and Pufendorf, we can see the forms, at least, of different and less purely conservative "justifications of private property," of the sorts discussed above. Locke's defense of private property, for instance, while undoubtedly conservative in many respects, was by no means a simple attempt to justify the entire private property system in place in English society in the 1670s and 1680s. It was rather an attempt to portray as clearly unjustified certain of the rights acknowledged within that system – especially those of the very wealthy, idle aristocracy – while presenting as clearly justified certain others – those of the landed gentry (who had rights to the products of the land worked by those they hired) and the commercial classes, as well as the more obvious cases of persons whose rights were in goods with which they had more directly mixed their labor (independent farmers and craftsmen, settlers of overseas wastelands, and so on).[14] Locke's was only a "local-*class*" justification. I will suggest later (in Section IV) that we can plausibly develop such arguments to produce a kind of *presumptive* justification of particular kinds of property claims within property systems that cannot themselves be justified in their entirety. Such selective, presumptive justifications, as we will see, advance admittedly defeasible claims about moral legitimacy (in the sense I will develop in Section IV), but seem to call in the absence of counterargument not for

---

14 See my *Lockean Theory of Rights*, pp. 288–306, 317–18.

the abandonment of property systems, but for revisions in unjustified practices around the solid center of presumptively justified claims.

Further, however, we can see in the arguments of both Locke and Pufendorf their common conviction that one can sufficiently "justify private property" by showing it to be merely a morally *permissible* (or morally possible) arrangement, even without any demonstration of its moral optimality. In Pufendorf this conviction is transparent. For according to his OA story, God's gift of "the earth, its products, and its creatures" to humankind came with no specific instructions about the kind of property system that ought to be instituted. On the contrary, "the law of nature approves all conventions which have been introduced about things by men, provided they involve no contradiction or do not overturn society."[15] Private property systems (of various sorts) are justified in the abstract, on Pufendorf's view, by virtue of their being members of that class of permissible systems on which persons might settle. And existing private property systems in actual societies are justified by virtue of their both belonging to that class and being systems on which people have in fact settled. Justifications of both *types* of systems and *existing* systems are "permissibility justifications"; they proceed without any demonstration of moral optimality.

Similarly, despite Locke's apparent argument that private property is in fact also morally optimal (meaning, in this case, that we are morally required to create it),[16] the main burden of Locke's case is *also*, like Pufendorf's, showing that a private property system is morally possible or permissible. This demonstration has, in fact, at least four distinct points, only the last three of which are of much continuing philosophical interest. First, of course, Locke intends to show how private property is morally possible in the face of apparent scriptural assertions of "original community." If God gave the earth to mankind in common, how could it be morally permissible for persons to take portions of the earth (or its resources) as private property? Locke's (not very convincing) answer is that God gave

---

15 Samuel Pufendorf, *De Jure Naturae et Gentium Libri Octo* (*The Law of Nature and Nations in Eight Books*) [1672], vol. 2, trans. C. H. and W. A. Oldfather (Oxford: Clarendon Press, and London: Humphrey Milford, 1934), bk. 4, ch. 4, section 4:

> Yet it was far from God to prescribe a universal manner of possessing things, which all men were bound to observe. And so things were created neither proper nor common (in positive community) by any express command of God, but these distinctions were later created by men as the peace of human society demanded.

16 I summarize Locke's argument below and in note 17.

the world to us for our productive *use*, and productive use requires private property.[17]

Second, Locke wants to show how it is morally possible for private property in external things to arise (without direct donation from God to individuals) from a condition in which there is no such property at all. The opponent here (again) is Robert Filmer, who argues that the proper way to understand the source of all subsequent private property is in terms of transfers from Adam's original dominion over all the world. If there is *no* original private property in parts of the world, as Locke contends, then (given the absence of any evidence of later donations by God) private property seems miraculously to spring from nothing. Locke's response is that the moral possibility of private property in external things is explained via our prior property in our persons and our labor (II, 27, 39, 44).

Third, Locke tries to show that, quite independent of worries about scripture, taking private property does not necessarily constitute a harm or wrong to other persons. If creating private property in originally unowned things inevitably and wrongfully deprived others of needed goods or fair opportunities, then one could attack private property as morally impermissible and attack existing private property systems as fundamentally and uniformly unjust (as did many of the Levellers writing shortly before Locke). Locke defends the moral permissibility of private property by arguing that in conditions of abundance, one's private appropriations harm no other persons (II, 33, 36), and that even in conditions of greater scarcity, acts of private appropriation need not either treat others unfairly or make anyone worse off than they would have been in the absence of those acts (II, 40–43).

Finally, Locke is attempting to show the moral possibility of meaningful,

---

17 This argument, of course, seems to show not only that private property is morally permissible, but also that it is obligatory to create it. For if (a) we are obligated to preserve ourselves (II, 6), (b) we need the earth's resources to survive, and (c) we can only productively use those resources by privately appropriating them, then it follows that we are obligated to appropriate. Premise (c), of course, is the weak premise in the argument, since productive use of *common* property seems quite possible. Locke's argument runs specifically as follows:

> [T]is very clear, that God . . . has given the Earth . . . to Mankind in common. But this being supposed, it seems to some a very great difficulty, how any one should ever come to have a *Property* in any thing . . . God . . . hath also given them reason to make use of [the world and its resources] to the best advantage of Life . . . yet being given for the use of Men, there must of necessity be a means *to appropriate* them some way or other before they can be of any use, or at all beneficial to any particular Man. (II, 25, 26; some italics deleted)

lasting private property rights by showing how they could arise in nonpolitical, nonlegal, noncontractual contexts. Once he discards the compact theorists' convenient but preposterous fiction of a historical agreement about the division of property, and then discards the Hobbesian, positivist derivation of private property rights from far-too-alterable civil law, Locke seems to face again the impossible task of pulling the private property rabbit from the hat of "the mere corporal act of one person."[18] Locke's strategy is to show that *some* private corporal acts (i.e., those involving purposive labor on unowned nature) are at least as morally significant as contracts between persons or civil laws backed by threat of sanctions.

Throughout these arguments, the *primary* force of Locke's OA justification of private property is to display private property rights as morally possible or permissible, and to articulate the conditions under which this permissibility is sustained. This is true despite Locke's further (unwarranted) conviction that creating private property is also morally *required*. The "permissibility arguments" constitute an attempted *justification* of private property in the sense specified earlier: if successful, they show that private property claims can be legitimate (i.e., morally acceptable), probably were once mostly legitimate, and may still be legitimate in certain (possibly quite widespread) contexts. Showing this, even without demonstrating the moral optimality of private property, would constitute a very significant justificatory achievement. Indeed, simply showing that (and how) private property claims *can* be legitimate under certain physically possible conditions – even when those conditions are now virtually unsatisfiable in most of the world – would still constitute a sort of permissibility justification of private property. The idea of "justification" at work in this most minimal sense of the term is simply the denial of "absolute" (i.e., necessary) wrongness. We might similarly try to give a minimal permissibility justification of, say, slavery, by arguing for its moral permissibility under possible conditions (e.g., dire and otherwise unavoidable societal poverty) that are admitted to be quite unusual or even nonexistent in modern societies. But, as we will see, OA justifications of private property in fact promise to advance well beyond such minimal justifications.

IV   Remoteness Objections

This understanding of the senses in which OA justifications are trying to justify private property can help us to see more clearly why some familiar

18 Pufendorf, *De Jure Naturae et Gentium*, bk. 4, ch. 4, section 5.

complaints about OA justifications are considerably less forceful than is often supposed. For instance, probably the most common criticisms of OA justifications emphasize the *distance* between the rights they attempt to justify and any rights we might today be interested in trying to justify. What OA justifications justify is too *remote* from our present concerns to be theoretically or practically important. These complaints take at least three forms.[19] First, it is claimed that the conditions under which OA justifications could actually justify anything are conditions impossibly remote from those in which we live today. OA arguments (at best) justify private property by appeal to the significance of, e.g., labor on, or occupancy of, or compact with respect to unowned goods in an unregulated time of abundance. But nobody deals with unowned goods anymore, since there are none left to deal with. And far from living in an unregulated time of abundance, we live under firmly established laws and conventions governing property and in circumstances of quite real scarcity of many natural resources. OA justifications may justify *something*, the argument goes, but they simply don't "apply" to concerns about property today, being based on a set of "unrealistic" assumptions.[20]

Second, and even worse (some argue), the conditions and actors imagined in OA histories are probably not even remotely accurate representations of those existing even at the times they concern, nor could we possibly know if they were. As Jeremy Waldron puts it:

---

19 One possible form of the complaint that I will not discuss here is that most OA justifications have concerned themselves exclusively or primarily with *tangible* property, where today our concerns about property centrally include such things as intellectual property, equity in companies, etc. I will simply assume here (without argument) that a suitably revised OA justification could deal satisfactorily with nontangible property as well.

20 Virginia Held claims that

> Locke's assumptions concerning the justifiable acquisition of property are, however, seldom plausible in the contemporary world. The unowned wilderness waiting to be appropriated, so central to Locke's argument, no longer exists. Rarely do we simply mix our labor with nature.... An even more serious difficulty... is that the Lockean proviso, in the contemporary world of overpopulation and scarce resources, can almost never be met. ("Introduction," *Property, Profits, and Economic Justice*, ed. Virginia Held [Belmont: Wadsworth, 1980], pp. 5–6)

See also James O. Grunebaum, *Private Ownership* (London: Routledge & Kegan Paul, 1987), pp. 53, 66–67, 85, and Grunebaum, "Ownership as Theft," *Monist*, vol. 73, no. 4 (October 1990), p. 544; Lawrence Becker, *Property Rights* (London: Routledge & Kegan Paul, 1977), p. 48; and Thomas Mautner, "Locke on Original Appropriation," *American Philosophical Quarterly*, vol. 19, no. 3 (July 1982), pp. 267–68. For a response specifically to concerns about the Lockean Proviso (on which I do not comment here), see David Schmidtz, *The Limits of Government* (Boulder: Westview Press, 1991), pp. 17–27.

One does not have to be an ethical relativist to see the difficulties here. What were conditions like when resources were first taken into ownership? How well developed was moral consciousness? Were those to whom the principle [of just acquisition] was supposed to apply capable of implementing it properly? Could it conceivably have been a principle which they held and abided by explicitly? Or in any way? If we turn from ancient to modern capabilities, how can *we* make sense *now* of principles whose only direct application was hundreds or perhaps thousands of years ago? If we cannot, does that not deprive such a principle of any right to be regarded as the generating basis of a system of entitlements that is to continue to constrain us today?[21]

Finally, even supposing that we are convinced by some OA justification that legitimate private property actually arose (or could have arisen) in the foggy past, in exactly the way specified in the OA history, it is not clear how this would bear on the property claims made by persons today. Even if original acquisitions of things were legitimate, and even if that property was transferred and exchanged as the theory imagines, our knowledge of the history of the process of acquisition and transfer is so spotty that we could not possibly reach any conclusions about who is entitled to what today. Any property rights that may legitimately have arisen at the time when things were first acquired have been so muddied by force, fraud, and our simple ignorance of the relevant histories that we may as well just forget about trying to reconstruct the history of property and accept some nonhistorical conception of property rights.[22]

I hope it is clear by now that much can be said on behalf of OA justifications of private property and against such criticisms. In response to the charge that the conditions of life are now very remote from those appealed to in OA justifications, we can note first that even if true, these charges do not affect at least the most minimal sort of permissibility justification of private property which might be accomplished by an OA argument. OA justifications, by specifying the range of principles and conditions for just original acquisition, can at the very least claim to have shown that legitimate private property is morally possible (i.e., permissible under physically

---

21 Waldron, *The Right to Private Property*, p. 259.

22 Mautner argues on these grounds that "a theory of original appropriation is irrelevant to questions concerning contemporary property rights" ("Locke on Original Appropriation," p. 268). See also Loren E. Lomasky, *Persons, Rights, and the Moral Community* (Oxford: Oxford University Press, 1987), pp. 115–16; Will Kymlicka, *Liberalism, Community, and Culture* (Oxford: Oxford University Press, 1989), pp. 158–59; and Schmidtz's reply in *The Limits of Government*, pp. 27–31. For a much earlier version of this style of argument, see Herbert Spencer, *Social Statics* (1851), ch. 9, section 3 (New York: Augustus M. Kelley, 1969), pp. 115–16.

possible conditions), even if it is seldom possible today. But further, the principles appealed to (explicitly or implicitly) in OA histories are not historically relative in any but the most contingent sense. They are not only principles that apply in conditions which are (merely) physically possible, but principles that *can* apply to our circumstances again, today or in the future, should the conditions of human life (or those for some specific group of humans) change in certain (easily imagined) ways.

Indeed, if the OA justification is alleged not to "apply" to contemporary life because of conditions of scarcity and the lack of unowned land and resources, it is possible to reply simply that there *are* vast quantities of unowned (or common) land and resources available to humankind today, both within the territories of existing political societies and external to them (in Antarctica, for instance, or on the moons and other planets of our solar system). The use of resources in these places, and even the colonization of our moon or of Mars, are not such fanciful possibilities that it is not meaningful or interesting to ask what could justly be claimed as private property in such enterprises. If the principles appealed to in some OA justification are valid, they are principles that may well apply again in the future in contexts such as these. While takings of these still-unowned things are, of course, regulated by domestic laws and international agreements, it is well worth considering both whether these laws and treaties are in fact morally *binding* on all of us, and what kinds of claims on things would be morally defensible in the absence of binding laws and treaties of this sort.[23]

Second, to the charge that OA justifications imagine wildly unrealistic (or at least unknowable) conditions for the acquisition of private property, we must first acknowledge that the classical OA accounts (such as those of Grotius, Pufendorf, and Locke) were so concerned with interpreting (or reinterpreting) scripture that their histories will naturally look bizarre to contemporary secular-humanist eyes. We cannot today think of primitive eras as populated with full-blown, self-conscious, socialized, morally aware persons; so we cannot think of these OA histories as accurate accounts of primitive life. But insofar as OA justifications of private property do not concern the first *brute takings by human beings*, but rather the first *creations of property by persons* (where persons are understood to be rational, morally

---

23 See my *Lockean Theory of Rights*, pp. 235–36. My *Moral Principles and Political Obligations* (Princeton: Princeton University Press, 1979) challenges the moral authority of existing governments or states to enforce such laws and to make treaties or agreements of this sort on our behalf.

developed, self-conscious, purposive agents), we can reasonably grant OA justifications this much: OA histories, suitably revised, might constitute roughly accurate accounts of the emergence of private property (i.e., moral rights in external things) at whatever period in our actual history persons (or groups of persons) began purposive appropriations. But even if we think that OA arguments have not given us even remotely accurate histories of the origins of property (leaving aside the history of mere brute takings by nonpersons), the *principles* of just acquisition defended in OA justifications of private property may still be defensible and applicable both to well-documented historical contexts (such as those instances of seventeenth- and eighteenth-century wilderness homesteads and settlements that did no harm to native inhabitants) and to contemporary or future contexts (such as the taking of goods in space).

Finally, to the charge that original acquisitions have no traceable relation to current holdings, and so are irrelevant to contemporary evaluations of property arrangements or distributions, consider the following response on behalf of OA justifications. Even if OA justifications cannot provide moral defenses of entire existing property systems and cannot provide proper pedigrees for any current property claims, they can provide *presumptive justifications* of certain classes of private property claims, even within systems that sanction some clear injustices. Take, for example, the central thesis (in my view) of Locke's OA justification: that your purposeful labor (using only what is yours) on what is either unowned or already owned by you, can yield property for you in the product of your labor (including as part of the product that which was labored upon, if it was unowned). This thesis, if defensible, can have real force even within existing property systems that are admitted to be unjust and that leave nothing unowned to be claimed by individual laborers. It can have force, for instance, if we allow that some current legal or conventional property rights – such as modest holdings which neither unfairly deprive nor permit unreasonable control over others – may still be morally defensible, and should be presumed to be so in the absence of evidence to the contrary, even within illegitimate property systems. This can be allowed for reasons similar to those advanced by theorists who allow that an illegitimate *government* may still be morally warranted in administering reasonable legal punishments to rapists and murderers, despite the availability of a sound critique of its overall legitimacy that condemns it for other aspects of its operations. Only an (in my view, unreasonable) insistence that all moral justification of property must be at the level of property *systems* (or, by analogy, governments or political systems) can block the

possibility of presumptive justifications of particular claims within unjustified systems.

Suppose, for instance, that we believe that existing private property
systems are indefensible because of, say, the inequality and human suffering they permit, or the impotence and lack of autonomy for the unfortunate that they sanction. OA justifications might still establish a presumptive
justification of some current private property claims within these systems,
provided there is no evidence that those claims are tainted by the problems that taint the system as a whole. If, say, I earn a modest wage as a gar-
dener on another's property, or I sell vegetables grown on a small plot of
my own, and I use the money to buy needed clothing and food for myself
and my family, one might argue for a presumptive justification of my (or
my family's) claim to property in the clothing and food, based squarely on
Lockean principles. I am entitled to the products of my labor (using self-
acquired skills) – or, in one of our cases, to the wages exchanged (by agreement) for labor on what belongs to another – provided that I do no harm
to others in my acquisitions or exchanges. If there is no evidence that the
land or resources I employ were wrongfully acquired, and no indication
that my possession or use harms or unfairly disadvantages others, we can
presume either a natural, historical entitlement or a justified institutional
entitlement (depending on our theoretical predilections) to the modest
holdings I use in my purposive labors. Justice may, of course, demand that
I receive, or live under a system which guarantees me, *more* than this modest
share. But insofar as my limited claims seem to objectionably disadvantage
or harm no others, it is not clear why my claims should be viewed as incapable of moral justification.[24] It is easy to imagine similar moral defenses
of claims to many kinds of small holdings, to handcrafts, or to noninstitutional ideas or inventions (provided, at least, that the knowledge employed
was fairly acquired). No *further* justification of such claims to private property (e.g., that they are recognized claims within a justified *system* of private
property) seems necessary.[25] For these claims are (*ex hypothesi*) not tainted

24 Indeed, even Marx and Engels allowed that "we by no means intend to abolish this per-
    sonal appropriation of the products of labour, an appropriation that is made for the main-
    tenance and reproduction of human life" (*The Communist Manifesto*, in *Karl Marx: Selected
    Writings*, ed. D. McLellan [Oxford: Oxford University Press, 1977], p. 232). See also
    Andrew Reeve's remarks on the "pure artisan" and "integrated production" models of pro-
    ductive activity in Reeve, *Property* (Atlantic Highlands: Humanities Press, 1986), pp.
    128–29.
25 Eric Mack argues for what he calls "the Practice theory of private property," claiming that
    we have a natural right to a justifiable *practice* of private property (Mack, "Self-Ownership
    and the Right to Property," *Monist*, vol. 73, no. 4 [October 1990], p. 535). That may seem

by what taints the system that is in place in the society; and (again, *ex hypothesi*) on the best historical evidence available these claims are consistent with defensible OA principles.

There are at least two very controversial assumptions made here, neither of which I can discuss fully in this essay. The first concerns shifting the burden of proof in the way we think about historical justifications. In the absence of both (a) a complete pedigree for some contemporary holding and (b) any historical or contemporary evidence which might count as a reason for denying entitlement to that holding, we can insist either that (1) we should presume entitlement (my view); (2) we can say nothing about entitlement (which is, I believe, the standard view); or (3) we should presume the holding is unjust, given that "force and fraud have reigned supreme in the history of mankind."[26] Given (among other things) the importance of holdings to persons' projects and life plans and the apparent innocence of the holdings in question, I think the first position takes more seriously than the others moral considerations at issue.

A second central and very controversial assumption involves my challenge to the most familiar way of distinguishing between historical-entitlement views, which supposedly concentrate on rights to *particular* goods, and "patterned" conceptions of justice, which focus on general rights to just *shares* of social goods. As stated I think the distinction is drawn too sharply. My own view is that any adequate *historical*-entitlement view will still need to refer centrally to (historically justified) rights to "shares" – both in connection with compensation for goods which are, e.g., stolen and then destroyed (where entitlement will then be to an appropriate share of the wrongdoer's goods), and in connection with initially just holdings which must be "downsized" to accommodate increased demands for fair access to the goods in question (where, e.g., the Lockean Proviso, applied now not to takings but to holdings, entitles others to a share of what you were initially entitled to acquire and keep). If genuinely historical entitlements can be to shares of goods (e.g., to shares of goods that were previously held legitimately in their entirety by others), *presumptive* justifications of small holdings, even in the absence of complete pedigrees for those holdings, seem much easier to motivate. For small shares seem likely to be ones which can still be justified after satisfying the historical requirements of "downsizing."

to amount to an insistence on justification solely at the level of systems of property. But Mack allows as well (as I do here) that certain "vivid instances" of property rights "stand on their own. They need not draw their moral force from their place within any larger normative system" (ibid., p. 529).

26 Mautner, "Locke on Original Appropriation" (*supra* note 20), p. 267.

None of this is quite to say, with Gerald Gaus and Loren Lomasky, that the "justificatory embarrassment" of OA stories can only be avoided if we discard their historical trappings, that we should understand them instead as trying to identify or emphasize "the *telos* of property rights," or as "fixing the spotlight" on the guiding intuitions of property justifications.[27] For the presumptive justifications imagined above are in a straightforward sense *historical* justifications, and such justifications have obvious historical applications.[28] But my arguments do suggest that insofar as OA principles successfully pick out a set of actions and conditions which generate property claims, they may not only apply within existing systems, but may also supply us with a conception of what the *point* of property systems ought to be (at least in part). Those arrangements that reliably produce distributions of institutional rights which *contradict* defensible OA principles (i.e., which disallow naturally permissible claims or allow naturally impermissible ones) are for that reason morally suspect, even if there may be *other* goals (e.g., distributive ones) which we think property systems should also advance or secure.

V   Partial Justification, Question-Begging, and Unfamiliar Obligations

Even if the "distance" between OA justifications and contemporary concerns is not as much of a problem as many critics of these accounts have alleged, there are two rather different lines of attack an OA justifications

---

27 Gerald Gaus and Loren Lomasky, "Are Property Rights Problematic?" *Monist*, vol. 73, no. 4 (October 1990), pp. 496–98.

28 OA justifications of the sort described here are historical in something like Nozick's sense: current justifiability of a particular claim depends (in the Lockean version of the argument) on past labor and on the (presumed) absence of past wrongs or presence of rectifying adjustments or developments in the history of the particular claim in question. There is no appeal to structural or patterned considerations – e.g., to an independent principle of desert or equality. And while the force of OA justifications does *not* turn on the plausibility of any story about the primitive historical origins of property (as Gaus and Lomasky rightly insist in ibid., p. 498), OA justifications do, of course, *apply* to historical circumstances in the same ways they apply to contemporary or future ones (as argued above). In this regard, Gaus and Lomasky are right to compare the use of OA histories in property theory with the use of state-of-nature stories in political philosophy (ibid.). The state of nature (in Locke, for instance) can be thought of as a particular relation among persons which may be exemplified at any time, including past, historical times. As such, the state of nature is not the first period, or any particular period, in human history, though it is a relation that has had many historical instantiations. On the state of nature, both as it is used by Locke and as a concept of general interest in political philosophy, see my *On the Edge of Anarchy: Locke, Consent, and the Limits of Society* (Princeton: Princeton University Press, 1993), ch. 1.

that are sufficiently compelling to require a reply here. The first line of attack has been most directly launched by James Grunebaum. OA justifications of private property, he argues, are defective because they are only partial and because they are question-begging. First, a defect shared by all OA justifications is the failure to show that *other*, nonprivate forms of property are not just as defensible as private property under the original conditions imagined in OA stories. OA justifications of private property invariably stress the advantages, in terms of mutual benefit, of private appropriation, making these advantages the centerpiece of their justifications. But in fact private usufruct or collective or social appropriations would yield the same kinds of advantages as private appropriation. The best justification of private property an OA argument could yield, then, would be only "partial."[29] Second, Grunebaum argues, OA justifications are uniformly question-begging. Such justifications specify the conditions for taking unowned goods; but "unowned" can mean many things, depending on which conception of ownership is being assumed. OA theorists mean by "unowned," "not *privately* owned." And this simply begs the question against alternative possible forms of ownership. For what is privately unowned may be owned in some other sense, and thus not available for private appropriation.[30]

To the charge that OA justifications can be at best only "partial;" several replies seem possible here, the most important of which has already been suggested above. For one thing, it is not at all clear that different kinds of appropriations *do* all yield the same advantages under the principles by which OA justifications of private property typically proceed. On Locke's argument, for instance, not just mutual advantage in material terms but the facilitation of *self-government* (i.e., nondependence in the widest sense) is a central concern. But it is easy to think of ways in which self-government might be more fully promoted by private appropriations than by social or collective appropriation.[31] "Mutual benefit," understood to *include* the good of self-government, might then be quite differentially served by different forms of appropriation and hence might select private property as uniquely justified or morally optimal.

29 In Grunebaum, "Ownership as Theft" (*supra* note 20), pp. 545–46, "partial" justifications are contrasted with "complete" ones. In Grunebaum, *Private Ownership*, pp. 57–59, 62–63, 66, the contrast is with "conclusive" justifications. See also Waldron, *The Right to Private Property*, p. 252.

30 Grunebaum, *Private Ownership*, pp. 53, 74, 80–81, 84–85. Grunebaum's primary target is Nozick, but he generalizes the attack on p. 85.

31 See my *Lockean Theory of Rights*, pp. 264–65, 275.

More important, however, is this. Even if private property is *not* uniquely justifiable within the terms of an OA argument, it is unclear why this should be taken to show that an OA justification of private property is objectionably "partial." As we have seen, demonstrations of moral possibility or permissibility (what I called "permissibility justifications") are perfectly respectable forms of moral justification, even if they are not the strongest possible form. So even if Grunebaum's point about other, nonprivate forms of appropriation is accepted, it seems that we should conclude *not* that private property is not justified by OA arguments, but rather that several forms of property can be so justified.[32] After all, we do not conclude from the fact that many possible acts are all morally permissible or acceptable for me that *no* act I perform can be fully justified. And in any event, the classical OA justifications did *not* typically involve maintaining that usufruct was not justifiable or that *groups* of persons could not collectively appropriate land or resources. Indeed, Pufendorf explicitly discussed original collective appropriation, regarding it as *also* justified (i.e., in addition to justified private appropriation).[33] Perhaps the real worry is that if several forms of appropriation are all equally justified, we cannot tell from any appropriative act(s) which form of property right has been acquired. But if this is the concern, it seems easy to dispel; for acquisition of property rights will always turn centrally on the nature of the intentions and purposes of the appropriating persons. These intentions and purposes could easily prove to be sufficient to determine the form of right acquired, just as they are central in determining the extent and duration of the right acquired.

To Grunebaum's second charge – that OA justifications are question-begging – our reply can be even briefer. When Locke, for example, talks about appropriating goods, he is, as Grunebaum suggests, thinking about "privately unowned" goods. But Locke's arguments in no sense beg the question against alternative conceptions of ownership, for he does not even talk about goods being "unowned" *simpliciter*. Locke does not use this "question-begging" language for the simple reason that he assumes that *common* ownership of the world is the relevant background condition against which private appropriation is to be understood.[34] His arguments

---

32 The possibility of parallel, equally justified, but quite different property systems (even within the same territory) is discussed by James Tully in the context of his interesting examination of Aboriginal and colonial property in North America. See Tully, "Aboriginal Property and Western Theory: Recovering a Middle Ground," in *Social Philosophy & Policy* 11:2 (Summer 1994).

33 Pufendorf, *De Jure Naturae et Gentium*, bk. 4, ch. 6, sections 3–4.

34 I have argued elsewhere that Locke's conception of original community is one of *positive* community (*Lockean Theory of Rights*, pp. 236–41, 279–81).

concern (1) the conditions under which claims to private property can *override* (or, in Locke's terms, "over-balance" [II, 40] or "exclude" [II, 27]) claims to alternative kinds of property, and (2) the facts that establish the superiority of private to other forms of property. Locke's arguments may fail, but they do not fail by begging the question against private ownership's competition.

The second line of attack on OA justifications of private property that I will discuss here has recently been advanced by Waldron. Typical OA justifications fail, the argument goes, because they involve trying to justify something that none of us on reflection can really regard as justifiable – namely, the deliberate, unilateral imposition by individuals of onerous obligations on all others. OA arguments normally entail that persons can, by their acts of acquisition, deliberately create for others universal moral duties of forbearance and noninterference with respect to holdings of possibly scarce resources. Such a power (to create significant moral burdens for others at will) is "radically unfamiliar" and "repugnant" to us, and it is therefore a power of which we should be highly suspicious. Needless to say, we should be equally suspicious of any argument which purports to justify such a power for individuals.[35]

Gaus and Lomasky have responded to Waldron's argument by maintaining that it is unreasonable to single out for this attack just those principles that purport to justify unilateral acquisition of original private property rights. *All* claim rights involve correlative moral burdens for others, burdens which may also be onerous. Original property rights in a thing are no different in this respect from other rights. The claim that there is a moral burden on others always requires justification, the same strength of justification for property rights (and their correlative obligations) as for any other rights. And, in any event, Gaus and Lomasky argue, we are quite familiar with cases of persons having the moral power to unilaterally and deliberately impose moral burdens on others. For instance, given the famil-

---

35 Waldron, *The Right to Private Property*, pp. 265–71. See also Becker, *Property Rights* (*supra* note 20), p. 44; and Allan Gibbard, "Natural Property Rights," in *Readings in Social and Political Philosophy*, ed. R. M. Stewart (New York: Oxford University Press, 1986), pp. 237–38. Waldron argues further that the kinds of principles defended in OA justifications fail the negative test of hypothetical consent (*The Right to Private Property*, pp. 272–78), but he allows that incorporating a strong Lockean Proviso may permit an OA justification to escape his attacks (ibid., pp. 281–83). I will not here discuss these additional components of Waldron's case. I should note here as well that Waldron's argument strikes primarily against Lockean-style OA justifications. OA justifications which appeal to compacts or agreements, of course, involve defending no rights of *unilateral* imposition of obligation. But such arguments face other obvious problems of their own.

iar moral obligation to reward desert, one person can pile obligations on others simply by doing things which ground desert claims.[36]

This response, I think, is inadequate to eliminate the sorts of concerns that motivate Waldron's attack on OA justifications of private property. For, in the first place, Waldron is clearly worried not so much by the mere existence of (or the need for justification of) onerous moral burdens, but rather by the suggestion that one person might have the right unilaterally to impose such burdens at will on others, deliberately and for the very purpose of limiting their freedom. And it is certainly not true of all claim rights that they subject others to that kind of liability. Most of the claim rights we take for granted (e.g., our "general" rights to noninterference) are not only not imposed unilaterally by anyone's deliberate acts, but are not imposed at all. They are, rather, part of the moral background conditions through which each person's moral agency is to be understood. But second, the example Gaus and Lomasky provide of a "familiar" right that is analogous to the right of property acquisition is not a very persuasive example. The right to be given what we deserve (and the correlative obligation of others to render to us what we deserve) is not, I expect, one that many of us take for granted. I doubt that I can find anyone who takes herself to be obligated to reward me for all of my meritorious conduct this year. Such rights and obligations only seem at all familiar in the kinds of institutional contexts Gaus and Lomasky's example actually involves, where, say, a department head is understood by all to have *agreed* to reward (academic!) merit in her colleagues – and thus has a purely *consensual* obligation to do so, *not* an (onerous?) obligation unilaterally and deliberately imposed at will by another.[37] Finally, of course, if one pursued acts which deserved reward for the very purpose of limiting another's liberty (i.e., in order to burden her with obligations), one's efforts would

---

36 Gaus and Lomasky, "Are Property Rights Problematic?" esp. pp. 492–93. For a different style of attack on Waldron's argument, but one which also emphasizes the significance of desert claims, see Stephen R. Munzer, "The Acquisition of Property Rights," *Notre Dame Law Review*, vol. 66, no. 3 (1991), pp. 669–78.

37 Gaus and Lomasky deny that this obligation is consensual ("Are Property Rights Problematic?" p. 492), although they say only that they "doubt" that both parties have consented to the "system." But all that is necessary to render the case hopelessly disanalogous to the one which worries Waldron is that the obligated party has himself agreed to bear this particular obligation. And it seems plain that this is our normal understanding of the position of a department head, at least in any context in which we *would* take her to have an obligation to reward merit. We do not think that just *anyone* has an obligation to reward *any* kind of merit in any other person; one's exceptional performance in an academic department surely imposes no new obligations on, say, Madonna or Mother Theresa.

very likely be self-defeating, such motives seeming, as they do, rather unmeritorious.

None of this is to say, however, that Waldron's complaint about OA justifications is unanswerable. I think, in fact, that Gaus and Lomasky are quite correct in asserting that the kinds of rights and obligations that worry Waldron are more familiar and considerably less repugnant than he suggests (even if the example they employ to illustrate their suggestion is an unpersuasive one). Such rights and obligations arise or are at issue in a wide range of contexts, particularly those involving certain special transactions, competitive situations, and the "activation" of general rights. For instance, I may make a legal will, unilaterally imposing on all others an obligation to respect its terms (which they previously lacked), for the very purpose of limiting others' freedom to dispose of my estate in ways contrary to my wishes. I may occupy a public tennis court to practice my serve, or we may take the softball field in the park for our game, unilaterally imposing on all others obligations to refrain from interference, and do so for the very purpose of enjoying our activities unhindered by such interference. Or I may rush to the patent office and register my invention, unilaterally imposing certain obligations of restraint on all others, for the very purpose of limiting others' freedom to likewise take advantage with their competing inventions. I may buy the rare stamp that many others are busy saving their money to buy, or I may organize a nature walk for children along trails many others use to seek solitude. How different are the rights and obligations involved in these contexts from the right of the original appropriator to take unowned goods, unilaterally imposing obligations of noninterference on all others, for the very purpose of restricting their liberty to impede her free use and enjoyment of the goods? Not, I think, very different. And the rights and obligations I have mentioned are both familiar and widely accepted, regarded by almost nobody as morally repugnant. Indeed, even though they all involve a background of (nonconsensual) institutional rules and expectations which sanction the entitlements and obligations at issue, it is easy to imagine *natural*, noninstitutional analogues for each case I mentioned (that is, to describe moral rules which play the same sanctioning role in these cases).

Now it is true that in my cases the unilaterally imposed obligations are typically not very "onerous" – though they might be if, e.g., others were relying heavily on an inheritance (or a share of what "reverts to common") or on proceeds from inventions. But, of course, the parallel obligations to respect originally acquired property need not be onerous either – though they might be if, e.g., such acquisitions "make it morally difficult or morally impossible for others to secure their own survival."[38] Perhaps, then, we should understand Waldron's complaint as addressed only to *some* of the rights (purportedly) justified by *some* OA arguments, rather than as a general condemnation of all OA justifications of private property (as Waldron's own closing remarks in fact suggest).[39] If so, however, only the most extreme of the libertarian versions of OA justifications are threatened by this attack, and perhaps even they are threatened only with a call for revision or limitation, not a call for abandonment. Certainly the well-known classical OA justifications all either insisted on serious limits on rights of acquisition – so that genuinely onerous obligations could *not* be unilaterally imposed – or defended parallel, overriding rights for others to *take* from an appropriator's surplus the justly acquired goods which are needed by those others for their survival (see, e.g., Locke, I, 42).

I conclude from this that neither the final, general attacks considered in this section, nor the arguments from "remoteness" considered in the previous section, really tell against OA justifications of private property in a way that should lead us to put them away, as antiquated reminders of less philosophically sophisticated times. On the contrary, I have suggested that OA arguments, properly developed, promise substantial justificatory punch and direct contemporary relevance. I believe, further, that an OA justification of private property can in fact be advanced that is both plausible and satisfies contemporary standards of argumentative rigor; but I have done little here that should convince others to share my belief.[40] Rather, I hope primarily to have supplied some reasons to believe that OA arguments ought not to be hastily brushed aside in contemporary discussions of the possible justifications of private property.

38 Waldron, *The Right to Private Property*, p. 268. Schmidtz takes issue with this characterization of the acquisitions of our forebears in *The Limits of Government* (*supra* note 20), ch. 2.

39 Waldron, *The Right to Private Property*, pp. 282–83. See Munzer, "Acquisition of Property Rights," pp. 667–68.

40 I try to sketch the outlines of such an argument, following a reconstruction of broadly Lockean claims, in my *Lockean Theory of Rights*, esp. pp. 271–77, 292–94.

11

HISTORICAL RIGHTS AND FAIR SHARES

I

My aim in this paper is to clarify, and in a certain very limited way to defend, historical theories of property rights (and their associated theories of social or distributive justice).[1] It is important, I think, to better understand historical rights for several reason: first, because of the extent to which historical theories capture commonsense, unphilosophical views about property and justice; next, because historical theories have fallen out of philosophical fashion, and are consequently not much scrutinized anymore; and finally, because of (what I see as) the continuing need to better understand the historical components of our society's responsibilities to the descendants of victims of systematic injustice in our own past. The case I will have in mind throughout is that of the property claims of Native American tribes, claims based on their historical standing as the original owners of certain lands and resources. And while I will concentrate here only on the question of rectifying past violations of property rights, this will constitute at least a start to answering more general questions about just rectification, which includes the more serious and less compensable wrongs of violence against persons.[2]

---

1 For their helpful comments on earlier drafts of this paper I would like to thank John Christman, Barbara Levenbook, Nancy Schauber, George Sher, Randy Barnett, Daniel Shapiro, Geoffrey Sayre-McCord, and audiences at V.P.I. & S.U. and at the Eighteenth Annual Greensboro Symposium in Philosophy.
2 I have in this first paragraph already used the languages of "reparation," "rectification," and "compensation" as if there were no interesting differences between them. Many will find this objectionable. But the many who agree that there are important differences here seem

By now we are all familiar with Robert Nozick's distinction between historical arguments for property rights (or for the justice of particular distributions of rights) and end-state arguments for rights or justice.[3] Historical arguments maintain that whether or not a holding or set of holdings is just (that is, whether or not we are entitled to or have a moral right to our holdings) depends on the moral character of the history that produced the holdings. We must see how holdings actually came about in order to know who has a right to what. End-state arguments maintain that the justice of holdings (and our rights to them) depends not on how they came about, but rather on the moral character of the structure (or pattern) of the set of holdings of which they are a part. We need only a "current time slice" of the set in order to morally evaluate the set and its component holdings.

Nozick, of course, claims that "most people . . . think it relevant in assessing the justice of a situation to consider not only the distribution it embodies, but also how that distribution came about." End-state arguments do not capture "the whole story" about rights and justice.[4] And this seems correct. Whether or not I have a right to the keyboard on which I type this paper seems to depend on whether I bought it (with money I legitimately acquired) or received it as a gift (from someone who had a right to it) or stole it from my trusting neighbor. But, contrary to the implications of the

unable to agree on just what those differences are. Loren Lomasky, for instance, distinguishes "rectification" ("restoring precisely that which was removed") from "compensation" ("providing something equivalent in value to that which has been lost") in *Persons, Right, and the Moral Community* (New York: Oxford University Press, 1987), p. 142. Onora O'Neill, on the other hand, considers "compensation" and "reparation" (both defined roughly as Lomasky defines "compensation") as kinds of "rectifications," with "restitution" as another kind, this last being defined in terms of restoring what obtained before some wrong ("Rights to Compensation," *Social Philosophy & Policy* 5 [1987]: 74–75). And Bernard Boxhill distinguishes "compensation" (a "forward-looking" concept) from "reparation" (a "backward-looking" concept, concerned with the righting of past wrongs) in "The Morality of Reparation," in B. Gross, ed., *Reverse Discrimination* (Buffalo: Prometheus Books, 1977), pp. 273–74. I will use "rectification," "compensation," and "reparation" loosely here, referring in all cases to that which is due the victim of a wrong in consequence of the wrong. As will become apparent, I regard "restitution" or "restoration" (in O'Neill's sense) as in one sense the ideal of rectification (or "correction"), from which we should depart only when it is impossible to achieve. Thus, the ideal is a return to the pre-wrong condition, with no losses for anyone but the wrongdoer. This ideal is, of course, typically impossible to achieve, so we must aim more generally to secure the conditions that would have obtained in the absence of the wrong. Punishment, another traditional branch of rectificatory or corrective justice, is normally taken to be due the wrongdoer, not the victim, and it will not be discussed here.

3 Robert Nozick, *Anarchy, State, and Utopia* (New York: Basic Books, 1974), pp. 153–55.
4 Ibid., p. 154.

exclusively historical theory Nozick ultimately embraces, it seems just as correct to assert that most of us think that historical arguments do not tell "the whole story" about rights and justice either.[5] Regardless of how the distribution actually came about, most of us think that a distribution could not possibly be just in which one group of people possessed virtually everything of any value, while many other people possessed nothing and were dependent for their survival on the charity and good will of the propertied. Indeed, we may think that historical considerations are only even relevant to rights or justice within a context in which a certain structure of broadly equal holdings and opportunities has first been guaranteed for all.

This kind of challenge to historical theories is, I think, compelling and important. But I want to ask that it be set aside for the purposes of my discussion here. I want to focus our attention instead on a different, more "internal" sort of criticism of historical views. And by doing so I hope to reveal more clearly the force that historical considerations should have in our theories of property rights and justice. For if historical principles can solve their internal difficulties, they can at least hope to have some claim to equal moral standing, perhaps alongside of end-state principles in a pluralistic theory of rights and justice, even if they cannot hope to satisfy Nozick's ambitions for exclusive moral dominion. Or perhaps historical principles could then be defended as the correct principles of property, as the principles which account for one kind of moral right, while acknowledging that other kinds of rights, or broader moral considerations of justice based in end-state principles, conflict with and limit the "trumping" power of property rights.

II

Suppose with me, then, that we have before us convincing historical principles of acquisition and transfer. Most likely, these principles will be broadly Lockean in nature. Our principle of acquisition, for instance, might hold that rights over previously unowned land or natural resources can be acquired by usefully employing these things in our projects and purposive activities – provided that a strong "Lockean Proviso" is satisfied, so that others will have equal opportunities to acquire such goods by their own labors. Our principle of transfer might hold that rights over the prop-

5 David Lyons, "The New Indian Claims and Original Rights to Land," *Social Theory and Practice* 4 (1977): 254.

erty of others can only be acquired by free, consensual transactions (such as trades, gifts, bequests, sales, and the like).[6]

Many will think, of course, that a historical theory of property rights cannot get even this far, perhaps believing that property is not a natural moral concept, as the Lockean suggests, but an essentially institutional one. It must be admitted even by such critics, though, that the intuitions underlying historical theories are strong. If I am the first settler of a vast uninhabited territory (in another solar system, say), and I build a home and cultivate the land needed to comfortably support me, surely the settlers coming after would wrong me (violate my property rights) if they simply seized my land and home, with ample and equally attractive land and resources available to them.[7]

What makes historical theories of property rights and justice look most questionable, I believe, lies not in their ideal theory – that is, not in their accounts of just acquisition and transfer – but rather in their nonideal accounts of rectification.[8] Historical theories of rights standardly include principles of rectification for situations of partial compliance, which specify the rights of persons who have suffered violations of their rights, as defined by the ideal principles of acquisition and transfer.[9] If you steal my bicycle, say, I have a right to the rectification of this wrong – usually assumed to amount to a right that the bicycle be returned to me, along with compensation for any damage to it and for any loss I suffered as a result of being temporarily deprived of its use. The idea seems to be that, in order to rectify a past rights-violation (injustice), we must, as far as it is within our power, "make it now as though the injustice had not happened."[10] We

---

6 I make no assumptions here about the content of Lockean property rights (i.e., about which of the "cluster" of ownership rights they include) beyond (a) their alienability and (b) their immunity from expropriation in the absence of competing moral claims.

7 In fact, I think that an "original acquisition" theory of property, of a Lockean sort, can be plausibly stated, motivated, and defended from the standard objections. See my *The Lockean Theory of Rights* (Princeton: Princeton University Press, 1992), ch. 5, and "Original-Acquisition Justifications of Private Property," *Social Philosophy & Policy* 11 (1994): 63–84.

8 "The rectification principle . . . seems to be the most problematic part of the entitlement theory. It is certainly an essential part; for, without it, . . . if there has been a single injustice in the history of a state, no matter how far back, the state will not be able to achieve a just distribution of goods in the present." Lawrence Davis, "Comments on Nozick's Entitlement Theory," *The Journal of Philosophy* 73 (1976): 839.

9 Nozick, *Anarchy, State, and Utopia*, p. 152.

10 Jeremy Waldron, "Superseding Historic Injustice," *Ethics* 103 (1992): 8.

cannot undo a past wrong, but we can try to minimize the effects of the wrong.[11]

This idea, familiar to us from the civil law, seems quite appealing in relatively simple cases of short-term rectification. But any of a wide variety of complications can quickly diminish its appeal. What if, instead of just stealing my bicycle, you then melt it down and turn it into cufflinks, various pairs of which are bought by innocent third parties and later left to their grandchildren as family heirlooms? What if I die or you die before rectification occurs? What if the injustice remains unrectified for several centuries? And how confidently, in any event, can we make the relevant counterfactual judgments even in relatively simple cases? For to make it as if the wrong had not occurred, we must judge what would have taken place in the absence of the wrong. But what would have taken place may depend on what choices people would have made and on other changes in context and circumstances that seem quite unpredictable.[12] Would I have met the perfect mate or found the perfect job had my mobility not been impaired by the theft of my bicycle? Or did the theft save me from being crushed by a delivery van while out riding?

Destruction of stolen property, changes in the cast of affected parties, innocent third parties, and the simple passage of time complicate the already complicated counterfactual judgments until we seem to have passed the breaking point. It is popular, for instance, in criticisms of historical theories of property rights, to cite instances of massive historical injustices – such as the theft of tribal lands and resources from aboriginal peoples – and then to note that all of these complications are present. It seems impossible to say with any confidence just what kinds of property transfers would satisfy a plausible historical principle of rectification in such cases. Must the struggling Asian immigrant return her hard-earned holding in commercial land, land which is now deforested and developed, to the distant descendants of the hunter-gatherers from whom the land was once stolen? The problems here are not just epistemological or evidentiary. It is

---

11 To reiterate, we are speaking here only about questions of reparation, which are independent of further questions about whether or what punishment is appropriate for the wrong. It is possible, of course, that reparation or compensation may be due the victim of a wrong simply for the breach of his rights, even when this breach is accompanied by no loss of well-being (or by a gain in well-being). I do not consider such cases here. For discussion, see Lomasky, "Compensation and the Bounds of Rights" and Gerald Gaus, "Does Compensation Restore Equality?," both in J. Chapman, *Compensatory Justice. Nomos XXXIII* (New York: New York University Press, 1991)), pp. 28, 33, 67, 69–72.
12 Waldron, "Superseding Historic Injustice": 8–13.

not just that we lack all of the relevant historical data to unravel the chains of historical entitlements.[13] The problems are also substantive difficulties of principle. It is very hard in such cases to see how we could find any satisfactory basis for specifying the exact content of historical rights to rectification. Someone was clearly wronged by someone somewhere in the murky past. But who has rights to what now? The players are now very different, the land is irreparably altered, and legitimate expectations of myriad sorts surround the present set of holdings. If just rectification is in many cases impossible in principle, because of the indeterminacy of the principles defining historical rights, such rights begin to look like only wishful shadows of real rights.[14]

A variety of responses to these difficulties seems possible. Defenders of historical rights might reply that any moral theory will face these kinds of problems in moving from ideal to nonideal theory. Any theory, historical or not, will have a hard time determining how to remedy injustice when faced with widespread, innocent expectations founded on the anticipated continuation of unjust arrangements. But this response is too feeble. The problem for historical theories seems not to be merely that situations of partial compliance require inevitably very complicated principles of rectification. The problem seems to be instead that historical theories cannot even state the desired principles of rectification in any plausible way. There is, for instance, no clear end toward which these principles aim us, as there is a clear end toward which end-state nonideal principles aim (namely, the achievement of a just structure of holdings in society). The nonideal theory of a historical account cannot be (as in an end-state account) a complicated set of practical rules for minimizing harm in the transition to a more perfectly just arrangement. Historical accounts, having no ideal just structure of holdings to aim us at, must defend the content of their principles of rectification in a way which is compelling independent of structural goals. And the complications we have been discussing seem to stand in the way of such a defense.

As a result, of course, a very common response to historical theories is simply to reject altogether the idea of historical entitlements. In anything but a world very close to moral perfection, historical rights will have no determinate content and hence will not be real rights at all. But this simple

13 Despite Nozick's apparent belief that this is the only real problem. Nozick suggests using nonhistorical patterned principles of distributive justice as "rough rules of thumb" for approximating historical rectification in real world cases where information about the past is incomplete (*Anarchy, State, and Utopia*, pp. 230–1).

14 Davis, "Comments on Nozick's Entitlement Theory": 844.

rejection of historical rights also seems feeble. For in our anything-but-ideal actual world, in both law and morals, we still take historical rights to rectification very seriously. Given the many reasons we have for taking practice to be relevant to theory, the best response to the problems of historical theories would seem to be neither to rationalize away the problems nor to dismiss the theories, but to see whether further clarifying our conception of historical rights can make the problems more manageable.

I will try in the remainder of this paper to undermine the standard complaint about historical theories of property rights that they cannot specify the precise content of rights to rectification in any even remotely complicated contexts. I will do so not by arguing that historical theories can specify precise contents for these rights, but rather by arguing that their inability to do so constitutes no defect in the theories. Historical theories can be coherent and plausible, I will suggest, and can thus define real rights, even when those rights do not have a perfectly determinate content. The best historical theory will entail that persons can sometimes have rights that give us only imprecise, but nonetheless principled, guidelines for rectification, rather than giving us determinate entitlements to particular things or performances.

III

I want to begin my argument by making two general points. First, I think it is easy to be a bit too sceptical about the possibility of making reliable contrary-to-fact judgments (and about the moral importance of such judgments). While the truth-conditions (or assertabiliy conditions) for various kinds of counterfactuals is obviously a controversial issue, it is clear that we do regularly make counterfactual judgments with a high degree of confidence and take them to be centrally relevant to determinations of praise and blame and moral or legal liability. "If he hadn't stolen my bicycle, I would have been better off (by so much and in these ways)." (Or: "If my father hadn't argued against it so passionately, I would have married that good-for-nothing bum.") We are not bothered by the fact that, during my bicycle's absence, I might otherwise have been shot by a deranged hater of bicyclists or might have been discovered by a talent scout for the Olympic cycling team. We do not hold the thief liable for dashing my Olympic hopes or reward him for saving my life. For purposes of assigning blame and liability we assume a normal unsurprising course of background events, roughly like the one that actually occurred. And we assume that our and others' choices would have likewise been more or less the same.

In saying "If he hadn't stolen my bicycle, I would have been better off," I am saying that those of my possible histories that most resemble my actual history (as closely as their including the non-theft of my bicycle allows them to resemble it) involve my being better off.[15] Possible worlds with Olympic talent scouts noticing my bicycling do not sufficiently resemble the actual world in which my bicycle is stolen to belong to the relevantly similar class of histories. Often, of course, our judgments concern not what would certainly have happened in any relevantly similar history, but rather what would have been most likely to have happened. The vagaries of individual choice and the complexity of background conditions often make stronger claims indefensible. They also force the moral (and legal) uses of counterfactual claims to be essentially conservative in nature. In ascribing blame or liability for losses, we take ourselves to be bound both to show a high probability that the losses would not otherwise have been suffered and to make only conservative assumptions about choices and background conditions.

In the absence of full knowledge of what would have occurred had a wrong not been committed, blaming a wrongdoer conservatively constitutes a fair compromise between assuming that his wrong would have had horrible consequences for the wronged party and assuming that his wrong would have had wonderful consequences. We instead conservatively assign him liability only for those losses that we can confidently attribute to his wrong, against background assumptions that things not directly affected by the wrong would in its absence have gone on more or less as they in fact did. We know that in the absence of the wrong, the wronged person (or some other) might have made wild or unpredictable choices, and that others might have been influenced to act differently because of this. But since we cannot know the likelihood or the consequences of such choices, we assume that rash choices would not have been made, trying to be fair in our determination of the extent of reparation required. If you hadn't stolen my money, I might have used it to rashly buy a stack of lottery tickets that included the winner, or I might have rashly invested it in penny stocks and lost everything. Even if I am a rash person, then, we assume an absence of rashness in our counterfactual judgments.[16]

---

15 This is roughly the analysis of counterfactuals suggested in David Lewis, *Counterfactuals* (Cambridge: Harvard University Press, 1973).

16 Obviously, our assumptions will be different if rash choices were made in the actual history, at least if these rash choices were not a direct consequence of the wrong. More generally, we assign moral liability to the wrongdoer only for those of the victim's subsequent losses which we take to be direct causal consequences of the wrong itself. To the extent that

None of this seems to me arbitrary or ad hoc. The difficulties of assessing counterfactual judgments are very real and substantial. But they are not theoretically insuperable; nor, I think, do they cast a pall over the whole project of explaining historical rights to rectification. People do make choices, and choices are sometimes unpredictable. Sometimes we will simply be unable to say what conditions would most likely have obtained in the absence of a wrong (perhaps because there simply is no fact of the matter available). But nothing in that admission (or in the nature of human freedom) justifies any stronger scepticism about counterfactuals involving persons or about their employment in moral judgment. Persons often have a (legal and/or moral) right to what they would have enjoyed in the absence of a prior wrong, according to our best conservative estimate of what that would have been. Nothing here involves assuming without warrant that "rational choice predictions" are "normatively conclusive," nor should such worries motivate a retreat from our efforts to understand historical rights counterfactually.[17] Indeed, even within nonhistorical, end-state conceptions of rights and justice, these same kinds of counterfactual judgments will very likely have to be relied upon to determine entitlements, even if these determinations are taken only to have force in the context of a just basic social structure.

A second general point about historical rights is this: I believe that the most prominent contemporary defenders of historical rights have importantly misdescribed such rights. Nozick, for instance, suggests that what is distinctive about the historical conception of rights is that, thus conceived, rights are to particular things; whereas on end-state conceptions of rights, rights are to shares of the total social product.[18] On historical accounts, the labor, say, that grounded a property right in the first place is invested in

---

these losses are taken to follow from the victim's own free choices and actions, we compare the actual history that includes those choices and actions to the closest possible histories that also include them, in order to determine the truth of counterfactual judgments about the consequences of wrongdoing.

17 Waldron, "Superseding Historic Injustice": 13–15. We can, for instance, confidently claim about Native American tribes that, in the absence of the deception and violence that in fact typically caused their loss of territories, they would not have given away or sold the land or resources necessary to the survival of their tribe or culture. This judgment is based not on some simple assumption about the authority of (hypothetical) rational choice, but rather on our knowledge of the actual prior histories of tribal choices and the vitality of their cultures, and on conservative assumptions about background conditions (and thus about the consequences of choice).

18 Nozick, *Anarchy, State, and Utopia*, pp. 238, 171–72. See also Lomasky: "Persons' rights are rights to particular performances and are rights over particular items of property" (*Persons, Rights, and the Moral Community*, p. 142).

some specific object, establishing a connection between the person and the object that persists even if the object is well-traveled afterwards. Rights depend on the actual history of acquisitions and transfers of particular things. When you steal my bicycle, my right to that particular bicycle persists not only through wrongful expropriations, but also through acquisitions by innocent third parties. Injustice permanently taints goods, because those particular goods are morally marked with the rights of their legitimate owners. As Locke puts it, "this labour being the unquestionable property of the labourer, no man but he can have a right to what that is once joined to."[19] Rectification calls for a return of unjustly appropriated objects to their rightful owners. By contrast, on end-state conceptions of rights, since rights are to shares of goods (i.e., to shares that satisfy the structural distributional requirements of the end-state theory in question), rectifying injustice is a simpler matter of adjusting the relative sizes of shares of goods. To rectify the theft of my bicycle, we need not return to me that particular bicycle, or any bicycle at all, provided that my overall share of goods is readjusted to its appropriate size and shape, the one specified by the favored pattern.

Nozick attempts, of course, to make the end-state view seem ill-motivated and oppressive, since it gives people claims on a share of the goods produced through the honest labors of other individuals. It pries apart production and distribution, treating created goods as if they were manna from heaven. But many of his readers respond instead by noticing that the end-state view makes the project of rectifying a long history of social injustice seem possible and attractive. We "simply" bring the shares of oppressed people into the range of those acceptable under the relevant end-state principle. On the historical view, on the other hand, this rectificatory project seems impossible, both for evidentiary reasons (we have no clear records of the complicated strands of entitlements to particular things) and for reasons of principle (the change of cast, the irreversible alteration or destruction of the things people were once entitled to, the passage of time, and so on, make it impossible even in principle to specify the holders or the contents of historical rights). If historical rights simply "dissolve" in these ways, why should we take them seriously as real rights at all?

An important part of the problem here for historical theories of rights is that the contrast with end-state theories has been badly drawn. Most obviously, of course, end-state theories will often also advocate the use of historical criteria for rights. If the end-state principles are taken as guides only

19 John Locke, *Second Treatise of Government*, para. 27.

for the basic structure of society (as on Rawls's view, for example), entitlements within a just structure of basic institutions will be historical claims on particular objects, not rights to shares of the total social product.[20]

Less obvious, perhaps, is the fact that no adequate historical theory can do without the idea of historical rights to shares of goods. This is most evident in two kinds of cases. In the first kind of case, the object to which I have a right is destroyed or irreversibly altered by some wrongdoer. You steal my bicycle and run it through a compactor or melt it down. What becomes of my right? How is the theft to be rectified, on an historical theory of rights? Surely my right in such a case is not any longer a right to a particular object, nor is it a right to a certain share of the total social product. It is rather a right to a certain-sized share of a particular set of holdings – namely, to a share of the holdings of the wrongdoer. Let me call this a historical right to a "particularized share." Now it may seem that such a right could not be a historical right at all, since I have no historical connection (say, through my labor) with the object on which I have a claim in this case. But this appearance is mistaken. One needn't oneself have any deep historical connection with an object, beyond a transactional connection, in order to have a historical right to the object. If you give me an object you own (or sell it to me), my right to it is perfectly historical, despite my having no prior connection to it.[21] Similarly, in the present case of theft

20 Nozick, of course, treats patterned theories as if their favored principles were intended to govern all distributions of goods within societies. Thus, in a perfectly just society, if you give me a more expensive gift than I give you, or if a judge awards compensation for an unintentional wrong, a patterned theory would require redistribution to restore the initially just pattern (since shares have now changed size). This understanding of patterned theories reduces them to a rather silly straw man. No real defender of a patterned theory believes that Christmas is a time for the redistribution police to be especially wary. As the discussion below indicates, I believe that Nozick's characterization of historical and end-state theories in fact badly distorts both approaches.

21 Historical theories are often criticized for their apparent inability to explain how alienation (transfer) of property rights is even possible. If my labor is mixed with an object, thus preventing any legitimate non-consensual appropriation of the object by another (since taking the object would involve taking my labor as well), why doesn't my labor continue to inhere in the object when I try to alienate my rights to the object, rendering consensual transfer impossible? See Jeremy Waldron, "Superseding Historic Injustice": 17, and *The Right to Private Property* (Oxford: Oxford University Press, 1988), pp. 259–62. The answer, I think, involves reinterpreting the Lockean idea of mixing one's labor with a thing in terms of incorporating that thing into legitimate purposive activities. One's rights over a thing are (in part) determined by its role in our pursuits or projects. Since one purpose we may have for a thing is that it be transferred to another person as a legitimate holding, our purposive incorporation of the thing (our "labor" in it) ends with the transfer. No "residue" of our "labor" persists in the thing, any more than it does when we abandon property, allowing it to "revert to common."

and destruction, you forfeit to me rights over a certain share of your legitimate holdings by virtue of your illegitimate theft and destruction of my property. But the right to this share is still perfectly historical. The claim in question depends on the past history of holdings and is justified by the importance of free acquisition and transfer. The claim is not based on any patterned or end-state insistence that the resulting shares meet a favored structural requirement – that they be equal, say, or that they be proportionate to the overall moral desert or virtue of the parties.

The second kind of case I have in mind is that of (what I will call) mandatory "downsizing" of legitimate holdings. Even the most thoroughly libertarian historical rights theorists acknowledge that historical rights must be sensitive in certain ways to changes in circumstances. Property claims that were once perfectly legitimate may cease to be so with decreases in the pool of resources or increases in the number of persons needing to draw on those resources. Thus, even Nozick allows that his Lockean Proviso applies to holding as well as to taking goods. If I legitimately appropriate a desert water hole, and all the other water holes subsequently dry up, the content of my rights over the water hole changes with the changed circumstances. I can no longer charge whatever I wish for the water. Nor does my legitimate appropriation of a desert island permit me to later deny a new castaway access to the island's meager resources.[22] No historical rights theory can be even remotely plausible unless it incorporates some version of a Lockean Proviso for takings and holdings – that is, unless it limits historical rights by some reasonable requirement that we leave "enough and as good" in common for others.[23]

I take the appropriate Lockean position on this issue to be something like the following. Persons have rights of fair access to available land and natural resources. These rights are opportunity rights, not rights of property in a fair share of the earth. Property rights in the earth and its resources are acquired by the incorporation of things (falling within our fair share) into our legitimate purposive activities. But changes in circumstances may change what constitutes a fair share. Thus, both access (opportunity) rights and property rights may change in their extent or content as circumstances change.

In the Nozickean example, simply imagine eight castaways, each of whom has an access right to one-eighth of the island's land and resources. Each of the eight takes property in his or her full fair share. But children,

---

22 Nozick, *Anarchy, State, and Utopia*, p. 180.
23 Locke, *Second Treatise of Government*, para. 27.

grandchildren, and additional castaways increase the population without any corresponding increase in land or resources. The original eight must then "downsize" their previously legitimate holdings, giving the new population fair access to their shares of the island. If the original owners refuse to yield, those of their holdings that exceed their fair shares may be justifiably seized by those who have rights of access (that is, seized by incorporating that surplus into their legitimate projects).[24]

As in our first kind of case – that of altered or destroyed stolen property – the point to notice here is that the mandatory downsizing creates for the original owners of the island an historical right to a share of their original holdings. And again it is a right to what I called a "particularized share." It is neither a right to just any fair share of the whole island nor a right to a particular piece of land or property. It is rather a right to some appropriate share of the specific original just holdings of that original castaway. And once again, as in our first kind of case, it may be thought that the right in question could not count as genuinely historical, since it rests on some apparently end-state idea of a fair division. Some of Nozick's critics, for instance, have suggested that his use of the Lockean Proviso undermines his theory, incorporating end-state considerations into what is supposed to be a purely historical theory.[25] Nozick explicitly denies that this is the case,[26] and I think he is right to do so. For, first, the idea of a fair share used in this account is motivated not by the need to insure some pattern of holdings, but by the requirement that our appropriations and holdings not harm or unfairly disadvantage others. Second, the idea of a fair division,

---

24 Lyons suggests that in such a situation it may be legitimate to require the original castaways to give up their private property altogether. If all the islanders are better served by a system of collective ownership, all may be obliged to pool their resources ("New Indian Claims": 263). My own view is that mandatory downsizing is the typical requirement in such circumstances, with collective property being a legitimate result only of voluntary joining of individual holdings or of collective purposive activities. To suppose otherwise is, I think, to suppose – mistakenly, in my view – that justifications of property must always be *optimality* justifications rather than *permissibility* justifications. See my "Original-Acquisition Justifications of Private Property," section. II. There may, of course, be some things that are not privately appropriable in the first place (because they are indivisible or because fair shares are unusably small, say). Locke, for instance, discusses the English common in these terms. And downsizing may in certain cases result in individual rights in undivided shares. Finally, considerations of charity may in some cases require that private property be surrendered. But while these kinds of possibilities may motivate a voluntary move to collective ownership, I take none of them to be equivalent to that of requiring the nonvoluntary conversion of private to collective property.

25 See, for one among many such arguments, Husain Sarkar, "The Lockean Proviso," *Canadian Journal of Philosophy* 12 (1982).

26 Nozick, *Anarchy, State, and Utopia*, p. 181.

on this model, is used only in determining rights of access to land or resources. Actual property rights continue on this account to be based in the actual history of acquisitions and transfers, not in the desirability of achieving any favored pattern of distribution of property rights. While rights of fair access limit the possible scope of property rights, they do not determine the content of those rights or the relative sizes of individuals' shares of property. Who owns what (if anything) within his or her fair shares is determined by what has actually taken place, by the specific history of actions and transactions.

IV

If I am right about this, then a properly developed historical theory of rights will accept the idea of property rights in shares of goods. But the historical rights in question will be to particularized shares – not rights either to particular objects or to general shares of the whole of the divisible resources. The historical theory thus still retains some of the essential particularity of historical claims.[27] But by acknowledging that some historical rights are not rights to particular things, the theory also gives us some reason to believe that the problem of rectifying complicated injustices may not be insoluble in principle. For even if we cannot say precisely to what particular thing some individual or group is entitled, we can now see that just rectification may be achieved in such a case by redistribution within a range of appropriate outcomes. And the theory now has something intelligent to say about why the content of historical rights is not always determinate – something to say, that is, that should not just lead us to conclude that the historical rights in question are not real rights at all (or that if real, they are only real because *reducible* to *end-state* rights). But it will undoubtedly seem that still I have left the content of historical rights to particularized shares too vague to do any real work in explaining the requirements of historical rectification of injustice. So let me add a few very brief remarks on how I think the idea of rights to particularized shares can be more fully specified.

Let me begin again with the case of destroyed or altered property. It was noticed long ago (by Lawrence Davis) that where stolen goods were

---

27 Some resources, of course are not divisible into shares. And where (if ever) the downsizing of artifacts is at issue, division will routinely be pointless. In such cases the relevant rights to shares will still be particularized in the right sense, even if they are rights only to undivided shares.

destroyed, no rectification seemed possible on Nozick's entitlement theory. It was noticed as well that the most obvious addition to make to his theory to handle such cases would be some sort of indifference principle:[28] where the stolen good is destroyed (or irreversibly altered), the victim's right is to some share of the wrongdoer's goods that raises the victim to at least as high an indifference curve as had the theft not taken place. The obvious worries about introducing an indifference principle are that (a) it leaves many possible just rectifications between which we must somehow choose, and (b) it ceases to preserve entitlements to particular objects.[29] Indeed, we might suppose that endorsing such a principle within an historical entitlement theory would mark a shift from a "deontic" to an "outcome-oriented" conception of rights. And then all historical entitlements to particular things would be threatened, since no rights would ever be violated if the victim's well-being were simply appropriately enhanced during the course of the apparent right-violation.[30]

These worries will be lessened, I think, by noting that rights of rectification in such cases may be more specific than the discussion has thus far indicated. In particular, if the motivation in rectifying wrongs is to as nearly as possible nullify the effects of the wrongdoing (i.e., to make it as if the wrong had not occurred), the best rectification in cases of theft will be that which returns the victim to the closest possible approximation of the condition that would have obtained in the absence of the theft. If you steal my bicycle but do not destroy it, I am entitled to the return of my bicycle (plus additional compensation for loss). I am not entitled to demand instead the cash amount that raises my indifference curve to an appropriate level. Nor are you entitled to decide to keep the bicycle and instead pay me that cash amount. This suggests that if you steal my bicycle and do destroy it, a genuinely historical theory must say that appropriate rectification is not just the return of any share of your goods that meets an indifference standard, but rather the return of a share that effectively facilitates my transition to the state I would have been in but for the theft. If you have another bicycle

28 Davis, "Comments on Nozick's Entitlement Theory": 840–1. As Davis notes, Nozick seems content to employ an indifference standard (earlier in his book) in formulating his Principle of Compensation.

29 Ibid., 842, 844.

30 Eric Mack, "Nozick on Unproductivity: The Unintended Consequences," in J. Paul, ed., *Reading Nozick* (Totowa: Rowman & Littlefield, 1981), 186–87. See also Robert P. Wolff, "Robert Nozick's Derivation of the Minimal State," in *Reading Nozick*, p. 86; Jeffrey Paul "Property, Entitlement, and Remedy," *The Monist* 73 (1990): 569–71; O'Neill, "Rights to Compensation": 78–79; Lomasky, *Persons, Rights, and the Moral Community*, p. 143.

of comparable quality, or you have the cash to allow me to replace my stolen bicycle with a similar one, giving me these would be better rectifications of the wrong than would giving me a pile of books that I would value as highly as my bicycle. I am not entitled to demand the books instead of an identical bicycle, nor are you entitled to insist on providing the books as compensation instead of exercising one of the other options. I conclude from this that (a) historical rights theories need not embrace a pure indifference principle (with all of its attendant difficulties) in cases of destroyed property; and (b) that claims to particularized shares in such cases, while not always claims to particular shares, will normally be claims to something in a relatively narrow range of options.

Let me return now to the second case of rights to particularized shares – the case of mandatory downsizing – and to our example of the desert island castaways. When the island's population increases, just what may the needy newcomers lay claim to and what must the original islanders surrender? My view is this: the original islanders must make available to the newcomers some portion of their holdings that will allow the newcomers access to a fair share of the island's land and natural resources. But the original islanders have the right to choose which portions of their holdings to relinquish, and they retain their rights over even the relinquished portions so long as the newcomers opt not to make property in them. The original islanders may choose to keep the fair share of their original holdings to which they feel most attached, for instance, or in which they have invested the most labor. And they are entitled to compensation from the newcomers for improvements they have made in the portions of their holdings they are obliged to surrender.

The newcomers, on the other hand, are entitled to take in their purposive activities their fair shares of the original islanders' previously legitimate holdings. But they may take only from the relinquished portions. If the original islanders resist downsizing their holdings and refuse to choose which portions to surrender, the newcomers may seize their shares without the original owners' consents. But they may not seize just whatever portions they choose. They must take those portions that are least central to the original owners' pursuits and that carry the least investment of labor by the original owners. The newcomers may not seize their shares without indicating to the original islanders their intention to do so and their need for fair access. And they must compensate the islanders for any improvements previously made to the portions seized.

Finally, both parties must compensate the other for any losses caused by holding or seizing property in a fashion that is illegitimate at the time, but that later becomes legitimate through changed circumstances. For instance, an original islander might retain control over more than his fair share, denying the newcomers full access; but later developments might increase the available land (a drought dries out swampland, say) or decrease the demand (some of the islanders die), rendering the retained share fair at this later time. In that case, compensation is owed the newcomers for losses suffered by not having had access to their fair shares during the intervening years. Or the newcomers could seize more than their fair shares, gradually distributing portions of these illegitimate holdings to their children or to other newcomers, until the shares they all hold are of an appropriate size. In that case, compensation is owed to the original islanders for the losses they suffered from having for a time less of their original property than that share to which they were entitled. In neither case has the historic injustice simply been "superseded," as Jeremy Waldron seems to suggest is true of such cases,[31] for compensation is still due for unjust losses suffered during the time before which circumstances (and fair shares) changed.

If I am right about this, then we should once again conclude that rights to particularized shares can in fact be given some reasonably specific content. The original islander's claim to a share of her initial holdings (in cases of mandatory downsizing) is not necessarily a claim to an antecedently specifiable holding, but it is a claim that is far more specific than simply a claim to any appropriately sized share of the island. Further, if my remarks here are plausible, we can see at least part of what a historical rights theorist should say about the effects on our rights of passing time and changed circumstances. This has always been a sore subject for historical rights theorists, for it has always looked ad hoc to claim that rights simply expire or fade away if we ignore or complicate injustices for long enough. In the face of an entire society historically descended from unjust land acquisitions, say, Nozick can hardly say, "We will start taking historical entitlements seriously *now*; these old entitlements don't count any more. But these *current* entitlements, grounded in precisely the same way as the old ones that we'll ignore, are supremely important morally."

We can now see some ways in which historical rights can change, shrink, or expand, and so be sensitive to passing time and changing circumstances, without their simply fading away.[32] My own view is that mere passage of

31 Waldron, "Superseding Historic Injustice": 24–25.
32 I do not, of course, wish to argue that historical rights can never disappear altogether due to changed circumstances. If you steal my banana, eat it, and die immediately (from an allergy to bananas, say), leaving no property behind with which to compensate me, my right to rectification simply disappears.

time, considered strictly by itself, can have no effects on the substance of our moral rights, including our rights to rectification of past injustices. I am aware, of course, of the legal doctrines of (positive and negative) prescription and adverse possession, and of statutes of limitations, all of which are based precisely on the idea that legal rights (or liabilities) of various sorts can simply fade away as a result of long periods of time during which they are not exercised or enforced. I can acquire a right of way on your property, for instance, by trespassing for long enough, and you can lose your right to exclude me. But these legal doctrines, insofar as they are defensible at all, are based on concerns about evidentiary difficulties and on the plights of innocent third parties or nonculpably ignorant wrongdoers, whose lives have been built up around legally indefensible expectations. The doctrines were never intended to legitimize the positions of those who, say, maliciously seize another's property and cleverly manage to hold it long enough for the prescriptive legal rules to apply. It is not, then, mere passage of time that is intended to affect our rights, even on these legal doctrines.[33]

It may seem, of course, that no account of historical rights (of the sort I've described) could deny that rights will fade away in the face of certain kinds of wrongs. If property rights are acquired over things by incorporating them into our activities and projects, surely stealing those things removes them from our activities and projects, and so ends our rights over them.[34] But this argument essentially destroys the moral distinction, crucial to Lockean theories of property, between abandonment and theft. Abandonment of property is accomplished by clear signs of one's intention not to ever use that property again. Theft of property may take that property out of my immediate plans and projects; but it will leave that property a part of my vague or long-term plans, provided only that I would be happy to get that property back (perhaps because I could advance my ends by selling the property or by charitably giving it away). When my wife tries to collect for the Salvation Army my various never-used mementos and assorted junk, my reply is usually that I still want these things (I may want to use them or just enjoy them some day). They have not been abandoned, nor would they count as abandoned by me if they were gathering dust instead in some thief's basement.

33 George Sher argues that there are "necessary conditions for desert of compensation which become progressively harder to satisfy over time." But his arguments are only to the conclusion that entitlements are very likely to diminish over time; and this diminution has nothing to do with the mere passage of time (*simpliciter*). "Ancient Wrongs and Modern Rights," *Philosophy & Public Affairs* 10 (1981): 6, 13.

34 Waldron, "Superseding Historic Injustice": 18–19.

Three final points on this subject: first, my response to this objection assumes, with the objector, that the conditions for continued possession of a right must mirror those for the initial acquisition of a right. And this is by no means obviously the case, as the example of promissory rights clearly shows.[35] Acquiring a promissory right from another requires the other's intention to convey the right (or at least the other's intention to use signs that he knows will lead you to believe he intends to convey it). Continued possession of a promissory right, however, does not depend on the promisor's continued intention that you should enjoy the right. The promisor's further intentions, after the binding promise is made, are irrelevant to your continuing to have a right that he perform as promised.

Second, with special rights other than rights to *things*, one cannot extinguish the right by eliminating the rightholder's capacity to use the right. If I have negotiated an unlimited contractual right to, say, enter your studio to view your art collection whenever I please, this right cannot be extinguished by crippling and blinding me. The right remains a moral asset, even if I cannot exercise it. (I might, for instance, sell the right to some third party.) It would be most odd, then, if theft of property, merely by removing the property from its owner's plans and control, affected the owner's rights over the property.

Third, I have deliberately ignored in all of this the most obvious and complicated way in which passing time and changed circumstances can affect the substance of our moral rights. That is when the rightholder or the violator of rights dies. In what ways does change of cast entail change of rights, particularly in the cases of unrectified property injustices with which I am chiefly concerned here? That, of course, is a central issue in attempts to rectify the actual long-term injustices which are included in our society's history, and I will discuss it very briefly in the final section of this paper.

V

I have said that I hope this discussion will help to illuminate the issues confronted in addressing systematic, large-scale injustices in our own history, such as the theft of tribal lands from Native American peoples. Unfortunately, I can give here only a brief sketch of how we might apply our theoretical results to such practical concerns. And I must begin with two quick

35 See my discussion of this issue in *On the Edge of Anarchy* (Princeton: Princeton University Press, 1993), pp. 111–12.

caveats. First, our discussion provides direct assistance in analyzing only property injustices, such as the theft of aboriginal land and resources – injustices which are surely not as serious as the more direct and violent personal wrongs done to aboriginal peoples. Second, the hopelessly incomplete or one-sided historical records of injustices and their aftermaths will present insuperable evidentiary barriers to reaching any very specific conclusions about just rectification. But we can still say a little about the principles of rectification to which we should appeal in such cases.

There are, I think, two broadly liberal approaches to dealing with the claims and problems of groups like the Native American peoples, only one of which is historical in the sense discussed here. Some theorists treat Native Americans simply as one of a number of disadvantaged groups in our society, all of whom need to be made better off until they enjoy the social and economic rights and goods that justice demands be provided to all. Native Americans may require some special rights, based on the special vulnerability of their cultural context; but their tribes' historical standings as the original occupants of the Americas are irrelevant to their current moral claims.[36] The alternative liberal approach to this end-state view is to take seriously the historical claims of Native Americans to land and resources as the basis of persistent rights to rectification, beyond anything to which they are entitled simply as equal citizens (or persons).[37] The virtue of the historical approach, as I see it, is that it preserves the particularity of Native American claims. Their rights are not, I think, just rights to some fair share of American resources; they are rights to a particular (or a particularized) fair share. Treating Native American rights as exclusively end-state rights means denying that the actual arguments made by Native American tribes for historical rights to particular lands and resources have any moral force at all, or any appeal beyond ungrounded emotionalism. But I do not think most of us regard Native American demands for control over portions of their historical homelands simply as unmotivated, sentimental nonsense.

36 This is roughly the approach taken by Will Kymlicka in *Liberalism, Community, and Culture* (Oxford: Oxford University Press, 1989). See especially the long footnote on pp. 158–61 in which Kymlicka expresses scepticism about the moral importance of "the fact of original occupancy." Lyons also concludes that "it is highly doubtful that [Native Americans] have any special claims based upon their distant ancestors' original occupation of the land" ("The New Indian Claims . . .": 268). Waldron seems sympathetic to this approach as well ("Superseding Historic Injustice": 26–28).

37 A good recent example of this approach can be found in James Tully, "Rediscovering America: the *Two Treatises* and Aboriginal Rights," in *An Approach to Political Philosophy: Locke in Contexts* (Cambridge: Cambridge University Press, 1993).

It is tempting to embrace the nonhistorical, end-state view if we think that passing time and changing circumstances simply wipe out such historical rights. But I have suggested some ways in which historical rights can be sensitive to changing circumstances without simply dissolving in the fact of change. I've argued that we can have genuinely historical rights whose content is nonetheless imprecise. This imprecision of content, however, does not reduce such rights to general, nonhistorical (i.e., end-state) rights to any fair share. Rather, such rights can be to particularized, though not particular, fair shares of land or resources.

These arguments enable us to defend a conception of Native American rights to rectification that preserves at least some of the particularity of the claims actually advanced in lawsuits and published arguments by (or on behalf of) Native American tribes.[38] There is, I think, a range of acceptable rectificatory outcomes in these cases. Native American historical rights are to particularized shares; but the relevant entitlements were seldom made precise by any freely chosen (or otherwise responsibly accomplished) just downsizing of holdings. This means the historical rights of Native Americans are in certain ways imprecise (in addition to being exceptionally difficult to trace). But their rights are to (currently) fair portions of the actual lands they lived, hunted, and worked on, not generic fair shares of American land. And these particularized rights are to portions of what were once their central holdings – for instance, to portions of lands they held sacred, lands on which they resided, or lands in which they invested labor through agriculture or other improvements (like ecological management). Where lands or resources within the acceptable range of particularized shares have

---

38 It may, of course, be maintained that end-state arguments can also particularize claims in the ways I am here suggesting can only be accomplished by historical arguments. For instance, showing equal respect or regard for all (within an egalitarian framework) might be thought to involve taking seriously the cultural contexts, religious beliefs, and emotional attachments of Native Americans (and all others), resulting in a favored distribution of property rights that would give to Native Americans portions of their historical homelands (and to others the property to which they are in various ways attached). I believe that this sort of argument in fact amounts to either just a disguised historical argument (where an alleged "end-state" goal like "equal respect for culture" illicitly incorporates historical elements) or an argument that has no real hope of succeeding. For any nonhistorical basis of claims to property can be easily satisfied by people other than those who seem intuitively to have special rights to the property in question. For instance, tribe A and tribe B might historically have lived in, hunted in, and defended adjacent and ecologically similar territories, both tribes regarding both territories as parts of sacred land. But only tribe B's lands were later expropriated by settlers and effectively destroyed (for tribal use) by industrial development. Equal regard for the cultures, religions, and attachments of the two tribes would likely give them equal claims on the historical homeland of tribe A. Only historical considerations could give tribe A any special rights with regard to that territory, rights of the sort actually claimed by Native American tribes.

been destroyed or irreversibly altered (by commercial development, say), the best rectification will be accomplished by returning lands or goods that most closely approximate those to which Native Americans have particularized rights, or lands or goods that best facilitate duplicating the condition they would have enjoyed in the absence of the original injustice. Our counterfactual judgments in these cases should be conservative, assuming an absence of rashness and of extraordinary developments. And additional compensation for losses incurred during the changing of circumstances that required downsizing must also be considered.

It will certainly turn out that some past property injustices are simply unrectifiable. And it will certainly turn out as well that our judgments about just rectification will be fuzzy at best, complicated as they are both by evidentiary problems and by the imprecision of historical rights to shares (and of the concept of a fair share generally). The calculations required to determine even a reasonably specific range of acceptable rectificatory outcomes will be, to say the least, extraordinarily complex. But the principles noted here can at least provide some very broad guidelines for the proper way to particularize the reparations made to Native American peoples. We will always face, of course, the problems of conflicting claims by current generations of (largely) innocent third parties, those "newcomers" to the Americas whose expectations are firmly based on an assumed continuation of current distributions of land and resources. Those of us in this group are not, of course, quite like the completely innocent person who unwittingly builds his life around holdings that just turn out to have been stolen by an earlier possessor. For we all know the history of theft, broken agreements, and brutal subjugation on which our holdings in land and natural resources historically rest. But the claims of current generations of Americans must still be taken seriously. They can only be taken seriously in the right measure, however, if we first understand at least some of the force of the historical rights of Native Americans with which these claims are alleged to conflict.

Now it may seem that in these suggestions I have blithely ignored the two largest obstacles to understanding or accepting historical rights: the changes in cast that accompany long passages of time, and the dramatically different conceptions of property in fact favored by most Native American tribes. I will close this discussion with a few brief remarks on these two problems. Taking changes of cast first, there are obviously two central, relevant possibilities of this sort: those involving the death of the victim of wrongdoing and those involving the death of the wrongdoer. Both sorts of cases are complicated. When the wrongdoer dies, he may leave behind nothing that could adequately compensate his victim for the wrong, in which case rectification will simply be impossible. Where land is at issue, of course, this will generally not be the case (though we will still need to deal with the conflicting claims on the land of the children or dependents of the wrong-doer or of innocent third party holders of stolen land). But set all of this aside for now; the impossibility of full rectification in certain kinds of cases is not, I think, any more of a problem here than is the impossibility of retributive justice in cases where offenders die before they can be punished. The more troubling questions, I believe, clearly concern those cases in which the victim of wrongdoing dies. If the victim's rights die with him, of course, then Native American rights cannot possibly have persisted through the centuries in the ways my previous remarks suggested.

And why should we suppose that rights of rectification have simply been passed down family lines, from the original victims of injustice all the way to their current descendants? After all, those original victims might, in the absence of the injustice, have later sold their holdings or lost them in a poker game or given them to a needy friend, so that the relevant rights never would have passed to their children anyway. Why should inheritance of rights to rectification simply be assumed in this way,[39] particularly when we know that inherited property is the source of many apparent social injustices?[40] To this I think there are three appropriate responses. First, our counterfactual judgments about how things would have gone on in the absence of the wrong should be conservative, as I argued earlier.[41] Second,

---

39 Waldron, "Superseding Historic Injustice": 15.

40 Lyons, "The New Indian Claims . . .": 258.

41 Some might argue, of course, that some of the counterfactual judgments necessary to the case for historical reparations are simply (necessarily?) false. Following the lead of Parfit, a number of philosophers have pointed to a set of "existential" difficulties allegedly involved in attempts to apply the historical theory of rectification to cases like those of the Native Americans. The central objection is put most clearly by Christopher Morris. If the idea of rectification is to restore victims to the conditions they would have enjoyed in the absence of the injustice (or to the closest approximation thereof), the historical theory cannot, Morris claims, sanction rights to rectification for persons conceived after the injustice occurs – for instance, for the descendants of wronged Native Americans. For insofar as the injustice certainly changed the conditions under which the children of victims were later conceived, those children are different persons than the ones who would have been born in the absence of the wrong done to their parents. There is, then, no condition that actual children would have been in had injustices prior to their conceptions not occurred; nor is there any sense in which they can claim that they would have been better off in the possible world without the injustices. "Existential Limits to the Rectification of Past Wrongs," *American Philosophical Quarterly* 21 (1984): 176–77. I can only quickly sketch here what I take to be the correct response to Morris (et al.). There can be no denying (and Morris does not try to deny) that Morris's conclusion is counterintuitive. Common sense has no trouble with the claim: "If my parents had not had all of their property stolen (before my conception), I would have had an easier life as a child." Yet on Morris's analysis, this claim is straightforwardly false. His analysis fails, I think, because it involves either:

I think children have rights against their parents to the receipt of property (including in this "property" parental rights to the return of stolen property) that is needed by those children for a decent life; and in the case of the children of hunter-gatherers, this will invariably mean rights to use of the land and natural resources. Even if the parents did freely give away or sell the land their children needed for a decent life, then, the children would still have claims against the recipients of that land to the portions they needed.[42] Their parents were not entitled to dispose of the land without regard for the needs of their offspring. Finally, and perhaps most obviously relevant, we have the fact that the land and resources at issue were taken by Native Americans to be tribal property, not individual property.[43] If the property was thus held jointly, so were the relevant rights to rectification of injustice; and then, of course, the death of individual Native Americans was irrelevant to the question of persisting historical rights, as was the question of inheritance of rights (since the tribe as a whole never died, in at least many actual historical cases).

Now this last response may seem to solve the problem of the changing cast of characters only at the price of introducing new difficulties into our attempts to make sense of historical rights. First, there is no doubt that most Native American tribes understood the nature of their property in land and resources quite differently than, say, Locke and Nozick understand property rights. Tribes regarded themselves as inseparably connected to certain territories, so that their identities depended on continued and in some cases exclusive use of the land. Tribal ownership (or, better, stew-

---

(a) a tacit assumption that a significant injustice *necessarily* alters subsequent conditions for the conception of offspring; (b) an assumption that the relevant claims always concern identity across possible worlds, rather than some version of the "counterpart" relation across worlds (see Lewis, *Counterfactuals*, pp. 39–43, 67); (c) an assumption that perfect identity of genetic makeup is the single privileged criterion of personal identity; or (d) some combination of these assumptions. I reject all three of these assumptions. The best analysis of the counterfactual above, I think, sees it as equivalent to: "In those possible worlds in which I (or my counterpart) exist and my parents do not have all of their property stolen (before my conception), I have an easier life as a child (than that which I had in the actual world)." Since there certainly *are* such possible worlds (i.e., since, contrary to assumption (a) above, the absence of the theft could not be claimed to *necessarily* exclude my existence [or the existence of my counterpart]), the counterfactual at issue will be perfectly capable of being true. For a more sceptical examination of these questions, see George Sher, "Compensation and Transworld Personal Identity," *The Monist* (1979): 381–83. I should add, for those who find my reply to Morris unconvincing, that the second and third responses in the text below in no way depend on this reply, since they do not turn on any claims of transworld identity (or on possible world counterparts).

42 I discuss this view in *The Lockean Theory of Rights*, pp. 204–12.
43 Waldron, "Superseding Historic Injustice": 15; Lyons, "The New Indian Claims . . .": 257.

ardship) of the land was typically viewed as essential and inalienable, with ownership not so much derived from productive use as demanding productive uses that harmonized with the land.[44] And this amounts, of course, to a view of property in land which is more national than simply joint or collective. On such a conception of property in land, mandatory downsizing to make room for newcomers makes no clear sense. Newcomers may be permitted to use (nonsacred) tribal lands, but they cannot come to have any kind of property in the land that excludes tribal use.

From a Lockean historical perspective, this Native American conception of property rights will probably be viewed as in certain ways simply mistaken. Persons have rights of fair access to land and natural resources, and even a nation is not entitled to insist on control over a territory of inflexible size.[45] We must make room for everyone.[46] Native American beliefs that they need not yield to newcomers exclusive control over portions of their territories would then be viewed as a kind of nonculpable moral ignorance, an ignorance that perhaps excuses their acts of resistance to settlement of their territories, but that in no way limits the rights of fair access (and self-defense) of newcomers. The alternative (i.e., non-Lockean) historical perspectives are either conventionalist, relativizing property claims within a territory to those acknowledged by the dominant conventions in that

44 Tully, "Rediscovering America," pp. 138, 153–54. This view of property thus had more in common with pre-Lockean (than with Lockean) European conceptions of property, according to which land was sometimes taken to define the family that possessed it and consequently to be inalienable for that family.

45 Locke himself regarded national territories as set by understandings or contracts (treaties) between nations, in which members of each society give up rights of fair access to land within the agreed-upon boundaries of other societies (*Second Treatise*, para 45). But it is unclear why such agreements should be taken to bind or protect (a) new residents of these societies (prior to their consenting to membership); (b) individuals in the state of nature (such as Locke imagined Native Americans to be); or (c) nations that lack this understanding or were not otherwise party to any tacit or express agreements concerning national territory. Locke could, of course, have tried recognizing the Native American nations as genuine political societies, and then placed them with the nations in group (c), thus justifying appropriation of their territories by European settlers. But this would have entailed that those same Native Americans were free to appropriate European territory. It was thus safer from Locke's perspective (which included his desire to defend European settlement of the Americas) to place Native Americans in class (b), as Locke in fact did.

46 This implication for national property is one of the least discussed features of historical rights theories. A Lockean alternative is to view the right of fair access as a right of access not to land and natural resources, but to the means for living a decent life. This right of fair access might, then, in developed societies entail, not rights to land for newcomers, but rights to wealth or to nonalienating opportunities for paid employment. See *The Lockean Theory of Rights*, pp. 293–94.

territory,[47] or use-oriented, denying that exclusive private property in land or natural resources is possible.

But it may seem that the problems for a Lockean historical theory run still deeper. We might think, for example, that Lockeans simply can't handle joint or collective property claims at all, that all Lockean property is individual. This view, I think, is clearly confused. Joint property is certainly possible on a Lockean view.[48] Any individual property that individuals freely join together is then the (private) joint property of that collective. And further, if property acquisition turns on labor or on the incorporation of objects into purposive activities, joint property will be produced wherever objects are incorporated into collective projects. Thus, Native American tribes can certainly be supposed even on a Lockean view to have joint property in bodies of land or in natural resources. They can thus have historical rights to land or resources that can persist through time; they can have rights to the rectification of property injustices (i.e., injustices consisting in violations of those historical rights); and they can have rights that may be affected (in the ways we have discussed) by changing circumstances.

This conclusion needs two final points of clarification. First, even joint or collective property is subject to the individualistic limit set by the idea of a fair share. Collectives may hold no more property than the sum of the fair shares of their individual members.[49] And mandatory downsizing will

47 The Lockean view "naturalizes" property rights, I think, precisely to avoid such conventionalism. For if property rests simply on social convention, our property cannot be secure, given the possibility of simple alterations in social convention. The Lockean has to argue that while agreements between persons or within groups may change property relations between those involved, such agreements cannot change the rights of those not party to the agreements – such as white settlers, who could insist, on natural moral grounds, on their rights of fair access to land and resources.

48 Indeed, national territory is for Locke in one sense all joint, for though it is composed of private land holdings, this private land is "united" to the commonwealth (*Second Treatise*, para. 120). And the commons within each nation's boundaries is the pure joint property of all the nation's members (ibid., para. 35). On the acquisition of collective property in Pufendorf and Locke, see my "Original Acquisition Theories," section III.

49 The truth of this claim rests on (at least) three assumptions. First, of course, I assume that collectives are the kinds of things that can possess rights. Second, I assume no insuperable difficulties are introduced by the changing composition of the collectives. Third, I assume that members of a collective may hold in trust the rights to fair shares of other members who have been wrongfully killed or who have died after being unjustly deprived of their shares. Thus, we cannot reduce the fair share of a tribe by killing off its members or by stealing their land and waiting for them to die off. Tribes are entitled to hold shares in trust for future members under such circumstances (for some reasonable time period, at least), just as family members are entitled to do in cases of joint familial property. Morris has objected to the second of these assumptions by suggesting that since the collective will have "radically different" histories in the possible worlds containing and not con-

be determined in terms of the proportionate downsizing of individual shares. Second, our Lockean conclusions about Native American tribal property cannot be derived by strict adherence to the letter of Locke's own arguments. Locke himself took Native Americans to have property only in their artifacts and in the products of their hunting and gathering. They had no property in land, for they did not use the land itself in any efficient way, as did the European settlers who enclosed and cultivated portions of the earth. Thus, for Locke there was no question of required reparations for encroachments on tribal lands, for those lands constituted vacant waste still awaiting original appropriation.[50]

If, though, we take seriously the idea that property can be acquired by incorporation into our purposive activities, then the collective tribal activities of hunting, fishing, migratory residence, nonsedentary agriculture, and the like, could certainly have grounded tribal property rights in land and resources. But while Locke may have been wrong on that point, he was certainly right about the inefficiency of aboriginal land use, at least in this one sense – there is not enough land in the world to support us all at the population density levels characteristic of original Native American tribal life. Even if hunting and gathering remain legitimate sources of property in land, the fair shares of land available for exclusive use by hunter-gatherers must be far smaller than those originally occupied by aboriginal Americans. Thus, mandatory downsizing enters our theory even if we reject Locke's assumptions about which activities constituted productive (hence, appropriative) uses of the land.

We are left, then, with a characteristically liberal idea, one that we can now see is embraced by both purely historical and purely end-state theories of property rights and social justice (and so, we can surmise, one that will be embraced by any hybrid theory as well). Justice cares about insuring to all persons (access to) their fair share of goods and resources; it cares far less about the manner in which persons use these goods to advance their life plans and particular projects, or in the perceived virtues of those plans or projects themselves.

taining the injustice, the actual and the possible collectives cannot be identical ("Existential Limits": 181). But here, unlike the case of individuals conceived after the injustice, the identity of the group across possible worlds can be supported by continuity with the previous (i.e., pre-injustice) history of the group in all similar worlds. Even more obviously, the "counterpart relation" (that can be used instead of identity in such cases) can be supported by that same previous history.

50 Tully, "Rediscovering America," pp. 148, 162.

12

MAKERS' RIGHTS

The theory of property defended by John Locke in chapter 5 of his *Second Treatise of Government* remains the most discussed in the history of its subject.[1] Supporters and detractors alike appear for the most part to agree that Locke's theory at least requires careful consideration. The central thesis of that theory – that labor is the original source of exclusive property rights – has proved to be enormously influential and durable. Indeed, it is usually difficult for contemporary readers of Locke (who approach the text without firm theoretical predilections) not to conclude that Locke's central thesis is simply true.

Locke's explanation of *why* labor grounds property, however, has proved far less persuasive to contemporary audiences. His initial claim appears to be that in laboring we mix what we own (our person and its labor) with what we do not own ("nature"), thereby making it wrong for others to take or use the product of our labor, that product "including" as it does the labor that is ours (II,27).[2] Locke's critics have not treated this argument kindly, suggesting that the principal inference in the argument is a *non sequitur*, that the argument as a whole involves a reasonably basic

---

1 In addition to dozens of articles, at least two complete books [Gopal Sreenivasan, *The Limits of Lockean Rights in Property* (New York: Oxford University Press, 1995); Matthew H. Kramer, *John Locke and the Origins of Private Property* (Cambridge: Cambridge University Press, 1997)] and significant portions of at least three others [A. John Simmons, *The Lockean Theory of Rights* (Princeton: Princeton University Press, 1992); James Tully, *An Approach to Political Philosophy: Locke in Contexts* (Cambridge: Cambridge University Press, 1993); Stephen Buckle, *Natural Law and the Theory of Property* (Oxford: Oxford University Press, 1991)] have been devoted to Locke's theory of property in the past few years alone.
2 References to Locke's *Two Treatises of Government* will be indicated by I or II, followed by section number.

category mistake, or that Locke's assertions, when taken literally, are simply unintelligible.

Locke's most recent interpreters, however, have sought to do better for Locke than he (initially) appears to do for himself, explaining *why* labor grounds property for Locke by placing his principal discussion of these matters (in Chapter 5 of the *Second Treatise*) in a more illuminating context. A more unified and historically sensitive reading of Locke, they suggest, explains the moral significance of labor in Locke by way of a broader "workmanship model" to which Locke committed himself in various of his works. James Tully's influential work, *A Discourse on Property*, for instance, has as one of its obvious goals to convince us of the superiority of this interpretation of Locke; and the majority of the most prominent Locke scholars writing during the past two decades seem to have followed Tully in this reading of chapter 5 of the *Second Treatise*.

This "workmanship model" at first appears to essentially involve an analogy between God's works and those of man. And that theistic content of the model might seem to reduce Locke's theory of property to one that few contemporary philosophers could take seriously, and so to greatly diminish its initial appeal. More recently, however, it has been suggested that the "workmanship interpretation" of Locke's theory of property in fact should make that theory *more* plausible to contemporary readers than do the traditional readings of the text, not less plausible. So what might have been dismissed as a topic of purely historical interest is being taken to be one of continuing philosophical interest and "contemporary relevance."[3] My purpose in this essay is to examine the workmanship model in both of its proposed roles: as part of the best interpretation of Locke's theory of property and as part of a defensible contemporary theory of property. I will argue that in neither capacity is it a model that we should find compelling.

I

Tully first characterizes the workmanship model – to which he takes Locke to be committed – as follows: it is "the relational model of man and his maker" which portrays "God as maker and man as his workmanship." Locke's employment of this model, Tully claims, is "a common theme uniting the *Essay* and the *Two Treatises*."[4] Taking this characterization of

---

3 Sreenivasan, p. 3.
4 James Tully, *A Discourse on Property* (Cambridge: Cambridge University Press, 1980), p. 4.

the model literally, Tully is certainly right that Locke explicitly embraced the workmanship model in many of his works, from his early *Essays on the Law of Nature*[5] to the *Two Treatises* (e.g., in I,53 and II,6) and the *Essay* (most prominently in II.xxviii.8 and IV.iii.18).[6] If this were all that Tully were claiming, or all that the workmanship model is thought by him to involve, there would be no controversy over his reading of Locke (or over the claim that virtually all of the Christian authors who influenced Locke accepted this model). Further, of course, the workmanship model would not be likely to be of much enduring philosophical interest, since so stated it seems just a relatively uncontroversial implication of most orthodox religious belief.

That Tully has more in mind than this "minimal" version of the workmanship model is indicated by his further claim that "in his many uses of this conceptual model Locke makes it clear that it is the ground of property relations as well as of many political relations."[7] That the workmanship model can be the ground of relations directly between *human beings* suggests, of course, that there must be more to the model than a simple account of man as God's workmanship (and property). Tully plainly intends, as do all those who have accepted his interpretation, that the model not only explain God's rights over man, based in his creation of man, but also analogous rights for man, based in man's analogous makings: "a maker has a right in and over his workmanship."[8] It is the claim that this *analogy* holds between God and man which is the more interesting thesis, and it is the claim that Locke defends the analogy that makes Tully's reading of Locke intriguing and controversial. I will call this more substantial body of claims the *full* workmanship model.

Leaving to one side Tully's claims about the bearing of this model on human political relations, let us concentrate on the analogy's alleged force for human property rights. Those who make new things (out of nothing or out of preexisting materials), the argument goes, acquire special rights of control over those things. Just as God acquires absolute dominion over what he creates – that is, over what he makes *ex nihilo* – man acquires a lesser (i.e., limited) dominion, or property, over what he makes from pre-

5 See e.g., Essay IV [in Mark Goldie, Editor, *Locke: Political Essays* (Cambridge: Cambridge University Press, 1997), pp. 103–105] and Essay VI (in Goldie, pp. 117–119).

6 Schneewind rightly notes that Locke was committed to "the principle of creator's right throughout his life" ["Locke's Moral Philosophy," in Vere Chappell (ed.), *The Cambridge Campanion to Locke* (Cambridge: Cambridge University Press, 1994), p. 214].

7 Tully, *A Discourse on Property*, p. 4.

8 Tully, *A Discourse on Property*, p. 42.

existing materials.[9] So when Locke writes that human labor is the original ground of individual property rights, he has this analogy in mind, according to those who argue that Locke accepted the workmanship model. Our labor is morally significant by virtue of its making new things, in (rather pale) imitation of God's creation. Human property rights, like God's rights over us, are thus "makers' rights." And Locke, the argument continues, took it to simply be self-evident that makers have rights over their workmanship.[10]

Different defenders of this reading of Locke present the essentials of the workmanship model in slightly different ways.[11] But all reject the more literal and traditional reading of chapter 5 of the *Second Treatise*, which, as Sreenivasan puts it, "has Locke taking property in one's person and labour for granted and arguing from there that labour legitimates appropriation because, in labouring one irretrievably mixes with the object something that one already owns, namely, one's labour."[12] Understood in this "traditional" way, Locke would be claiming that God's dominion over the earth and man's property in the products of his labor have no common foundation. God's dominion is based in God's self-evident right of creation; man's property is based in man's mixing of his labor with unowned nature. God's property is based on his having created new things; man's property is based on extending his property in his person by acts of labor, which may or may not "make" new things, but which never make them in a way suffi-

---

9 In Locke's account of the distinction, a "maker" is one who "effects the material realisation of some idea of his, one which constitutes the essence of the thing made." "Creation" is simply "making *ex nihilo*" (Sreenivasan, p. 64. See also pp. 62–63, 74–76).

10 Tully, *A Discourse on Property*, pp. 40–42; Sreenivasan, pp. 62, 72.

11 John Colman, *John Locke's Moral Philosophy* (Edinburgh: Edinburgh University Press, 1983), pp. 187–192; Sibyl Schwarzenbach, "Locke's Two Conceptions of Property," *Social Theory and Practice* 14 (1988), p. 150, and Sreenivasan (p. 62), along with Tully, seem to present Locke's argument more or less as I have described it above. Buckle characterizes the workmanship model more in terms of improving the world, mirroring God's creative act, and carrying out God's purposes (p. 151). Ashcraft stresses the ways in which Locke's creationism place limits on his conception of property [Richard Ashcraft, *Revolutionary Politics & Locke's "Two Treatises of Government"* (Princeton: Princeton University Press, 1986), pp. 258–263; Richard Ashcraft, *Locke's Two Treatises of Government* (London: Unwin Hyman, 1987), pp. 134–135]. Shapiro identifies the "workmanship ideal" as involving man's ownership of his productive capacities and his right to own the product [Ian Shapiro, *The Evolution of Rights in Liberal Theory* (Cambridge: Cambridge University Press, 1986), p. 96; Ian Shapiro, "Resources, Capacities, and Ownership: The Workmanship Ideal and Distributive Justice," *Political Theory* 19 (1991), pp. 47–48]. It is not obvious that this last characterization of the model in fact requires one who embraces it to accept the makers' rights doctrine, instead of the more traditional labor-mixing doctrine.

12 Sreenivasam, p. 59.

ciently like God's *ex nihilo* creations to bring the two kinds of "making" under a common principle.

Some defenders of the "workmanship interpretation" of Locke[13] regard Locke's references in II,27 to "mixing labor" as a "metaphor" for the makers' rights doctrine.[14] Others say instead that the labor-mixing argument in fact detracts from and is unnecessary to Locke's real (workmanship) theory.[15] The latter seems a better interpretive strategy, perhaps, but still a questionable one: a good interpretation of the text should not have to explain away or dismiss the first and most direct and explicit of Locke's attempts to locate the origin of human private property.

Where the *minimal* workmanship model had the virtue of being plainly in Locke's texts, it also possessed the drawback of being philosophically uninteresting. The *full* workmanship model, by contrast (and as we shall see) is not so obviously one which Locke accepted. But advocates of the workmanship interpretation of Locke have claimed that it is a model in which we *should* continue to be interested (and this, by itself, would speak at least softly in favor of the interpretation). For the workmanship model in one form can be defended independent of any commitment to God's existence. If we understand the workmanship model as asserting that it is God's having *made* the world and his or her creatures that gives him or her property in them, then if man's makings are sufficiently similar to those ascribed to God, humankind should have property in what he or she makes *regardless* of whether or not God in fact exists.[16] The heart of the model is just the claim that makers have rights over what they make, and this aspect of the model seems to be one that contemporary philosophers could accept. Indeed, it is one that we could easily take many other historical theorists to have been committed to, along with Locke.[17] And, thus understood, the workmanship model can be said by its defenders to "retain a

---

13 As I shall call the interpretation that ascribes to Locke acceptance of Tully's full workmanship model, complete with the strong analogy between God's makings and man's, and including the doctrine of makers' rights.

14 Sreenivasan, p. 89.

15 Buckle, pp. 171, 174, 193.

16 Sreenivasan, pp. 63, 125. While Sreenivasan suggests that Tully's remarks (in Tully, *A Discourse on Property*) appear to *deny* the independence of the workmanship model from theistic commitments, Tully at least now appears to agree with Sreenivasan [James Tully, "Property, Self Government and Consent," *Canadian Journal of Political Science* 28 (1995), p. 115].

17 See, for instance, Shapiro's ascription of the secularized workmanship ideal to Karl Marx and to the "neoclassical political and economic theorists" [Ian Shapiro, "Resources, Capacities, and Ownership: The Worksmanship Ideal of Distributive Justice," *Political Theory* 19 (1991), pp. 51, 55].

certain plausibility even in our day. What is more, [this] plausibility is strictly independent of any theistic assumption."[18]

In the following sections of this essay, I shall address some of the issues I have just raised concerning the workmanship model. First, in section II, I will try to assess the weight of the textual (and other) evidence for the workmanship interpretation of Locke. Next, in section III, I will try to compare the virtues of the workmanship interpretation with a labor-mixing interpretation of Locke's theory of property. Finally, in section IV, I will assess the *independent* plausibility of the (secularized) workmanship model, divorced from any questions of its adequacy as part of an interpretation of Locke's moral and political philosophy.

II

Given the obvious popularity of the workmanship interpretation of Locke's labor theory of property acquisition – and especially given its acceptance by so many of the most distinguished contemporary Locke scholars – the actual textual evidence that has been adduced to support this reading of Locke is astonishingly slight.[19] Nowhere in the *Second Treatise*, for instance, does Locke defend anything like the full workmanship model or explicitly refer to makers' rights for humans, nor do any of his remarks there even directly imply a commitment to these views. Locke does, of course, prominently assert God's "right of creation" over man, invoking the "minimal" workmanship model: "Men being all the workmanship of one omnipotent and infinitely wise maker . . . they are his property whose workmanship they are . . ." (II,6). But Locke does not in that passage (or in *any other* passage in his writings in which he discusses God's right of creation) take the obvious opportunity to suggest an analogous maker's right for humans. And chapter 5 of the *Second Treatise* – the text that we are supposed to read in the light cast by the workmanship interpretation – simply makes no direct mention at all of makers' rights. Nowhere does Locke say or imply that labor grounds property because by our labor we make new things.

While Tully is correct in asserting that Locke uses "the word 'make' consistently and repeatedly" in chapter 5,[20] Locke uses "make" there exclusively

18 Sreenivasan, p. 125.
19 Despite Sreenivasan's somewhat wishful assertion that this evidence is "ample and impressive" (Sreenivasan, p. 88), Tully also takes Sreenivasan's defense of the workmanship interpretation to be "persuasive" (James Tully, "Property, Self-Government, and Consent," p. 115).
20 Tully, *A Discourse on Property*, p. 120.

to describe "making a property," "making use" of something, "making" something one's own, and "making value."[21] In no instance does Locke speak of "making a new thing" or of property being a consequence of such makings, as Tully's reading of the text requires. Surely this simple fact about the text in question should be deeply troubling to those who defend the workmanship interpretation.[22]

We might, however, argue that this troubling absence of solid evidence in the *Second Treatise* is not really fatal to the workmanship interpretation, provided we remember to read chapter 5 in the proper context of Locke's *other* works and in the correct historical context of the "creationist" works by others that influenced Locke. On the latter point, for instance, Tully cites "the judicious" Richard Hooker's reference to the analogy between God and man in their "manner of working."[23]

What Hooker actually wrote, however, is this:

> Man in perfection of nature being made according to the likeness of his maker resembleth him also in the manner of working; so that whatsoever we work as men, the same we do wittingly work and freely, neither are we according to the manner of natural agents any way so tied, but that it is in our power to leave the things we do undone.[24]

The "working" of which Hooker writes is plainly not "laboring," but merely "acting" (or "behaving"). He is discussing "how things work." And the analogy between God and man that Hooker is stressing in this passage is clearly only that man (like God) has knowledge and will, hence the freedom to choose to act or to leave things undone. Hooker is contrasting man with what he calls "natural agents," such as fire, that lack knowledge

---

21 See my discussion of this point (Simmons, p. 259) and Waldron's similar claims [Jeremy Waldron, *The Right to Private Property* (Oxford: Oxford University Press, 1988), pp. 199–200].

22 Sreenivasan (in a bit of understatement) does admit that it would be "disappointing" if no evidence could be found in "the text of the *Two Treatises* itself" (Sreenivasan, p. 77); but he takes comfort in finding (what he takes to count as) some direct evidence in the *First Treatise* (which I discuss below). Given that the principal material being interpreted is Locke's labor theory as this is presented in the *Second Treatise*, however, even this comfort should be relatively *cold* comfort – especially if we take seriously Laslett's contention that the *Second Treatise* was written *before* the *First* [Peter Laslett (ed.), *Locke: Two Treatises of Government* (Cambridge: Cambridge University Press, 1960), pp. 61–62], and note the obvious fact that it was in the *Second* that Locke tried to give his principal statement of his *own* views (with the *First* being primarily a polemic against Filmer).

23 Tully, *A Discourse on Property*, p. 110.

24 *Of the Laws of Ecclesiastical Polity*, I.7.2 [in Arthur Stephen McGrade (ed.), *Hooker: Of the Laws of Ecclesiastical Polity* (Cambridge: Cambridge University Press, 1989), pp. 70–71].

and will and so "work" without the liberty to do or forbear. Nothing in this passage even hints at the view that man has "maker's rights" over what he makes, analogous to God's self-evident right of creation. Indeed, Hooker is not discussing creation or making or labor or property at all, so that only a misreading of Hooker by Locke could have influenced Locke to follow by defending the full workmanship model.

Not surprisingly, perhaps, the passage in Locke's own works that is most frequently cited as demonstrating his commitment to makers' rights for humans in fact only points to an analogy between God and man that is very similar to the one to which Hooker was pointing (in the passage just discussed). Defenders of the workmanship interpretation have argued that we must read the *Second Treatise* in light of the *First Treatise*'s clear commitment to the doctrine of makers' rights. They point chiefly to I,30,[25] in which Locke asserts that "God makes [man] in his own image after his own likeness, makes him an intellectual creature, and so capable of dominion."

Notice that Locke does not in I,30 claim that the similarity to God which makes us capable of dominion (i.e., property) is that we, like God, can *make* new things. Locke mentions only our similarity in both being "intellectual creatures" – that is, in both being what Locke elsewhere calls "rational beings" or "free and intelligent agents" (II,57). Now this assertion is, of course, *consistent* with Locke's embracing the doctrine of makers' rights, since our making something plainly requires "intellect" in our acting on the idea of that thing. But it does not in any way *imply* the makers' rights doctrine, as defenders of the workmanship interpretation contend, and it is in fact also consistent with any *other* reasonable interpretation of Locke's theory of property. To see this it is necessary only to recall that for Locke beings that lack reason ("intellect") are not "under" the "law of reason" (or law of nature), and so do not enjoy the equality and freedom which is the "natural condition" of rational beings (II,55,57). That fact by itself, independent of any commitment to makers' rights, entails that only "intellectual creatures" are "capable of dominion," dominion being a complex right defined by the law of reason/nature.[26] Rightholders must be rational for Locke. Since Locke's *overall* point in I,30 (like Hooker's in the passage considered above) is only that rational man is superior to the rest of nature

---

25 See, e.g., Tully, *A Discourse on Property*, p. 37; Sreenivasan, pp. 65, 75; Colman, p. 187. Sreenivasan also cites I,40, in which Locke says almost identical things.

26 Sreenivasan is thus mistaken in suggesting that (only?) Locke's commitment to the makers' rights doctrine can explain *why* our godlike intellectual nature makes men capable of dominion (Sreenivasan, p. 65).

and thus "enabled to have dominion over the inferior creatures" (I,30) – and since the dominion of man in question (i.e., that over the lower animals) is created by a direct grant from God, not by any "making" activities by man – it is hard to find any reason to interpret I,30 as showing Locke's support for or commitment to the doctrine of makers' rights.

As far as I can see, the only other passage in the *Treatises* that defenders of the workmanship interpretation even attempt to cite as support for their view is Locke's refutation (again, in the *First Treatise*) of Filmer's arguments for absolute paternal power, where Locke denies that fathers make their children (I,52–55). Sreenivasan, for instance, claims that this passage "is very obviously informed by the assumption that the doctrine of maker's right applies to man"[27] – though it takes him four pages of explanation to demonstrate this obviousness. Without trying here to fully summarize Sreenivasan's reasoning, it is perhaps sufficient for my purposes to point out the following: even on Sreenivasan's preferred reading of this text, he is forced to ascribe to Locke a "slip" or a careless acceptance of one of Filmer's doctrines, for Locke on Sreenivasan's reading turns out to be committed to the view that makers have *absolute* rights over their workmanship.[28] This, of course, is a view that Locke plainly *denies* in the case of *human* makers, as all defenders of the workmanship interpretation acknowledge. It is hard to accept a very elaborate reading of a passage that must still, in the end, ask us to disregard one of its clear implications. Locke never in I,52–55 directly affirms the makers' rights doctrine or even directly ascribes it to Filmer; it thus seems more reasonable to take the passage as either just making a case, *arguendo*, against Filmer or as simply being confused and irrelevant to Locke's considered position on labor and property.

Indeed, one of Locke's principal aims in I,52–55 is precisely to point to a *dissimilarity* between the "makings" of man and God: God's making involves "incomprehensible works" (such as "breathing life" into man) (I,53), where man's making plainly does not. But, of course, *none* of man's makings, not just his alleged "making" of his children, are like God's in that respect. Locke is willing to grant that *if* "parents made their children, gave them life and being," *then* parents might enjoy an "absolute power" over them (like God's absolute power over us) (I,55). But man enjoys absolute dominion over nothing, in Locke's view, for man gives "life and being" to nothing, being incapable of creation (i.e., making *ex nihilo*).

27 Sreenivasan, p. 77.
28 Sreenivasan, pp. 80–81.

Locke simply never says or implies – despite ample opportunity to do so – that *lesser* kinds of "making" analogously create lesser kinds of dominion, as the workmanship interpretation asserts.

Without clear support from the *Treatises* themselves, the workmanship interpretation of the *Treatises* seems doomed to failure. Perhaps if evidence from Locke's other writings unambiguously showed him committed to the full workmanship model, we might be persuaded to view the makers' rights doctrine as a background assumption of the *Treatises*, never stated by Locke because he regarded its truth as simply obvious. But the evidence from Locke's other writings it at least as weak as is that from the *Treatises*. The only such passages that even seem to stand a chance of supporting the workmanship interpretation are drawn (by Colman and Sreenivasan) from Book II of Locke's *Essay* and from his little unfinished (and unpublished) essay called "Morality."

In "Morality," Sreenivasan contends, Locke's argument "constitutes a clear case of the maker's right doctrine being applied specifically to man."[29] There Locke argues that because man makes neither himself nor the world into which he is born, man can have at birth no exclusive right to anything in the world. This certainly seems to imply – though, once again, not to *state* – that man's "makings" are what give him exclusive property rights. Sreenivasan declines to quote, however, the sentence that immediately follows the argument in question: "Men must therefore either enjoy all things in common or by compact determine their rights."[30] Here Locke plainly asserts a doctrine that is both inconsistent with the later, developed argument of the *Second Treatise* – where Locke specifically *rejects* the compact theory of private property, insisting that a person's labor can legitimately individuate the commons without the consent of the other commoners (II,25,27) – and clearly inconsistent with the doctrine of makers' rights.[31] "Making" cannot be the source of man's private property if a

---

29 Sreenivasan, p. 76.

30 The full passage reads: "Man made not himself nor any other man. Man made not the world which he found made at his birth. Therefore man at his birth can have no right to anything in the world more than another. Men therefore must either enjoy all things in common or by compact determine their rights" [Mark Goldie (ed.), *Locke: Political Essays* (Cambridge: Cambridge University Press, 1997), p. 268].

31 Colman tries to deny that Locke is in "Morality" defending a compact theory of exclusive property (Colman, p. 196). He argues that Locke's remarks there refer only to (what Locke calls in the *Second Treatise*) the "settling" in civil society of the property "that labor and industry began" (II,45) (Colman, pp. 196, 264–265 [note 22]). But this is not, of course, what Locke *says* in "Morality"; nor does it make sense that the exclusive alternatives offered there – either "all things in common" or "compact to determine rights" –

compact is necessary to divide the earth, originally held by mankind in common, into private shares.[32] We have good reason, then, not only to regard the whole argument of Locke's peculiar little unfinished essay as of dubious relevance to the proper interpretation of the *Second Treatise*, but also to regard with great skepticism any attempt to use this argument as good evidence for the workmanship interpretation.

Locke's *Essay* might initially appear to hold more promise for supporting the workmanship interpretation of the *Treatises*. There Locke claims:

> The dominion of man, in this little world of his own understanding, being muchwhat the same as it is in the great world of visible things; wherein his power, however managed by art and skill, reaches no farther than to compound and divide the materials that are made to his hand; but can do nothing towards the making the least particle of new matter, or destroying one atom of what is already in being."[33]

Now this passage could, I suppose, be read to say (or at least to imply) that man's dominion, or property, in "the great world of visible things" derives solely from his making new things out of those things that were first created by God (despite Locke's saying that man's dominion in the two worlds is only "muchwhat the same"). But such a reading would have to ignore two rather obvious obstacles to it. First, the word "dominion" in this passage from the *Essay* is not most naturally read as meaning "property," but rather as meaning something like "domain" or "area of control." Locke's point

could describe the same situation of which Locke in the *Second Treatise* says "labour, in the beginning, gave a right of property, wherever anyone was pleased to employ it, upon what was common" (*also* from II,45). Colman may have been led to his misinterpretation by the mistaken impression that "Morality" *postdates* the *Treatises* (as Sargentich's dating of the essay's composition in the 1690s would suggest). It would, of course, be disturbing if Locke had simply, without explanation, contradicted his earlier emphatic rejection of compact theories in the fully developed theory of property in the *Second Treatise*. But the more reliable datings of "Morality" by Marshall, who puts it between 1676 and 1680 [John Marshall, *John Locke: Resistance, Religion and Responsibility* (Cambridge: Cambridge University Press, 1994), p. 193], and Goldie, who puts it in 1677–1678 (Goldie, p. 267), place its composition *prior to* that of the *Treatises*. Marshall also correctly states that Locke was still at that stage in his thought defending a compact theory of exclusive property (Marshall, pp. 206, 280).

32 Unless the idea is that we "make" the compact that determines our rights. But that would be to turn the doctrine of makers' rights into a completely different doctrine, with labor having no special status as a routine source of property, and only some very specific kinds of "makings" turning out to be relevant to the appropriation of property.

33 *An Essay Concerning Human Understanding*, II.ii. 2 (Peter H. Nidditch (ed.), *John Locke: An Essay Concerning Human Understanding* (Oxford: Oxford University Press, 1975), p. 120). Colman (p. 190) and Sreenivasan (p. 75) both cite this passage as evidence for Locke's support of the full workmanship model.

would then be to simply deny man's capacity for *ex nihilo* creation, *not* to affirm his property in that which he *does* make. And it should be remembered that Locke frequently uses the word "dominion" in ways that are *contrasted to*, rather than *identified with*, ownership or property.[34]

Second, we must emphasize that the context of Locke's remarks in the *Essay* is his distinction between simple and complex ideas, and his point in the quoted passage is just to deny that persons can make their own simple ideas (independent of sensation and reflection), in the same way that they cannot make (or destroy) new matter. Locke is not here concerned with our *ownership* of either our ideas or those material things we make, but only with the analogous limits on our capabilities in the two "worlds." Indeed, he emphasizes not only our inability to create matter, but also our inability to destroy it (which would not be germane to a discussion of *property* in what we *make*). Locke's *Essay*, then, will not supply evidence with which to defend the workmanship interpretation.

Our conclusion must be that neither the *Treatises* themselves nor any of Locke's other (published or unpublished) works offers any compelling evidence that Locke was committed to the doctrine of makers' rights. Indeed, as we have seen, Locke worked far harder to stress the *disanalogies* between the "makings" of God and man than he ever did to argue for the analogy between them on which that doctrine relies. We would do well, then, to look to other possible readings of Locke's labor theory of property. The workmanship interpretation, for all its apparent appeal and symmetry, fails to capture Locke's intended explanation of why labor gives rise to property.

III

In the face of this distinct paucity of direct textual evidence, one might well wonder how the workmanship interpretation of Locke can have achieved such a substantial and influential following. One reason, of course, is that the interpretation offers a unified account of the various instances of property mentioned by Locke, and it does so in a way that takes seriously Locke's very serious theological commitments. And this might be reason enough.

---

34 In the *Second Treatise*, for instance, Locke uses "dominion" to mean "government jurisdiction" – the right of the government to "secure and regulate" property – which he plainly intends to be consistent with "possession," "property," and "proprietorship" by individual members of the society (II,120). My ownership rights in my land are limited by, not superseded or replaced by, the "dominion" of my government over that land. For a fuller defense of this reading of Locke, see Simmons, pp. 310–318.

For much recent Locke scholarship has been driven by the desire to give an appropriately prominent place to Locke's theology, in response to the preceding decades of Locke interpretation having largely ignored the role of Locke's religious beliefs in his moral and political philosophy.

But an equally important factor behind the popularity of the workmanship interpretation has been the (allegedly) obvious failure of Locke's theory when it is read in a more traditional manner. In particular, if we take Locke's "labor-mixing" argument, as this is usually presented, to be blatantly fallacious – as most defenders of the workmanship interpretation do – it is natural to think that Locke *must* have had in mind a better explanation than *that* of why labor grounds property. The workmanship model is then taken to supply the necessary "better explanation." But the premise from which this conclusion is drawn is false. Locke's labor-mixing argument is not only plainly *in* the text, where the doctrine of makers' rights is not. It also can be naturally read in a fashion that reveals it to be not only non-fallacious, but quite persuasive. And so read it is clearly better able to explain the range of instances of property that Locke mentions than is the competing argument from makers' rights.

The most often noted defects of that "labor-mixing" argument are the following: first, it simply makes no sense to talk of literally mixing labor with nature, but Locke's argument requires us to take this literally.[35] Second, the crucial inference in Locke's argument is a *non sequitur*, for Locke gives no explanation of why, when we mix our labor with a thing, we come to own that thing instead of just losing our labor.[36] Third, if we take the labor-mixing argument literally, we make it impossible for Locke to explain why those kinds of laboring that *don't* involve "making" *don't* create property – for instance, the labor of parents, which Locke *denies* gives them property in their children (because children aren't *made* in the proper sense by their parents).[37] Fourth, as it is ordinarily understood, the labor-mixing argument treats our property in our persons and labor as simply axiomatic, and so it is forced to give asymmetrical accounts of our ownership of our persons and our ownership of what we labor on.[38]

But any moderately sympathetic reading of Locke's labor-mixing argu-

---

35 E.g., Waldron, pp. 184–188.
36 E.g., Robert Nozick, *Anarchy, State and Utopia* (New York: Basic Books, 1974), pp. 174–175; Waldron, pp. 189–190; Sreenivasan, pp. 60–61.
37 E.g., Sreenivasan, pp. 83–84; James Tully, "Property, Self-Government, and Consent," p. 117.
38 E.g., Sreenivasan, pp. 61, 89.

ment should show us how Locke can easily address these difficulties.[39] What Locke writes about labor suggests that he thinks of labor as free, intentional, purposive action aimed at satisfying needs or supplying the conveniences of life.[40] To "mix" my labor with an object for Locke is simply for me to make productive use of the object, within the scope of my labor's purpose. My labor "marks" the object ("removes it from common") by thus usefully bringing it within the realistic sphere of my plans or projects. And this "marking" makes any use of the object by others (without my consent) a violation of my right to govern myself (within the bounds of morality) – what Locke calls my "natural freedom" or "natural liberty" (II,22,54,191).

Similarly, Locke's claim that I have property in my person and actions is best understood as being Locke's way of saying simply that nobody but I myself may rightly use or govern me, unless they have my consent. This is why Locke follows his claim that each has property in his person by explaining that "this nobody has any right to but himself" (II,27).[41] Both my property in myself and my property in what I labor on are thus based in what is necessary for self-government to be possible. There is, then, a perfectly natural (and not at all unintelligible) sense that can be given to Locke's claim that in laboring on nature I "mix" my property in myself with nature: I bring (part of) nature within my legitimate sphere of self-government by physically imposing my plan for its useful employment upon it. My plan, which is the product of my mental labor, is "mixed" with the object through the purposive activity that constitutes my physical labor. There is nothing incoherent about such an account. Indeed, it seems to me broadly correct.[42]

39 I offer a much longer and more detailed version of such a reading in Simmons, chapter 5.

40 Simmons, pp. 271–273.

41 Each man has "a right of freedom to his person, which no other man has a power over, but the free disposal of it lies in himself" (II,190). Since Locke in this passage says that "every man is born with a double right," but never mentions a man's right of *property* in his person and actions, it is natural to understand this "right of freedom" as simply *identical to* the "property in his own person" that "nobody has any right to but himself." It is, then, no coincidence that the two rights are similarly described as simply being the *exclusions* of the rights of others. See also Waldron, p. 181.

42 See my argument for this conclusion in Simmons, pp. 273–277. Any Lockean account of this sort will obviously have to begin in an argument for the existence of the right of self-government (or for "self-ownership," so conceived) that I have described. I favor a "Kantian" version of this argument, which appeals to the irrationality of "using" rational agents; but whatever version one favors, some such argument must, in my view, be at the foundation of *any* theory of natural rights. For a convincing defense of the view that the thesis of self-ownership does not have obviously objectionable consequences, see John Christman, "Self-Ownership, Equality, and the Structure of Property of Rights," *Political Theory* 19 (1991), pp. 28–46.

Understanding the labor-mixing argument in this way also supplies ready answers to the other alleged defects of that argument that I mentioned. Mixing labor is not a way of losing our labor (instead of gaining property) because our labor never "leaves" us in being mixed with nature. Our labor extends our selves (that is, our legitimate spheres of self-government) into the natural world. Our purposive activities are inseparable from our selves. We come to own that part of what we labor on that is necessary to those activities (within the limits on property acquisition and retention set by the "Lockean provisos"). This typically includes the "object" on which we labor, and not just the value that we add to it, because adequate self-government and the living of a purposive existence typically require that sort of control over objects.[43]

Some kinds of labor-mixing *cannot* create property in the object of labor, because that which is labored on is *itself* a being born to natural freedom/self-government and so is already owned (i.e., by itself [and/or by God]). Examples are cases in which I labor to save the life of an accident victim, the slaver labors to capture his victims, or parents labor to conceive, deliver, and raise their children. Similarly, some labor on *objects* (i.e., on non-persons) cannot create property because the object is already owned by another – as when I surreptitiously wax your car. This is because our exercises of self-government commit us to respecting the similar exercises of others who are similarly endowed with natural freedom.

This account does, admittedly, give different (though plainly related) explanations of our property in our own persons and our property in "external" goods. But this asymmetry seems to me an asymmetry that properly reflects the differences between the two cases. Exclusive control over our persons and actions is in itself essential to self-government.[44] Control over nature is only essential to self-government when the goods necessary to self-government are not otherwise supplied (as they might be, for instance, in property regimes that substituted satisfactory alternatives for access to land and natural resources).

Where the labor-mixing argument thus seems capable of being under-

---

43 This provides the answer to another familiar criticism of the labor-mixing argument – i.e., that it cannot explain why we come to own more than merely the added value labor produces (Nozick, pp. 174–175; Waldron, pp. 189–190).

44 Nor need we simply take this "property" in ourselves to be axiomatic, as the criticism we originally considered maintained. Locke took such property to be a function of God's having entrusted each of us with the care and living of a life. And any secular rights theory will have to say something about the clear centrality of such self-government (or "self-ownership") to any plausible conception of *personhood*.

stood as a forceful argument, consistent with Locke's texts and purposes, the argument from makers' rights is not. One of the goals of the workmanship interpretation, remember, is to try to present a unified account of Lockean property, according to which all exclusive property – God's in the universe, ours in our persons and actions, and ours in external goods – originates in acts of "making." But the workmanship model is only a plausible account of – and the workmanship interpretation of Locke can only explain – the *first* of these three instances of exclusive property. Locke plainly defends God's "right of creation" in his *ex nihilo* makings. And (I suppose), however loath we might be to accept Locke's (or anyone's) appeal to the self-evidence of such a right, even those who deny God's existence might be persuaded to allow that genuine *creation* (that is, *ex nihilo* making) would be a special enough sort of act that special rights might well be based upon it.

Neither the workmanship model nor the workmanship interpretation of Locke, however, can deal with the second instance of exclusive property: our property in our persons and actions. Not only do we not make our *bodies* (as all defenders of the workmanship model concede), there is simply no plausible sense in which *we* – as opposed to our parents, our teachers, our friends, our societies, our psychotherapists, our God – are solely responsible for *making* our *persons*, so that we might have sole property in our persons based on a principle of makers' rights. This, of course, is why contemporary action theorists have expressed so much skepticism about the idea that we are fully responsible for our *characters*, in addition to our free *actions*. Similarly, Locke never suggests – nor *could* he, given his stated views of the importance of parents and teachers in making children into persons – that we *make* our persons, and that this making is the source of our property in our persons.[45] While there is, perhaps, a plausible sense in which we could be said to "make" our *actions*, it is far less plausible to claim that it is this "making" – as opposed to the importance of freedom of action to living our lives – that gives us rightful control over ("property" in) those actions. And the text that is typically cited to defend the position that *Locke* had such a view in mind clearly cannot bear the stretching these claims require.[46]

---

45 As even many defenders of the workmanship interpretation find themselves forced to acknowledge. See, e.g., Sreenivasan, p. 68; Tully, *A Discourse on Property*, p. 109; Colman, p. 189.

46 The passages cited to support this reading – i.e., that Locke believed that it is our making our actions that gives us property in them – are drawn from II.xxvii. of the *Essay*. There Locke suggests both that agents freely bring their actions into existence and that persons

Last, and by far *worst* for the workmanship interpretation, its explanation of our property in external goods is plainly inadequate (as I argue in section IV below), and its attempts to account for the examples of external property actually given by Locke clearly fail. Locke's principal examples of the exclusive property in external goods that originates in labor are these: (1) acorns and apples (plums and nuts [II,46], moss and leaves [II,42]) "gathered from the trees in the wood" (II,26,28,31,46), and timber cut in the wood (II,43); (2) the grass my horse eats, turfs my servant cuts, and ore (iron, coal, stone, lime [II,43]) I dig up (II,28); (3) water drawn from a fountain (II,29) or drunk from a river (II,38); (4) deer killed (or animals caught or tamed [II,37]), fish caught in the ocean, "ambergriese" gathered from the water (II,30); (5) land that is tilled, planted, improved, cultivated (II,32,37–38,42–43); (6) bread, wine, cloth, bricks, masts, ropes that people make (II,42–43); (7) shells, sparkling pebbles, diamonds that people pick up (II,46).

Notice that (1), (2), (3), (4), and (7) – which includes *all* of the examples Locke uses in II,26–31 to clarify his initial presentation of the labor theory of property acquisition – involve only gathering or catching things that are fully "made" by nature/God. We establish exclusive properties for ourselves by gathering fruits, nuts, wood, or pebbles, by digging ore, by catching deer and fish. Locke's examples of agriculture, manufacture, and domestication of animals are all introduced *after* he has presented and given examples of the essentials of his theory. But there is simply no way that anyone (at least, anyone not in the grip of a theory) could take the activities of gathering and hunting to involve "making" something new. The labor that grounds property *may* involve making for Locke, as when I make bread or grow a field of corn; but it plainly *need* not.

Tully tries to argue that labor in these cases of gathering and hunting still "transforms the earthly provisions provided *for* use into manmade objects *of* use."[47] But this most minimal sort of "making" could hardly be thought by Locke to be sufficiently like God's glorious creation to bring them both under a common principle of makers' rights. I can establish a

---

"own" the actions that they attribute to themselves. But Locke *never* there suggests that the "making" of our actions gives us *property* in them. His use of "owning actions" plainly refers not to our property in them, but simply to our taking responsibility for them, to our accepting them as *our* actions – as when we "own up to" some act. Locke says that "personality . . . owns and imputes to itself *past* actions," thereby "appropriating actions *and their merits*" (II.xxvii.26 [my emphases]; in Nidditch, p. 346). This would be a *very* odd way of trying to make a point about our *property rights* in our actions!

47 Tully, *A Discourse on Property*, p. 117.

property in an acorn or in a sparkling pebble simply by picking it up with the intention of using it; but the "change" that I bring about in the object by moving it a few inches does not look like much of a "making." And, of course, I can turn things into "objects of use" *without* making property in them, on Locke's view: I can turn the North Star into an object of use by finding my way with it, or turn a tree into an object of use by moving into its shade. In neither case do I come to own the object. So the kind of "transformation" Tully describes to cover cases of gathering and hunting seems, in Locke's own terms, neither necessary nor sufficient (even *within* the stated Lockean limits on takings) for property acquisition.

Sreenivasan, more realistically, simply admits that the workmanship interpretation cannot account for Locke's belief that we have property "in natural things prior to their entry in productive processes."[48] But he concludes that this problem "is one which merely reflects a genuine difficulty in Locke's own account, one generated by his overly extended application of the theory";[49] and he justifies this interpretive liberty by insisting that "no interpretation of Locke's theory will be able to handle without difficulty all of the cases he presents."[50]

But, of course, we are not speaking here of the workmanship interpretation's failure to handle one or two of Locke's minor examples (such as his confused discussion of the hare in II,30, the case Sreenivasan cites). We are speaking of an interpretation that can make sense of *none* of the examples Locke initially uses to explain his theory, and only a minority of the examples he uses anywhere in chapter 5. And I, for one, do not share Sreenivasan's opinion that Locke has plainly *overextended* his theory by trying to explain the baker's property in the apples he has gathered (*before* he makes the apple pies) or the brewer's property in the water he draws from the stream (*before* he begins to turn it into beer). These activities do plainly involve labor, and control over the objects of labor (i.e., that which is gathered) is clearly important to the viability of any subsequent production. These thus seem to me to be precisely the kinds of cases that a labor theory of property acquisition *should* be able to explain, but that it *cannot* explain on the workmanship model of such a theory.

That the "traditional" understanding of Locke's labor-mixing argument *does* allow it to explain Locke's conclusions about these kinds of examples – and about virtually all of Locke's *other* examples as well – speaks very

48 Sreenivasan, p. 87.
49 Sreenivasan, p. 88.
50 Sreenivasan, p. 87.

strongly in favor of that reading of Locke, as the failure to do so speaks strongly against the workmanship interpretation. That the argument is plainly in the text on the former reading of it, but not on the latter, also speaks volumes. Finally, I think it can be reasonably claimed that the traditional labor-mixing interpretation of Locke's theory squares better with Locke's *theological* commitments than does the workmanship interpretation, despite the fact that the desire for such a fit was a prime motivation for the development of the workmanship interpretation. For, as we have seen, Locke works quite hard in many places to impress upon his readers the enormous *differences* between God's works and man's, combatting the hubris involved in supposing that we can make new things in ways at all similar to God's creation. The labor-mixing interpretation of Locke marks these differences clearly: God's absolute dominion is based in creation; man's limited property is based in his labor on what is provided for him (and, ultimately, in God's having entrusted men with their own lives). The workmanship interpretation actually obscures these differences, trying to bring all rightful exclusive control under a single principle of makers' rights.

IV

Let us turn, finally, to the question of whether the workmanship model provides us with (all or part of) an *acceptable* account of original property acquisition, leaving behind now the question of whether *Locke* should be understood as having embraced that model. We can, remember, regard the workmanship model as having force independent of any commitment to God's existence or dominion, since the heart of the model is simply the doctrine of makers' rights. When Sreenivasan, for instance, takes up "the question of [the model's] tenability in *secular* terms," he summarizes it as follows:

1. If one makes something *ex nihilo*, then one is entitled to it.
2. Making something from pre-existing materials is sufficiently like making something *ex nihilo* (so that if one makes something, then one is entitled to it, *provided* no one has a legitimate objection to one's use of the relevant materials).

According to Sreenivasan, it "is difficult to deny . . . that, at some level of entitlement, premisses (1) and (2) retain a certain plausibility, even in our day."[51]

---

51 Sreenivasan, pp. 124–125.

We should begin by stating clearly which claim(s) it is whose plausibility we are assessing. We have already seen, for instance, that the principle of makers' rights cannot provide us with a *complete* theory of original property acquisition, or even a complete theory of that original property which is grounded in *labor*. For the property we acquire by gathering natural things, for example, cannot reasonably be said to be the result of "making" something new. And it seems to me that it would be foolish to deny either that we *can* have property in such cases – i.e., in cases involving gathered natural things, prior to their entry into productive processes – or that the property we have in such cases is due to our labor. The baker surely requires rightful control over the apples he gathers from the woods, *before* he makes them into pies, if apple pie-making is to be a rational endeavor. And surely the explanation of *why* it is wrong to take from the baker the apples he has gathered is precisely that he has invested his labor in their acquisition. That is, he has, through his purposive physical activity, brought the apples within the scope of a legitimate plan for their use. To deprive the baker of his apples is to illegitimately frustrate that plan by appropriating for oneself (without his consent) the labor invested in their gathering.

The doctrine of makers' rights, then, will not provide by itself an intuitively satisfying complete account either of how we can acquire property from unowned nature or of how we can acquire property by laboring on unowned nature. As such, it can at best play only a limited role in a defensible theory of property acquisition. But it is possible that its role in such a theory might be far more limited than this suggests, even if we take Sreenivasan's premises (1) and (2) to be *true*. For it might be true that makers *are* entitled to what they make, but not *because of* the making. If making something is just one instance of a broader category of activity, and if all instances of that broader category create entitlements, then it is unlikely to be the *making* that explains or justifies the resulting entitlement. This, of course, was just my understanding of Locke's position: makers (typically) acquire property in what they make, but only because making is one kind of productive labor, one way of bringing material from nature within one's legitimate sphere of self-government.

So it seems worth asking whether there is anything about *making itself* that we should regard as important to a plausible theory of property acquisition. Sreenivasan and most others who have discussed the workmanship model appear to believe that there is. I am more doubtful. To begin, it is difficult to understand why, according to the doctrine of makers' rights, *certain* kinds of makings do *not* create property. I can, for instance, make new things during idle or pointless activity – as when I make a design on the unowned forest floor while resting from my hike – or during purely recreational activity – as when I build a snowman on an unowned meadow. I acquire no *property* through these makings, but it is hard for the defender of makers' rights to explain *why* I don't (at least partly because makers' rights are taken to be something like "self-evident"). My activities may not have interestingly *improved* the world, but it is unclear just what relevance this should have to a doctrine that is focussed on the moral significance of *making*. I can plainly make new things without improving anything (e.g., a trash pile or a dreadful painting); and I can improve things without any making (as I do when I remove a boulder from the roadway or garbage from the beach). By contrast, it is easy for a "labor-mixing" account to explain why no property is created by idle or recreational makings. Such makings are not a part of any productive activity that is aimed at and requires for its success continuing control over the newly made things.

Similarly, it is hard for defenders of the doctrine of makers' rights to explain why I acquire no property when I turn something that *you* own (by virtue of a prior making) into something new, as I do if I make the chair you built into a coffee table.[52] If it is simply making that is morally important, and not the intended role of the made thing in the maker's life, then there seems to be *no* reason why a second making is not as significant as a first. Indeed, to make the more general point that is applicable here, it is unclear why making, considered by itself, should be thought to produce entitlements of any one particular extent or duration, rather than another. If anything, *absolute* dominion over what one makes seems the most "natural" position for a makers' rights principle to fix on; but defenders of the doctrine uniformly deny (as, of course, did Locke) that human property is ever equivalent to absolute dominion. Again, by contrast, it is easy for a labor-mixing theory to explain these matters. As we have seen, when we labor to acquire things, exercising our rights of self-government, we are thereby committed to respecting the similar exercises of others with those same rights – in this case, by not taking (or, more generally, by not laboring on) what others have previously taken (without their consent). And the extent and duration of the property that "labor-mixing" grounds is determined perfectly naturally by appeal to what is necessary to the (legitimate) project or plan of which that laboring activity is a part.

It is difficult, then, to see why we should be inclined to take *making itself* to be morally significant in the ways that the doctrine of makers' rights

---

52 Put in Sreenivasan's terms, it is hard to see why, on the makers' rights doctrine, your objection to my re-making your made thing counts as a legitimate objection.

requires us to. There is, of course, no denying that we *do* celebrate the achievements of great creators and "makers": inventors who fabricate the things that make our lives more comfortable and productive, craftsmen who make objects of great utility and beauty, innovative theorists, great artists, and so on. We take their "makings" to be performances of great significance. But we do not celebrate these performances because they originate especially obvious *property rights* for the makers. We celebrate them because of their great social utility, because these makers enrich and improve our lives. Thomas Jefferson helped to "make" a great nation, and we celebrate his accomplishment; but we do not take him to have acquired any special property or entitlement by so doing. Perhaps we will say that such makers *deserve* reward for their achievements, and that the best form for this reward to take would be increased personal property. But such assertions are neither obviously true nor in any way directly relevant to the assessment of a doctrine which maintains that makings by themselves *create* entitlements.[53]

The *property* that makers actually acquire (as opposed to what they might "deserve"), they acquire by virtue of incorporating their creations into plans for their continued use, just as do those who acquire property *without* making new things. Inventors, craftsmen, artists, and the like often make new things at least partly in the course of attempting to make a satisfactory living, by selling or exchanging what they make for other things that they need or want. Where they make useful things *without* these (or other) plans or intentions for their creations, without actually employing (or intending the future employment of) what they make, we think of them less as creators of exclusive property and more as simply benefactors of mankind.

Makers may often *deserve* our admiration and the rewards that might flow from it. They may also deserve blame or contempt (as when they make a new "weapon of mass destruction," or another mindless television sitcom). But makers' *rights* are just the same rights that can be enjoyed by nonmakers: rights to control over those things, drawn or made by labor from their fair share of unowned resources, that are necessary to the successful government of their lives. We do Locke no favor, then, by ascribing to him a special principle of makers' rights. *Makers'* rights are, at least in Locke's sense of the term, just *laborers'* rights.

---

53 People might *deserve* property (say, greater wealth or material comfort) for all sorts of reasons besides "makings," such as simply living virtuous lives. But there is plainly a logical gap between any such assertions of desert and assertions of entitlement to (i.e., property in) some particular object.

INDEX